Jefferson's
Second Revolution

Books by Susan Dunn

George Washington
(coauthored with James MacGregor Burns)

The Three Roosevelts:
Patrician Leaders Who Transformed America
(coauthored with James MacGregor Burns)

Sister Revolutions:
French Lightning, American Light

Rousseau: The Social Contract
and *The First and Second Discourses*
(editor and translator)

The Deaths of Louis XVI:
Regicide and the French Political Imagination

Diversity and Citizenship:
New Challenges for American Nationhood
(coedited with Gary Jacobsohn)

Nerval et le roman historique

Jefferson's
Second Revolution

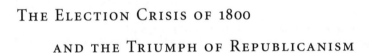

The Election Crisis of 1800
and the Triumph of Republicanism

Susan Dunn

HOUGHTON MIFFLIN COMPANY
Boston · New York   2004

For information about permission to reproduce selections
from this book, write to Permissions, Houghton Mifflin Company,
215 Park Avenue South, New York, New York 10003.

Visit our Web site: www.houghtonmifflinbooks.com.

Library of Congress Cataloging-in-Publication Data
Dunn, Susan, date.
Jefferson's second revolution : the election crisis of 1800 and the
triumph of republicanism / Susan Dunn.
p.   cm.
Includes bibliographical references (p.) and index.
ISBN 0-618-13164-7
1. Presidents—United States—Election—1800. 2. Jefferson, Thomas,
1743–1826. 3. Adams, John, 1735–1826. 4. United States—Politics
and government—1797–1801. 5. Republicanism—United States—
History—19th century. 6. Political culture—United States—
History—19th century. I. Title.
E330.D86 2004
324.973'044—dc22   2004047489

Printed in the United States of America

Book design by Robert Overholtzer

QUM 10 9 8 7 6 5 4 3 2 1

FOR JIM

Contents

Illustrations

Jefferson's Second Revolution

1

On the Brink

MURDER, ROBBERY, rape, adultery, and incest will all be openly taught and practiced," predicted the *Connecticut Courant* in the fall of 1800. "The air will be rent with the cries of distress, the soil will be soaked with blood, and the nation black with crimes." Hardly more than a dozen years after the path-breaking Constitutional Convention in Philadelphia in 1787, the outlook for American democracy suddenly appeared grim. There was "scarcely a possibility that we shall escape a Civil War," the *Courant* editorialized.

The stability and prosperity of the young republic would abruptly halt if Thomas Jefferson, the vice president of the country and the leader of the Republicans, were to defeat President John Adams in the Electoral College in December 1800 — or so Federalists believed. Reasonable, dependable government seemed unlikely to survive the leadership of a man who blithely held that "a little rebellion now and then is a good thing," indeed, that rebellion was "a medicine necessary for the sound health of government." Jefferson was a "fanatic," they exclaimed, as they drew lurid pictures of the starry-eyed visionary in love with radical revolution, the "great arch priest of Jacobinism and infidelity." The Virginian and his Republicans would turn America upside down, permitting the hoi polloi to govern the nation and unseating the wealthy social elite, long accustomed to wielding political power and governing the nation. Jefferson's election, wrote a Federalist in western Massachusetts, would produce "the most serious and alarming evils to this Country."

Something had to be done to save the country from the "fangs of

Jefferson," cried an anxious Alexander Hamilton. The Virginian's radical promises of liberty, equal rights, and a redistribution of wealth and property, another Federalist declared, would introduce anarchy, which would surely terminate, as it had in France, in military despotism. People whispered about his "Congo Harem" and "dusky Sally Hemings." They were incensed at his lack of respect for religion. It had come to light, an outraged Robert Troup reported to his friend Rufus King, the American minister in London, that Jefferson had once been indiscreet enough to attend a public entertainment in Virginia on a *Sunday!* What better proof of his "contempt for the Christian religion and his devotion to the new religion of France"?

For months during the spring and summer of 1800, Federalist editors throughout the country had been fulminating against the Virginian, smearing him for being an atheist, a dreamer, a coward, a man entirely lacking in conscience, religion, and charity. "Do you believe in the strangest of all paradoxes," demanded one of Jefferson's foes in the *New York Commercial Advertiser,* "that a spendthrift, a libertine, or an atheist is qualified to make your laws and govern you and your posterity?" Writers denounced him for seeking to poison the minds and destroy the morals of the people while spreading the seeds of confusion, anarchy, and slavery throughout the United States. And not only morality, but economic prosperity too, they concluded, would suffer. Commerce would be plundered, farmers impoverished, and merchants ruined. "Shadows, clouds, and darkness rest on our future prospects," wrote Troup dejectedly to his friend King.

And then, in the middle of the summer heat, jolting news! Jefferson was dead! For more than a week in early July 1800, newspapers carried shocking but unconfirmed reports of the Virginian's sudden death. Sadly the *Baltimore American* relayed an "alarming and truly melancholy report" that Thomas Jefferson "is no more." He seemed to have died in a sudden manner, the Philadelphia *True American* informed its startled readers the following day. The next day, the Federalist newspaper, the *Gazette of the United States,* affirmed that "the report of Mr. Jefferson's death appears to be entitled to some credit." Had the author of the Declaration of Independence fallen ill — or been assassinated? Three days later, the *American Daily Advertiser* still could not disprove the "distressing information" that Jefferson had mysteriously died. "Old Tories" and "haters of our independence" were giving one another sly "winks of congratulations," reported the Republican newspaper, the *Aurora.*

A week later, the story still remained in doubt. One Federalist, writing in the *Connecticut Courant,* explained tongue-in-cheek that it had been a slow news week, and "some *compassionate* being," seeking to provide the country with noteworthy news, had "very humanely killed Mr. Jefferson." When the reports were exposed as false, Republican newspapers took aim at the Federalists' glee. "The asses of aristocracy, fearing the paws of this republican lion, reported his death — because they wished him so!"

"I have never enjoyed better and more uninterrupted health," a vigorous, unperturbed Jefferson wrote upon receiving news of his own passing. His friend, Pierre Samuel Dupont de Nemours, had just written to him to describe his great relief when he learned that the reports of Jefferson's death were false. "I am much indebted to my enemies," Jefferson responded, "for proving by their recitals of my death, that I have friends."

The fifty-seven-year-old vice president was alive and well in Monticello. The presiding officer of the Senate, he had been delighted to leave Philadelphia in May of 1800 for his hilltop home in Virginia. The Senate, he felt, did not have enough business to occupy it for a half-hour a day, while the beloved estate he had so carefully planned and created for himself fully occupied his mind and, as he said, gratified his esthetic senses.

In Monticello, he would wake at dawn, slip out of his alcove bed, and spend the first hours of the morning in the adjacent "cabinet," reading and working on his voluminous correspondence. Then came breakfast with other members of the household at eight o'clock. After breakfast there was time to give thought to the university he was planning, to contemplate more alterations to his house, which was in a state of perpetual redesign and reconstruction, and to pursue his scientific inquiries and inventions. Science, he told his friends and family, was his "passion," whereas politics was a "duty" as well as a "torment."

Letters streamed in from all over the country keeping him in close touch with political events. Still, Jefferson wanted to be passive during these election months, trusting his friends and collaborators to campaign on his behalf — as well as to respond to the "calumnies of the newspapers." The "only truth to be relied on in a newspaper," he quipped, was contained in its advertisements. Surveying his land on horseback, attending to his crops, playing with his grandchildren, conversing with his guests, he was content to spend his time in his refuge of mountains, forests, rivers, gardens, books, inventions, and ideas.

"Is this the violent democrat, the vulgar demagogue, the bold atheist . . . I have so often heard denounced by the federalists?" wondered a captivated Margaret Bayard Smith, the wife of the editor of the *National Intelligencer,* when she first met Jefferson in December of 1800. "Can this man so meek and mild, yet dignified in his manners, with a voice so soft and low, with a countenance so benignant and intelligent, can he be that daring leader of a faction, that disturber of the peace, that enemy of all rank and order?"

But Federalists were not as enchanted by the Virginian's courtly manners, pensive eyes, and gentle, lilting voice. His intellectual stature and distinguished public service — author of the Declaration of Independence, member of the Virginia House of Burgesses at the age of twenty-six, wartime governor of Virginia, delegate to the Continental Congress, minister to France, secretary of state under George Washington, vice president under John Adams — left them unimpressed. Perhaps in the little republic of St. Marino Jefferson's political "experiments" could be tolerated, observed Charles Carroll of Carrollton, but in America the Virginian's "fantastic tricks" would most assuredly dissolve the union.

Carroll and his patrician Federalist friends not only wanted to remain at the helm, from which they had so ably steered the country toward stability and prosperity, but they believed that they were *entitled* to remain there. Clinging to the myth of the virtue of the elite few, they were convinced that only they possessed a deep commitment to public service and an unerring sense of the common good. How could the nation survive and flourish without them, "the wise & good," asked Alexander Hamilton, one of the Federalist leaders. "Obedience and submission to the powers that be," a Pennsylvania congressman declared, "is the duty of all." In private, the Federalist governor of New York, John Jay, was just as blunt. Conflating power and property, he candidly confided to a friend that "those who own the country ought to participate in the government of it."

Oddly, the pedigreed, patrician Jefferson was one of those "owners" of the country — wealthier and from a more distinguished family than Federalists like Adams and the self-made Hamilton. And yet Jefferson sought to challenge their hold on power — their "strident exclusivism," in the words of historians Stanley Elkins and Eric McKitrick — and even challenge the legacy of the great George Washington. The father of the country and his closest disciples, Federalists believed, had created and bequeathed to America an orderly society and well-functioning institutions. "Our government is as free as it is capable of being — the country as happy as a government can make it," they crowed. "What more do you want? Will you grasp at a shadow, and lose the substance?"

What principles guided Jefferson and his so-called Republicans? The Jeffersonian brand of republicanism, Federalists scoffed, simply meant "an essential want of integrity, and an unprincipled pursuit of whatever promotes the interests, or gratifies the passions of the individuals." In short, Republicans were motivated only by base "self-interest" whereas Federalists were proud to be anti-individualists, committed to the notion of the common good of all.

Violence and anarchy would spread through the nation, a "Christian Federalist" warned in a political pamphlet, if Jefferson won the presidency. Serious, thoughtful men could not doubt, he wrote, that if Jefferson was elected, he and his Jacobin cronies would trample and explode "those morals which protect our lives from the knife of the assassin — which guard the chastity of our wives and daughters from seduction and violence — defend our property from plunder and devastation, and shield our religion from contempt and profanation." Just as wild, radical Jacobins and their guillotines had transformed France into a vast cemetery, Republicans too would leave in their wake a nation in ruins. By what right were these brazen Republicans calling into question the precious status quo?

Surely in a democracy in which the people were sovereign, the Republicans, though political outsiders, had the right to criticize and oppose those who governed. And yet, some Federalists proposed that "a few BOLD STROKES" be used to silence all opposition to government. But Republicans refused to be silent. They offered voters a forceful platform and an aggressive agenda for change. They blasted John Jay's recent one-sided treaty with Great Britain in which the English had made few concessions to American claims. They attacked Adams and the other Federalists for passing the repressive Sedition Act in 1798, designed to smother opposition to the Federalist regime. They denounced the standing federal army, warning that it could be used to quash domestic dissent. They condemned the dispatching of federal troops in 1799 to crush a tax revolt — Fries's Rebellion — in Pennsylvania. Republicans pounded home their message: a simple government, low taxes, state militias instead of a standing army, repeal of the Sedition Act, and free schools. In the South and the burgeoning West, they attracted voters by offering security for slavery, access to new unsettled lands, and markets for their agricultural products. In New England, their democratic message appealed to voters with aspirations of upward mobility.

Most of all, Republicans criticized the Federalist "monocrats" for upholding the rights of the few and ignoring the rights of the many, for catering to the social and financial elite, for disdaining the people and democracy itself. Even Federalist Gouverneur Morris, the former minister to France and now the junior senator from New York, conceded that his Federalist colleagues had given Republicans reason to believe that they wished to establish a monarchy. The Republicans' affinity for inclusion contrasted sharply with Federalist elitism. The election, declared Massachusetts Republican Elbridge Gerry, was a battle between the people and a party "utterly devoted to a monarchical system." A Republican victory was essential, insisted Governor James Monroe of Virginia, to restore to Americans the principles of 1776, to "secure to us forever those liberties that were acquired by our revolution, which ought never to have been put in danger."

By the late fall of 1800, most of the electors to the Electoral College had been selected. State legislatures had either chosen their presidential electors themselves or permitted voters to choose them in statewide or districtwide elections. In some states, it was winner-take-all.

The Electoral College was an indirect and largely undemocratic method for choosing a president. At the Constitutional Convention, it had been less the product of consensus or compromise than of delegates simply throwing up their hands in frustration. Indeed, no subject at the Philadelphia convention had perplexed the delegates more than the mode of choosing the president. Three times delegates had approved motions that the executive be chosen by the national legislature — the equivalent of a parliamentary system — but toward the end of the convention they were back to square one, having rejected every proposal for electing the executive. A Committee on Detail finally settled on the system of electors, and, by that time, the other fatigued and impatient delegates were in no mood to revisit the question again.

Now, after months of campaigning, it appeared that Federalists would win all of New England's electoral votes, along with those of New Jersey, and would split the votes of Pennsylvania, North Carolina and Maryland, gaining 65 votes. Republicans had won all the electoral votes of New York State and most of the South: they too could count on 65 votes. It was unclear for whom South Carolina would cast its 8 electoral votes.

"This is the day appointed for the election of President and Vice President," Troup wrote to King from New York on a cool December morning. On that day, December 3, 1800, presidential electors all met in their respective states and cast their votes. "The calculations now are that Adams and Pinckney will outrun Jefferson & Burr," Troup informed his friend. But he was wrong.

Official Electoral College results from the outlying states trickled in slowly, but there was little doubt that Republicans had won. Jefferson seemed to have 73 votes; John Adams, 65. The mood of the country had swung around. On December 15, the *National Intelligencer* reported a victory for Republicans — and for democracy: "The storm, which has so long raged in the political world, has at length subsided," the *Intelligencer* declared, encouraging Americans to celebrate an event that was "auspicious to the destinies of the world."

But December 15 found Jefferson brooding. To his running mate Aaron Burr he revealed his doubts about the outcome of the race — not questioning that he had defeated Adams, but troubled that one particular thing had been "badly managed" and "left to hazard." He and Burr might have each received an equal number of votes, creating a tie — and a crisis.

The Electoral College's voting system was deeply flawed. According to Article II, section 1 of the Constitution, each state could appoint a number of electors equal to the total number of senators and representatives of that state. Each elector was entitled to cast 2 votes, but there was no way to differentiate between the votes cast for a presidential candidate and those for a vice-presidential candidate. Electors could indicate a clear preference for the man they wanted to be president only if they all agreed that at least one elector would cast 1 of his 2 electoral votes for a man who had no chance of winning. But Jefferson worried that that had not happened.

It appeared, he reported to Burr, that Republican electors might have cast all their ballots for Jefferson and Burr, forgetting to withhold at least 1 vote from Burr so that Jefferson would be the undisputed victor. "I never once asked whether arrangements had been made to prevent so many from dropping votes intentionally," he confided to the New Yorker, bitterly reproaching himself for his own "passivity" and negligence. Still, he ended his letter on a positive note, anticipating their inauguration day: "We shall of course see you before the 4th of March."

Now a worried Jefferson recognized the "probable equality" of the two Republican candidates, and by the 19th, his unease had intensified, becoming distress. Jefferson and Burr had each received 73 votes. Disciplined Republican electors had toed the party line — too much! The tie, Jefferson reported to Madison, had "produced great dismay and gloom on the republican gentlemen here, and equal exultation on the federalists."

In the case of a tie in the Electoral College, the choice, according to the Constitution, would be thrown into the House of Representatives — the lame-duck House controlled by Federalists, not the newly elected Republican House — for a special tie-breaking presidential election in which each state would cast 1 vote, a system even more undemocratic than that of the Electoral College. The House, however, would not begin the process until February 11. And so a tense waiting — and maneuvering — period began.

"Federalists will have to Choose among Rotten Apples," a despondent politician grumbled to Alexander Hamilton. But while some were resigned to relinquishing power to their enemies, others predicted chaos and violence. An alliance of "men of desperate fortunes" stood at the threshold of power, wishing "for nothing so much as a *revolution*," warned the conservative *Gazette of the United States*. "It is fallacious, therefore, to imagine that we shall experience only a change of men. . . . We are now in the high road which has uniformly led to despotism, through the dark valley of anarchy." Some overwrought Federalists predicted that Jefferson would soon call upon France and Napoleon's soldiers to invade the United States.

And some were determined not to take their loss lying down. On

December 19, Jefferson heard reports about a Federalist plot to "stretch" the Constitution and steal the presidency. Federalists were openly declaring their intention to prevent an election, he informed Madison. If Federalists could prolong the deadlock beyond the expiration of Adams's term on March 4, the country would be without a president, and then all bets were off. The Constitution said nothing about such an eventuality. Federalists were seeking to "reverse what has been understood to have been the wishes of the people," a gloomy Jefferson wrote. "This opens upon us an abyss, at which every sincere patriot must shudder."

A week later more pieces of the plot came to light. The "feds," Jefferson wrote to Madison, intended to pass a bill giving executive power either to John Jay, whom they would first reappoint chief justice, or to John Marshall, John Adams's secretary of state. Their backup plan was to let the presidency "devolve" on the Federalist president pro tem of the Senate. Could Federalists be capable of such a "Degree of boldness as well as wickedness?" wondered a horrified James Monroe.

The tie in the Electoral College presented Federalists with an unexpected golden opportunity. They could delay the transition, or better still, block it altogether. The Sedition Act had already compromised the right of citizens to criticize and oppose the men in power. The Federalists' refusal to let Republicans govern would constitute just one more step in that same direction.

Still, how could Federalists convince themselves — and the American public — that it was not a major blow to democratic process and to the principles of the Declaration of Independence and the Constitution to impede the election of the people's choice? Theodore Sedgwick of Massachusetts, the Federalist Speaker of the House, admitted that the majority's clear intention had been to elect Jefferson. But, he asked in a letter to Alexander Hamilton, why had this preference been given to Jefferson? Sedgwick believed that Jefferson had won because he was a fiery democrat, crafty, opportunistic, servilely devoted to revolutionary France. "Ought we then," he concluded, "to respect the preference which is given to this man from such *motives,* and by such *friends?*" If the majority was mistaken, poorly informed, or misguided, and if its judgment was so flawed as to harm the nation, Sedgwick reasoned, its decisions should be declared null and void. He insisted that the Constitution had intended elections "to secure to prominent talents and virtue the first honors of our country." The virtuous elite had the obligation to direct — or disqualify — the majority. Such a course struck Sedgwick as justified, rational, and wise.

Most Federalists were stunned that the American people had thrown the party of Washington, Adams, and Hamilton out of power. Would they — the men who had created the republic and governed it so successfully since its founding — meekly accept an unjust, undeserved defeat? "Resistance must be bold, determined and unshrinking, or it is ineffectual," declared the *Gazette of the United States.*

But neither would Republicans shrink from confrontation. They were not about to let their victory be snatched away from them. They stood ready to fight. "We are resolv'd never to yield," one Republican wrote to James Madison, "and sooner hazard every thing than to prevent the voice and wishes of people being carried into effect." Federalist usurpation would signal the start of another revolution and even a civil war, predicted Virginia political activist John Beckley. "If any man should be thus appointed President by law and accept the office," threatened Albert Gallatin, the leader of Republicans in the House of Representatives, "he would *instantaneously be put to death.*" In the event of a Federalist attempt to install one of their own in the presidency, the middle states would arm, Jefferson declared, emphasizing that "no such usurpation, even for a single day, should be submitted to."

The fundamental consensus about the Constitution and the union was collapsing. During the turmoil, Jefferson wrote that his "sincere wish" was to see the government "brought back to its republican principles." And yet he and the other great architects of the republic, on both sides of the political spectrum, appeared equally willing to dissolve the federal union and institutions that were their masterpiece.

"There is nothing more common," wrote Dr. Benjamin Rush of Philadelphia in 1786, "than to confound the terms of the American Revolution with those of the late American war. The American war is over; but this is far from being the case with the American revolution. On the contrary, nothing but the first act of the great drama is closed. It remains yet to establish and perfect our new forms of government; and to prepare the principles, morals, and manners of our citizens, for these forms of government, after they are established and brought to perfection."

In 1786, Rush captured the significance of the dilemma that would confront Americans in 1800. The American Revolution could not be equated solely with the War of Independence. On the contrary, there were crucial political transformations and social reforms to come to make that Revolution complete. Indeed, before the winter of 1800, the Revolution had been proceeding successfully from stage to stage — from the war of 1776 to the Constitutional Convention of 1787 to the ratification of the Bill of Rights in 1791. But then, in the 1790s, things seemed to go awry. It was a decade of turmoil and conflict: profound ideological disagreements in the nation as well as in Washington's own cabinet; pressure from the top to maintain the authority of the nation's elite leaders and populist movements from the bottom demanding a more open and inclusive political arena; two clashing visions — agricultural in the South and commercial in the North — of the nation's future; the rise of embryonic political parties in an atmosphere of hostility to parties; attempts to undermine the Bill of Rights and quash opposition to elected leaders; and forceful assertions of states' rights. Adding to the brew was the toxic enmity among the founders themselves, the band of brothers who, only a dozen years earlier, had worked so harmoniously together.

Now, at the beginning of the new century, the colliding ideologies and personalities congealed into an acute electoral and constitutional crisis. It would be the revolutionary drama's final act. In 1796, power had been easily transferred from one Federalist to another, from outgoing president George Washington to his vice president, John Adams. But now, would Federalists willingly and peacefully hand power over to their political enemies, to these Republicans, men whom they not only loathed but also considered dangerous to the republic, to private property, to economic growth and a strong federal government, to everything they respected and cherished?

Why, after all, should the nation's distinguished, successful leaders recognize an insurgency of homespun zealots and upstarts? Why would the elite willingly transfer power to a populist party? Why should they recognize the legitimacy of the opposition? Which heads of state had ever voluntarily ceded power to their enemies? The Constitution had enshrined checks and balances, not a party system. In what land had two fiercely opposing parties agreed to respect each other and alternately govern? Surely a coup d'état or an assassination was more in keeping with Western political tradition. Even in the twenty-first century, elected leaders often refuse to step aside and allow voters to choose a successor; parties that win elections are often outlawed by would-be dictators. Again and again, budding democracies are quashed, their constitutions suspended.

Jefferson, Madison, Gallatin, and others fully grasped the frightening dimensions of the crisis. A few Federalists candidly acknowledged their party's malice. "Understand that the democrats in Congress are in a rage for having acted with good faith," one Federalist explained to Rufus King. So polarized were the two parties, so severe the strain between them, that their differences appeared unbridgeable.

In the cold, overcast winter of 1800, the federal republic tottered on the brink, its future shrouded in a grim, menacing fog.

2

"If the people be governors, who shall be governed?"

D RESSED IN HIS USUAL BLACK, a slight, thin, studious-looking man, about forty years old, quietly entered the president's office. Towering over him, the president smiled and greeted his old friend. It was May 5, 1792. Washington came right to the point. Would the younger man advise him how and when he should announce to the country his intention to retire from office?

The second presidential election was to take place seven months later, when presidential electors would vote in December, but strain and exhaustion showed on Washington's face. He complained that he was becoming deaf; his sight was weakening, too. There were troubling lapses in his memory; illnesses had plagued him in 1790 and again in 1791; now, he sighed, he found the fatigues of his position "scarcely tolerable." Attacks and abuse from the press both surprised and disheartened him; unexpected party divisions within his own cabinet posed a "fresh source of difficulty," and, more and more, he sensed discontent among the people. Nor was he convinced that he alone was indispensable to the effective administration of the government. His "disinclination to remain in office," he admitted to Madison, was "becoming every day more & more fixed." After a lifetime of public service, the sixty-year-old president — the former commander in chief of the Revolutionary forces and president of the Constitutional Convention — longed to return to his farm, "take his spade in his hand, and work for his bread."

Madison's reaction was one of acute alarm. Washington's retirement, he told the president, would give a "surprize and shock to the public mind." While he made sympathetic murmurs about the "severe sacrifice" the president had made for his country and the ugliness of the divisive spirit of party, he insisted that Washington was simply the only person who could conciliate and unite the opposing factions. In the present "unsettled condition" of the young government, Madison concluded, "no possible successor" to Washington could perform as well in the presidency. No one else had demonstrated such consistently wise judgment. In short, the consequences of Washington's leaving office "ought not to be hazarded."

Unconvinced and disappointed, Washington turned to other matters. But before Madison took his leave, the president once again urged him to give thought to the best time and means for announcing his decision to retire.

The president also consulted with his secretary of state, Thomas Jefferson, and his secretary of the treasury, Alexander Hamilton. The Virginian and the New Yorker, famous for agreeing on little, for once agreed absolutely. "The confidence of the whole union is centered in you," Jefferson wrote. Worried about deep geographical divisions in the nation, Jefferson was convinced that only with Washington "at the helm" would there be tranquility. "North & South will hang together, if they have you to hang on." Hoping to soothe and persuade the weary president, he suggested that perhaps Washington would not have to complete a second term — one or two more years of his leadership might be enough to stabilize the nation.

"The greatest evil, that could befall the country at the present juncture," Hamilton concurred, would be Washington's retirement from politics. Knowing that the president placed supreme importance on his reputation in history, Hamilton suggested to Washington that his premature withdrawal from politics might lower him in the estimation of posterity. The nation's new institutions, moreover, were not yet firmly established; the president must not leave them in danger of being undone. The only path open to Washington, Hamilton wrote, was to "obey the voice of your country," and that voice, Hamilton promised, "will be as earnest and as unanimous as ever."

By the end of the summer, it appeared to Hamilton that Washington had "relaxed" his determination to retire. Madison, Jefferson, and Hamilton had their way. Still, though Washington was willing to make sacrifices for the country, to serve the people, to accept another four-year term — he was not willing to campaign. Competition for political office held no appeal for him. "It was scarcely possible that, with such a transcendent reputation," Massachusetts congressman Fisher Ames would later say, "he should have rivals." The reluctant candidate never threw his hat into the ring in 1792; on the contrary, only by his public silence did he indicate that he would not refuse the highest office. He took no part in the contest.

In November 1792, Washington was elected to a second term with 132 electoral votes. Every elector in the Electoral College had cast a vote for him. John Adams won a majority of the electors' second ballots and was elected vice president with 77 votes; Governor George Clinton of New York received 50 votes, Jefferson 4, and Aaron Burr 1. It was not Washington's first landslide victory: he had been unanimously elected commander in chief of the Revolutionary army in 1775, unanimously chosen president of the Constitutional Convention in 1787, and unanimously elected president of the United States in 1789. The first two American presidential elections and inaugurations resembled coronations more than political contests. Washington had expected nothing less. He "would have experienced chagrin," he confessed in 1793, had he not been returned to the presidency by "a pretty respectable vote."

For men like Madison and Hamilton, Washington was politically indispensable, but for tens of thousands of Americans, he was emotionally indispensable, too. They revered him as the father of the nation. "The liberties of America depend upon him," wrote John Adams to his wife, two days after Washington was chosen commander in chief in 1775. As early as 1778, an almanac termed him "Father of his country."

"I cannot describe the impression that the first sight of that great man made upon me," recounted one officer who saw Washington at Valley Forge. "I could not keep my eyes from that imposing countenance; grave, yet not severe; affable, without familiarity. . . . Its predominant expression was calm dignity through which you could . . . discern *the father* as well as the commander of his soldiers."

During the War of Independence and the first decades of the republic, American civilians as well as soldiers venerated Washington as their national father. Exhorting Washington to lend his prestige to the forthcoming Constitutional Convention, Henry Knox, the future secretary of war, assured Washington that such a gesture would "doubly entitle

A View of the Federal Hall of the City of New York, 1797,
by H. R. Robinson, 1847. Washington began his presidency
in New York in 1789. In December 1790 the government moved to Philadelphia.

you to the glorious republican epithet — The Father of Your Country."
By the time Washington toured the southern states as president of the
young republic, the emotional bond between him and his people had
deepened even more.

Indeed, during his travels in the northern states in 1789 and in the
South in 1791, the president cemented his bond with the people. The
trips had a double purpose. As the *ceremonial* leader of the nation, he
wanted to make himself visible as the emblem of national unity and
identity. By presenting himself to Americans in celebratory public
events, he hoped that they would — through him — transcend their local loyalties and develop an attachment to the concept of their federal
government and to the idea of a unified American people. As the *political* leader of the nation, Washington wished to see with his own eyes
the conditions in the country and gauge the mood of his fellow citizens.

In the fall of 1789, accompanied by two secretaries and six servants (Martha having decided to stay in New York with her grandchil-

Inauguration of George Washington by Montbaron and Gautschi.

dren), Washington visited all the New England states except Vermont and Rhode Island, which were not yet members of the union. He dined with the notables, watched parades, listened to songs and odes, received accolades, and strolled in the countryside. He was mostly pleased by the receptions he received, especially by the attention of the "very handsome" ladies, though he appeared at times overwhelmed by the welcome. "He looked oppressed by the attention that was paid him," commented one observer in the joyful crowd that greeted the president in Salem, Massachusetts. "As he cast his eye around, I thought it seemed to sink at the notice he attracted." When the songs and cheering stopped, "he bowed very low, and as if he could bear no more turned hastily around and went into the house."

Nor was travel easy. In New England, Washington found "intolerable" roads and "indifferent" accommodations. He was turned away from one tavern because the owner was absent and his wife sick. Frustrated and irritated after getting lost in the Massachusetts countryside, he wrote in his diary that "the roads in every part of this state are amazingly crooked to suit the convenience of every man's fields; and the directions you receive from the people equally blind and ignorant." One Sunday, he found himself trapped in the village of Ashford, Connecticut, where it was illegal to travel on the Sabbath. A church service provided the only activity, but he grumbled about the minister's "very lame discourse." Still, his travels permitted him to see firsthand the country at work.

In Boston he toured a sail manufactory, noticing the twenty-eight water-powered looms at work and the fourteen girls spinning. "They are the daughters of decayed families," he wrote, "and are girls of Character — none others are admitted." At another factory in Boston, he saw that each spinner had a "small girl" to turn the wheel. Though he remarked that the girls worked from eight o'clock in the morning until six o'clock in the evening, he did not comment on the broader social issues of women's and children's labor. In Beverly, Massachusetts, he stopped at a cotton manufactory and admired the new carding and spinning machines, especially one, operated by a single person, that could spin eighty-four threads at a time. In Marblehead, he viewed a fleet of a hundred shipping vessels but wrote that the houses were old, the streets dirty, "and the common people not very clean." Portsmouth had stagnated after the war, but, Washington happily reported, "it is beginning now to revive again." In Springfield, he examined arms and ammunitions depots. In Hartford, he visited Colonel Wadsworth's woolen manufactory and ordered a suit of broadcloth to be sent to him in New York. "There is a great equality in the People of this State," he jotted down in his diary while visiting Connecticut. "Few or no opulent Men and no poor — great similitude in their buildings."

Factories, bridges and roads, crops and fish, gristmills and sawmills, harbors and ships — everything that moved, grew, and made the country work captured his attention.

Touring the southern states a year and a half later, in the spring of 1791, he saw that the South was not as industrialized and prosperous as the North. As he made his way toward Georgia, he commented on the poor, thinly populated land, the ever-present pines. On the road between Charleston and Savannah, only a few homes had "anything of an elegant appearance." Most houses, he noted in his diary, were made of logs; a few had brick chimneys, but generally the chimneys were constructed with "split sticks filled with dirt between them." Occasionally the accommodations were so poor and dirty that he felt compelled to move on. Still, the crops in the South had been good for the past few years, and people seemed in good humor and generally satisfied with their lives and their government.

It was the first time Washington had traveled south of Virginia, but he seemed to feel more at home there than in the Northeast, commenting on the prosperous people's homes, paying a visit to the widow of his friend, General Nathanael Greene. In Charleston, he found a number of very fine houses. The people there were wealthy, gay, hospitable, and happy. The guest of honor at "a very elegant dancing assembly at the Exchange," the president danced happily with some of the "elegantly dressed and handsome ladies," who had adorned their gowns with red, white, and blue ribbons.

As his journey approached its end, he wrote to a friend that the South

> appears to be in a very improving state, and industry and frugality are becoming much more fashionable than they have hitherto been there. Tranquillity reigns among the people, with that disposition towards the general government which is likely to preserve it. They begin to feel the good effects of equal laws and equal protection. The farmer finds a ready market for his produce, and the merchant calculates with more certainty on his payments. Manufacturers have as yet made but little progress in that part of the country, and it will probably be a long time before they are brought to that state to which they have already arrived in the middle and eastern parts of the Union.

While Washington studied the country, the country studied — and applauded — him. That applause served a purpose. Tributes to the first president, commented the British minister to the United States, "tend to elevate the spirit of the people, and contribute to the formation of a *national character.*" Americans were the gainers, he concluded, from the recital of the feats of the Revolutionary War and their praise of Washington. As for the president himself, he was pleased with "the marks of respect shewn to my official Character." He had accomplished his goal. He had fashioned himself into the ideal unifying emblem of the nation.

"I wish he had a *Son,*" wrote Brigadier General Anthony Wayne to the Marquis de Lafayette in 1788, failing to grasp the symbolic importance of Washington's childlessness. "I have no child," Washington had once written, "no family to build in greatness upon my country's ruins." Why had God denied Washington a son? Gouverneur Morris would cry out in his funeral oration for the president in 1799. Morris knew full well the answer to his own question. "AMERICANS! he had no child — BUT YOU!"

The king, George III, the presumptive *pater familias* of the colonies, had proved a bad father, an unnatural one. The people had beseeched him to show them fatherly goodness and protection, but he had refused. During the Revolutionary War, people's antipathy for him, as John Dickinson wrote at the time, lay in "the resentment of dutiful children who have received unmerited blows from a beloved parent." George the Bad had been ousted and replaced by George the Good.

Washington was a man for all: a courageous military leader who could be gentle and restrained, dignified yet unassuming, who, like the Roman military hero Cincinnatus, wanted nothing more than to return to his plow and field; a political leader who seemed devoid of political ambition, more eager to resign from positions of power than to cling to them, who seemed to stand above factions and intrigue; a public servant who refused to accept any salary for the privilege of leading his people; a man of tolerance who welcomed Jews as well as Christians; a wealthy man who represented the sovereignty of ordinary people.

Always stressing the paramount importance of Americans' unity, which, he would tell them in his Farewell Address, made them one people and was the "Pillar" of their independence and security, Washington himself symbolized that unity. He incarnated the "sacramental center" of the American polity, in the words of historian Catherine Albanese; he was "a living 'tribal' totem for an emerging nation-state." His birthday, by the mid-1790s, had begun to displace the Fourth of July as the most important patriotic holiday in America. His very name, declared John Adams in his inaugural address in 1797, was a "rampart."

A few skeptics wisely urged restraint, noting that "to raise Washington up anymore would be to unseat the omnipotent." Even Adams complained that deference toward Washington had transformed the Virginian into the object of a cult that dispensed with people's rational faculties. "Instead of adoring a Washington," he wrote in 1785, "mankind should applaud the nation which educated him." Indeed, the president was so popular, Jefferson concurred, that people were willing to support him unquestioningly, "without appealing to their own reason or to anything but their feelings toward him." The adoration of

Washington, wrote a Republican Boston newspaper, was a Federalist attempt to cut away the liberties that had been gained.

Cracks in the edifice were appearing. Could Washington's national fatherhood be reconciled with the autonomy of free, rational, and dissenting Americans, with a self-governing citizenry, with the rise of vociferous political factions?

"Fourscore and seven years ago, our fathers brought forth on this continent a new nation . . . ," Abraham Lincoln intoned on the battlefield of Gettysburg. Lincoln deliberately turned to the nation's forefathers to understand the past — as well as the present — of the United States. Today, too, Americans look to our pantheon of fathers and framers — Pilgrim forefathers, Revolutionary fathers, constitutional fathers — to not only make sense of our history but even to chart our future. We ask, What were the "original" intentions of our Founding Fathers? What would they think of our innovations? Are we faithfully and intelligently following their constitutional blueprint for our political lives?

But in the seventeenth and eighteenth centuries, the figure of the father signified even more than a means for national self-understanding: many Americans had long sought to weave the fabric of their society and to design the institutions of their polities around the complex image of the caring, protective, authoritative father. This patriarchal, familial model of political relationships furnished average Americans with a sense of security and order while also reflecting their deference to the well-born, well-educated "fathers" who governed their communities.

Were the existence of an elite class of governing fathers and deference to that class purely negative features of the political life of the colonies and young states? Thomas Jefferson thought so. His top priority would always be to defeat the hold that birth and wealth had on the public trusts. And yet, the influence that certain wealthy, distinguished families had on political power had contributed immeasurably to the strength and stability of American society. The combination of birth, wealth, education, and ambition had indeed made possible the leadership of a cadre of extraordinary men — including Jefferson himself. As historian Gordon Wood argued, the brilliant, creative, and bold *political* leadership of the galaxy of Founding Fathers was a consequence of their *social* standing and leadership — of the obligations to others that their high social rank imposed upon them.

Still, toward the end of the eighteenth century, Americans, for better or for worse, were ready for a change. Though the gentlemen-politicians of the Revolutionary epoch did not see themselves as standing in an adversarial relationship to the populace, many Americans nevertheless resented the reign of the fathers and their hold on political power. These men would seek to replace the patriarchal model with a more egalitarian, republican model of political leadership — a more impersonal, institutional structure that would legitimize the private interests of individuals, that would accord them their own portion of esteem, and that, instead of emphasizing subordination, would even incorporate channels for dissent, factions, and conflict.

"There can never be any regular government of a nation without a marked *subordination* of mothers and children to the father," John Adams wrote to his son Thomas in 1799, issuing a tongue-in-cheek warning about the dangers of marriage. He requested that his son keep these thoughts "between you and me." Should his wife, Abigail, hear such an opinion, it would "infallibly raise a rebellion." Though in his own family Adams was reluctant to undermine his wife's autonomy or disparage her authority, he did not shrink from advocating the subordination of American citizens to the stabilizing and wise authority of the governing fathers. A republic, Adams suggested in that letter, could find at least temporary respite and protection from the onslaught of menaces like revolution and unfettered democracy by strictly maintaining — socially and politically — "*true family authority.*" Indeed, as president, Adams wanted to cast himself in the Washingtonian role of father in the nation's collective consciousness — and regretted his lack of success in the endeavor. "I always consider the whole nation as my *children,*" he said bitterly, "but they have almost all proved undutiful to me."

My children. Adams and other socially conservative American leaders often spoke of their communities as a large family, a metaphor that evoked for them not equality or fraternity, but rather the hierarchy and deference that, in their minds, were essential to a civilized, ordered society. Indeed, Adams would maintain until the end of his life, deference and hierarchy were natural to man. Most people, he wrote in 1791, live in a "habitual state of deference," willing to admire, support, and serve their "superiors," men of wealth, birth, and talent. Thus it was not only vain, he felt, but also counterproductive to try to obliterate all signs of "distinction and degree."

As far as the governing elite was concerned, it was understood that some Americans — the fathers — would pilot society, as they piloted their families, while other Americans — the wives, the children, the "people" — would sit in the back of the boat, obediently rowing. Even in the act of voting, it was expected that the common folk would follow the lead of the well-born, choosing between men of rank and probity, not between rival programs or ideologies. The exercise of political power by the elite, not by the people, seemed to some of the conservative fathers the most logical form of prudent government. "If the people be governors," John Cotton had asked in the seventeenth century, "who shall be governed?" Even by the late eighteenth century, that attitude had not entirely disappeared. It was quite proper that society be divided into two groups, maintained conservative Connecticut congressman Samuel Dana, "the rich, the few, the rulers" and "the poor, the many, the ruled."

It was a long-established tradition, Jefferson remarked, that political influence and power belonged to certain "canonized" families. Especially in New England, he wrote, there seemed to be so great a "traditionary reverence" for certain families that most government offices had become "nearly hereditary" in those families. In other states, too, agreed John Adams, there had been a "constant respect for certain old Families." The Randolphs and Carters in Virginia no less than the Winthrops and Saltonstalls in Massachusetts, he added, "are preferred to all others." The elite families — Livingstons, Clintons, Schuylers, Van Rensselaers, and Morrises in New York; Watsons and Greens in Rhode Island; Carrolls and Chases in Maryland; Rutherfords and Cadwaladers in New Jersey; Pinckneys and Habershams in South Carolina — not only socialized together, mingling at the theater, dinner parties, receptions, and balls, but were interrelated, too. Jefferson's mother was a Randolph; in Massachusetts, Lowells, Cabots, Lymans, and Dwights married one another; in New York, John Jay married a Livingston, and Alexander Hamilton boosted his social standing by marrying a Schuyler.

What the men from the notable families were believed to have in common, in addition to wealth (especially landed wealth), education, and breeding, was virtue. Indeed, virtue was the prerequisite for political leadership in eighteenth-century America. Stemming from the Latin word *vir* for "man" and originally meaning virile strength and courage, virtue had come to mean the ability to transcend one's own self-interest. A virtuous leader, motivated by his dedication to the community, by a sense of noblesse oblige, was supposedly prepared to sacrifice his own private interests for the public good.

The people, on the other hand, were assumed to be interested only in their own personal well-being. In general, the lower class possessed, Gouverneur Morris wrote, "no Moral but their Interest." Thus, the stability and prosperity of the young republic, the ruling elite was convinced, depended on people's deference to the virtuous, enlightened few. Conservatives like Fisher Ames remained convinced that only "the miracle of virtue, that loves others first, then one's-self," could save the nation from the selfishness and ignorance of the many.

Most average Americans fell into line, obediently and timidly deferring to men of social and political distinction. "We were accustomed to look upon, what we called *gentle folks,* as beings of a superior order," confessed Reverend Devereaux Jarratt, remembering his boyhood as the son of a Virginia carpenter and farmer. "For my part, I was quite shy of them and kept off at a humble distance." Not only did Jarratt believe that his feelings of respect for the gentry were universal among those of his rank and age, but he was also convinced that good government required subordination and "proper distinctions between the various orders of the people."

But conspicuous inequality rankled others, who made known their impatience with hierarchy and their unwillingness to play their submissive parts. Already in the mid-1750s, an irritated Reverend Jacob Duché, the future chaplain of the Continental Congress, muttered that the "meanest" among men in Pennsylvania believed they had a right to civility from the "greatest." And a decade later, Charles Carroll noticed that, prey to "a mean, low, dirty envy," people stood ready to challenge any man of superior fortune or merit. In western Massachusetts, Theodore Sedgwick glowered when a "free-and-easy mechanic" dared to come to the front door of his home. The mechanic as well as Sedgwick understood that attitudes were changing. "The aristocracy of virtue is destroyed," Sedgwick bemoaned; the "personal influence" of the elite few, he wrote, seemed to have come to an end. William Henry Drayton of South Carolina complained of having to participate in government alongside butchers and cobblers.

The arrogant attempts of the conservative fathers to assert their privileged status betrayed their glum recognition of the dissent, unrest, and challenges to authority that had been swirling around them for decades. They could not ignore legislation that abolished primogeniture and entail, preventing families from passing down undiluted economic power from one generation to the next. Nor could they disregard the religious dissent of Presbyterians and Baptists from the Anglican Church in the 1750s and 1760s; the disobedience of some militias in the 1750s; land riots in New York in the 1760s; armed movements in the 1760s and 1770s like the North Carolina Regulators protesting against "the unequal chances the poor and the weak have in contentions with the rich and the powerful"; and Shays's Rebellion in 1786.

Nor could they pretend not to notice the "Democratic-Republican societies" that were springing up in towns and cities in the 1790s or clubs like the Society of St. Tammany. A fraternal, charitable organization, St. Tammany was open to men of the middle and working classes and offered an alternative to the closed society of the elite New York families. Looking down on St. Tammany, some members of the Cincinnati, the hereditary fraternal club of Revolutionary officers, branded its meeting place, called the "Wigwam," the "Pig Pen."

American society was far less of a pyramid than the conservative fathers wanted to believe, for there were few great extremes of wealth. Most Americans were small and moderate property owners. Very poor people constituted a small fraction of the population, and most of the rich were well-to-do but not fabulously wealthy. It was also a land of great social mobility. In one Virginia county, 75 percent of the men who owned no property in the 1760s would acquire land within twenty years. In Boston, 50 percent of the city's merchants after the Revolution were self-made men, and the proportion of self-made men in the elites all over the country was steadily increasing.

The nation indeed was in tremendous flux — so much so that people at both ends of the economic spectrum were beginning to suspect that their social and economic situations were open to change — and *exchange*. At the Constitutional Convention, George Mason, one of the wealthiest landowners in Virginia, voiced astonishment at the "indifference of the superior classes of society" to the rights of ordinary citizens. The wealthy elite should realize, he explained, that within the course of a few years, members of their families would certainly be found "throughout the lowest classes of Society." Thus it was in their interest, he concluded, to provide just as carefully for the rights and happiness of the lowest order of citizens as for the highest. And several decades later, Jefferson would similarly suggest that wealthy men should make a greater contribution to subsidizing public schools, for their descendants, he predicted, would become poor within three generations, and their only chance to rise again would be through education. For his part, James Madison would write of "a constant rotation of property" in free societies, noting that when the rich man contributes to public education, "he is providing for that of his own descendants."

While some people, like Senator John Rutherford of New Jersey, worried that farmers and other middle-class people "run too much to sending their sons to Colleges," thereby giving them "ideas beyond their circumstance," others knew that the key to democratization and equality was education. "If those who know much are few," editorialized the Philadelphia *General Advertiser* in 1792, "and those who know little are many, an aristocracy exists." Several years later, tavern keeper and political radical William Manning would acerbically comment that "it is the universal custom and practice of monarchical and arbitrary governments to train up their subjects as much in ignorance as they can . . . and to teach them to reverence and worship great men in office and to take for truth whatever they say."

So fundamental was the idea of an educated citizenry in a republic that the most enlightened and distinguished fathers, Federalists as well as Republicans, called for educational opportunities for all. Knowledge, wrote John Jay, is the "soul of a republic" and should be open to "all ranks of people." And though George Washington had stated in 1785 that education for the "lower class of citizens" should encompass no more than writing and arithmetic, "so as to fit them for mechanical purposes," in 1796 he would propose a national university at which "a portion of our youth from every quarter" would study, so as to create a more egalitarian society and "homogeneous" citizenry.

Americans were rethinking the relationship between education and citizenship. The true purpose of education, wrote Benjamin Rush, was to "convert men into republican machines." A pupil should be taught to love his family, he wrote, but even more important was the welfare of his country. "He must watch for the state." Old allegiances to a privileged class of men and to a social system based on hierarchy would be discarded in favor of new allegiances to political institutions open to all (that is, to all white men). But education had another purpose, too, for Rush: it would open the door to social mobility and prosperity. Rush envisaged his students studying the "origin and present state of COMMERCE" as well as the "nature and principles of MONEY." Students would learn to "love life and endeavor to acquire as many of its conveniences as possible"; they would learn both responsible citizenship and material acquisition.

This novel synthesis of dedication both to the republic and one's own self-interest spelled a new kind of virtue that called into question the virtue of the old elite, that is, its valorization of self-sacrifice and renunciation. Indeed, some people began to suspect that the ruling fathers' supposed dedication to the public good — for example, their celebrated willingness to serve in office without any compensation — was merely a pretext for protecting their own status, power, and wealth.

In the 1780s, Pennsylvania politician William Findley explained that, while patrician leaders might make claims about their own disinterestedness, self-made men like himself had their own interests to promote. Findley went even further: it was legitimate, he held, for candidates to campaign on behalf of the interests of their constituents. Findley was anticipating not only competitive politics and political parties but also, as historian Gordon Wood noted, the eventual weakening of the classical republican ideal that portrayed legislators as so many disinterested umpires, standing above the play of interests.

People like Findley had glimpsed a new world: an open government in which average citizens could hold public office and promote the interests of certain groups. It would no longer fall to the elite to discern the "public good." Rather, autonomous individuals — some engaged in their governments, others working hard in private occupations, all pursuing their own happiness — would together create the "public good." The public interest, Jefferson was heard to say, was best promoted "by the exertion of each individual seeking his own good in his own way."

But there would be no easy transition to that modern world. The clash between elitism and equality, between an aristocratic republic and a democratic one, underlay many of the debates at the Constitutional Convention. Some of the delegates to the convention spoke up passionately for equality. Equality was the "leading feature" of the United

States, declared William Pinckney of South Carolina. The new federal republic would comprise "one great & equal body of citizens" among whom there would be few if any distinctions of rank or fortune. Every member of society, he continued, "will enjoy an equal power of arriving at the supreme offices & consequently of directing the strength & sentiments of the whole Community." The new republic would contain "but one order . . . the order of Commons," said Charles Pinckney, also of South Carolina, at the Philadelphia convention.

But most of the fifty-five delegates to the convention belonged to the "well-bred, well-fed, well-read, and well-wed" of the nation, and few of them felt that they could rely solely on the wisdom and prudence of the people as a basis for the new government. Meeting in the high-windowed first-floor chamber of the State House in Philadelphia during the sultry summer of 1787, the delegates discussed and debated the new government for four months, six days a week, from ten o'clock in the morning until four in the afternoon, pausing only once for a ten-day recess. The result of their deliberations, the Constitution, mirrored their ambivalence about equality and democracy.

After agreeing to scuttle the weak, ineffective Articles of Confederation, the delegates decided to follow the broad outlines of James Madison's "Virginia Plan," expanding the authority of the national government, to which the states would now be subordinate. The new federal legislature would be the engine of law and policy. Still, they were unwilling to permit it to "absorb all power into its vortex," as Madison warned, and decided that there would be two legislative chambers, the lower one based on popular representation, the upper one, the Senate, based on equality between large and small states. The Senate, moreover, would be able to check the popular House by defeating its bills or simply by ignoring them. Representatives would be elected directly by voters every two years, while senators would be chosen by the state legislatures for six-year terms. Senators would be insulated from the pressure of popular majorities not only by their long terms but also by their staggered elections: a third of their terms would expire every two years. As for the executive branch, after much debate and over objections that it might be the "foetus of monarchy," delegates decided on a one-person executive, elected for a four-year term by electors chosen by the states. Though the president could veto legislation, two-thirds of the members of both houses of Congress could override his veto. And the delegates designed a federal judiciary that would hold at least enough power over the political branches to protect its own independence.

The underlying scheme of the new government was the separation and division of powers: division of power between the national government and the state governments; a separation of power, commonly called a system of checks and balances, among the branches of government; different processes — mostly indirect — for electing president, senators, and representatives; and staggered elections. The delegates had designed a representative government, but it was representation with a twist. For the aim of the delegates in Philadelphia, as political scientist James MacGregor Burns noted, was to pass the interests and passions of the voting populace "through a filter of overlapping and mutually checking representative processes and bodies." Representation would act as a kind of "sieve" that would, delegates hoped, select the most virtuous Americans to be the political leaders of the new republic.

Though the constitutional system sought to hinder individual, average Americans from rising to leadership roles, more importantly, it sought to thwart the power of the people as a whole. The greatest — perhaps the only — strength of the people lies in their numbers, in their ability to mobilize tens of thousands or hundreds of thousands of voters in elections. But the Framers designed the Constitution to impede popular power by breaking it up through separated elections as well as through separated institutions. If the people's principal weapon to achieve equality was elections, elections were precisely what many of the Founders feared. "Elections, my dear sir," John Adams wrote to Jefferson a few months after the Constitutional Convention, "I look at with terror."

But what about the Declaration of Independence's ringing affirmation of equality? Was the Constitution reneging on that promise? Alexander Hamilton seemed to embrace equality of opportunity, noting in *Federalist* No. 36, that "the door ought to be equally open to all." There were "strong minds in every walk of life," the meritocratic Hamilton explained, that could, with opportunity and encouragement, rise above their social and economic circumstances. But at the convention, he had praised England's hereditary House of Lords, "a permanent barrier against every pernicious innovation" and a useful check on "the imprudence of democracy." Doors wide shut?

For his part, Gouverneur Morris openly trumpeted government by the elite. "There never was, and never will be," he told his colleagues at the convention in Philadelphia, "a civilized Society without an Aristocracy." Echoing traditional paternalistic, monarchical ideas, he spoke up for a strong president who, he said, would be the "guardian of the people, even of the lower classes." And yet, following a certain logic, Morris took the radical position of advocating popular election of the president. If the executive is "to be the Guardian of the people," he said, "let him be appointed by the people."

Not even the hard-working, self-made Benjamin Franklin could free himself entirely from the vestiges of elitism. At the Constitutional Convention, he argued that officeholders in the executive branch should receive no salaries whatsoever, for wealthy aristocrats, he held, posed less of a danger to republican government than profit-seeking men engaged in "selfish pursuits." So misguided was his proposal that, Madison noted, "no debate ensued."

Contradictions surfaced even in Madison's political thinking. In the new republic, he envisaged no qualification of wealth, birth, religion, or civil profession for election to office. Voters, too, would belong to the "great body of the people"; they would be as much "the humble sons of obscurity and unpropitious fortune" as "the haughty heirs of distinguished names." And yet, there were subjects, such as that of the acceptance of the Constitution itself, that the "bulk of mankind" could simply not comprehend. In those cases, he explained, the people "must and will be governed by those with whom they happen to have acquaintance and confidence," that is, men who "possess most wisdom to discern, and most virtue to pursue, the common good of the society." But Madison also acknowledged that "enlightened statesmen will not always be at the helm." How then would the common good emerge if one could place confidence neither in the "bulk of mankind" nor in the certainty that men of wisdom would hold high public office? A combination of checks and balances and the supremacy of national interests over local ones, Madison suggested, would ultimately defend the people against "their own temporary errors and delusions" so that the "cool and deliberate sense of the community" — the public good — could "ultimately prevail."

Still, Madison's reservations about the "bulk of mankind" and especially Hamilton's and Morris's praise of aristocratic institutions reinforced the disquieting specter of aristocracy that, for some delegates, loomed over the convention in Philadelphia as well as the ratifying conventions in the states. The new government, George Mason of Virginia charged, would commence in a "moderate aristocracy" and then degenerate into a monarchy or "a corrupt oppressive aristocracy." Others opposed to the Constitution darkly predicted that the members of Congress would inevitably be of "the *well born*" and that the thirteen former colonies would find themselves "consolidated into one despotic monarchy." Amos Singletary warned his colleagues at the Massachusetts ratifying convention to beware of "men of learning, and moneyed men, that talk so finely, and gloss over matters so smoothly." Those men, he said, expected to be the "managers of this Constitution"; they would get all the power and all the money into their own hands, and then "swallow all us little folks like the great Leviathan; yes, just as the whale swallowed up Jonah!" "The great consider themselves above the common people," Melancton Smith remarked at the New York ratifying convention. "Will any one say," he asked, "that there does not exist in this country the pride of family, of wealth, of talents, and that they do not command influence and respect among the common people?" His conclusion? "We ought to guard against the government being placed in the hands of this class."

Despite democratizing trends, high turnover in the First Congress, social movements, and the great preponderance of property owners in America, an elite, privileged class, as Mason, Singletary, and Smith suspected, still tended to dominate American politics. Indeed, within a few years, even Madison would express deep disappointment with the elitism he discerned in American politics. Though he had designed the constitutional system of checks and balances to block especially an "overbearing," oppressive majority, he came to fear, more than a popular majority, an overbearing elite — though now *elite* signified for him not just a privileged social class but a privileged financial class, too. He also came to fear that the influence of the supposedly sovereign people in the government had been "lessened" by the electoral processes by which the people delegated their authority.

In a stinging newspaper essay, written seven months after he exhorted President Washington to remain in office for another term, Madison denounced certain "anti-republicans" who persisted in believing that the people were "stupid" and who demanded their "*Submission* and *Confidence.*" He lashed out at those politicians who, though they had an "interest" in "betraying" the people, nevertheless urged the people to leave "the care of their liberties to their wiser rulers." But those "wise rulers," Madison asserted, wanted to "enrich" the government with influence, expand its powers at the expense of the states, and "arm it with force." *Wise rulers, enrich, force:* Madison had employed all the code words of a battle he himself would lead against fathers and financiers.

Was there another revolution to be fought — one against the dual menace of inequality and paternalism, against economic as well as social aristocrats? The political history of the 1790s would largely be the contentious prelude to that revolution.

Would Americans remain children forever? asked Thomas Jefferson. "We both consider the people as our children," he wrote to his friend Dupont de Nemours, "and love them with parental affection. But you love them as infants whom you are afraid to trust without nurses; and I as adults whom I freely leave to self-government."

As the eighteenth century drew to a close, Americans were trying to liberate themselves from the reign of the fathers, from the vise of paternalism. New leaders — forward-looking, creative, democratic — were emerging, breaking up, in Jefferson's words, the "hereditary and high-handed aristocracy" of America. Jefferson trumpeted a new breed of men, "not so well dressed, nor so politely educated, nor so highly born" as the refined gentlemen of the founding generation. These average men were "the People's men (and the People in general are right). They are plain and of consequence less distinguished, . . . less intriguing, more sincere."

Was Jefferson, the cultivated, soft-spoken Enlightenment gentleman whose mother was a Randolph, even acquainted with such ordinary men? Perhaps not. But his intelligence and his personality, his whole being, embraced the future, and these plain men belonged to the future, and the future would be theirs. Though born into the landed aristocracy of America, Jefferson was drawn, not to the traditions of the fathers, but rather to the experiments of the sons. Freedom, democracy, and inclusion ignited his imagination, not hierarchy, privilege, and patriarchy. Part of the brief inscription he would request to be engraved on his tombstone was "*Father* of the University of Virginia" — the paternity he chose for himself was one of ideas and enlightenment.

In a letter he wrote to John Adams in 1813, Jefferson contrasted his notion of the new kind of politician who could chart a bold course for the nation's future with the fearful individuals who cling to old ways

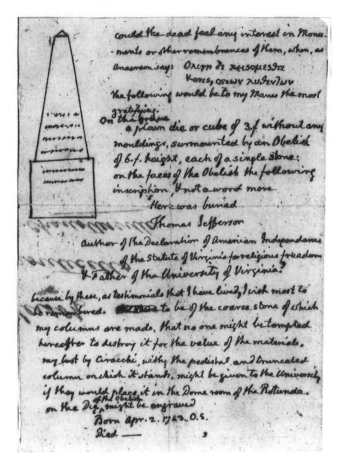

Jefferson's design for his tombstone. Jefferson designed his own
tombstone and wrote his epitaph in 1826, a few months before he died.
It reads: "Thomas Jefferson, Author of the Declaration of American
Independence, of the Statute of Virginia for religious freedom
& Father of the University of Virginia."

and old lessons. "Those who advocated reformation of institutions," he
wrote, "maintained that no definite limits could be assigned to that
progress. The enemies of reform, on the other hand, denied improvement, and advocated steady adherence to the principles, practices and
institutions of our fathers, which they represented as the consumma-
tion of wisdom, and akmé of excellence, beyond which the human
mind could never advance."

The shift that was taking place in political relationships at the end of the eighteenth century from a familial model of authority to Madison's constitutional model reflected, in a sense, the clash of two different visions of time. While conservatives, prey to anxiety about the forces that were transforming American life, lamented the disintegration of social order and hierarchy, and while men like John Adams found in antiquity "eternal, unchangeable truth" and consulted the lessons of the past in order to predict and chart the future, other men, like Jefferson and Madison, unafraid of the future, were seizing the freedom to experiment against history.

They were embarking on a second revolutionary journey along an untraveled path, a course strewn with obstacles and defeats until the final showdown of 1800.

3

Farewell to Harmony

E LEGANTLY ATTIRED IN DARK VELVET and satin, his dia-
mond knee buckles glittering, his wig well powdered, Washington did not dance at his birthday ball, but he mingled happily
with the guests, chatting with the diplomats adorned in medals and
swords, smiling at the captivating young Philadelphia ladies in their
jewels and décolletage. To say that he felt pleasure in commencing his
second term in office, he confided in a friend early in 1793, would have
been a departure from the truth, but he could rejoice in presiding over
a young republic in which "the light of truth and reason" had triumphed. And he had much to be proud of. His administration had
overseen the passage of the Bill of Rights and the creation of a national
bank and system of currency and credit; and his brilliant cabinet members — Secretary of the Treasury Hamilton and Secretary of State Jefferson — along with advisers like Representative James Madison, Chief
Justice John Jay, and Vice President John Adams, assisted him in establishing a strong and determined executive office and a stable, moderate
government for the United States.

The young republic now included fifteen states, Vermont and Kentucky having joined the union. The census of 1790 counted about 4
million inhabitants, including 60,000 free blacks and 700,000 slaves.
Only Massachusetts reported having no slaves. While 50,000 new immigrants — Germans, Dutch, English, Irish, even French royalists —
were disembarking in Atlantic ports in the 1790s, settlers from New
England and New York, Virginia and Maryland, were pushing west-
ward, crossing the Appalachians, moving toward the Ohio and the

Mississippi Rivers, creating new towns and villages, often by ousting and uprooting American Indians. The most populous state was Virginia, with 820,000 inhabitants; Georgia, Delaware, and Rhode Island were the smallest and had less than 100,000 each. Philadelphia, with 42,000 residents, was the capital and the nation's largest city.

On the streets of Philadelphia, Washington could see laborers in their striped trousers, servants and stable boys in their rough clothes, mechanics in their leather aprons, and wealthy merchants in their fashionable English garb. Their clothes told the story: socially and economically, Americans were still stratified. And yet, despite visible signs of inequality, people of all classes were working energetically to improve their communities — and their lives. Everywhere one looked there was activity, commotion, ferment. New associations, groups, and societies were springing up all over: trade unions; fraternal, charitable, and political organizations; societies for penal reform; temperance societies; historical associations like the Massachusetts Historical Society; clubs for intellectuals and scientists, like the American Philosophical Society; and new religious sects, like the Universalists, led by the Reverend Elhanan Winchester and Dr. Benjamin Rush.

Two months before his birthday ball, on a cold, clear January morning, Washington had watched the first balloon flight in America. To the cheers of excited spectators, Frenchman Jean-Pierre François Blanchard, who had crossed the English Channel by balloon in 1785, now slowly rose in the sky above Philadelphia, reaching a height of 6,000 feet. Culturally, scientifically, industrially, Washington's nation was alive. New schools were opening their doors; laws banning stage plays had been repealed; a new copyright act, called for by Noah Webster, protected books, maps, and other artistic property; the first American novel, William Hill Brown's *The Power of Sympathy*, advocating the education of women, was published in 1789; publication of the first American edition of the Encyclopedia Britannica had begun in 1790; a new almanac was published in 1791 by Benjamin Banneker, the son of a free black family, who had also surveyed the site of the planned federal capital on the Potomac; and American naturalist William Bartram published his *Travels*, describing his botanizing expeditions in the southern states. After circumnavigating the globe for the second time, Boston Captain Robert Gray discovered the Columbia River in the Washington-Oregon territory in 1792. In the Atlantic states and in the South, new turnpikes were slashing through forests and hills. In mechanized cotton mills in the Northeast, clamorous spindle and cording machines announced the arrival of the industrial revolution.

The band played "The President's March" when President and Mrs. Washington arrived and again when they departed the birthday ball. The guests all cheered them and applauded warmly.

Ten days later, on March 4, 1793, a brooding Washington delivered his Second Inaugural Address in the red-brick building in Philadelphia called Congress Hall. It was a curt speech of fewer than 150 words. Sullenly he announced only that if he were found guilty of having willingly or knowingly violated his oath of office, he would be "subject to the upbraidings of all who are now witnesses of the present solemn ceremony."

The president was shaken by negative reactions to the birthday ball. The affair resembled a "monarchical farce," the *National Gazette* sneered. Five months earlier the *Gazette* had welcomed Washington's reelection; now it ridiculed his government for indulging in "every species of royal pomp and parade." What were the "gee-gaws of a court" compared to "the manliness of freemen who are resolved not to erect a funeral pyre for their liberties?" The president's formal entertainments, the *Gazette* charged, were the "offspring of inequality, begotten by the aristocracy and monarchy upon corruption." Though Americans had not yet heard the news that radicals in France had just beheaded their hapless monarch, many sympathized with the ravenous hunger of their French brethren for liberty and equality.

With his head still attached to his shoulders, Washington had abruptly descended from the heights of the immortal gods to the swamp of fallible politicians. "Tranquillity reigns among the people," he had contentedly observed when he traveled through the South in the spring of 1791, accepting accolades and toasts, making speeches, greeting admiring followers. But little by little, that appearance of tranquility had been shattered.

Although Washington wished for nothing more than to preside over a unified government and nation, he was dismayed by the opposition to his administration's policies. The abusive attacks on public officers and government policies, Washington believed, were "insidious"; they were destroying people's confidence in their public servants and, he predicted, would ultimately destroy the union. But he was particularly stung by personal criticism of himself, of his superb state dinners and

levees, of his cream-colored coach drawn by four horses. "Ah, thought I
to myself, the times are changed," wrote "A Farmer" to the Philadelphia
Aurora, after seeing Washington's coach pass by, "and have changed
with them *plain and republican General Washington* into a being, which
my neighbour Tribble took to be a Prince."

Washington had claimed that "the arrows of malevolence" could
never reach the "most vulnerable part of me," but they did in fact reach
their target. Attacks on him in the Republican press were "outrages on
common decency," he fumed, that could only be met with contempt
and silence. Coldly explaining Washington's sensitivity to criticism, Jefferson wrote that the president wore "the rags of royalty" and that they
could "hardly be torn off without laceration." "Gratitude no longer
blinds the public mind," another American wrote.

And Congress, too, had chimed in, defeating in 1792 a proposal to
place the image of Washington's head on coins. Such a symbol, congressmen warned, might encourage a future president to emulate a
Caesar, a Nero, or a Caligula. The practice of placing a leader's image
on coins represented an "almost idolatrous practice of Monarchies,"
declared Virginia representative John Page. Other Americans objected
to celebrations of the president's birthday, calling them "incompatible"
with their republican character. They insisted that revolutionary and
republican principles — not men — should be honored and applauded.
These "frenchified zelots," John Adams reported to Abigail, were bent
on ruining the president's character, destroying his peace, and injuring
his health.

But most troubling of all to Washington were opposition and conflict within his own executive branch of government. Already during
his first term, the chagrined president had witnessed strife and acrimony overwhelm his cabinet. "Internal dissentions," he bitterly commented, were "harrowing and tearing our vitals." The nation's father
was deeply opposed to factions and parties. But could he prevent
them?

If one cabinet secretary "pulls this way and another that," he carefully explained, government "must inevitably be torn asunder." Divisions within the executive branch, he believed, would produce only
deadlock. The president's leadership strategy was to govern through
consensus and unity. Hamilton had similarly conceived the executive
branch in terms of unity. Advocating an executive composed of a single individual rather than a council of men, Hamilton explained in

Federalist No. 70 that "no favorable circumstances palliate or atone for the disadvantages of dissension in the executive department." Nor did Hamilton countenance a council of advisers, which, he felt, would be "nothing better than a clog" upon the good intentions of the president.

Washington and Hamilton's antipathy for parties and dissent in government was not unreasonable. It was predicated on the historical vulnerability of republics and on the long tradition that viewed factions as evil, the tools of special interests that prevented a national consensus and stable government. But Washington and Hamilton also sensed that the United States was not yet a unified nation, that the commitment to constitutional government was not yet so strong and deep that ideological divisions would not damage tenuous feelings of nationhood.

"United we stand; divided we fall," Patrick Henry had written to Thomas Jefferson in 1785, underlining the crucial importance of political concord. "Let us not split into factions which must destroy that union upon which our existence hangs." John Jay also sought to ground the young republic in a myth of unity. In *Federalist* No. 2, he portrayed Americans as "one united people — a people descended from the same ancestors, speaking the same language, professing the same religion, attached to the same principles of government, very similar in their manners and customs." Though this fictional romance of homogeneity was clearly at odds with the reality of American diversity, Jay's point was that "Providence" itself had bestowed on America a Constitution that would strengthen the unity and solidarity of the "band of brethren."

Almost without exception the leaders of the founding generation idealized and advocated unity and harmony, agreeing that factions and parties — whether in the legislative or executive branch — were harmful to good government. "There is nothing which I dread so much," John Adams had remarked in 1780, "as a division of the republic into two great parties, each arranged under its leader, and concerting measures in opposition to each other." In *Federalist* No. 10, Madison had cautioned against the "instability, injustice, and confusion" that result from faction. Still, he realized that it was impossible to eliminate factions, since the cost of that would be freedom itself. Even Thomas Jefferson, the future leader of the Republican opposition, spoke out against parties. "If I could not go to heaven but with a party," he quipped, "I would not go there at all." For many, nonpartisan unanimity seemed the key to good government — and yet, even while these leaders were spurning the idea of party, they were aligning themselves with certain policies and giving shape to nascent parties.

On the other side of the ocean, Edmund Burke, a leader of the opposition Whig party in Great Britain, had, in 1770, already offered a convincing explanation for the need for parties in a representative government. Why would like-minded politicians who want to see their ideas and principles translated into practice not associate and cooperate with one another? he wondered. He was certain that "no men could act with effect, who did not act in concert; that no men could act in concert, who did not act with confidence; that no men could act with confidence, who were not bound together by common opinions, common affections and common interests." The thought that men would choose *not* to act in concert with others struck Burke as "utterly incomprehensible."

Indeed, groups of American politicians did act in concert. In the 1780s, rudimentary "parties" or legislative blocs already existed: though politicians formed no organizations and articulated no platforms, they possessed and acted on "principles of concert" — for example, one bloc was willing to tax and expand government, whereas the other wanted to hold down taxes and government costs. Their groups, wrote historian Jackson Turner Main, "in many ways anticipated the political alignments of the post-Revolutionary era." But these blocs also aroused much ire, provoking warnings against "violent party spirit" and complaints that politicians were not pursuing the public good.

Washington and Hamilton were adamant in their rejection of parties, offering instead a philosophical basis for their faith in unity: they both believed that there existed only one true overriding public interest. After all, the Constitution had been created "to unite all parties for the general welfare," Hamilton had explained shortly after the Philadelphia convention in 1787. Dedicated personally to "the aggregate happiness of society," Washington fully concurred. Though the country might be "diversified in local & smaller matters," the president wrote in 1792, he was persuaded that the public good "is the same in all the great & essential concerns of the Nation." If there was one and only one common good, how could there be two competing versions of it? "Truth is a thing, not of divisibility into conflicting parts," pronounced John Taylor of Caroline.

The problem was that the "public good" is a purely abstract, theoretical concept. In a free, open society — as Madison intuited in *Federalist*

No. 10 — people all have their own opinions, interests, beliefs, and passions. While they might agree on a public good consisting of "life, liberty, and the pursuit of happiness," it was unlikely that they would agree on much else.

Some Americans were beginning to feel that the public good existed only insofar as it could reflect the needs and wants of disparate and even clashing individuals and groups, each with its own idea of what constituted the public good. Indeed, a new spirit of individualism would soon surface, one that would countenance multiple interests and multiple pursuits of happiness. But Hamilton and Washington did not question the existence of the public good; they questioned only the ability of ordinary people, "turbulent and changing," "steadily to pursue the public good." But to whom, if not to a majority of unruly citizens, would it fall to discover, formulate, and articulate the public good? A handful of virtuous, wise fathers? Hamilton indeed believed that the health and survival of the republic depended on stable government by men who were, as he wrote, "faithful to the national interest." These virtuous and enlightened few, Hamilton wrote, "would look down with contempt upon every mean or interested pursuit."

Convinced that there was only one public interest, Washington expected the brilliant gentlemen in his administration to recognize it and then to craft and implement the best policies for the nation — rationally and harmoniously.

In later years, Jefferson credited Washington with avoiding deadlock and inaction in his cabinet, even though its "monarchists" and "republicans" could not have been more divided. Washington's strategy was to listen to his cabinet members, hear their opinions and reasons, and then decide the course to be pursued and keep "the government steadily in it, unaffected by the agitation."

But agitation there was. Jefferson and Hamilton were "daily pitted in the cabinet like two cocks," Jefferson would later recall. Despite Washington's pleas for harmony, deep ideological fault lines slashed through his administration. There may have been a consensus on constitutional government itself, but there was agreement on little else. Hamilton and Jefferson battled on all the important issues of the day — a national bank, tariffs, foreign policy, the site of the new national capital, and the bloody revolution convulsing France.

In the summer of 1792, before the end of his first term, the president had finally had enough. He wrote a stern letter to Jefferson. "Without more charity for the opinions and acts of one another in Governmental matters," he lectured his fellow Virginian, "it will be difficult, if not impracticable, to manage the Reins of Government or to keep the parts of it together." Because he deeply valued both Jefferson and Hamilton, he counseled "liberal allowances and mutual forbearances" and an end to "wounding suspicions and irritable charges."

The following day, he composed another letter, this time to reform his other protégé, Alexander Hamilton. More melancholy than severe, the president repeated his message that "internal obstructions" in the government were "harrowing our vitals." Differences in political opinions, he recognized, were unavoidable, but he insisted that issues be discussed with civility, without individuals' motives being challenged. Washington hoped that Hamilton and Jefferson, men of vast abilities as well as "upright intentions," would "exercise more charity" toward each other. Could they not strive to compromise, to find a "middle course"? he asked. How could they be so sure that their own opinions were correct? After all, mortals possessed no "*infallible* rule by which we could *fore* judge events." Like a gentle doctor, Washington hoped that "balsam may be poured into all the wounds which have been given." But it was becoming increasingly difficult, he confided in his attorney general, Edmund Randolph, on that same day, "to keep the machine together."

Indeed, there was nothing conciliatory in Jefferson's reply to the president. Days after receiving Washington's letter, he responded with a lengthy detailed catalogue of his grievances against Hamilton. As for Hamilton's allies, they were "deserters from the rights & interests of the people," men who had "nothing in view but to enrich themselves." Jefferson's conclusion? He wished to return to private life in Monticello and would shortly resign from the government. "My farm, my family, and my books call me to them irresistibly," he wrote, after having insisted, four months earlier, that Washington, who panted to return to domestic life at Mount Vernon, should not do the same.

Hamilton's response was more generous. He offered to help Washington "smooth the path" of his administration. "If any prospect shall open of healing or terminating the differences which exist, I shall most chearfully embrace it." But sandwiched in between Hamilton's pacifying phrases was his own attack on Jefferson. Presenting himself as the "injured party" and a "silent sufferer," he gave his own list of Jefferson's outrageous actions.

At his wits' end, the president could not comprehend the enduring enmity in his cabinet and again appealed to Jefferson for "harmony." He assured him of his "sincere esteem and regard" for him as well as for Hamilton and oddly remarked that he was persuaded that, at bottom, there was "no discordance" in Jefferson's and Hamilton's views.

Trusting that the government was a kind of neutral umpire in national affairs, Washington was puzzled that men he knew to be completely devoted to the republic could be so ideologically divided. He was equally mystified by the absence of tolerance and civility. Washington himself had always shown respect for the opinions of others. Should he "set up [his] judgment as the standard of perfection?" he had written in his draft notes for his first inaugural speech. "And shall I arrogantly pronounce that whosoever differs from me must discern the subject through a distorting medium, or be influenced by some nefarious design?" Only through "good dispositions, and mutual allowances" was effective government possible. "Suspicions unfounded, jealousies too lively" would produce only evil.

Washington kept both Hamilton and Jefferson in his cabinet, profiting from their counsel and ideas, until Jefferson resigned at the end of 1793. His relations with James Madison were more complex.

During Washington's first term, Madison had been his closest and most trusted adviser, even closer to him than Alexander Hamilton. "What do you think I had best do?" he asked Madison again and again as he worked at setting up his new government. Apologizing for so many "troublesome" requests, he wrote warmly, "Ascribe it to friendship and confidence." The president ended his letters to Madison with "Yours ever" and with "affectionate regard," while Hamilton received only a "Yours sincerely." But the deep trust between the two Virginians was about to end.

In the first months of Washington's presidency, Madison, as congressman from Virginia in the House of Representatives, and Hamilton, as secretary of the treasury, had worked well in tandem on a variety of issues, including banking, taxation, and trade. Hamilton was not only brilliant but charming and generous, too, and Madison must have appreciated his lively imagination. But Madison the Virginian quickly grew wary of the New Yorker's motives, viewing them as antithetical to the interests of ordinary citizens and republican government. The tension between the two men erupted over the issue of certificates of debt in 1789 and early 1790.

Some speculators, poised to reap huge windfall profits, were paying anywhere from one to ten cents on the dollar to soldiers and others for debt certificates that would eventually be paid back at full value by the government. Was the government collaborating with America's financial gamblers at the expense of her veterans? Veterans had "been cheated out of their honest dues, by speculators, monopolizers, sharpers and oppressors," charged the *New Hampshire Recorder*. How could the great George Washington "endure seeing the pay of the impoverished soldiers go into the coffers of parasites?" demanded the *New-York Packet*. But Hamilton's allies displayed little sympathy for these veterans. "Esau had sold his birthright for a mess of pottage," one congressman commented, "and heaven and earth had confirmed the sale."

Something was rotten. The term *speculation* had once meant deep thought on some original problem, but it had come to signify a risky business enterprise or transaction for the purpose of great gain. "Speculation" on the debt, James Madison concluded, was "wrong, radically & morally & politically wrong." He proposed a motion in Congress to indemnify the original owners of certificates of debt at full value and the present holders at a lesser value. For him, at stake was something more fundamental than economic policy: traffic in certificates of debt posed a moral problem. Shouldn't the holder of a certificate of debt, he asked, feel remorse for having bought that certificate for one-tenth of its value from a distressed fellow citizen?

For his part, Hamilton feared that Madison's plan would render American debt nonfungible in the future. Believing that public credit was the "powerful cement of our union," imagining that federal promissory notes could even substitute for money, he felt strongly that Madison's proposal rewarded those who were unwilling to bet on the American future, unwilling to believe that America would repay her debt. While Hamilton's avowed intention was to ally the interests of the moneyed class with those of the government, to encourage them to become America's creditors, making them partners in ensuring the economic development of the nation ("He never meant for monied men to use the government. He intended the reverse," argued one historian), different considerations of class, morality, and economic justice were creeping into Madison's political consciousness.

Whereas Hamilton wanted to keep capital concentrated in the hands of the small class of men who would develop the American economy and build manufactories, ships, and infrastructure, thereby strengthening the nation, Madison, for his part, believed that in a just society the government would aid average citizens, farmers, and small manufacturers, not just large financial interests. Madison, the cultivated member of the landed Virginia gentry, seemed to be temperamentally repelled by urban financial dealings. He and other southerners were convinced that in the cultivation of the land and in the yeoman farmer resided the true moral strength of the nation; they were temperamentally opposed to the expansion of government that Hamilton's economic programs required. Not only was Madison acquiring an awareness of the sectional and cultural differences between himself and Hamilton, but he also appeared to be acquiring a new sense of social justice. "Thank God," wrote a "real Soldier" to the Boston *Columbian Centinel,* "there lives a Madison to propose justice [for] the poor emaciated soldier."

Many rushed to Hamilton's defense. For Vice President John Adams, Madison's motions were nothing short of "stupid" testimony to his "Infamy." Representative John Trumbull of Connecticut assured Adams that Madison had become "the insignificant leader of an impotent Minority" and had "lost all his popularity." Madison had made himself the leader of the opposition to Hamilton's economic plans, Theodore Sedgwick of Massachusetts contended, charging that the Virginian stood "at the head of the discontented in America."

Madison's motion for "discrimination" in the matter of certificates of debt was defeated, but that did not stop him from continuing to oppose Hamilton's other economic policies, his plans for the federal government's assumption of the states' debts and for a national bank. Hamilton's schemes, Madison charged in Congress, were aimed only at helping speculators — some of whom were in Congress — and wealthy merchants. The explicit goal of his national bank was to promote industrialization by concentrating capital solely in the hands of big entrepreneurs and financiers. Under Hamilton's aegis, wealth would shift from the South to the industrializing North, and power would shift from the states to the executive branch of the federal government, significantly reshaping the country.

Indeed, Madison's objections to Hamilton's funding scheme reflected more than mere concern for the average man; he also wanted to protect the autonomy of state governments and southern agrarianism and keep at bay the economic forces of corruption. The sale of shares in the new bank, he wrote, signified a "scramble for so much public plunder"; it was an ominous sign of the "daring depravity of the times." Jefferson, too, saw in Hamilton's concept of a permanent national debt the seeds of corruption. "I would wish the debt paid tomorrow," Jefferson grumbled. "[Hamilton] wishes it never to be paid." Jefferson's aversion to a national debt may have been colored by his personal feelings; in debt all of his adult life, as historian Edmund Morgan remarked, "he hated debt and hated anything that made him a debtor" because it limited what was most precious to him: his freedom. Wouldn't a national economy founded on debt similarly undermine American liberty and independence? Even so, Madison and Jefferson did finally accept Hamilton's plan for the national assumption of state debts — in exchange for Hamilton's agreement that the country's new permanent capital would be located not, as he had dreamt, in the center of the banking and trading community of Manhattan, but rather on the Potomac, near their own state of Virginia. They were apparently as transactional in their opposition to Hamilton's policies as Hamilton was in his grab for influence. The two gentlemen from Virginia even managed to maintain cordial relations with Hamilton — temporarily.

Hamilton's concept of an active, central government that planned the nation's economic future was stunningly modern, and his economic policies would prove to be hugely successful. He was a brilliant, forward-looking thinker and a daring political and economic venturer. "There are epochs in human affairs," he had written in 1780, "when *novelty* even is useful." But he never was able to counter the impression that he was an inegalitarian; nor was he able to articulate if and how the American people were to share in the economic prosperity he sought to promote and how that prosperity might contribute to the welfare and happiness of average Americans. Unlike Hamilton, Madison had struck a chord, and many ordinary Americans were sticking with him. After the failure of Madison's motion for discrimination, the Boston *Columbian Centinel* applauded his courage in defending "the right of the widows and orphans, the original creditors and the

war worn soldier." And the *Pennsylvania Gazette* editorialized with
a poem:

> A soldier's pay are rags and fame,
> A wooden leg — a deathless name.
> To Specs, both *in* and *out* of Cong,
> The four and six percents belong.

After an early breakfast in New York, its streets already bustling with
every manner of vendors from knife grinders to ragmen and orange
girls, all calling out their trade, Thomas Jefferson and James Madison
set sail on the Hudson. It was May 1791. They left behind them the
clamorous, smelly streets, the mansions, counting houses, taverns, refuse piles, construction sites, hogs, and goats. On the water, the two
friends marveled at the springtime beauty of the Hudson highlands,
rejoicing in the vistas of the wide river, in the astonishing variety of
trees — white cedar, silver fir, and candleberry myrtle — and flowering
shrubs — juniper, azalea. "Not a sprig of grass shoots uninteresting to
me," Jefferson wrote to his daughter.

In Poughkeepsie, they left their boat and traveled slowly by phaeton
to Albany, Madison's horse trotting after the carriage, their two servants on horseback following behind. Jefferson noted in his diary still
more varieties of trees — oak, sugar maple, white birch, spruce pine,
red cedar. The air was rich with fragrant honeysuckle. Red squirrels
and chipmunks darted past them; seagulls, loons, and wild ducks flew
above. It was early spring, but the weather was "sultry hot," Jefferson
wrote, as unpleasant as summertime heat in Carolina or Georgia. In
point of climate, he remarked, Virginia had nothing to envy in New
England, where "they are locked up in ice and snow for six months."

In the town of Albany, the two Virginians were welcomed by Alexander Hamilton's father-in-law, General Philip Schuyler, who had just
been defeated for the Senate by Aaron Burr. In Saratoga, General
Schuyler's son John showed them around the battleground. "Lake
George is without comparison the most beautiful water I ever saw,"
Jefferson wrote to his daughter Martha, after sailing up the lake. Nes-
tled in a mountain basin, it was dotted with small islands and surrounded by silver fir, white pine, aspen, and paper birch trees as well as
wild cherries and "strawberries in abundance." Continuing on to Lake
Champlain, Jefferson noted that the water of that lake was less pleasant

than that of Lake George, but it was also "less infested with musketoes and insects." The eastern shore of Lake Champlain was well settled, Madison jotted in his diary, but east of Lake George the only inhabitant was a "free negro" who, Madison commented with surprise, ran a large farm with "white hirelings" and was "intelligent, reads, writes, understands accounts [and] is dexterous in his affairs." Jefferson kept busy, scribbling notes for a study he had undertaken for the American Philosophical Society on the damage inflicted by the dreaded Hessian fly on wheat production. Newspapers along their route carried stories about the arrival of the two notables from Virginia.

Heading back south, they stopped in Bennington, then the capital of the new state — since March 1791 — of Vermont. Governor Moses Robinson welcomed them to his home overlooking the Walloomsac River and then accompanied them to the Congregational church, Jefferson and Madison admitting that they hadn't been to church in several years. It was unlawful to travel on the sabbath, and the Virginians had to bide their time in Bennington until they could continue their journey into Massachusetts the next day. They traveled on through the Berkshires to Williamstown and Pittsfield, the region of Shays's Rebellion in 1786, and then down to Northampton in the Connecticut River valley, passing through Springfield and Hartford and then sailing across Long Island Sound, going as far as the northeastern tip of Long Island. Finally the Brooklyn ferry carried them back to their starting point.

Had their journey been nothing more than an enjoyable botanical excursion, a naturalist's interlude? Or did the political landscape hold more interest for them than the natural one? New York politicians had been intently, narrowly watching the tourists as they journeyed through their state. John Hamilton, Alexander Hamilton's son and biographer, later claimed that the trees, lakes, and squirrels of the Northeast were a mere "pretext," a convenient cover for scouting out the political terrain. Was Jefferson and Madison's trip, historians have wondered ever since, the first phase in their creation of a nationwide opposition party?

Before setting sail on the Hudson, Jefferson and Madison had met in New York with New York senator Rufus King, with newly elected senator Aaron Burr, and with Robert Livingston, chancellor of the state of New York. Livingston, happy to combat the "Anglocrats," had helped Burr win his race. "Are the people in your quarter as well contented with the proceedings of our government, as their representatives say they are?" Jefferson had pointedly asked Livingston in a letter written a few months before the excursion. "There is a vast mass of discontent gathered in the South, and how and when it will break god knows."

Livingston's reply contained good news and bad news. "Our delegates deceive themselves," he answered, "if they believe their constituents are satisfied with all the Measures of Government." But would it be possible to mobilize people to return to true republican principles and ideals? Livingston was dubious. The rapidly expanding prosperity was diminishing civic engagement. People "have no idea of a more perfect government," Livingston wrote, "than that which enriches them in six months."

Did those discussions continue in New York? Probably. Was Jefferson and Madison's goal to forge an opposition alliance of New York and Virginia politicians? Probably. "There was every appearance of a passionate courtship" among Livingston, Burr, Jefferson, and Madison, a worried Robert Troup quickly reported to Hamilton, warning that if the conspirators succeeded, "they will tumble the fabric of the government in ruins to the ground." The planter aristocrats had embarked on a secret mission, Nathaniel Hazard revealed to Hamilton. They "scouted silently through the Country, shunning the Gentry, communing with and pitying the Shaysites."

The friends had indeed avoided the political luminaries, preferring to see firsthand how ordinary people lived and worked. In Hudson, New York, Jefferson tried to convince Captain Seth Jenkins, the founder of that port town, that better spirits could be made from wine instead of molasses, thereby increasing trade with France and diminishing dependence upon the British West Indies for sugar. In Waterford, New York, Jefferson visited a nail factory, and in Springfield and Hartford, he and Madison looked at a few small manufactures.

In Bennington, they focused on politics. Moses Robinson, the governor who had just been elected to the Senate, Joseph Fay, a Vermont Revolutionary leader, and Anthony Haswell, editor of the *Vermont Gazette,* reported on state politics, relations with Canada, the cultivation of maple orchards, and Thomas Paine's reply to Edmund Burke's lacerating criticism of the revolution in France. After Madison and Jefferson left Bennington, the *Vermont Gazette* noted that the Virginians had "secured to themselves a fund of political knowledge."

What had they chatted about as they breakfasted, journeyed, hiked, rode, and dined in New York, Vermont, Massachusetts, and Connecticut? The scenery, animals, rivers, and lakes? Their lives, their families, their feelings? Or their ideas, political visions, and embryonic plan to form a political opposition? The "mutual influence of these two mighty minds upon each other," wrote John Quincy Adams, "is a phenomenon, like the invisible and mysterious movements of the magnet in the physical world."

The two friends pronounced the trip a grand success; even the headaches that had plagued Jefferson during the winter of 1790–91 had disappeared. Jefferson returned to Philadelphia, while Madison stayed on at Mrs. Elsworth's boarding house on Maiden Lane. Did he linger in New York for more conversations with Burr and Livingston, or for more intimate tête-à-têtes with a certain mysterious Mrs. Colden?

Frustrated by the undiluted praise of Washington's administration that appeared in John Fenno's *Gazette of the United States,* Jefferson and Madison cried out for an antidote. In New York they had met with Philip Freneau, Madison's old classmate at Princeton, and had persuaded him to found a newspaper in Philadelphia that would oppose the administration's policies. There was surely room for another newspaper in a city in which almost all citizens were literate.

Jefferson sweetened the proposal to Freneau with the offer of a position of translator in the Department of State, along with the promise of printing for the government and access to the secretary of state's foreign correspondence. Hamilton was livid. "Is it possible," he asked in an anonymous newspaper essay, "that Mr. Jefferson, the head of a principal department of the Government can be the Patron of a Paper, the evident object of which is to decry the Government and its measures?" Hamilton had posed an important ethical question, to which Jefferson tortuously replied — to President Washington — that he had not really recruited Freneau and that he had never attempted to influence Freneau's editorial policies. The real miscreant, he added, was Hamilton, who penned anonymous articles for the *Gazette of the United States.* Party alignments were forming, and yet neither side was willing to admit it openly. Indeed, precisely this lack of openness on the subject of party, as historian Lance Banning remarks, "favored a conspiratorial interpretation of opponents' motives." One remark in Jefferson's letter to Washington, however, was more forthright. "No government ought to be without censors," he stated, "& where the press is free, no one ever will."

In the early 1790s, the United States had about a hundred newspapers. Most of them, two to four pages long, were weeklies, but there were a few dailies. One page at a time, on a block of type, printers cranked them out, on rough, grayish or bluish paper. They were "not much to look at," commented historian James MacGregor Burns, and yet they added tremendous vitality to the public arena. Along with advertisements, arrival and departure schedules of sailing vessels, and notices of runaway slaves, the papers covered international as well as national news, often quoting from congressional debates.

In general, newspapers were not yet openly partisan. At the time of the Philadelphia convention and state-ratifying conventions, the press had "monolithically" supported the Constitution, commented a historian of the American press. One editor, Alexander Dallas, was even fired for reporting on speeches of the antifederalist as well as federalist side at the Pennsylvania ratifying convention. But American newspapers were on the verge of developing into the partisan organs of burgeoning political parties.

The first issue of Freneau's *National Gazette* appeared in late October 1791. Within weeks, Madison, coauthor of the *Federalist* essays that had originally appeared in New York newspapers, once again jumped into political journalism, writing a series of a dozen unsigned articles explaining the principles underlying his opposition to the administration's — and Hamilton's — policies. As if he were the leader of a shadow government, Madison outlined his vision of the national purpose, a vision more multidimensional and inclusive than Hamilton's hard-nosed goal of national wealth, military might, and power. The essays, published between November 1791 and April 1792, are a startling attack on Hamilton's values and policies from one of Washington's closest and most trusted advisers.

In an article entitled "Property," Madison redefined the concept of property. Property, he argued, is not merely a man's land or wealth — or slaves. On the contrary, it has a "larger and juster meaning" — more democratic and egalitarian. A man's property includes his opinions, his religious faith, his free use of his faculties, and "the most sacred of all property," his conscience.

Governments, Madison reminded his readers, are typically accorded high praise for protecting the property of the wealthy. But far more important to the health of a republic and to the vitality of an open political arena than the financial well-being of a small number of individuals, Madison contended, is the government's protection of all citizens' "free use of their faculties, and free choice of their occupations" as well as protection of their intangible property, that is, their rights and labor. Just as Jefferson had changed the classic Lockean formula from "life, liberty and estate" to "Life, Liberty, and the pursuit of Happiness," Madison, too, was drawing a distinction between a conservative government that safeguards the material property of the wealthy few and a truly "republican" government that safeguards the interests and the freedom of expression of the many. Madison was awakening the class consciousness of average Americans, advising them that they too possessed "property" interests that were as worthy of their government's attention — and even intervention — as the economic interests of the moneyed elite that Hamilton's economic programs favored.

James Madison, a connoisseur of style? One essay, entitled "Fashion," was inspired by a news item from England. The Prince of Wales had just created a new vogue: buckles on shoes were out, shoestrings and slippers were "in" for the fashionable crowd. But the abandonment of buckles meant that the more than 20,000 people employed in that industry had been laid off. They were hungry and destitute, victims of the "mutability of fashion." The least desirable jobs in an economy, Madison observed, are those that "produce the most servile dependence of one class of citizens on another class." And when the two classes are unequal — when the needs of one class are those that are truly necessary to its survival and the needs of another class are only "caprices of fancy" — the evil is in the extreme.

The jobs and welfare of ordinary working people, Madison concluded, must be protected from the fickle, trivial desires of the wealthy elite. The ultimate solution he proposed to the problem of job insecurity and economic exploitation was an agricultural economy. In part, this was Madison's response to Hamilton's recent *Report on the Subject of Manufactures,* recommending government support for industry. Like Jefferson, Madison argued that people who cultivate the soil are uniquely able to be independent citizens. In an agricultural economy, there is "a reciprocity of dependence" rather than the dependency of one class on another. But whatever a community's economic base might be — agriculture or manufacturing and commerce — in order to have a society in which people have a "dignified sense of social rights," their ability to work should not depend on "fashion and superfluity." On the contrary, the wants of all citizens, Madison argued, should be "founded in solid utility," not in an economy dominated by the production of luxury goods. Stressing the economic underpinnings of freedom, Madison was convinced that unless there was a "*mutuality* of wants" in society, some citizens, those who experience the "horrors of want," could not be free.

In another article entitled "Parties," Madison again brought up the subject of economic inequality, but this time he linked it to the question of political parties. In *Federalist* No. 10, he had noted that the "unequal distribution of property" was the "most common and durable source of factions." While recognizing that parties are "unavoidable" in a free, diverse society, he now argued that the best way to eliminate the "evil" of parties was to diminish the "differences of interests" that are responsible for their rise.

How did Madison propose to lessen these differences of interests among citizens? First, there should be "political equality" among citizens. Second, "*unnecessary* opportunities" should be withheld from the wealthy few so that they cannot increase the inequality of property "by an immoderate, and especially *unmerited*, accumulation of riches." Third, "extreme wealth" should be reduced "towards a state of mediocrity" while "extreme indigence" should be raised toward a "state of comfort" — in short, economic leveling and redistribution of wealth. Fourth, the government should not favor certain interests at the expense of others.

Madison's idea was that as citizens' conditions become more equal and as they come to conceive the public interest in similar terms, divisive parties based on class interests might fade from view. But if it were impossible to obtain such equality and political concord, he offered a fifth suggestion: he proposed that a political party representing the interests of ordinary Americans could try to "check" the party opposite representing the interests of the wealthy. On the one hand, Madison seemed to want ideally to do away with parties; on the other, he believed that the "great art of politicians lies in making one party a check on the other." That "art" would be a means through which an organized majority of citizens could overcome his constitutional system of majority-pulverizing checks and balances.

A few months later, Madison again broached the issue of parties. His essay, "A Candid State of Parties," is indeed candid. Parties in America, Madison declared, reflect class and economic dichotomies. One party, he explained, is "more partial to the opulent" and believes that government should be carried on only by the "pageantry of rank, the influence of money and emoluments and the tenor of military force." Simply put, this party, enamored of debts, financial speculation, taxes, and armies (clearly Hamilton's capitalist, pro-military party), governs in the interest of the few. In Madison's mind, the secretary of the treasury was surrounded by so many Tory aristocrats who selfishly profited from exemptions, monopolies, and all manner of arbitrary privileges that the government accorded to the "few" but denied to the "many." But even worse, these financial royalists were supposedly conniving to narrow the government into ever fewer hands, a process that would ultimately change the government into "an hereditary form."

In other words, the old "Fathers," the members of the social elite to whom the people had for decades been obliged to defer, had metamorphosed into a pernicious, aristocratic party of financial speculators and pro-military, nationalist politicians, the Hamiltonian "Federalists." Indeed, through the code word *aristocrat,* which, in the absence of the epithet *capitalist,* was the all-purpose term for any powerful, privileged in-group, Madison exploited the specter of monarchy, caste, and hereditary government, not merely to inflame old class resentments but rather to conflate the privileged social elite of the past with the new privileged class, the capitalist elite.

Even though the backward-looking, landowning, conservative elite of the past had little if anything in common with the rising class of wealthy bankers and speculators, Madison had discovered a way to mobilize class resentments in opposition to the modernizing trends of capitalism and industrialization. Monarchists, aristocrats, speculators, bankers: in Madison's mind, they had all become one and the same foe of the people. Indeed, if the antipaternalistic revolt against "aristocracy" of Madison, Jefferson, George Mason, and others seemed at times exaggerated, it was in part because they often used words like *aristocracy* to refer to the economically privileged as well as the socially privileged.

In contrast to the party of Hamiltonian aristocratic "Federalists," the other party, the "republican" party, Madison held, is founded on the notion that mankind is capable of governing itself in the general interest of all the members of the community. While the "antirepublican party" is weak in numbers, Madison noted, the republican party could count on the support of a majority of Americans. And yet, he also recognized that in politics "stratagem is often an overmatch for numbers." Still, so superior was the size of the republican party that, predicted Madison, it would eventually govern in the name of the "great body of the people."

But what point was Madison making about political parties? Was he still ambivalent about them? The hope he expressed in "A Candid State of Parties" was for the ultimate victory of his own party, the creation of a new consensus about the public good, and the disappearance of the opposition, not for a system of two parties that, equally legitimate, might alternately govern.

Another openly partisan essay trumpeted even louder the class divisions underlying the two adversarial political factions. In his article, "Who Are the Best Keepers of the People's Liberties?" Madison asserted that "anti-republicans" are convinced that "the people are stupid." They scornfully dismiss the idea that the people can be trusted with self-government. The only political role that antirepublicans bestow on the people is "obedience, leaving the care of their liberties to their wiser rulers." But the Republican party, Madison emphasized (using that label for the second time), holds that the people are the best keepers of their own liberties. Like a real party operator, Madison wanted to see the people "enlightened, awakened, *united*" against the antirepublicans. One sentence sums up Madison's critique of Hamilton: "What a perversion of the natural order of things! to make *power* the primary and central object of the social system, and *Liberty* but its satellite."

Madison had come a long way from his political masterpiece, *Federalist* No. 10. In that essay, he had located the most dangerous threat to the stability of the republic in a majority of citizens who, unchecked, could tyrannize individuals and minorities and infringe upon their rights. To counter such a majority, he had devised his system of checks and balances as a way to fragment authority and prevent a concentration of power. The government would be divided against itself, institutionally split "between different bodies of men, who might watch and check each other." In addition, Madison's blueprint for government required so many different methods for choosing senators, representatives, and president that the different branches of government ultimately represented different and possibly conflicting majorities, thereby thwarting the power and thrust of the real majority of citi-

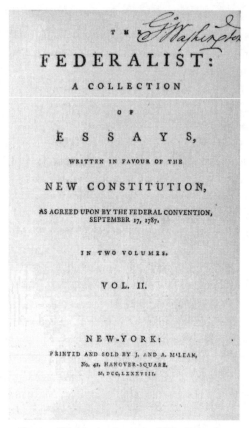

George Washington's copy of *The Federalist*.

zens — or, as Madison would have phrased it, an "oppressive" majority. That way, a certain balance and stability — if not deadlock — in government could be achieved. And, of course, Madison also counted on a vast array of diverse interest groups and factions scattered throughout the nation to prevent a majority of citizens from invading the rights of others.

And yet, only a few years after composing *Federalist* No. 10, in which he had argued in favor of institutional and other ways to foil the majority and strengthen the rights of minority groups, Madison had come to believe that a wealthy, privileged minority controlled the government and shaped its policies. Now he was embracing the idea of party conflict as a means for achieving a more egalitarian society and a more majoritarian government. Washington's close adviser was writing both as a theorist and as a politician, a champion of ordinary Americans, and the leader and proponent of the opposition.

The author of the most important American work of political theory had begun to see America's fundamental public values through a different lens. Like the other founders, he had always emphasized "liberty" over "equality." But as American politics and economic policies evolved, Madison's political views also evolved, and his focus shifted to equality. In *Federalist* No. 10, he had written that "the first object of government" was to protect the "diversity" in people's faculties that permits some to acquire more wealth and property than others — although, in *Federalist* No. 62 he had warned against giving an "unreasonable advantage" to the moneyed few at the expense of the "uninformed mass of the people." Less than five years later, on behalf of that "uninformed mass of the people," he was pleading for more equality.

Whether writing about fashion or parties, Madison was taking aim at elitism, class divisions, and inequality. But it would not be easy for him to trump his own brilliant constitutional design or easy for an opposition party to check his blueprint for checks and balances. Moreover, Madison had not yet embraced the idea of a two-party system.

Theory had not yet caught up with reality.

Modern political parties did not yet exist in America, some historians, like Ronald Formisano and others, have forcefully argued. It is true that parties had not yet developed on a national level. And yet, some states were in fact developing a system of statewide and local party committees. Coalitions were forming in Congress; many representatives were regularly voting for or against measures supported by Madison; and, on the local level, everything from barbecues and parades to handbills and pamphlets injected partisanship into American life.

Even without the various structures that characterize modern party politics, party politics was evolving in America. Within government, faction "glowed like a coal-pit," wrote Federalist congressman Fisher Ames of Massachusetts in late 1791. The following spring, he noted that Madison's anti-Hamiltonian faction functioned as "a regular, well-disciplined opposition party"; and a few months later he remarked that the discipline of Madison's Virginia followers had become "as severe as the Prussian." Although people were still deeply ambivalent about political parties, although one party did not necessarily recognize the legitimacy of the other, and although men on both sides were nostalgic — at one time or another — for an imaginary golden age of political harmony, few people could be found in the early 1790s who believed that parties did not exist. The parties even had names: Federalist and Republican.

"The plot thickens," Alexander Hamilton wrote to John Adams, calling his attention to Madison's articles in the *National Gazette*. By the spring of 1792 Hamilton recognized that battle lines had been drawn and that Madison had metamorphosed into his personal and ideological enemy, "*the head of a faction decidedly hostile to me and my administration.*" In the past, the two men had shared a "similarity in thinking," and even in recent months, Hamilton remarked, he had never suspected "a lisp of [Madison's] new system." Unburdening himself in a letter to Edward Carrington, Hamilton voiced dismay that Madison had "become personally unfriendly to me." Even worse, Madison was "*actuated by views in my judgement subversive of the principles of good government and dangerous to the union, peace and happiness of the Country.*" Hamilton blamed Madison for opposing his economic measures, pursuing a course that would lead to war with Great Britain, possessing a character that "is the reverse of that *simple, fair, candid* one, which he has assumed," and even abusing the president's confidence. "In giving you this picture of political parties," he concluded to Carrington, "my design is I confess, to awaken your attention." As far as Hamilton was concerned, Madison and Jefferson both belonged to the enemy camp.

Mayhem erupted in western Pennsylvania during the spring and summer of 1794. Two people were killed and tax offices destroyed by mobs. The small excise tax on the production of liquor that Hamilton had advocated as part of his plan to fund the national debt inflamed Pennsylvania farmers. Political opposition had exploded in violence — the nightmare scenario of Federalists.

For Pennsylvania farmers who shipped wheat and rye over the mountains in liquid form, the tax was especially punitive. They were even taxed on the brew they made and drank for their own refreshment! Even worse, the tax had to be paid in cash, which was rare in that part of the country, where jugs of whiskey were often used instead of currency. Though the farmers were adept at circumventing the tax men, they objected to the *principle* of the thing. The funding system was "founded upon injustice," editorialized the anonymous but class-conscious "Franklin" in the *General Advertiser,* explaining that unless corruption was eradicated, "a privileged order of men will be established among us who shall enjoy the honors, the emoluments, and the patronage of government, without contributing a farthing to its support."

Denouncing the tax as unequal and oppressive, farmers ransacked the tax offices. But the problem went even deeper. No good men were willing to support the government, excise collector George Clymer had earlier informed Alexander Hamilton. Instead of "men of distinction" serving in the Pennsylvania government, only "sordid shopkeepers and crafty lawyers" were candidates for public office, men "not inclined to make personal sacrifices to truth or honor." Revolted by the "political putrefaction" of Pennsylvania, Hamilton demanded swift military action against the Whiskey Rebellion, insisting that without "rigor" the "next storm will be infinitely worse than the present one." Washington agreed. Still unhappily remembering Shays's Rebellion in western Massachusetts in 1786, he knew that the national government had been established to put down precisely such revolts against law and order. "If the laws are to be so trampled on with impunity," the president now said, "there is an end put, at one stroke, to republican government."

It was a remarkable scene: the sixty-two-year-old president, in full military attire, the martial embodiment of the federal government's authority to enforce national order, riding on horseback to western Pennsylvania in the fall of 1794 — the only president ever to lead an army in the field. With him marched more than twelve thousand troops — as well as the man who was the principal target of rebel fury, Alexander Hamilton, the original excise man himself, whom the president, in an impolitic move, had named "acting secretary of war." It was an immense overreaction to a paltry demonstration. Most of the "rioters and delinquent distillers" had already agreed to disarm. When the president visited the scene of battle, he found it empty of rebels. Still, Washington and Hamilton believed that the forces of order had triumphed; for Madison and Jefferson, it was an excessive show of might, an "armament," Jefferson wrote, "against people at their ploughs."

It was also an armament against nascent political parties. In his next annual message to Congress in November 1794, Washington took sharp aim at what he termed "self-created societies," blaming them for encouraging dissension and fomenting disorder in Pennsylvania, accusing them of spreading their "nefarious doctrines with a view to poison and discontent the minds of the people." These cliques, so many clandestine conspiracies, preferred to meet, he wrote, "under the shade of Night in a conclave."

Washington was referring to the "Democratic-Republican societies." These were political clubs that were spreading in the 1790s throughout the country and, between 1793 and 1800, numbered over forty. There was the Society for the Preservation of Liberty in Virginia, the Sons of St. Tammany and the Democratic Society in New York, the Constitutional Society in Boston, the Society of Political Inquiries, the German Republican Society and the Democratic Society of Pennsylvania in Philadelphia, and similar groups scattered in all the states.

The purpose of the Republican Society of Norwalk, Connecticut, was, according to a report in the *New London Bee*, "to exercise the right of speech and freedom to debate, recognized by the Constitution; to perpetuate the equal rights of man, to propagate political knowledge, and to revive the republican spirit of '76." Members circulated petitions, drew up manifestos, passed resolutions, held celebrations, organized libraries and library societies, voiced their demands — often for public education and free schools. Perhaps the only thing that distinguished them from full-fledged political parties was that they usually did not promote candidates for office. Through the clubs, citizens from many walks of life — merchants, politicians, landowners, slave owners, professionals, small tradesmen, mechanics, seamen, laborers, and newspaper publishers — participated in political discussions, defining for themselves and their communities the important issues of the day, pronouncing on everything from local roads to the startling revolution taking place in France.

Members of the Democratic-Republican societies believed they were fulfilling the obligations of citizenship. They recognized that the magnetic allure of prosperity and comfort was seducing many citizens away from playing active roles in the political arena. "The charms of wealth, the allurements of luxury," wrote a member of the New York Democratic Society in May 1796, were threatening "the ardor of liberty," diminishing people's attachment to the "sacred interests of our country." One Democratic-Republican observed that the clubs were more a "safeguard to our Constitution and liberties than standing armies and sedition laws." The editor of the *National Gazette* considered the clubs "absolutely necessary." Without citizens actively engaged in political discussions and debates, he wrote, "what is every man's business soon becomes no man's business."

A Peep into the Antifederal Club. Federalist cartoon from 1793 showing Jefferson (with gavel in hand) presiding over the Philadelphia "Democratic Society." The scroll in the upper left corner announces the Creed of the Democratic Club: "The People are All and we are the People. All Power in one body and that Body Ourselves. Governments but another name for Aristocracy."

But Federalists preferred a silent, passive people to a vociferous, unruly, independent — and Frenchified — one. In New England, a Federalist newspaper railed against "the vapors of putrefying democracy." The clubs were "perverting the truth and spreading jealousy and intrigue through the land," railed Fisher Ames. Above all, Federalists feared that the Democratic-Republican societies were cousins of the radical revolutionary Jacobin clubs in France and were importing into America violence, extremism, and anarchy from France.

The French and the Americans had once been joined at the hip. In the 1770s, many in France had been swept away by the excitement of a struggle for freedom and equality in faraway America. Even the king found himself caught up in the prospect of revolution — which also presented him with a chance to humiliate Great Britain. Borrowing staggering amounts of money that would eventually precipitate an economic crisis in France, destabilize the monarchy, and put his own life in jeopardy, Louis XVI had sent fleets of vessels as well as admirals, generals, sailors, and soldiers to America. Led by General Rochambeau, the French had helped turn the tide — and win, in 1781, the battle of Yorktown, at which French soldiers had outnumbered Americans. It was the decisive victory of the War of Independence. After the war, a generation of French officers had returned home from America, hailing the revolution that had just taken place across the ocean, praising the idealistic zeal they had witnessed, and spreading the contagion of liberty to France.

For their own revolution, the French could have found in America a prudent model to copy. It was France's for the taking — after all, she had paid for it, and her officers and soldiers had fought and died for it. True, some of the challenges facing the two nations were different. Unlike the Americans, the French had a feudal heritage to extirpate, a hereditary aristocracy to democratize, and wretched poverty and domestic insurrections to eliminate.

And yet, as different as the historical, military, and social circumstances were, as different the size of their populations — 24 million people in France, fewer than 4 million in the thirteen colonies — both revolutions wanted to install representative governments based on popular sovereignty and the will of the majority.

When the French set about drafting a constitution and establishing unfamiliar political and judicial institutions, advice and wisdom from thoughtful Americans might not have been unreasonable. Eager to assist his French friends, Jefferson, the American minister in Paris until the end of 1789, had sketched out his recommendations, giving advice, over dinner, to Lafayette and others on a representative legislature and individual rights. Lafayette would send his friend George Washington the key to the Bastille, but the French were confident that they could open their own doors.

They were convinced that they could improve upon the American model. The Americans, revolutionaries in France pointed out, had just ratified a constitution that did not contain a bill of rights, and they still tolerated slavery. And were Americans not setting the clock back by retaining a Senate that mirrored the English hereditary House of Lords? The French wanted no part of a system of checks and balances that thwarted the people's will. They wanted energy, not stability, in government. And while the American founders had emphasized liberty, calling it their "darling" and their "precious jewel," the mantra of the revolution in France was equality. After centuries of the wrenching inequality of a rigid caste system, revolutionaries in France hungered first and foremost for equality; liberty and individual rights might come later. Alas, they did not.

By the end of 1793, Americans had learned that the French Revolution had been taken over by Jacobin radicals and that it was plunging into a downward spiral, devolving into Terror, devouring its children and its leaders. News had reached the United States about the guillotining of the pitiable monarch and Queen Marie-Antoinette, about summary arrests, mass drownings, and the decapitation of thousands of French men and women. The Jacobins — Robespierre, St. Just, and company — had become experts in suspending constitutions and rights, making the judiciary subordinate to the legislature, purging French society of all "counterrevolutionary" elements, denying rights to the accused, and beheading the Revolution's former leaders, Danton, Vergniaud, and others.

The news was grim, and yet Jefferson and other idealistic Americans remained hopeful about the prospects for eventual change in France. The dream of universal freedom and of a fraternity of revolutionary nations was far too precious, too heady, to let go. "We are not to expect to be translated from despotism to liberty in a feather-bed," a sanguine Jefferson had written in 1790 to his friend Lafayette. In 1793, when the French Revolution was beginning to implode in violence, Jefferson penned his famous "Adam and Eve" letter. "Rather than [that the French Revolution] should have failed," he wrote to his colleague William Short, "I would have seen half the earth desolated. Were there but an Adam and an Eve left in every country, and left free, it would be better than as it now is." His enthusiastic though ill-considered apologia for political violence may shock, but Jefferson's dream of a new race of free men is also powerful testimony to the boldness of his revolutionary vision. This boldness, for Jefferson, was the spirit of '76. Despite the violence in France, Jefferson and other intrepid Republicans would not be deterred from embracing a new spirit of change.

But the Federalists had seen and heard more than enough about revolution in France. "When will these savages be satiated with blood?" sneered John Adams. For his part, Hamilton expressed scorn for the "horrid and disgusting scenes" taking place in Paris, for the "atrocious depravity" of the Revolution's leaders, so many "assassins still reeking with the blood of murdered fellow Citizens." For Hamilton, only slightly more than a decade after Yorktown, both *revolution* and *France* had become scare words. Americans were becoming polarized by the revolution in France. Those who looked upon the French as their revolutionary brethren moved into the Republican orbit with Jefferson and Madison; those who deplored the upheaval and violence in France joined hands with Hamilton and his Federalist colleagues.

Those Federalists feared that the Democratic clubs in America were spreading French anarchy to America. These Democratic-Republican clubs "were born of sin, the impure off-spring" of the radical ambassador, Edmond Genêt, from revolutionary France, Fisher Ames grumbled. Club members were "hot-headed, ignorant or wicked men devoted entirely to the views of France," Oliver Wolcott wrote. While Democrats sported red, white, and blue ribbons, tricolored cockades that symbolized the radical ideals of the French and American Revolutions, Federalists wore black rosettes that stood for "a pledge of friendship among Federalists, and of attachment to our Constitution and Government," according to the *Massachusetts Mercury*.

Though few in America may have realized it at the time, the anti-democratic nature of the revolution in France ironically had the effect of consolidating democracy in the United States. Galvanized by devotion or disgust for France, more and more American citizens were taking sides and participating in the political culture of their times.

Danger emanated not only from radicals in France. Pointing to history's usual suspects and scapegoats, Federalists also raised the tattered banner of anti-Semitism, declaring that the "tribe of Israel" was bent on controlling American politics through the Democratic-Republican clubs. The Democratic Society in New York, founded in 1794, constituted an "itinerant gang," wrote Federalist publisher James Rivington in 1795. Led by a Jewish vice president, merchant Solomon Simpson, "they all seem to be . . . of the tribe of Shylock: they have that leering underlook, and malicious grin, that seem to say to the honest man — *approach me not.*" "If by the word Shylock," retorted a reader in an anti-Federalist newspaper, "you mean a Jew, from my knowledge of the Vice-President, I dare say he would think himself honoured by the appellation, Judaism being his religious profession, as Democracy is his political creed." In Pennsylvania, when a man named Israel Israel ran for the state senate on the Republican ticket in 1797, the anti-Republican *Porcupine's Gazette* discerned a Jewish plot to take over the state.

"Since the Jews obtained such a complete triumph over the Gentiles," the newspaper announced, "it is said they have conceived the idea of imposing on us a *general* circumcision. Ah! poor Pennsylvania."

But Francophiles and Jews were not the only source of Federalist anxiety: *Porcupine's* William Cobbett worried that women might be drawn to the Democratic-Republican clubs. "No; you are too mild, too lovely, to become the tribune of a Democratic Club," he wrote. "You want no rights, no power but what you possess." Still, he fretted that the result of democratic agitation might well be a take-over of the House of Representatives by women! Perhaps even by pregnant women!

And so, when Washington condemned "self-created societies" in November 1794, he was igniting a powder keg.

"It is wonderful indeed," an astonished Jefferson wrote, "that the President should have permitted himself to be the organ of such an attack on the freedom of discussion, the freedom of writing, printing and publishing." But the Senate jumped to Washington's defense, passing a motion commending him and denouncing the societies, claiming that they had been "founded in error" and had been "influential in misleading our fellow citizens." The House of Representatives chimed in too, introducing an amendment condemning the societies for having "stimulated and urged the insurrection" in Pennsylvania. While there had been no debate on the motion in the Senate, in the House the debate lasted for three days.

James Madison's words on the floor of the House were reasoned but strong. "Opinions," Madison said, "are not the objects of legislation." Was the government considering withholding from the people their rights to "liberty of speech and of the press?" A few weeks later, he remarked to Jefferson that the president's and the Senate's "indiscriminate censure" of the societies was nothing less than an "attack made on the essential & constitutional right of the Citizen," an attack that "must be felt by every man who values liberty."

The president and Congress had set a dangerous and indefensible precedent, Madison contended, for if the government succeeded in censuring political clubs, it could also censure criticism flowing from any other source, "from the press and from individuals as well as from Societies." Moreover, if the government itself was the judge, "it will never allow any censures to be just." Unbeknownst to him, Madison was accurately predicting the repressive Sedition Act that would be enacted four years later.

For Madison, Washington's condemnation of the clubs was "the greatest error of his political life." It would "wound" the president's popularity more than any other action. Washington's "game," Madison believed, had been to connect the Democratic-Republican societies with the "odium of insurrection" and to connect the Republicans in Congress with those clubs. But his condemnation of the clubs was backfiring: it was having the reverse effect, Madison wrote, of contributing to "the invigorated exertions" of Democratic societies.

Indeed, Republican newspapers shouted out for freedom. "Is it for assembling, that we are accused?" demanded the New York *Journal.* "What law forbids it? for deliberating, for thinking, for exercising the faculties of the mind; what statute has deprived us of the right?" Were Americans to be muzzled every time they disagreed with the government? asked the *Independent Chronicle.* If the President and Congress aimed at voiding citizens' constitutional rights to freedom of speech and petition, who then, inquired the *Aurora,* were the true enemies of the national welfare?

The "mobocrats" were taking over, Fisher Ames sighed.

There were other *causes célèbres,* too, in the 1790s, that bitterly divided Americans. In the wake of the Terror in France and the incendiary and even conspiratorial machinations of Genêt, the volatile French minister to the United States, and especially in the wake of armed confrontation between Great Britain and France, Washington and Hamilton prudently wanted to declare American neutrality while Jefferson insisted on honoring America's treaty of amity with France. While the members of Washington's cabinet and other politicians grappled with the issue of neutrality on constitutional grounds relating to presidential power — could the president unilaterally declare neutrality or was a treaty relating to war and peace the domain of the Senate? — emotional citizens rallied passionately to the cause of France or the cause of Britain. But when Washington proclaimed American neutrality in April 1793, Jefferson reluctantly signed on. Neutrality might be a "disagreeable pill," he wrote to Madison, "tho' necessary to keep out of the calamities of a war."

But tensions escalated in 1795, when John Jay, the chief justice, returned from London with a new trade treaty in his hands, a treaty that, he hoped, would prevent a war with the English and secure strong economic relations between the two countries. When the terms of the treaty leaked out to the public, many citizens were shocked by the lack of British concessions to American claims. While Britain received Most Favored Nation status, the United States received little in return, only the long-overdue evacuation of British northwest posts in America. Some citizens proclaimed July 4, 1795, a day of mourning. In Philadelphia, five thousand people turned out to oppose the treaty and burn Jay in effigy. While some Americans threatened to guillotine Jay, others rushed to voice their outrage at local meetings of the Democratic societies. In the South as well as in the North, the treaty was condemned. In private Hamilton admitted that the treaty was "execrable" and made by "an old woman," but when he attempted to defend the treaty in public, some men hurled stones at him, and he challenged two of them to duels. There were anti-Jay disturbances in Boston and riots in Portsmouth, New Hampshire. At one point Jay dryly remarked that he could have made his way across the country by the light of his burning effigies.

Madison accused Jay of the "blindest partiality to the British Nation" and nothing short of the "most vindictive" feelings toward the French Republic. He expressed pleasure that the "sentiment & voice" of the people in Virginia against the treaty were "as decided & as loud as could be wished." Jefferson called the treaty "nothing more than a treaty of alliance between England and the Anglomen of this country."

For both sides, the treaty contained a mine of powerful, emotionally charged symbols. Americans rallied to the "Anglomen" or to the "Gallomen," branding their adversaries "monocrats" or "Jacobins." Protesters surrounded Washington's house in Philadelphia, John Adams later remembered, "demanding war against England, cursing Washington, and crying success to the French patriots and virtuous Republicans."

Predilection for England or good will toward France now colored — even *defined* — political divisions in America. Americans might think in English, as Hamilton had remarked in 1789, but Republicans believed that they felt and acted in French! For Federalists, England represented the side of order; for Republicans, France represented the side of *man.* "To deny that there has been a French Influence and an English Influence in this Country," observed John Adams a few years later, "is to deny that the sun and Moon have shone upon the earth."

The Times: A Political Portrait, c. 1795–99. Thomas Jefferson,
along with Madison and Gallatin, attempts to block the wheels of
Federalism, symbolized by the chariot drawn by Washington.
The caption reads: "Triumph Government: perish all its enemies.
Traitors, be warned: justice, though slow, is sure."

In the spring of 1795, the Senate ratified the treaty, and that summer, Washington signed it. Though admitting that it was a flawed treaty and that his own opinion was "not favorable to it," he recognized the vulnerability of the United States and concluded that it was more prudent to approve it "than to suffer matters to remain as they are, unsettled."

But the following spring, 1796, the Republican-dominated House of Representatives, under Madison's leadership, jumped into the act, threatening to withhold appropriations to put the treaty into effect and demanding that the president turn over copies of Jay's diplomatic instructions. Indeed, a few months earlier, Jefferson had expressed the hope that the "popular branch" of the legislature would find a way to "rid us of this infamous act." But for Washington, the House's demand for documents was clearly unconstitutional. When the Framers gave the president and Senate the power to make treaties, Washington insisted, it was not their intention to give the House a veto on their decision. "A crisis now exists," wrote Federalist representative Fisher Ames, as the House and the president locked horns, "the most serious I ever witnessed." Though some Republicans believed that the president was demonstrating "monarchical privilege," the tide turned when Ames made an immensely effective and emotional speech, and the House went on to pass the necessary appropriations for the treaty. Madison was crushed. He appeared "pale, withered, haggard," observed John Adams.

Were Jefferson and Madison right to oppose the treaty? Their grasp of the geopolitical situation of the young republic may have been less sophisticated than that of Washington and Hamilton. Washington signed the Jay Treaty knowing that he held no trumps in his hand: England possessed a monopoly on commercial might. Even so, Washington did not lose the game. American commerce would flourish as a result of the treaty; after the British finally evacuated their northwest posts in 1796, new settlements — Cleveland, Dayton, Youngstown — quickly sprang up. In accepting the treaty, Americans sacrificed a "measure of their own national self-esteem," historians Elkins and McKitrick observed, though had they rejected it, they would have "sacrificed their own material prosperity."

But Jefferson dismissed the advantages that improved relations with England might bring, attributing instead the success of the treaty in the House to the colossal influence of Washington. People simply "supported his judgment against their own." A disappointed Madison searched for other reasons for the upset. Republicans had lost in the House, not because of the "strength or dexterity or malice of our opponents," he concluded, but rather because of "the unsteadiness, the follies, the perverseness and the defections among our friends." In other words, the defeat in the House was a defeat of nascent party, of organization, of discipline. When House Republicans had caucused to discuss strategy, Albert Gallatin observed, caucus members "were left at full liberty to vote as they pleased, without being on that account proscribed or considered as having abandoned the principles of the party." Now, from this defeat in Congress, Madison inferred not the importance of a more nuanced Republican foreign policy but rather the need for a strong party organization, tight discipline, and a clear, compelling, galvanizing ideology.

For their part, Washington, Hamilton, and other Federalists adamantly held to their view that the opposition was undermining constitutional government itself. "No attempts," Washington wrote, were "left unessayed to destroy all confidence in the Constituted authorities of this country." It was a "childish comfort," observed Fisher Ames, for

Federalists to believe that Republicans did not aim "at the overthrow of government."

And so the issue of political parties took on a larger dimension, becoming a question of the legitimacy of opposition itself and the right of citizens to disagree with, criticize, and work to oust public officials.

While Madison and Jefferson already saw themselves as the leaders of an opposition party, Washington adamantly refused to entertain the idea that he himself might actually belong to a party or that his administration reflected the ideology of a party. "I was no party man myself," he insisted, "and the first wish of my heart was, if parties did exist, to reconcile them." And yet by the mid-1790s, American politics was thoroughly colored by party ideology and party spirit — in the legislative branch of government as well as the executive branch. Historians who have analyzed voting patterns in Congress confirm the existence of clear partisan voting blocs at least as early as 1794. By 1795, there were no Republicans left in Washington's cabinet. Not only did the president's appointments reflect Federalist ideology, but the president himself, Madison remarked, had successfully cloistered himself from opposition sentiment. "Through what official interstice," asked Madison, "can a ray of republican truths now penetrate to the President?"

Washington might cloister himself from the rays of republican truths, but not from attacks in the press. Not only were the acts of his government subject to the "grossest and most insidious misrepresentations," he complained bitterly to Jefferson in the summer of 1796, but he himself was attacked in "indecent terms as could scarcely be applied to a Nero, a notorious defaulter, or even to a common pick-pocket." Every manner of malicious falsehood had been invented to "wound my reputation and feelings." The president comforted himself with the knowledge that during his entire administration, he had not "been guilty of a *willful* error, however numerous they may have been from other causes."

Still, the criticism, acrimony, and strife had taken their toll. In 1796, Washington was bone tired. "The trouble and perplexities" with which he had been burdened as president, he explained to John Jay, added to the "weight of years which have passed over me, have worn away my mind more than my body." Now both "ease and retirement" had become indispensably necessary to his mental and physical health.

An election was approaching, and this time the nation's father refused to be persuaded to run for another term. He was determined to close his public life on March 4, 1797. Unlike in 1792, this time no one could persuade the president to run for another term. "No consideration under heaven that I can foresee," the president wrote after eight contentious years in office, "shall again draw me from the walks of private life." But there was an even more important reason impelling the battle-weary president to retire: he wished to give "an early example of rotation" in the nation's highest office. It was a principle, he wrote, that accorded with "the republican spirit" of the Constitution as well as with people's ideas of "liberty and safety." Did he also reason that, if he accepted a third term, he might die in office and the "succession" might appear monarchical in form? But if the president wished to establish the precedent of rotation in office, it was not his intention to set the precedent for a two-term limit on presidents.

Alexander Hamilton had, for a decade, objected to term limits for the president. In *Federalist* No. 72, he had rejected the idea of depriving the president of the chance to serve another four years in office. Term limits for the chief executive, Hamilton forcefully argued, would diminish inducements to good behavior, discourage the president from undertaking new projects, deny the community the advantage of his experience, and preclude political stability. Finally, Hamilton contended, term limits would ignore certain emergency situations when the president's continuance in office would be "of the greatest moment to the public interest or safety."

Less than a decade after composing *Federalist* No. 72, Hamilton envisaged precisely such an emergency situation. Thus, in the summer of 1796, he convinced Washington to wait until the fall to announce his retirement. "*Hold the thing undecided to the last moment,*" he counseled. "If a storm gathers, how can you retreat?" And so, in September 1796, just when American politicians were most polarized around issues like the Jay Treaty, most divided by personal antipathy and mutual suspicions, the president presented his famous Farewell Address, drafted by Hamilton though containing phrases from a speech Madison had composed for him in 1792. Cloaked in the mantra of harmony and unity, the "address" — which was never delivered in person by Washington but rather communicated to Americans through their newspapers — constituted an attack on parties in general and on the opposition Republican party in particular.

The president stressed the theme of unity. The unity of government, which "constitutes you one people," comprised the "Pillar in the Edifice" of American freedom, independence, and tranquility. He expressed the hope that Americans' "Union and brotherly affection" would be "perpetual." And why should it not be? "You have the same Religion, Manners, Habits and political Principles. You have in a common cause fought and triumphed together." In other words, united by similar backgrounds and similar mores, all Americans could recognize one overriding public interest. And because the elected constitutional government, in Washington's mind, mirrored the public interest and the common good of the sovereign people, neither individuals nor groups had the right to oppose the government. On the contrary, it was "the duty of every Individual to *obey the established Government.*" Having undermined the right of people to oppose those who govern, the president then went on to condemn parties. "Combinations and associations," he announced, subverted good government because they put "in the place of the delegated will of the Nation, the will of a party; often a small but artful and enterprising minority of the Community."

He went further. He branded parties "potent engines, by which cunning, ambitious, and unprincipled men will be enabled to subvert the Power of the People, and to usurp for themselves the reins of Government." And, as if taking Republicans to task for their pro-French, anti-English stance, he warned against "excessive partiality" for one foreign nation and "excessive dislike" of another. If allowed to spread, party spirit was a "fire not to be quenched." Ultimately it could cause so much disorder and suffering that people, hungry for security and calm, would turn to the "absolute power of an Individual" — and a "frightful despotism" would reign. Washington had sketched a nightmare descent into tyranny — produced by parties. The nation's father would believe, until the end of his term in office and the end of his life, that, at best, parties rendered "alien to each other" those who ought to be bound together by "fraternal affection."

Despite the enormous weight and prestige of the president's opinions, a strange gap was opening. It was clear that antiparty political rhetoric no longer reflected political reality. Parties — alternately unrecognized, scorned, and condemned, by Republicans no less than by Federalists — had already become a feature of the young republic's political landscape. Tens of thousands of citizens no longer believed that it was, as Washington had asserted, "the duty of every Individual to *obey the established Government.*" They had a different notion of the rights and responsibilities of citizens. Washington's conviction that the administration was always in the right, remarked the *Albany Register*, perniciously aped the ancient monarchical idea that "the king can do no wrong." Citizens had not only the privilege but also the responsibility of assembling, organizing, and expressing themselves on the policies of their government, judged *Bartgis's Federal Gazette* of Fredericktown, Maryland.

"The moment he retires," Jefferson predicted to James Monroe about the president, Republicans would be back in the fight. Especially after the debacle of the Jay Treaty, public opinion, Jefferson believed, was shifting toward the opposition. Republicans might soon find themselves in a strong position to capture the government. Then, far from establishing a two-party system, they would, as Jefferson said, "lead things into the channel of *harmony* between the governors & governed." "In the mean time," he counseled, "patience."

4

Heir Apparent

I AM HEIR APPARENT, you know," John Adams wrote to his wife Abigail in January 1796, cheerfully confident that "a succession" was about to take place. Though he had been excluded from decision making in the Washington administration, he had been a loyal vice president for seven years. The unwavering support he had given the president, he said, constituted "the pride and boast of [his] life." Now it was his turn.

Would it be a traumatic succession from charismatic national father to acerbic, prickly New Englander? Adams saw "no more danger in the change than there would be in changing a member of the Senate," he assured Abigail. Others were less sanguine. The first national election after Washington, Oliver Wolcott confided in his son, "will probably ascertain whether our system and union can be preserved." How indeed would the system cope with candidates who simultaneously sought political power and disdained it, candidates who were ambivalent about party conflict and party leadership? The election of 1796 would push to center stage political actors who were unsure of their parts, still polishing their script, still rehearsing their roles.

Adams harbored reservations about running for president. Perhaps it would be a more glorious if not safer destiny to follow Cincinnatus and Washington and, as he proposed to Abigail, "make a voluntary retreat" from politics, spending the rest of his days "in a very humble style" with her. After all, the "mode of becoming great," he would later remark, "is to retire." Indeed, during the summer of 1796, he seemed to be enjoying living and working on his home in Quincy, Massachusetts, cutting wood himself, supervising the construction of a new red barn, and riding around his fields of barley and corn.

But his more serious reservations about the upcoming presidential election concerned his distaste for party strife, the lack of civility in the political arena, and his own thin-skinned vulnerability to criticism. Not unlike Washington, he was willing to govern — but not to fight for office. Why would he do battle for what he considered rightly his? He was especially reluctant to fight the men he called the "demagogues." "I have no very ardent desire to be the butt of party malevolence," he confessed. "Having tasted of that cup I find it bitter, nauseous, and unwholesome."

Indeed, even before Washington let his noncandidacy be known, before he delivered his Farewell Address, and before candidates were chosen for the 1796 election, people were buzzing about the different possibilities. Newspapers were jumping into the fray, taking sides, declaring their preferences. In the spring of 1796, the *Aurora* announced that Jefferson, the "good patriot, statesman, and philosopher," should be the people's choice.

"I am determined to be a *silent spectator* of the silly and wicked game," an irritated Adams wrote to his son on the same day the *Aurora*'s premature endorsement appeared. Adams had decided to regard the whole election process "as a comedy, a farce." He was "very indifferent" to the outcome, he told his son John Quincy, "really, truly and sincerely." Should he lose the election, he assured his wife, he would retire from public life, without a complaint, without the smallest dread of private life. Perhaps he was a "fool," he mused, to serve at all.

But as diffident as Adams wished to appear, as much of a "farce" as he considered electoral and partisan politics, he knew that the stakes were high. In his mind, his political adversaries comprised a deranged combination of anti-Federalists, "desperate debtors," and "Frenchified tools." Together they would work to "murder all good men among us and destroy all the wisdom and virtue of the country." How could he remain indifferent, on the sidelines? As dirty a game as politics was, "I don't know how I should live out of it," he candidly admitted to his great confidante, Abigail. Five days later, in another letter to her, he seemed calmer about his political foes. If Jefferson should win, he acknowledged, "the government will go on as well as ever." Indeed, the Virginian "could not stir a step in any other system than that which is begun." But two weeks later, he made another about-face, reporting to Abigail that people were saying that Jefferson might "endanger too much." While Adams tried to deal with his contradictory feelings about running for office (he would leave it to historians, he said, to decipher his true feelings and "detect my errors"), Republicans had decided that Jefferson was the only logical candidate to oppose him.

But was Jefferson even remotely interested in running?

"I have never seen a Philadelphia paper since I left it," a placid Thomas Jefferson revealed to James Madison in the spring of 1794. He considered himself "thoroughly weaned" from the interest he used to take in politics. "I find my mind totally absorbed in my rural occupations," he told his old friend. Jefferson had resigned from Washington's cabinet in 1793, leaving Madison in command of the Republican opposition in Congress. With only Federalists now surrounding the president in his cabinet, the Republican party would have to evolve in Congress. Madison had asked Jefferson to delay leaving office, but he would hear nothing of it. "Never let there be more between you and me, on this subject," Jefferson scolded.

Surrounded by his 152 slaves, Jefferson rejoiced in his Eden. He boasted that he never ventured more than seven miles from his Virginia hilltop. Only at Monticello did he consider himself really at home, able to carry on experiments in agriculture: crop rotation, fruit trees, peas, clover, and fertilizer. One pint of "essence of dung," he reported to George Washington, might be enough to fertilize an acre. In addition to setting up a small nail manufacture, he was occupied and preoccupied with the redesign and rebuilding of Monticello, planning an octagonal dome to replace the attic, doubling the size of the house, transforming it to resemble Palladio's Villa Rotunda in northern Italy with elements from the elegant Hôtel de Salm he had visited in Paris. Busily he was seeing to every detail, from the dumbwaiter to the window sashes to the alcove for his bed.

"I put off answering my letters, now, farmerlike, till a rainy day," he wrote to Adams. Had he no regrets? Perhaps only that he hadn't retired from politics four years earlier. "I return to farming with an ardor which I scarcely knew in my youth," he wrote, "and which has got the better entirely of my love of study." He looked the part, too. Casually dressed, his tall frame slouched over, his face freckled, he cheerfully portrayed himself as "living like an Antediluvian patriarch among my children & grand children, and tilling my soil." "No circumstances, my dear Sir," Jefferson wrote to his friend Edmund Randolph, the secretary of state, "will ever more tempt me to engage in anything public. I thought myself perfectly fixed in this determination when I left Philadelphia, but every day & hour since has added to it's inflexibility." To another friend he wrote that he considered himself but a "passenger" in life, "leaving the world, and its government to those who are likely to live longer in it." Doth the farmer protest too much?

Jefferson would have argued that he was a gentleman, not a professional politician. Already in 1782, at the budding age of thirty-nine, he had confided in James Monroe his determination to retire from public life. The private self, too, had rights. "If we are made in some degree for others," he explained, "yet in a greater are we made for ourselves." Public service and private misery were, unfortunately, inextricably linked, he noted, adding that "I have not the vanity to count myself among those whom the state would think worth oppressing with perpetual service."

And so, more than a dozen years later, back on his Virginia mountaintop, he crowed about "having interdicted to myself the reading of newspapers, & thinking or saying anything on public matters." But the tart, skeptical Adams knew better — or so he believed. He informed his family that he could see through the Virginian's rural charade. "Jefferson thinks by this step to get a reputation of an humble, modest, meek man, wholly without ambition or vanity," Adams observed to his son John Quincy. "He may even have deceived himself into this belief. But if a prospect opens, the world will see and he will feel that he is as ambitious as Oliver Cromwell." Adams would never budge from his opinion that Jefferson's retirement had been a calculated ploy, a way for his allies to advertise him as "unambitious, unavaricious and perfectly disinterested."

Jefferson's agricultural occupations in Monticello did not prevent him from giving his opinions at length and in detail on current affairs. From his rural retreat, he commented on all facets of political life, from the "shameless corruption" of a portion of the representatives in Congress and the recall of the French ambassador Genêt, to taxes, Senate bills, Washington's denunciation of "self-created" Democratic-Republican societies, and especially the Jay Treaty, which he discussed in person with Madison at Monticello in the fall of 1795. Nor did the farmer's life prevent him from receiving the visit of Aaron Burr in October 1795, an occasion to discuss Republican prospects in New York. And a few months after insisting that he was nothing but "a passenger," leaving politics to others, Jefferson sent eight dollars to Benjamin Franklin Bache for a subscription to his Republican newspaper, the *Aurora*.

However much Jefferson might proclaim that he would not give up retirement "for the empire of the universe," he understood fully the leadership obligations of a man of his standing, intellect, and class. "Hold on then, my dear friend," he urged Madison in 1794 upon learning that Madison too might withdraw from public life. "I do not see . . . a greater affliction than the fear of your retirement; but this must not be, unless to a more splendid & a more efficacious post." Did Jefferson sense a contradiction? In 1792 he had begged Washington to run for a second term; nothing was more indispensable than his remaining "at the helm." Now, writing to Madison, he wondered how he could "justify wishing one whose happiness I have so much at heart as yours, to take the front of the battle which is fighting for my security." It would be easy, he concluded, to explain this contradiction, but "not at the heel of a lengthy epistle."

Jefferson was adamant that he would play no role in the presidential election of 1796. Emphasizing to Madison that there was no "opening for future discussion," he went on to describe his "essay in red clover" and the expense of seeding an acre. And yet, in February 1796, Jefferson recognized that the time he was living in was "the age of experiments in government." Would he, the political visionary par excellence, passively withdraw from such an epoch? And could Madison convince his unwilling friend to run for the highest office? Republicans meant to "push" Jefferson for the presidency, Madison reported to James Monroe in the winter of 1796, adding that he feared that Jefferson would "mar the project and insure Adams's election by a peremptory and public protest."

Nothing could be official until after Washington's Farewell Address in September. That speech was, Fisher Ames wrote, "a signal, like dropping a hat, for the party racers to start." But after Washington's address, Jefferson would still not throw his hat into the ring. And Madison accepted it that way, preferring ambiguity to an outright refusal. In a bit of comic improvisation, Madison pounced on the strategy of avoiding a meeting with Jefferson. "I have not seen Jefferson," he wrote to Monroe after the Farewell Address, "and have thought it best to present him no opportunity of protesting to his friends against being embarked in the contest." Without ever agreeing to run, without ever declaring his candidacy, Jefferson would be the Republican candidate for the presidency in 1796. The door he had shut to politics had somehow inched its way open.

"The question is forever closed with me," Jefferson had categorically stated. Why had he changed his mind? Was it the decision of a disappointed farmer who concluded that "the unprofitable conditions of Virginia estates" made it almost impossible to avoid financial ruin?

Or was it a political decision, the return of his will to fight for ideology? "An Anglican monarchical aristocratical party has sprung up," he wrote to his friend Philip Mazzei in the spring of 1796. The government had fallen into the hands of the "timid men who prefer the calm of despotism to the boisterous sea of liberty." Was he now willing to fight for his own political principles? In a letter to Madison, he admitted that he would do everything in his power to defend "the Southern interest," though after penning the word "*Southern*" he crossed it out and wrote in "*Republican*" — underscoring the centrality of the agrarian south in his political vision and the interchangeability of the terms *Republican* and *Southern* in his mind. Did Jefferson come to believe that true republican — and southern — principles could be restored? Perhaps, but "only by unremitting labors and perils." Had he decided to share those labors and face those perils?

Or was it a moral decision to reenter politics, the realization that he had a responsibility to lead his young nation? "There is a debt of service due from every man to his country," he reminded Edward Rutledge in December 1796, exhorting his friend to play an active role in the public life of the country. "Come forward & pay your own debts. . . . I love to see honest and honorable men at the helm."

Or was it a personal decision, a need for a more active, extroverted, purposeful life, a response to the gnawing sense that the occupations of the farmer did not really satisfy his mind? "I do expect that your farm will not sufficiently employ your time to shield you from ennui," he would write two years later to James Monroe, trying to dissuade him from retiring from politics. "Your mind is active, & would suffer if unemployed."

In 1802, Jefferson would look back at the psychological cost of his retreat from public life in the mid-1790s, describing the "ill effect" of his isolation. It had rendered him "unfit for society" and had given him "a misanthropic state of mind." "Happiness," he counseled his own daughter, "requires that we should continue to mix with the world . . .

and every person who retires from free communication with it is severely punished afterwards by the state of mind into which they get."

So new were Americans to the game of presidential elections that no mechanisms yet existed for nominating presidential candidates. No one publicly declared his candidacy. No one could be so presumptuous as to say that he was *not* a candidate. Two small groups of men each nominated two candidates. Federalists recognized Adams as Washington's heir. As their vice-presidential nominee they chose Thomas Pinckney of South Carolina, the former governor of the state who had recently negotiated the treaty with Spain giving the United States navigation rights on the Mississippi. Perhaps Pinckney might drain some southern support away from Jefferson, Federalists hoped. At any rate, no one consulted with Pinckney, who was in the middle of the Atlantic, returning from Europe. Madison, Gallatin, and their group in the House of Representatives nominated Jefferson and selected Aaron Burr of New York as his running mate — to give some northern balance to the ticket.

Federalists presented their man as calm, rational, and stable, someone who would continue Washington's administration and pursue his policies. Republicans touted Jefferson as a believer in equality and republican principles.

The Federalist press blasted Jefferson for possessing a feeble commitment to public service. They accused him of twice abandoning his trust, first when he resigned as governor of Virginia during the British invasion and then when he resigned as secretary of state in 1793. But mostly Federalists denounced him as an atheist, a utopian dreamer, a representative of "Virginianism," a radical French Jacobin, a lover of revolution intent on subverting American government. In a poem interestingly entitled "The Guillotina," Connecticut Federalist Lemuel Hopkins attacked Jefferson for burning to "o-er turn" the Constitution.

Republicans accused Adams of being an "avowed friend of monarchy." His sons were waiting in the wings to succeed him, they noted, while Jefferson only had daughters. The smoking gun was a text Adams had written in 1786, *Defence of the Constitutions of Government of the United States of America.* His own words, Republicans railed, were nothing but "a continued eulogium upon the British form of government." One candidate was mesmerized by England, the other was the tool of France. The Republican Committee of Pennsylvania declared that voters had a choice between a man who was "the uniform advocate of equal rights among citizens" and another who was "the champion of rank, titles and hereditary distinctions."

It was not all political ideology. There were some clear sectional differences, too, between the parties. The "moral and political habits of the citizens of the southern states," one writer announced in the *Connecticut Courant,* seemed to make an enduring union unlikely. Perhaps the nation should split along geographical lines, some people in New England felt. For his part, Jefferson did not go that far, though he saw himself as committed to protecting "the Southern interest." Despite their different sectional biases, both parties claimed that only they expressed the public good and could represent all Americans who were committed to constitutional government.

Adams and Jefferson, dignified, aloof, kept above the fray. Although Washington had created a powerful executive branch of government — surely more powerful than the Framers had envisaged — and made the presidency the one big political prize in the United States, and although bitter disputes over foreign policy were polarizing Americans and politicizing their society, Adams and Jefferson were non-participants in the race, neither active candidates nor party leaders nor party builders. They made no speeches, they shook no hands. Jefferson remained hidden away the entire time in Monticello. Only Aaron Burr was willing to dirty his hands by tirelessly campaigning for six weeks in New England. Otherwise, it was local party leaders who organized rallies and distributed pamphlets. Republicans were more active than Federalists, cultivating grass-roots support, aiming their message at ordinary citizens. Adams complained that the people were being "abused and deceived" and that "little care or pain" was taken by Federalists to "undeceive and disabuse them."

In some states, like Pennsylvania, Republicans were becoming adept at organizing at the local and state-wide level and at marketing their message and candidates. In Pennsylvania, Republican organizer John Beckley energetically took charge of distributing campaign literature as well as 30,000 copies of the Republican ballot (in a state in which there were 12,000 voters). Heading a committee of five, he employed eleven clerks and did his utmost to animate a generally listless and indifferent electorate. Republicans won 14 of Pennsylvania's 15 electoral votes. In another state, South Carolina, there was not yet a deeply rooted sense of party loyalty, and, though Federalists dominated the state, representatives in the state legislature overwhelmingly chose a Pinckney-Jefferson ticket.

At the last minute, the French minister to the United States, Pierre Auguste Adet, injected himself into American presidential politics by complaining publicly about Washington's administration, an intrusion that, on the one hand, encouraged many Francophile Republicans and, on the other, fortified Federalists in their belief that Republicans were Jacobin tools. But in general the public was poorly informed about the candidates and their messages and unaroused by the election.

The campaign continued right up to December, when members of the Electoral College would cast their votes for a president and a vice president. Electors, even after they had been chosen by the states, were not bound to vote for certain candidates, and so people tried, until the last minute, to influence their votes. In leaving to the discretion of the state legislatures the method for choosing electors and the rules that bound them, as historian Jack Rakove remarked, the Constitution had granted not only a "license to innovate" but also a license to manipulate — one that Hamilton eagerly pounced on.

Hamilton had always been a reluctant supporter of Adams, preferring his running mate Pinckney. Adams was probably "too headstrong" to be the "puppet" Hamilton wanted to manipulate, Madison surmised. And so Hamilton came up with a plan to elect Pinckney instead of Adams. What if all Federalist electors cast their votes for Adams and Pinckney, he mused, except in South Carolina, where Adams would inevitably lose votes to Jefferson? That way, Hamilton hoped, Pinckney would garner more votes than Adams. If Hamilton's strategy was successful, Robert Troup bragged, "we [will] have Mr. Pinckney completely in our power."

The tactic misfired. Some New York Federalists heard of the plan and withheld some votes from Pinckney. More important, the hostility between Hamilton and Adams burst out into the open, fracturing Federalist unity. Hamilton was "as ambitious as Julius Caesar," an angry Abigail snapped afterwards. The New Yorker, her husband concurred, was "as great a hypocrite as any in the U.S." Even Jefferson chimed in, pointing out to Adams that he had almost been cheated out of his "succession" by "the subtlety of your arch-friend of New York."

But the Electoral College presented other stumbling blocks too. Because the Constitution did not recognize political parties — none had existed in 1787 — no one had perceived the need for a team ticket, that is, for a president and a vice president united by political philosophy. Thus there was no mechanism for preventing two political enemies — the two highest vote-getters — from being elected, one as president, the other as vice president. And, to make matters worse, if the president were to die in office, he could be succeeded by his ideological opponent, thereby negating the thrust of the presidential election. "It will be a dangerous crisis in public affairs," Adams observed, "if the President and the Vice President should be in opposite boxes."

And still one other potential problem existed. The Electoral College could be tied. Before the vote in the college was officially known, in December of 1796, Jefferson feared just such an outcome. If there was an "equal division" in the votes, he authorized Madison "to solicit on my behalf that Mr. Adams may be preferred. He has always been my senior, from the commencement of my public life." Adams agreed with Jefferson's assessment: "Jefferson was but a Boy to me," Adams wrote years later. "I was at least ten years older than him in age and more than twenty years older than him in Politicks."

In late December 1796, the results of the election were still not clear, and again Jefferson expressed his reluctance to assume the highest office. "On principles of public respect," he wrote to Edward Rutledge, "I should not have refused; but I protest before my god, that I shall, from the bottom of my heart, rejoice at escaping." Predicting that the "honey moon" would be short and that any brief pleasure in governing would inevitably be followed by "years of torment & hatred," Jefferson insisted that he had "no ambition to govern men; no passion which would lead me to delight to ride in a storm." The moment, moreover, was not propitious. He would be content to plant his corn and peas. Did Jefferson realize that it would be far easier for the third president of the United States to change course after the great Washington than for the second? Adams himself remarked that if Jefferson won the presidency, he would not be able to "stir a step in any other system than that which is begun."

A candidate anxious to concede the election to his opponent — even before the vote is tallied? Has such a creature ever existed? Skeptical Federalists dismissed Jefferson's pleas to be relieved of office. For Theo-

dore Sedgwick, Jefferson's deference to Adams was part of "an insidious deception." "Such hypocrisy may dupe very great fools," wrote
Fisher Ames, "but it should alarm all other persons." Even as vice president, Jefferson would pose "a most formidable danger." Despite the
limited powers of the vice-presidency, Ames concluded, the Virginian
would be able to "go on affecting zeal for the people."

The outcome of the election still uncertain, Jefferson rushed to compliment Adams on his imminent victory, assuring him of his support.
"No one will congratulate you with purer disinterestedness than myself," Jefferson wrote.

In 1796, Jefferson's goal was conciliation — he had no appetite for re-
igniting party conflict, no taste for combating the "monocrats." On the
contrary, he feared only that Hamilton's "machinations" might "alienate" the president from his vice president. Thus he assured Adams of
his "sentiments of respect & affectionate attachment," underscoring his
"solid esteem" for his old friend. He minimized the "various little inci-
dents" that in the past had been "contrived to separate" them, and he
papered over their differences on policy. He even convinced himself
that Adams was not so very much unlike him. "I do not believe Mr.
Adams wishes war with France; nor do I believe he will truckle to England as servilely as has been done." Jefferson promised to be a loyal vice
president; he would counsel Adams to avoid war and promote prosperity and progress — not only for the sake of the nation but also for the
sake of Adams's own reputation. Acquainted with the Bostonian's frag-
ile ego, he guaranteed his old friend that "the glory will be all your
own" and that his administration too would be "filled with glory" if the
country continued on its pacific path.

A new political religion of unity, civility, cooperation, and bipartisanship seemed to be the logical choice for someone who longed to
spend a large fraction of his time as vice president in Monticello, enjoying "philosophical evenings in the winter, & rural days in the summer." Jefferson expressed pleasure that Adams had spoken of him
"with great friendship, and with satisfaction in the prospect of *admin-
istering the government in concurrence with me.*" To seal the bond, Jefferson was prepared to make certain promises to Adams, especially regarding Republican support for Adams's "future elections," if Adams,
in turn, agreed to take a less Federalist tack in his new administration,
that is, to "administer the government on it's true principles, & relin-

quish his bias to an English constitution." Jefferson drafted a letter to Adams, outlining the concessions he would make. But, slightly uncertain of all the possible implications, he sent the letter first to Madison for his perusal.

Madison was surprised and disturbed — and revealed himself to be a tougher opposition leader than Jefferson. Madison was highly skeptical of Jefferson's offer of consensus government. Yes, Adams and Jefferson had established a mutual and respectful cordiality, but sooner or later Adams's policies would force Republicans into opposition, Madison predicted, and then Jefferson's premature assurances of support would compromise his independence. "Considering the probability that Mr. A's course of administration may force an opposition from the Republican quarter," Madison responded, "there may be real embarrassments from giving written possession to him of the degree of compliment and confidence which your personal delicacy and friendship have suggested." In other words, the Republicans had nothing to gain by rapprochement. They were the "opposition," not to be confused with the government, and Jefferson was their leader. The letter to Adams was never sent. It remained in Madison's files.

After it became clear that Adams had won the election, Madison published the earlier letter that Jefferson had written him, authorizing Madison to request that preference be given to Adams over Jefferson. Adams was delighted. The letter was evidence, the pleased Bostonian reported to his wife, "of his friendship for me — and of his modesty and moderation." Abigail buttressed John's optimism, noting that her own friendship for Jefferson "has ever been unshaken" though she pronounced the Virginian "wrong in politics."

In February 1797, Adams, as presiding officer of the Senate, announced the official results of the election. The vote was close. Adams received 71 electoral votes while Jefferson won 68. Despite the two principals' expressions of respect and friendship for each other, the vote nevertheless revealed a certain level of party unity and discipline: Federalists had cast all their votes for Adams and 59 votes for Thomas Pinckney. John Jay and George Washington each had received a few token votes. Republicans were a little less disciplined; most Republican electors had voted for Jefferson, but they had scattered their second votes, casting ballots not just for Burr but also for George Clinton, Samuel Adams, and Charles Pinckney. The vote reflected sectionalism, too. Jefferson won no votes at all in New England, and Adams won a mere 2 votes in the South. Burr captured only 1 vote in Virginia, a humiliation he would revisit four years later.

While the president-elect seemed to want an administration that would stand above party and while some Republicans, like the Unitarian theologian Joseph Priestley, were cheered by the hope that Adams and Jefferson would "act harmoniously together" and reduce party animosity, many High Federalists sneered at the new "fraternizing" among political adversaries. The Adams clique, a friend of Hamilton gloomily reported, seemed happier to have Jefferson as vice president than Pinckney, for Jefferson would "serve readily under Mr. Adams, and will be influenced by and coincide with him." Hamilton, like Madison, was skeptical of the new game of making nice. "The *Lion* & the *Lamb*" were going to lie down together, he snickered to Rufus King, mocking the hopes of Adams and his followers for harmony with "our Jacobins." Such soft-headed Federalists, Hamilton wrote, were jabbering among themselves that "Mr. Jefferson is not half so ill a man as we have been accustomed to think him. There is to be a *united* and a vigorous administration."

Fisher Ames, too, scorned the idea of harmony in government, but from a different angle. In a cogent analysis, he perceived that the absence of two sharply adversarial parties with strong leadership was making divided government even more stagnant than it had been designed to be. For Ames, the solution to the stasis of checks and balances was party. "One might have hoped," he wrote to Hamilton after the election results became known, "that Govt would find in party all the combination & energy that is excluded from its organization." Though he loathed the "Jeffs" and the "Jacobins," he realized that effective government called for not one but two energized parties — to oppose and galvanize each other. His own Federalist party, he wrote in the winter of 1797, "unless compacted together by the violent action of the rival party will subdivide or fall into inaction."

Just as Ames had predicted, after Adams's victory, in the new climate of conciliation between the parties and division among the Federalists, both parties found themselves enervated and rudderless. Who was willing to fight, to lead? Party, "even when roused to the utmost," Ames had understood, "is in need of a clear Sighted guide." Adams's win did not buoy the Federalists. On the contrary, key Federalists were withdrawing from politics, Adams reported to Abigail, and those who remained were "divided and crumbling to pieces."

And Federalists were not the only ones leaving politics. The day before Adams took his oath of office, Madison retired from the House of Representatives. After eight years in Congress, the leader of the Republicans wanted to return to his estate facing the Blue Ridge Mountains of Virginia with his young wife, Dolley, to whom he had been introduced in 1794 by Aaron Burr. In Montpelier, Madison was eager to manage the family plantation, look after his aging father, his many nieces and nephews, and, of course, his slaves.

Now Jefferson's and Madison's roles were reversed: from Philadelphia Jefferson would pass on political intelligence to Madison, rusticating on his land, as Jefferson had for several years. As vice president, Jefferson felt that he would have to give up the partisan fight. Now the chance was lost, he wrote, "to put our vessel on her republican tack before she should be thrown too much to leeward of her true principles."

Had the embryonic political parties in the United States already run their course? Were the antipathy for strife, the ambivalence about party, and the yearning for "harmony" all weakening Americans' commitment to their political principles and ideals?

George Washington arrived at Adams's inauguration, one witness noted, "unattended and on foot, with the modest appearance of a private citizen." It was an unforgettable, emotional scene. The burst of applause that greeted him, Theodore Sedgwick reported, was as "impossible to describe, as my own sensations produced by it." Attired simply and in black, Washington was seated at the podium next to Adams and Jefferson. The three men represented the past, present, and future of the young republic. Many people wept during the ceremony. With more than a trace of envy, Adams grumbled that "it is all grief for the loss of their beloved." But one newspaper editorialized that the country was fortunate to be governed finally by the "talents and science" of Adams rather than by the "mysterious influence of a name." The new president agreed.

In his inaugural speech, addressing himself to all who "call themselves Christians," the sixty-one-year-old president echoed Washington, condemning the "spirit of party, spirit of intrigue," warning against "anything partial or extraneous" that might "infect the purity of our free, fair, virtuous, and independent elections." Parties, with their "artifice or corruption," would push for candidates for the sake of their "own ends, not of the nation for the national good." Blind to the momentum of politics and history, Adams stubbornly stood against the tide of parties. Finally, appearing to champion an established religion, he declared that it was his "duty" to end by reminding Americans that a "decent respect for Christianity" was the best recommendation for public service. "Nothing is more dreaded," he would write years later — perhaps apologetically — "than the national government meddling with religion."

After the ceremony, Washington congratulated his successor and wished him well. Then, the slightly aloof, white-haired man in his old-fashioned black coat, at six feet four inches still towering majestically over everyone else, displayed his noblesse by deferring to the new president and vice president, ushering them out of the House chamber ahead of himself. People rushed after him into the street to catch a final glimpse of their hero. He stole the show.

The nation's father was already grieving for the many compatriots he would never see again, though he felt relief at abandoning the duties and pressures of office. Indeed, Jefferson considered him "fortunate to get off just as the bubble is bursting." The transition was well timed, he wrote Madison, because Washington was "leaving others to hold the bag." Adams, too, imagined Washington secretly joyful. On Adams's inauguration day, did Washington feel that he, not Adams, had triumphed? Adams wondered. "Ay! I am fairly out and you fairly in!" he fantasized Washington saying to himself. "See which of us will be happiest." Adams said that he had never lived through "a more trying day."

Would Adams become, as newspaper editor Benjamin Franklin Bache optimistically chirped, a great conciliator, "a man of incorruptible integrity," a "friend of France, of peace, an admirer of republicanism"? Adams and Jefferson "appear in the amiable light of friends," Bache's *Aurora* declared. "Surely this harmony presages the most happy consequences to our country." Under the new administration, the *Aurora* confidently predicted, the "VIOLENCE OF PARTY" would wither and disappear. Adams and Jefferson even shared the same Philadelphia boarding house in 1797 — a most hopeful sign. "It carries conciliation and healing with it," wrote one charmed observer, "and may have a happy effect on parties." The observer, Judge William Paterson, concluded that "it is high time that we should have done with parties." And Edward Rutledge, too, could only have been pleased with the new spirit of harmony, for he was convinced that "*unanimity* is . . . absolutely essential to the happiness, & I had almost said Independence of America."

In his new administration Adams insisted that political ideology would not prevent him from appointing the most able and "influential" men in the nation — though he would later admit that he had wanted to be more cautious than Washington in appointing "democrats and jacobins of the deepest die." Still, Adams wished for an inclusive government, free from party ideology and party domination. A government run solely by one party, a government that excluded men of virtue and talent, appalled him. "It is intolerance!" he remonstrated. "It is despotism!"

One person Adams eagerly wished to include in his government was James Madison. He confided in a friend that he was "extreamly desirous of availing myself of Mr. Madison's abilities, experience, Reputation and amiable qualities." One day, early in his administration, Adams met with his secretary of the treasury, Oliver Wolcott, and broached the subject of sending Madison to France as a member of a bipartisan team of special envoys. Wolcott frowned, his face suddenly darkened by a "profound gloom." "Mr. President," he said curtly, "we are willing to resign." Adams was shocked. He reflected that he had said "nothing that could possibly displease, except pronouncing the name of Madison." That, of course, had been enough.

For this fiasco, Adams blamed the "violent Party Spirit of Hamilton's Friends." Little did he know that Hamilton, too, had favored Madison. "Unless Mr. Madison will go," Hamilton had written to Washington, "there is scarcely another character that will afford advantage." Still, Adams was not wrong to conclude that party passions had "deep and extensive roots." Despite Washington's recent warning against the spirit of party, Federalists now scoffed at bipartisanship. The "Jacobins are flattering [Adams]," one Federalist remarked, "and trying to cajole him to admit the V. P. into the Council." But they were hardly the only ones to disdain the idea of a "unity" government. Madison himself would have refused Adams's invitation to go to France. He was convinced that foreign travel would harm his health, but more important, he did not wish to negotiate on behalf of a "hot-headed executive" and a Federalist administration that was the successor to the one that had imposed the hated Jay Treaty on the United States.

Between Adams and Jefferson, too, mutual mistrust quickly dispelled illusions of cooperation. Late that spring, after being informed that Jefferson had criticized him for endangering the country's peace, Adams angrily sputtered that Jefferson was "unfit for office" and "a dupe of party!" After all the assurances of friendship, respect, and loyalty, after the promises of harmonious collaboration, the two men rarely saw or spoke to each other. Adams never sought his counsel, Jefferson later remarked, about "any measures of the government." And Adams reported the same. "We consulted very little together," he admitted. Party "violence," he explained, made any such meetings "impracticable, or at least useless."

Despite Jefferson's continuing ambivalence about party, far from being a loyal vice president, he was metamorphosing into a strong opposition leader. With Madison in Montpelier, Jefferson would take his place as the Republican chief. In his personal life, Jefferson yearned for harmony and conciliation, advising his friends to "take things always by their smooth handle" and cautioning his grandson to "never enter into dispute or argument with another." But in politics, while preferring persuasion and conciliation, he did not shrink from conflict. Criticizing the loose commitments to parties and principles of some members of Congress, he commented that they had "no fixed system at all." He had little patience for politicians who were governed "by the panic or the prowess of the moment, flap as the breeze blows against the republican or the aristocratic bodies, and give to the one or the other a preponderance entirely accidental." Jefferson had become "the very life and soul of the opposition," Sedgwick reported in 1798 to Rufus King in London.

The eighteenth-century version of political "cohabitation" was overwhelmed by the reality of party and ideology. Harmony and unanimity were a short-lived dream: Adams had to yield to the spirit of party, filling his cabinet with Federalists who had not only served under Washington but who were still loyal to Hamilton. While Adams naively believed that Secretary of State Pickering "and all his colleagues are as much attached to me as I desire," Pickering revealed his true loyalties in a letter to Hamilton. "I wish you were in a situation not only 'to see all the cards,' but to play them," he wrote. Adams later justified keeping in his cabinet men who were loyal to Hamilton with the claim that "I knew if I removed any one of them, it would turn the world upside down." But ironically, Adams turned the political world upside down because he could establish cooperation and harmony neither with the Republican party nor with his own Federalist party.

However inclusive Adams wished his administration to be, however much, in Jefferson's words, he wanted to "steer impartially between the parties," he had no choice but to lead a party government; and this he would do ineffectively. His denunciations of party — along with his split with Hamilton and Hamilton's High Federalist allies — only left him isolated within his own party. He admitted that he felt "shackled." "I had all the officers and half the Crew," he later recalled, "always ready to throw me overboard."

With a two-thirds majority in the Senate, Federalists could be "confident, exclusive, and presumptuous," Adams remarked, noting that they were easily able to veto his proposals and thwart any attempts he might have wanted to make at conciliation and collaboration with Republicans. And for their part, Republicans, more unified than Federalists, were also bent on opposing the administration, certainly not on cooperating with their political enemies. They now constituted the loyal opposition.

Adams improbably claimed to have the instincts of a mediator. There existed two parties in America, he remarked a few years later, Aristocrats and Democrats, and only a president "capable of mediating between two infuriated Parties," he believed, would be able to govern well. But he was pessimistic about that prospect. Indeed, far from bringing both parties together, Adams recognized that he had been "abjured and abhorred by all Parties."

There was a silver lining to Adams's failure as a party leader. One of the great achievements of his administration — peace with Europe — was the result of his courageous struggle against his own party and his determination to place country above politics and party. "Great is the guilt of an unnecessary war," he had written to Abigail.

In February 1799, while France, angered by the pro-British Jay Treaty, was preying on American vessels, seizing them and plundering their cargo, Adams nominated William Vans Murray to be the American minister plenipotentiary to the French Republic. The president wanted negotiations with France; he wanted peace. But the High Federalists, itching for war, were outraged. Secretary of State Pickering furiously exclaimed that all real patriots were "thunderstruck." Hamilton angrily strode into Adams's office to "remonstrate" against the mission to France, working himself up, Adams later recalled, to a paroxysm of "heat and effervescence."

Despite his own disdain for "the babyish and womanly blubbering for peace," John Adams succeeded in avoiding war with France by behaving responsibly and independently, by resisting Federalist demands for war, by purging his cabinet of two of Hamilton's most loyal allies, Secretary of State Pickering and Secretary of War James McHenry, by insisting on negotiations, and by pursuing all avenues for peace. "Here lies John Adams," Adams suggested years later as the inscription for his tombstone, "who took upon himself the responsibility of the peace with France in the year 1800." At the time, Adams's fellow Federalists ranted that he was mentally unfit to be president. In the next election in 1800, wrote Robert Troup to Rufus King, Federalists would want only "to get rid of Mr. Adams." "The men of most importance," concurred another Federalist, "were disgusted and entirely alienated from the President."

In securing peace with France, Adams won the respect of historians but not of his fellow Federalists. His prudent, restrained foreign policy along with his subjugation of the pro-war faction in his own party would doom both him and his party, fatally dividing Federalists and wrecking his own career. By reversing his administration's and his party's policies — and those of Washington's administration — and by not building up a base of support within his party, he incited his Federalist enemies to plot his fall. The lesson? A president and his party need each other.

Successful presidents have their parties behind them. They might give lip service to the ideal of national unity, to the mantra of consensus and the ideal of the public good, they might repeat in their inaugural addresses that patriotism comes before party and that we are all Americans, but — as Madison had already intuited — to be strong national leaders, presidents have to build and lead their parties, articulate clear platforms, solidify their base, galvanize popular support, strive for unity within their own parties, and offer clear and forceful alternatives to the policies of the party opposite.

Adams refused to accept the idea that presidential leadership also meant party leadership; he did not see how a president, who was the leader of his party, could also be the leader of the nation. "We can never have a national President," a disenchanted Adams wrote in 1821. "In spite of his own judgment, he must be the President, not to say the tool, of a party." But the most successful presidents have not followed the model of Washington's anti-party leadership. On the contrary, presidents such as Jefferson, Andrew Jackson, Abraham Lincoln, Theodore Roosevelt, Franklin Roosevelt, Lyndon Johnson, and Ronald Reagan were effective precisely because they were able to balance two contradictory roles, the symbolic role of "President of all the people" and the practical role of head politician and party leader — two roles that complemented each other and held each other in check. As party leaders, they had clear political visions and worked for progress and change by relying on their strong party base and by exploiting conflict with their political opponents. Their strategy was party building, party leadership, and confrontation — not compromise, mediation, or consensus. "Legislative leadership is not possible without party leadership," said John F. Kennedy. "No president, it seems to me, can escape politics."

Already in 1796 party was becoming part of the fabric of American politics. However polarizing parties were, it was too late to dismiss or condemn them: their power had to be harnessed and exploited to make government work.

In 1796, an election had taken place. It was neither a "succession" nor the anointing of another charismatic leader. It had been a contest. A president had been elected democratically — albeit indirectly — from among a field of candidates. In the new post-Washington age, the fatherless children had not run amok. "The machine has worked without a creak," one observer commented in the spring of 1797. Even Washington had taken the conflict in stride, reminding a friend that "in all free governments, contention in elections will take place."

The American political future no longer appeared uncharted. Every four years — crisis or calm, depression or prosperity, war or peace — an election would take place, the uncertainty of future time and the fear of political turmoil conquered by four-year historical bites. Washington the patriarch could probably have "reigned" as long as he would have wished. But now, the mundane routine of a political timetable would replace the magic atemporality of charismatic leadership.

Still, the new president belonged to the same party as the outgoing one. A governing, incumbent party had not yet met the critical test of handing over power peacefully to its political enemies. The real test of democracy would come in four years.

5

Sedition

A TORRID, STEAMY HEAT WAVE washed over Philadelphia. "The mornings instead of being pleasant, are stagnant," Abigail Adams told her sister in June 1798. "Not a leaf stirs." The sultry days smothered the city. "The extreem heat of yesterday & the no less prospect of it this day, is beyond any thing I ever experienced in my Life," she wrote. "Live here I cannot an other week unless a change takes place in the weather. You had as good be in an oven the bricks are so Hot." Philadelphia streets, she added, had become "nausious," and people had begun to complain about bowel trouble and "inflamitory Soar Throat." America's coastal cities, another witness reported, were "again scourged by the Introduction of an epidemic disorder of the most malignant Character."

The old fever, the "destroying angel," one newspaper reported, had returned.

As soon as the congressional session was over in July, President Adams and his wife fled Philadelphia for their home in Quincy, south of Boston. Coastal cities from Wilmington to Boston were being abandoned en masse, one man observed, their inhabitants running "in every Direction, to seek an Asylum." Robert Troup, in New York, reported that two-thirds of New Yorkers had left for the country; in Philadelphia, too, he noted, citizens sought "safety in flight." Poorer people, living in the most fetid areas and without the resources to flee, were suffering the most, another witness remarked.

By the end of the summer, deaths in Philadelphia were averaging seventy a day. "Some days last week," Robert Troup informed Rufus

King, "they have exceeded 100." Life as usual had come to a standstill. "All private business is at an end," Troup sighed, "and nothing but distress, deep distress, prevails." Fifteen hundred of Philadelphia's poorest residents camped out on the common in September, Oliver Wolcott wrote to President Adams; and fifty orphans had been taken in by the city's almshouses.

What was this dreadful fever, this plague? "The Physicians," commented William Bingham, senator from Pennsylvania, "are disputing whether it is contagious, infectious, or epidemic." The disease "was found to baffle all medical skill," lamented Troup. Could the key lie in the climate? "In the midst of our heat," he wrote, "we had the longest heaviest shower ever remembered here; and this by filling cellars, choking drains, etc. put our whole mass of filth into a state of violent fermentation."

No one took notice of the tiny mosquitoes whining above.

That summer another fever was gripping the city. War fever.

France was permitting private, armed French vessels to look for contraband and raid or capture American ships. In June 1797, Secretary of State Pickering announced that the French had already seized hundreds of American trading vessels, mostly in the Caribbean. On February 5, 1798, President Adams informed Congress that a French privateer had attacked a British merchant ship inside Charleston harbor. In May, Congress passed a bill empowering American war vessels to patrol the water and seize all armed French cruisers and privateers.

The political situation in France itself was hardly stable. In 1794 the "Thermidorean" reaction, or counterrevolution, had put an end to Jacobin excesses, only to be replaced in 1795 by the Directory government. Why had the new government in France turned against the United States, the land she had rescued only seventeen years earlier? For their part, the French placed the blame squarely on the treaty that Jay had negotiated with England. After having lost much of her ocean commerce as a result of her maritime war with Great Britain, France was suffering economically. Seeking to recover from her losses, Paris now accused the United States of violating not only its old alliance with France but even Washington's 1793 proclamation of neutrality vis-à-vis France and England. According to the French, it was the Americans, not the French, who had forgotten Yorktown.

France was intent on retaliation. She started raiding American ships and cargo, just as England had done before the Jay Treaty. Diplomatic relations were severed, and President Adams urged Congress to take adequate defense measures. Even so, he kept his head, dismissing fears of French invasion. "Where is it possible for her to get ships to send thirty thousand men here?" he asked. "What would 30,000 men do here?" Making a good faith attempt to head off war, the president asked Elbridge Gerry of Massachusetts and John Marshall of Virginia to join the American minister to France, South Carolinian Charles Cotesworth Pinckney, in negotiating a peace. But the French grandly refused to deal with the Americans — that is, unless they received a bribe of a quarter of a million dollars. "No, no! not a sixpence!" the outraged envoys indignantly replied. The French had demonstrated "unparalleled stupidity," muttered Madison. But worse was soon to come.

In March 1798, news broke about this scandal, this XYZ affair — the letters standing for the three unidentified, corrupt Frenchmen who demanded bribes. The revelations, Fisher Ames recalled, "electrified all classes." John Marshall returned home in June 1798 to a tumultuous hero's welcome. "Millions for defense, but not a cent for tribute!" patriots shouted.

France's conduct toward the United States, exclaimed George Washington in May 1798, was "outrageous." Still, the former president was not yet convinced that "open war" was inevitable.

Others were more belligerent. Secretary of State Pickering happily gloated that the majority of Americans were coming to view France "in all its deformities and horrors." There was too much talk of peace, Fisher Ames objected in early June, adding that a passive Congress appeared "too much afraid of measures of self-defense." The people, on the other hand, unlike congressional leaders, were ready for action. "A spirit of warm and high resentment against the rulers of France," Troup wrote to King, "has suddenly burst forth in every part of the United States." One week later, Troup bestowed high praise on the governor of Pennsylvania, Thomas Mifflin, for speaking in "very harsh terms" of the government of France. In New York ordinary citizens were roused as well. That city was putting on "quite a military face," Troup wrote. Volunteer companies of horse and infantry declared themselves prepared for battle, old officers of the army and navy were holding meetings, and people gathered to discuss measures for defending the port. "If the French invade their shores," Troup confidently predicted, "I have no doubt the Yankee Doodle will triumph over ça-ira."

Some Federalists demanded more than talk, even more than preparedness: they wanted war. "Every day's delay is perilous," Ames warned. "Everybody asks, shall we have war? My answer is, we have war, and the man who now wishes for peace holds his country's honor and safety too cheap." Abigail Adams jeered at the reluctance of Congress to declare war. "Why, when we have the thing," she wrote a friend, "should we boggle at the name?"

Finally, Congress permitted calling up a provisional army of 12,000 men. Fears of an imminent invasion were so real that General Washington was willing to come out of retirement and serve as official commander. "I could not remain an unconcerned spectator," he confided to Lafayette. Still, the old general would take an active role only if the United States was invaded. The army would be placed under the active field direction of Major General Alexander Hamilton. What choice did Adams have when Washington intervened on Hamilton's behalf, insisting that the New Yorker was a "man to excel in whatever he takes in hand"? The loss of Hamilton's services, Washington warned, would be "irreparable." A department of navy was also established; American naval vessels were permitted to seize armed French ships, and American merchantmen were allowed to repel French searches. Money was approved to fortify harbors, and Congress levied a $2 million direct tax — based on the number of windowpanes in each household — to finance the army and navy.

Why were members of his own party so passionately urging war? Adams wondered. Did they have a hidden political agenda? In a letter to Elbridge Gerry, he suggested that Hamilton's enthusiasm for hostilities with France was a pretext for his own reactionary political designs. "Hamilton and a Party," Adams said, "were endeavoring to get an army on foot to give Hamilton the command of it & then to proclaim a Regal Government, place Hamilton at the Head of it & prepare the way for a Province of Great Britain." *A Province of Great Britain?* Fortunately there was no basis in reality for Adams's colonial scenario. But Hamilton was spinning bizarre fantasies of his own.

"We may have to enter into a very serious struggle with France," Hamilton informed George Washington. Hamilton warned of Republican ties to the French enemy, insisting that Republicans stood "ready to new model our constitution under the influence or coercion of France." Ultimately, Jefferson and his cronies, Hamilton wrote, wanted nothing less than "to make this country a province of France." *A prov-*

ince of France? Interesting work for the author of the Declaration of Independence.

Nor was Washington immune to the odd fantasies of his friends. He, too, discerned the "Agents and Partizans of France" determined to weaken the American government and divide Americans. But a few months later, though still deploring Republican machinations, he no longer bought into Hamilton's French conspiracy theory. Republicans might want to "subvert the constitution," Washington allowed, but it was not out of loyalty to France. Republicans had "no more regard for [France]," he wrote to Lafayette, "than for the Grand Turk." A month later he repeated his belief that Republicans, whom he called the "discontented among ourselves," had no affection for France but simply wanted to undermine and change the American government. Still, the general was sufficiently apprehensive about Republican ties with France that he urged his cherished friend Lafayette to postpone a voyage to the United States. His visit "would be injudicious in every point of view," Washington confided to the American ambassador in Paris, "Embarrassing to himself, Embarrassing to his friends, and possibly embarrassing to the government."

Against the background of war fever and calls for national unity, with barbarians at — and perhaps within — the gates, the country turned, as had ancient societies, to its aristocrats, its elite "warriors," for protection and leadership. The duty of all Americans had become "self-preservation," wrote Federalists. Anti-Republican feeling soared to new heights. In this heated crisis atmosphere, political opposition had become tantamount to subversion. Republicans had an "intimate acquaintance with treason," charged Representative John Allen of Connecticut; they "vomited" falsehood on "everything sacred, human and divine."

Many Americans stopped wearing the tricolored cockades that symbolized French and American Revolutionary ideals. One young Republican, wearing the red, white, and blue cockade on his hat, ventured into a Congregational church. After the service, Federalist worshipers tore the cockade from his hat and hurled him and his hat into the street. Several butcher boys, gathered in front of the State House in Philadelphia, were thrown into jail for wearing the tricolored cockade. It was no time for public displays of pro-French sentiments. Americans sporting the Revolutionary ribbon, commented the *Boston Gazette,* "will skulk through the streets, marks of public scorn." They would be made to feel so unwelcome that they "will finally be obliged to flee to their beloved France, or meet the doom which traitors deserve." Even Harvard College decided to omit the French oration from its graduation exercises.

In May 1798, twelve hundred excited young men of Philadelphia marched down Market Street to the president's house, gallantly offering their lives in war against France. Decked out in full military regalia, the president received them warmly. A few weeks later, having decided to whip up anti-French and anti-Republican feeling, Adams publicly denounced Republicans as "dangerous and restless men" who purposefully sought to mislead "well-meaning citizens" with the design of prostrating American liberties "at the feet of France." The crowd erupted in cheers. For the first time, a surprised Adams experienced the adulation of the public. People greeted him and his wife in the streets of Philadelphia with a new respect and enthusiasm. "We are now wonderfully popular," Abigail marveled.

Citizens congratulated Adams for awakening the country from its heedless slumber, for saving the nation from the pacifist Jefferson and his Francophile followers. On the Fourth of July 1798, the president of Yale predicted that, if left to his own devices, Jefferson would "see the Bible cast into a bonfire . . . our wives and daughters the victims of legal prostitution . . . our sons become the disciples of Voltaire, and the dragoons of Marat."

While lambasting the "war party," Jefferson and Madison recognized the unpopularity of their pro-French position. In their minds, the culprit was the Jay Treaty: the United States now found itself in the ironic position of defending a treaty, Madison remarked, that had been adopted "as a defense against war." But what tack could the opposition responsibly take? The Republican attacks on the Federalist monocrats and Anglomen were, next to French depredations, ringing increasingly hollow. "The best that can be done by the republicans," Madison concluded, "will be to leave the responsibility on the real authors of whatever evils may ensue."

Opposition to Federalist policies had become unseasonable during the months of war fever. But would opposition and dissent also become illegal? In his address to Congress in March 1798, President Adams had asked Americans for "unanimity" in their "half-war" against France. "*He that is not for us, is against us,*" roared the Federalist *Gazette of the United States.* Who would dare to breach American "unanimity" at such a critical point?

Federalists now viewed Republicans as America's domestic enemies and began thinking about how to quash them militarily. Hamilton in private admitted as much, arguing that a large military force was necessary "with a view to the possibility of internal disorders." A state militia, he stressed, would not be sufficient to keep order in as "*refractory & powerful*" a state as Virginia. There was clearly a "close connection between the Infernals of France & those in our own Bosoms," Abigail Adams wrote. True "republicans" and true patriots, one Boston editor held, were those who were friends to the present American administration. "Whatever American opposes the administration," the editor asserted, "is an anarchist, a jacobin, and a traitor. . . . It is Patriotism to write in favor of our government — it is *Sedition* to write against it."

Fantasies of Republican conspiracies, Federalists' moral indignation at Republican criticism of them, and their apocalyptic visions of the demise of the union and the Federalist way of life all seem to correspond to what historian Richard Hofstadter termed the "paranoid style" of American politics — a political pathology he discerned in the 1950s no less than in the 1790s. If there was "paranoia," however, it also existed among Republicans, who were similarly convinced that the Federalist Anglomen were conspiring to "monarchize" the United States.

Could these supremely rational men — this galaxy of brilliant leaders — really have descended into the depths of paranoia? Perhaps not. Federalists were searching for a means to crush the Republican opposition. Above all, they wanted to protect their hold on power, threatened by Republicans. The accusations they would hurl at their opponents of conspiring with France were the result not of paranoia but of a rational plan to suppress opposition — a plan that would prove to be a hugely miscalculated strategy.

Sedition. A new word entered the public consciousness and the political arena.

Wasn't it logical — as well as prudent — for a government, in a time of national emergency, to prohibit public criticism of its policies, to limit freedom of the press, to insist on national unity and unanimity, to be on guard against a fifth column of traitors, to criminalize dissent?

Wasn't it *illogical*, in a time of national emergency, for a government to permit its domestic enemies to attack it with impunity, insulting and libeling the people's elected representatives? Wasn't it irresponsible for a government to countenance subversion, sedition?

"Every independent Government," explained Massachusetts representative Harrison Gray Otis, "has a right to preserve and defend itself against injuries and outrages which endanger its existence." How could a government expect to be effective, asked South Carolinian Robert Goodloe Harper, if sedition and libel went unpunished? Already in 1795 Fisher Ames had yearned to inflict punishment on an opposition senator, wishing that "the crackbrain could be convicted for libeling the government." Many Federalists had come to agree with Ames. Republicans were "morbid excrescences upon the body politic," remarked Connecticut representative John Allen. If necessary they would have to be removed "by a surgical operation." He did not say if he had in mind surgery by the guillotine.

From campaigns waged by two adversarial parties during the election of 1796, from Adams's talk of amity and harmony with the opposition in 1797, the nation had moved — or descended — to a new stage in its political development. The party in power in 1798 came to believe that there should be just one party, one press, one truth, one foreign policy, and one notion of the common good — its own. "How mischievous a thing it is," wrote James Lloyd, senator from Maryland who proposed the first draft of the Sedition Act, "to oppose the government of the state." Federalists could not accept disapproval of their administration, nor could they swallow criticism of themselves coming from an opposition party. And so, people who objected to their policies, their authority, or their personalities would simply be indicted for sedition. Some Federalists, however, had a more subtle agenda, too. Fisher Ames, for one, believed that the severity of the Sedition Act would purge his own party of moderates, cowards, and hypocrites, all those who, as historian Saul Cornell remarked, were not entirely devoted to the party's ideals.

During the torrid season of yellow fever and war fever of 1798, desperately clinging to their elitist ideology, Federalists would attempt something as shattering and virulent to democracy as the lethal malady was to public health. Oddly, for President Adams, the lethal malady was democracy itself. Comparing democracy to yellow fever, he would remark in 1805 that he could not "help thinking that Democracy is a distemper of this kind, and when it is once set in motion and obtains a majority it converts everything good, bad, and indifferent into the dominant epidemic."

Is there anything in a democracy more important than a free press? For Thomas Jefferson, the press was the "bulwark of liberty." In 1787 he had made the unforgettable pronouncement that "were it left to me to decide whether we should have a government without newspapers or newspapers without a government, I should not hesitate a moment to prefer the latter." What could be more crucial in a democracy, asked Benjamin Franklin, than the open political forum provided by newspapers? "If by the Liberty of the Press were understood merely the Liberty of discussing the Propriety of Public Measures and political opinions," Franklin wrote in 1789, "let us have as much of it as you please."

No one could deny that some American newspaper editors were an unruly lot, delighting and indulging in all manner of abusive, extravagant, witty, hyperbolic, outrageous, obscene, and *ad hominem* attacks. Benjamin Franklin Bache's *Aurora* had even taken on George Washington, claiming that "Louis XVI, in the meridian of his power, never treated his subjects with as much insult." "Damn!" Washington was heard to explode, as he angrily threw down a copy of the newspaper. Adams provided an even juicier object of derision. For the New York *Time Piece*, Adams was "a person without patriotism, without philosophy, and a mock monarch." The *Aurora* pronounced him "old, bald, blind, querulous, toothless, crippled."

Even so, in the spring of 1798, most of the nation's newspapers were Federalist. Only about a quarter of American papers took pro-Republican positions, and less than a dozen of them — the *Aurora*, the Boston *Independent Chronicle*, the New York *Journal*, the *Vermont Gazette*, and a few others — embraced Republicanism aggressively. Not only did Federalist merchants support their newspapers with advertising, but it was Federalists who controlled the flow of information from the government. "The national government," wrote historian Jeffrey Pasley, "could easily disseminate its version of events through the government documents, presidential speeches, and congressional proceedings that the commercial newspapers printed in quantity, as authoritative fact. This advantage was difficult for a scattered handful of opposition editors to counter." And yet, though Federalists had little to fear from the

Republican press, they were determined to suppress any influence it might have.

The ostensible target of the Sedition Act was newspapers, but its *real* target was the opposition Republican party — for newspapers were the crucial organs of parties, their voice boxes and lungs. Could a party exist without a newspaper? No, answered the great political sociologist, Alexis de Tocqueville. People who want to organize, with some collective purpose in mind, he remarked, "need a way to speak with one another every day without seeing one another, a way to march together without actually meeting." A newspaper provides people with the means to carry out together their plans; it is the point of contact among disparate citizens, the means through which they can meet and become unified. "The newspaper has brought them together," Tocqueville observed, "and continues to be necessary to keep them together." Freedom of the press and freedom of association, he perceived, are virtually one and the same. Parties and newspapers were the lifeblood of a democracy. Was it all going to come to an end?

Only seven years earlier, Congress had ratified ten amendments — the Bill of Rights — to the Constitution. The first one proclaimed that "Congress shall make no law . . . abridging the freedom of speech, or of the press." By "no," James Madison had meant *no*. His intent in drafting the First Amendment was to guarantee protection to individuals and minorities against a tyrannical majority or against the government itself. "The censorial power," Madison had memorably stated in 1794, "is in the people over the Government, and not in the Government over the people." But now, in a bizarre reversal, it was the government that claimed the right to protect itself against individuals and minorities. Who could legitimately ask for protection — individuals, in all their vulnerability and fragility, or the government, with all its authority and monopoly on might? "A licentious press," wrote newly appointed Supreme Court Justice Samuel Chase in 1796, "is the bane of freedom, and the peril of Society." The bane of freedom? There was clearly no agreement as to the meaning of freedom.

Among themselves, Federalists were disarmingly frank about their true agenda, candidly admitting that they sought to suppress dissent, not because they were concerned about the crisis situation with France, but because they wanted to suffocate the Republican party. The whole episode with France, Theodore Sedgwick predicted, "will afford a glorious opportunity to destroy faction." "I believe faction and Jacobinism," wrote Wolcott to Hamilton in April, "to be the natural and immortal enemies of our system." According to Federalist John Allen, Republicans had tried to keep the weapon of the press in their own hands, but now it was time for Federalists "to wrest it from them." Realpolitik — not paranoia.

This was the pull of the age-old dream of unchallenged power. At the same time, Federalists dreamt of a society of docile if not contented citizens, all concurring with what their wise leaders and elite Fathers considered the common good. Using their considerable intellectual powers to deny that the essence of politics is conflict, not consensus, Federalists struggled to create a political arena in which acquiescence and deference displaced strife.

And yet, as Americans would eventually learn, the right to criticize and oppose those who occupy the offices of power — and the right to work to oust them — is the sine qua non of a free government. Such a government must be able to tolerate opponents and permit them to organize; and, if its opponents win an election, it must be willing to transfer power to them peacefully. Nonviolent political conflict, not tranquility or harmony, always characterizes an open, healthy democratic society. Should citizens not agree on *anything?* The only consensus that is necessary in a free society is the *constitutional consensus,* an agreement among citizens about their institutions and principles of government. Opposition is then directed against certain officeholders and their policies, not against the legitimacy of the constitutional government itself.

But what if an administration in power — let us say, the Adams administration — believes that the opposition seeks to subvert constitutional government? What if it considers any criticism of itself seditious? What if the administration deems it appropriate and reasonable to arrest political critics, impose fines, and shut down opposition newspapers? This was the political climate during the feverish summer of 1798 when Congress began to debate the Sedition Act — the "Gag-bill," as Republicans branded it.

Republicans — like lawyer Thomas Cooper — charged that the purpose of the bill was to enable one party "to suppress the opinions of those who differ from them," thereby imposing upon the opposition "a degrading and unjustifiable subjection." And the *Washington Gazette* pointed out that since today's minority might become tomorrow's majority, it should not be crucified for expressing its opinions. To Republican complaints and protests, high-minded Federalists self-righteously and cynically responded that newspapers and writers would *not* be deprived of the right to publish as they wished — provided that what they wrote was the "truth." The "truth" standard was not new. Perhaps Jefferson had forgotten his own proposal for a Charter of Rights for France in 1789, in which he had stipulated that French printers would be liable for printing "false facts," a startling precursor of his own to the Sedition Act.

But Federalists went even further: not only would facts have to meet the test of truth — so would *opinions*. But what test can measure the truth of opinions? Far from eliminating political lies, the *Aurora* maintained, the Sedition Act would encourage them, for it obliged printers to bow obsequiously to the Adams administration. And yet, wasn't it precisely such deference and obsequiousness to their social, intellectual, and political leadership to which Federalists felt entitled?

In 1791 Madison had argued that people possessed "property" in their opinions. Now that "larger and juster meaning" of private property had also come under attack by Federalists, who defined property solely in terms of wealth. All opinions were not equal, Federalists declared, suggesting that certain opinions were not deserving of protection. "Truth has but one side," declared Pennsylvania jurist Alexander Addison, "and listening to error and falsehood is a strange way to discover truth." But in a political arena that was opening up to all, Republicans insisted that all opinions be tolerated. Not fancy words, Greek and Latin expressions, or esoteric allusions to Pufendorf and Locke were needed to express an opinion but just people's sincerity and honesty. As for "truth," Republicans, if not others, were beginning to view it, in the words of historian Gordon Wood, as the "combined product of multitudes of minds thinking and reflecting independently, communicating their ideas in different ways, causing opinions to collide and blend with one another, to refine and correct themselves."

But Federalists, stung by the combined thrust of the popularization of American political culture and vituperative political opposition, purposefully continued their march down the road toward repression. One Federalist, Samuel Dana of Connecticut, argued that, although the people had the right to publish the truth, they also had the "right" to utter "what is not injurious to others." Thus even true statements could be punishable if they were "injurious" to others. The final bill struck out the word "injurious," replacing it with "false, scandalous, and malicious." Other punishable offenses were proposed, including statements "tending to justify the hostile conduct of the French government" and attempts to defame the president and other federal officers by questioning "their motives in any official transaction." For her part, Abigail Adams was losing patience with the legal quibbling. "In any other Country," she objected, "Bache & all his paper would have been seazd and ought to be here, but congress are dilly dallying about passing a Bill enabling the President to seize suspicious persons, and their papers."

Few prominent Federalists opposed the Sedition Act. One who did oppose it was the future congressman and chief justice of the United States, John Marshall. Marshall was "the meanest of cowards, the falsest of hypocrites," Fisher Ames charged, for abandoning Federalists on the alien and sedition bills. Marshall opposed the acts because he considered them "useless" and "calculated to create unnecessary discontents and jealousies." But he did not hold that the acts were unconstitutional. On the contrary, when the Virginia legislature would later pass its famous Resolution condemning the sedition bill, Marshall would write the Federalist response, defending its constitutionality. Another Federalist too, Theodore Sedgwick of Massachusetts, opposed the bill, but only because it restricted Federalists in the aggressive actions they could take. Without the alien and sedition laws, Sedgwick wrote, "we might have hanged traitors and exported frenchmen. This was the policy I would have pursued instantly."

In late June, Congress passed the Naturalization Act, changing from five to fourteen years the period of probationary residence for immigrants, and also the Alien Act, giving the president the power to deport aliens in times of peace. On July 10, 1798, the House of Representatives passed the Sedition Act by a vote of 44 to 41, with only two representatives from south of the Potomac voting for the act. The Sedition Act criminalized the writing, publishing, or saying of anything of a "false, scandalous and malicious nature" against the houses of Congress or the president with the intent to defame them. Four days later, President Adams signed the statute into law. "Until lately," observed Adams in an address on July 19, "licentiousness has been too little restrained." For his part, Vice President Jefferson, the most passionate advocate of the Bill of Rights, had fled to Monticello, not wishing to be present at the debacle.

Ironically, it was John Adams who, in 1770, had given to the old

Boston Gazette its motto, "*A Free Press maintains the Majesty of the People*," and it was he who, in 1778, had proposed that the Massachusetts state constitution contain an article guaranteeing the people's right to speak, write, and publish their "sentiments." But, at the same time, he consistently held, during those early years, that antigovernment talk was seditious.

By 1798, Adams's feelings about a free press had hardened. "I cannot but be of the opinion," he wrote to the citizens of Boston a month after signing the sedition bill, "that the profligate spirit of falsehood and malignity are serious evils, and bear a threatening aspect upon the Union of the States, their Constitution of Government, and the moral character of the Nation." Adams decided not to follow the Washington model of standing above party; in this case, he permitted one party to use the law to crush the opposition. Apparently the Federalist party believed, the Boston *Independent Chronicle* caustically remarked, that there should "be but *one freeman* in this country and Mr. Adams ought to be the man."

Can responsibility for the Alien and Sedition Acts be laid at Adams's door? Historians are divided. No, say Stanley Elkins and Eric McKitrick: sedition was not one of Adams's primary concerns. Yes, concludes Merrill Peterson, contending that Adams "helped to create the climate of opinion in which they were enacted; he articulated the principles and fears they embodied; and despite later disclaimers, he cooperated in their enforcement." Indeed, proclaiming that the nation's "worst enemy" was "obloquy," Adams encouraged the prosecutions of editors Thomas Cooper and William Duane, refused to pardon editor Anthony Haswell and itinerant Democratic speaker David Brown, and fulminated that United States Attorney William Rawle was unfit for office for not prosecuting the *Aurora* with greater zeal. In later years Adams professed to be puzzled by "the hideous clamour" against the Alien and Sedition Acts, which he insisted had been "constitutional and salutary, if not necessary."

There were odd historical precedents for the Federalist foray into coercion. The British monarch's method of choice for repressing his colonial subjects was the accusation of sedition. When the King wanted to crush colonial opposition, he looked to the law of seditious libel. The title of George III's writ against the rebellion in the American colonies in 1775 was "A Proclamation, By the King for Suppressing Rebellion and Sedition."

Recent French history, too, offered a model for repression. Indeed, by criminalizing dissent and making political opposition illegitimate, the Sedition Act approached the kind of repression so ably practiced by the Jacobin terrorists in France whom Federalists purported to loathe. One Federalist was heard to say, according to a Republican newspaper, that once the Sedition Act became law, they would "begin first with JEFFERSON *and* GALLATIN, *banish* them and then . . . take the *others one by one.*"

Americans would witness their nation's analogue of the French Terror — the purge of all the French men and women deemed not sufficiently loyal to the Revolution. Fortunately, the American terror was a half-hearted one that consisted more of words than deeds and that demanded fines and jail time for the guilty, not decapitation. It was a milder Inquisition, though Inquisitors would once again proclaim that they were seeking only the "truth." Federalist Harrison Gray Otis wrote that his fellow Federalists selflessly bowed to the "necessity of *purifying* the country from the sources of *pollution.*" Sometimes the "pollution" even flowed from Congress itself. Making short shrift of congressional immunity, Federalists were not inhibited about targeting members of Congress, seeking to impugn and arrest elected representatives for the crime of voicing dissent. Indeed, it was all the more important to stop these representatives from uttering heresy, maintained Federalist Robert Goodloe Harper, precisely because they carried "weight with the people." Thus Harper wanted to censor representatives' private correspondence and especially to restrict their circular letters to their constituents — a masterstroke that could make it virtually impossible for Republicans to campaign for office. For his part, Secretary of the Treasury Wolcott voiced astonishment at the outcry against the Sedition Act, since its "principles," he asserted, "are among the most ancient principles of our government [and] have long been recognized in the jurisprudence of these states."

The Sedition Act was designed to protect Federalists from opposition. The whole intent of the bill, Pennsylvania representative Albert Gallatin, the leader of the Republican opposition in the House, lucidly explained, was to suppress the free circulation of political opinion so that citizens would hear no point of view contrary to the Federalist point of view. The law enabled "one party to oppress the other," Gallatin wrote, and "perpetuate themselves in power." Federalists were safe. Printing presses, Jefferson noted, had simply been put under the imprimatur of the executive branch of government. Republicanism had become not only unprofitable but also hazardous. Indeed, all the defendants prosecuted under the Sedition Act would be Republicans, all the judges and most jury members Federalists.

The bill would be a "harmonizer of parties," quipped the New York *Time Piece,* noting that all parties would have to "sing to the same tune!" Was there "more safety and liberty to be enjoyed," demanded the *Aurora* in the midst of the debates, "at Constantinople or Philadelphia?" Two weeks after the bill passed, the *Aurora* advised Republicans to "hold their tongues and make tooth picks of their pens." Another newspaper reported on one citizen's plan to form a "THINKING CLUB." Since the Sedition Act would not only muzzle the press but also censor verbal communication, he came up with the idea of a club that would begin to meet at 7:30 and begin to think precisely at 8:00 P.M. "The first question to be thought of is — How long shall we be permitted to think? Dumb waiters are provided."

That humorous touch not withstanding, for Jefferson, the gravity of the potential consequences of the Alien and Sedition Acts could hardly be overstated. The sedition law was "so palpably in the teeth of the Constitution," the dejected vice president remarked to Madison, "as to shew they mean to pay no respect to it." When Republicans tried to reason with them on the floor of the House of Representatives, Jefferson noted with dismay, Federalists drowned them out with loud conversations, coughing, and laughing, making it impossible to proceed. Federalists had embarked on an "*experiment* on the American mind," Jefferson said, "to see how far it will bear an avowed violation of the Constitution." And he feared that more Federalist "experiments" lay ahead — congressional acts declaring that the president shall continue in office for life, that presidents can choose their own successors, and that senators have lifetime terms. Madison sadly concurred with Jefferson's dire prediction. Federalists aimed at nothing less than transforming "the present republican system of the United States into an absolute, or, at best, a mixed monarchy." The guardian of every other right that citizens possessed, Madison believed, lay in the "right of freely examining public characters and measures, and of free communication thereon." And that primary right had been blatantly violated.

And so Jefferson and Madison countered with experiments of their own: first, Jefferson came to the aid of indicted editors of the *New Lon-*

don (Conn.) *Bee,* the *Albany Register,* and other papers, contributing money to the support of printers who, he wrote, were "staggering under the sedition law."

Second, and most important, Madison and Jefferson drafted the Virginia and Kentucky Resolutions. The Kentucky Resolutions, in their original form drafted by Jefferson, had stated that the federal union was a compact among states and that if any acts of the federal government went beyond that government's delegated powers, states had the right "to nullify of their own authority all assumptions of power." While Madison's more moderate Virginia Resolutions did not contain the scare word *nullification,* the point of the resolutions was that states could judge for themselves the constitutionality of acts of Congress. Still, Jefferson and Madison's aim was not to offer a theory of nullification and states' rights but rather to protect the integrity of the First Amendment. Indeed, Madison explicitly referred to the Bill of Rights, rights of conscience, and freedom of the press, as well as the "right of freely examining public characters and measures." But Jefferson went further down the path to disunion. In a letter to Madison, while mentioning his "warm attachment to union with our sister-states," he acknowledged that, rather than forfeit the rights of self-government, Virginians would "sever ourselves from that union we so much value." Certain fundamental rights took precedence for him over union. In defense of freedom of the human mind and freedom of the press, he wrote, "every spirit should be ready to devote itself to martyrdom."

But for Hamilton, the resolutions meant nothing less than "a conspiracy to overturn the government." Was the resolutions' theory of "nullification" or unconstitutionality a prescription for eventual secession and disunion? Madison would have said no; he objected to the right of any one state to withdraw unilaterally from the union and intended that the Virginia Resolutions apply only to the states as a whole. And even though Jefferson had written, in incendiary French style, that the Sedition Act would "necessarily drive these states into *revolution and blood,*" the calmer and more prudent Madison succeeded in tempering his friend's views; in the future Jefferson would limit himself to advocating only "protestations against violations of the true principles of our constitution."

The Virginia and Kentucky Resolutions nevertheless constituted a backward step toward southern sectionalism and especially toward the

Articles of Confederation. They implied that the way to overcome a bad administration or bad legislation was to regress back toward weak federal power. Politicians skilled at playing the game of party politics would logically take a different tack: organize, win supporters, and, at the next election, force the administration out of power. Still, if Republicans suggested that they were less than fully committed to playing that political game in 1798, it was understandable. Federalists, with their Sedition Act, had already broken and changed the rules of the game, destroying the level playing field, compromising Republicans' right to campaign freely and criticize the government's policies. But when Republicans were ready to jump into the national political contest, they would have two effective and — to some voters — appealing tools at their disposal: their opposition to the Sedition Act and the specter of states' rights.

In the fall of 1799, Madison ended his brief retirement from politics: he accepted a seat in the Virginia state assembly and threw himself into vindicating the Virginia Resolutions. The combination of Federalist repression and the retrograde response of the Kentucky and Virginia Resolutions, calling into question the "consolidation" of authority in the central government, placed the very survival of the union in jeopardy.

Under the Sedition Act, twenty-five people were arrested; there were seventeen prosecutions, mostly Republican printers and proponents. Only one man was found not guilty. Sixteen of the seventeen prosecutions took place in New England, where Federalists dominated the political and judicial scene.

The chief hound and enforcer was Secretary of State Pickering. He busied himself scouring newspapers for evidence of libel against the government and its officers. "Those who complain of legal provisions for punishing intentional defamation and lies," Pickering insisted with a hyperbolic flourish, "may with equal propriety complain against laws made for punishing assault and murder."

One of the first to be prosecuted under the new law was Benjamin Franklin's grandson, Benjamin Franklin Bache, whose newspaper, the *Aurora*, had steadily heaped abuse on Federalist follies. After his indictment, the twenty-nine-year-old Bache eloquently denounced laws that limited the right of a citizen to speak or publish his sentiments. But before his trial could take place, he died of the fever sweeping Philadelphia in September 1798.

Bache's assistant, an Irishman named William Duane, took over the *Aurora* after his death and kept up the drumroll of attacks on the administration and on the Alien Act. After Duane and two Irish friends canvassed for signatures on petitions requesting the repeal of the Alien Act, Duane and his friends were accused of seditious rioting with intent to subvert the United States government. Duane and company were tried and acquitted, but that was only the first skirmish. A few months later, in July 1799, Duane claimed to have in his possession a letter in which President Adams himself lamented British influence in America. Because Duane had insisted that Great Britain was influencing American affairs, Pickering proposed a double prosecution of Duane, under both the Alien and Sedition Acts. Even George Washington weighed in, remarking that "there seems to be no bounds to [Duane's] attempts to destroy all confidence that the People might . . . and ought, to have in their government."

When Duane appeared in court to stand trial for seditious libel, he fired his bombshell: he would produce the letter in Adams's own hand. Taken completely by surprise, the judges in the case hastily decided to postpone the trial until June 1800. The trial would never take place, but Pickering was not through hounding William Duane.

Jedidiah Peck — remembered as the father of the public school system in New York — was a good Federalist from central New York State, first appointed to a judgeship in the Otsego County Court of Common Appeals and then elected to the state Assembly. But there he did not always side with Federalists: he supported resolutions condemning the Alien and Sedition Acts and also asked for the direct election of presidential electors by the people of New York. In March 1799, angry Federalists secured Peck's dismissal as judge on the court. Less than two months later, Peck won reelection to the state Assembly, but this time as a Jeffersonian Republican. In September 1799, Peck was indicted under the Sedition Act for circulating a false, scandalous, and malicious petition protesting the Alien and Sedition Acts and for denouncing the Sedition Act as the wicked attempt to "convert Freemen into Slaves." He was arrested in Cooperstown, manacled, and taken to New York City. The five-day journey, remarked historian James Morton Smith, became a "triumphant processional rather than the march of a doomed man," the public exhibition of a "suffering martyr" in the cause of freedom to speak, publish, and petition. Peck's trial was scheduled to take place in April 1800, in the middle of the New York election campaign. Only then did Federalists realize their blunder in pursuing a man who was both an assemblyman and a judge, and with President Adams's consent, the charges were dropped.

In July 1798, President and Mrs. Adams, slowly making their way from fetid Philadelphia to their slightly cooler refuge in Quincy, Massachusetts, stopped in Newark, New Jersey. Happy crowds cheered them, flags waved in the breeze, and church bells rang. Just after President and Mrs. Adams had driven down Broad Street, followed by the boom of cannons firing a sixteen-gun salute, one inebriated Republican, Luther Baldwin, shouted out, "There goes the President and they are firing at his a — !" That "ridiculous expression," the New York *Argus* reported with astonishment, resulted in a formal trial and criminal penalties for speaking seditious and defamatory words. Baldwin was sentenced to jail in 1799 and not released until he could pay a fine of $200. It was a "*heinous joke*," the *Argus* commented, noting that European royalists would be pleased to learn that their cause "might yet succeed in this country."

David Brown, a poor laborer in Dedham, Massachusetts, charged that a clique of oligarchs controlled the federal government and ruled in their own interest. There always had been, he held, a "struggle between the laboring part of the community" and the class of "lazy rascals." Testimony at Brown's trial showed that not only had he stirred up the hoi polloi against the government, but he had also held a ladder from which another man had nailed an anti-Federalist poster to a liberty pole! Even worse, witnesses had overheard Brown discussing Thomas Paine's *Age of Reason*! Brown was sentenced to eighteen months in prison and ordered to pay a $480 fine — the harshest sentence imposed at any of the sedition trials, a sentence lengthened by his inability to pay the fine. Not until President Thomas Jefferson pardoned Brown in March 1801 was he released from jail.

On the floor of the House of Representatives, Vermont Republican Matthew Lyon was defending his own military record against disparaging comments by Federalist Roger Griswold of Connecticut, when Griswold marched across the chamber floor, grabbed Lyon by the arm, and insulted him again. At that point Lyon shot a stream of tobacco

Cartoon showing Republican Matthew Lyon with fire tongs
and Federalist Roger Griswold with cane coming to blows
on the floor of Congress, 1798.

juice in Griswold's face. Two weeks later, again on the House floor, Griswold struck Lyon with his cane, and the two men proceeded to wrestle each other to the ground. But Lyon did more: he started his own publication called *The Scourge of Aristocracy and Repository of Important Political Truths,* edited by his oldest son. Four days after the first appearance of *The Scourge* on October 1, 1798, a grand jury, presided over by Supreme Court Justice William Paterson, indicted "Spitting Lyon" for sedition. He was found guilty of libelous attacks on the president, fined, and sentenced to four months in jail. Lyon's imprisonment and fine did a splendid job of "inculcating a proper submission to our rulers," wrote Republican editor Philip Freneau, tongue-in-cheek, adding that "cutting off his head" would also have been efficacious though "*wrong* in itself." Freneau signed his opus "A Monarchist." From his prison cell not only did Lyon continue his denunciations, but he even won reelection to the House.

In November 1798, a month after Lyon's sentencing, the editor of the

Vermont Gazette, Anthony Haswell, whom Madison and Jefferson had visited in Bennington in 1791, decided to help Lyon. Haswell condemned Lyon's trial as a "persecution," not a prosecution. But for attacking the Sedition Act and for printing attacks on Adams's administration, Haswell found himself indicted for "false, malicious, wicked and seditious libel." In October 1799, eight months after Lyon was released from prison, two deputy marshals arrived in Bennington to serve Haswell with an arrest warrant. After several postponements, Haswell was tried by Justice Paterson, who sentenced him to two months in federal prison and fined him $200. Reduced to poverty, unable to support his family and his ill son, Haswell appealed to President Adams for a pardon. Adams refused. When he was finally freed from prison in Bennington, Haswell received a hero's welcome — the town had postponed its Fourth of July celebration until the day of his release.

Not just the shocking abrogation of Americans' constitutional rights or the anachronistic infringement on a free press, the Sedition Act represented one of the last mean gasps of the Federalists' political philosophy — a philosophy that was still rooted in their belief in their social and intellectual superiority, their old sense of their entitlement to govern, their reverence for hierarchy. The new law, charged the Boston *Independent Chronicle,* was the final breath of an "expiring Aristocracy."

In ramming the sedition bill through Congress, Federalists were attempting — unconstitutionally, self-destructively — to return to the old status quo when "a speaking Aristocracy" ruled over "a silent Democracy." They insisted that the insults hurled at the nation's elected leaders undermined their ability to command respect and govern well. The Sedition Act, they believed, would restore to them the deference and respect that were their due. Didn't the president, didn't congressmen and senators have any rights of their own against Republican lies? "How can the Congress protect the people, their constituents," demanded Robert Treat Paine of Massachusetts, "if they are not able to protect themselves?" Should Federalist politicians then stand above criticism? countered Republicans. Were Federalists "the peculiar favorites of heaven" who "partake of the divine essence?" asked the Norfolk *Epitome of the Times.* "It is a sacrilege to look askance at them and to wound their hallowed ears with the recital of unpleasant truths." Federalists apparently possessed, concluded the *Epitome*, a "divine right to rule uncontrolled over the mighty multitude."

Or did this mighty multitude retain the right to criticize as well as praise those they put into power? Were politicians elected to lead or to rule? The author of the Bill of Rights minced no words. "In no case," James Madison wrote in 1799, "ought the eyes of the people to be shut on the conduct of those entrusted with power; nor their tongues tied from a wholesome censure on it, any more than from merited commendations." It was nothing short of "folly or mischief," Madison continued, for politicians to claim a right to the people's "unlimited confidence." The political duty of citizens, he insisted, was not terminated "when they have chosen their representatives."

Political freedom, for Madison, involved more than citizens' casting votes at election time, more than these isolated expressions of choice and consent. Only a decade and a half earlier, at the Philadelphia Constitutional Convention, Americans had extolled liberty as a "jewel," praising it with verbal caresses as if it were a darling loved one. And four years after that, senators and congressmen had approved a Bill of Rights guaranteeing individual liberties *against* government. But what did liberty mean now?

It took only a subtle sleight of hand for Federalists to conflate liberty and acquiescence. In his Farewell Address, Washington had reminded his fellow citizens that their government was "the offspring of our own choice" and therefore had a "just claim to your confidence and your support." Once citizens had freely consented to their social contract, he implied, they could assume that the government mirrored their collective will and had "claim" to their support. Americans' "respect for [the government's] authority, compliance with its Laws, *acquiescence* in its measures," Washington continued, "are duties enjoined by the fundamental maxims of true *Liberty*." By "measures," Washington doubtless meant not just the paying of taxes but also controversial policies like the Jay Treaty. By obliterating any distinction between constitutional government and the men and "measures" of the current administration, Washington could claim that it was "the duty of every Individual to *obey* the established Government." Astonishingly, liberty had metamorphosed into deference toward a ruling elite. Did freedom now mean obedience?

Surely Federalists still believed in freedom. But what did freedom mean for them? Freedom for whom? Freedom to do what? Freedom from what? In their scheme of things, the officers of government would be free from the criticism of citizens. As for citizens, they would not be free *from* government but they would be free *to* consent to constitutional government, free *to* vote for certain candidates, and then free *to* defer to their wise judgment. In other words, the people were free to obey, free to concur with the eminently wise judgment of men who claimed to represent the public good. Ultimately, the law of seditious libel was, as historian James Morton Smith remarked, "the product of the view that the government was master." The Bill of Rights was turned upside down.

But elected leaders, too, had responsibilities, John Adams suggested. In Adams's view, their judicious and enlightened leadership would inspire rather than impose respect and deference. "The moderation, dignity, and wisdom of government" would, Adams proclaimed in 1798, "awe into silence the clamors of faction and pals[y] the thousand tongues of calumny." In this way good government would succeed in crushing "every attempt at disorganization, disunion, and anarchy." Leaders would be wise, followers would be acquiescent. Was this the dismal fate of the precious jewel, liberty?

Or did Federalists feel that something even more important than freedom was at stake — the stability of the entire constitutional order? And at the heart of that order lay, at least for some Federalists, neither freedom nor equality, but oddly the anachronistic value of Honor.

Just days before signing into law the Sedition Act, President Adams addressed the students of the College of New Jersey. "Reputation," he told his audience, "is of as much importance to nations, in proportion as to individuals. Honor is a higher interest than reputation. The man or the nation without attachment to reputation, or honor, is undone. What is animal life, or national existence, without either?" Adams was deftly equating the nation's honor with the honor of its elected officials and arguing that there could be no "national existence," no breathing life, without honor. He was implying that criticism of him and his administration in effect could destroy the honor — the very essence — of the nation. "Your *approbation* of the conduct of government," he pointedly counseled the students, "and confidence in its authorities, are very acceptable." By refusing to distinguish between approbation of the "conduct of the government" and approbation of the constitutional system itself, Adams had delegitimized criticism of elected officials. To criticize the "conduct of government" was to dishonor it.

Adams had evoked the political code that had reigned in the medieval world, a code that valorized the "honor" of the lord on the one hand, and fidelity to one's lord on the other. The failure to be loyal was called a *felony*. There was no concept in that feudal world of loyalty to the nation or of patriotism. As if the officers of American government were so many feudal lords, Adams was demanding people's loyalty to them, demanding people's respect for their honor, demanding people's "confidence" in the "authorities" of government. Adams undoubtedly knew the Latin root (*auctor*) of *authorities:* author, founder, father. Loyalty — as well as deference — to certain men, to the Federalist "fathers," had superseded loyalty to a rational, legal constitutional system.

Such eighteenth-century politicians with thin skins and delicate egos, undone by criticism and concerned more with their own honor than with citizens' First Amendment rights, attempted to replace the Revolutionary passion for liberty with a retrograde cult of "honor" and loyalty. Ironically, it was their own repressive actions and bills — not attacks on their "honor" — that would forever stain their historical reputations.

Federalists were astonishingly deaf. They refused to give up the illusion that, if they could not mold public opinion and channel it in one direction, they could coerce it; that, if they could not inform public opinion and make it responsive to their elite leadership, they could make it subservient to their repressive laws. Though Alexander Hamilton would come to embrace the Sedition Act, his first reaction had been extremely different — and far more politically sensitive. Hamilton initially feared that the Sedition Act would backfire, giving ammunition to the opposition, unifying Republicans. "Let us not establish a tyranny," he had warned about the harsh wording of an early version of the sedition bill. "If we push things to an extreme, we shall then give to faction *body* and *solidity*." But surprisingly, although the Sedition Act would present Republicans with a potent campaign weapon to use against Federalists in 1800, in 1798 not only did the tide *not* turn against Federalists, but they won the midterm congressional elections that fall. "We have broken the democratic fetters with which we have lately been bound," exulted Robert Troup, a bit prematurely.

In 1800, with tensions heightened by yellow fever, naval war with France, and fears of foreign invasion, election battles would be waged. But how? Without a free press? With the sedition law hanging like a sword from above? With newspaper editors arrested, indicted, thrown in jail? How would Republicans conduct political campaigns while prevented from criticizing the opposition candidate? Could a democratic election — with one party gagged — take place?

6

Life Without Father

"THE DEATH OF THE GENERAL!" exclaimed one Federalist in late December 1799. "God help us!"

Just five days before Washington died, Gouverneur Morris, at the urging of Hamilton and his friends, had written a letter imploring him to run again for president, listing no fewer than eight reasons why it was imperative for the sixty-seven-year-old former president to return to public life. "Should you decline," Morris wrote, "no man will be chosen, whom you would wish to see in that high office."

For months Washington had been receiving similar pleas to run again. But he could feel his energy ebbing. "I am too far advanced into the vale of life," he somberly wrote to a friend, "to bear such buffiting as I should meet with, in such an event." He was adamant. "No eye, no tongue, no thought," he insisted, could induce him to hold office again. Moreover, the president's view of the political terrain had changed radically. The man who had wanted to be the leader of all Americans and who had repudiated the very notion of political factions came to see that there was no circumventing political reality. Turning down the invitation to run again in 1800, he wrote, "I am thoroughly convinced I should not draw a single vote from the anti-federal side." He explained that his Democratic opponents could choose as their candidate "a broomstick," but, by calling the broomstick a "true son of Liberty," the broom would undoubtedly command "their votes in toto!"

In mid-December, on a gray, cold, windy morning, Washington mounted his horse and set out from Mount Vernon to inspect his farms. As hail turned to snow, then to rain and back again to snow, he rode through the fields until mid-afternoon. When he returned home, he sat down to dinner without changing his clothes. His assistant Tobias Lear noticed that his neck appeared wet and that snow was hanging on his hair.

The following morning, Washington's voice was hoarse, and he had a sore throat. "You know I never take anything for a cold," he said when Lear urged him to take some medication. In the middle of the night, Washington awoke, scarcely able to speak, his breathing labored. The next morning, an overseer who attended to sick slaves bled him before the doctors could be summoned.

Three physicians soon arrived, examined the patient, and consulted among themselves. Should he be bled? Should they perform a tracheotomy? Should they recommend purges? Was the patient suffering from acute tonsillitis? A violent inflammation of the membranes of the throat? They could not agree on a diagnosis but decided to bleed the patient again.

"I find I am going," Washington murmured to Lear. "My breath cannot continue long. I believed from the first attack it would be fatal." He asked that his accounts and books be settled and took a last look at his will. Several times, in a voice almost impossible to understand, he asked what time it was. "I am not afraid to go," he whispered when his old friend Dr. Craik approached his bedside. "Let me go off quietly," he begged. But the doctors desperately embarked on more procedures. Again Washington asked what time it was. "Have me decently buried," he said softly to Lear, "and do not let my body be put into the vault in less than three days after I am dead." Unable to utter a reply, the grief-stricken Lear could only nod in agreement. "Do you understand me?" Washington insisted. "Yes, sir," Lear said. "'Tis well" were the president's final words.

The funeral took place on the afternoon of December 18, a clear, crisp day. Citizens from miles around flocked to Mount Vernon to honor their general. At three o'clock, a schooner on the Potomac started firing its minute guns. Cavalry and infantry, arms reversed, began the slow, somber funeral procession to the beat of muffled drums. The general's horse, his saddle empty, followed two postilions dressed in mourning. Four lieutenants from the Virginia militia, surrounded by six honorary pallbearers, carried the bier.

Apotheosis of George Washington

That same day, Americans learned of their hero's death. "The whole United States," wrote Benjamin Rush, "mourned for him as a father." It was a "national calamity," declared congressman John Marshall before he quickly adjourned the House of Representatives. Washington's friend, Edmund Rutledge, suffered a stroke upon hearing of the general's death.

"Our country mourns her father," announced the Senate on December 19, in an official message. "I feel myself alone," Adams wrote in his official response, "bereaved of my last brother." "From a calamity, which is common to a mourning nation," commiserated Alexander Hamilton with Martha Washington, "who can expect to be exempt?"

December 26 would be the official day of mourning. Marshall, speaking for the Senate and House, decreed that a marble monument be erected at the Capitol in Washington and that, with the permission of the general's family, his body be interred under it. A thirty-day period of national mourning, during which all Americans would "wear crape on their left arm," was declared. Public buildings were draped in black; bells tolled. Vice President Jefferson, presiding over the Senate, occupied a chair draped in black — despite accusations that his absence from all funeral ceremonies had been a deliberate slight.

Hundreds of funeral processions took place throughout the country, and no fewer than three hundred funeral orations were pronounced, each one printed and distributed to members of the community. Margaret Bayard Smith wanted to hear Gouverneur Morris's eulogy in New York, but wrote that it would be "almost an impossibility for ladies to be present, as the crowd will be so large." At Harvard, Washington was extolled as one of the "gods upon earth." In a eulogy in Boston on February 8, Fisher Ames emotionally recalled that, following Washington's death, "every man looked round for the consolation of other men's tears." The loss was "irreparable," Ames explained, for "two WASH-INGTONS come not in one age." But, he concluded, Washington's name "is hung up by history as conspicuously as if it sparkled in one of the constellations of the sky."

That same day, February 8, 1800, hundreds of French men and women, garbed in black, solemnly flocked to the Temple of Mars in the Hôtel des Invalides in Paris. Napoleon Bonaparte — now the First Consul in the new Consulate government — upon learning of Washington's death, had commanded a grandiose pageant of mourning for the liberator of the New World. Flags — the same ones that had recently accompanied French troops on their military campaign in Egypt — adorned the temple. The minister of war, Alexandre Berthier, who had fought in the American Revolution in 1781, and other government ministers and hundreds of war veterans, stood silently at attention. Finally one man, the poet and professor Louis de Fontanes, came forward to speak.

"I praise a man who never yielded to the impulses of ambition," he intoned, "and who devoted himself to the needs of his country; a man who . . . died quietly as a private individual, in his native land." Then Fontanes went on to consider the unpredictable, tumultuous aftermath of a great revolution. "A nation in the throes of a revolution no longer has allies or friends," he said. "People run away from it as they do from a volcano. Following such great political convulsions a man out of the ordinary must manifest himself and through the sole power of his glory check the daring of all factions and restore order from the midst of confusion. He must, if I dare say it, resemble that god of mythology, that sovereign ruler of the winds and the seas, who silences all the raging storms when he raises his brow above the waves." Volcanoes, raging storms, an extraordinary man, a mythological god, glory, order, calm, silence. No mention of freedom, the Constitution, the Bill of Rights, or representative political institutions. Was it Washington about whom Fontanes was orating — or Napoleon?

Napoleon was puzzled by Washington. Who was this virtuous, self-sacrificing Virginian? The handsome young Corsican general of oceanic ambition could hardly fathom the American Cincinnatus. "I could only be a crowned Washington," he later explained. Only after he had mastered all the other kings of Europe and become a "world dictator," Napoleon confessed, could he "have possibly displayed Washington's moderation, disinterestedness, and wisdom." In truth, the two men had nothing in common. Washington had fervently believed in rotation in office, preferring to resign as president rather than create the appearance or the possibility of a "succession" after him; Napoleon would declare himself consul for life in 1802 and would soon thereafter crown himself emperor.

Napoleon had justified his coup d'état of 18 Brumaire 1799 as the only means possible to restore stability to France, to quash the lawlessness, violence, and anarchy that had plagued France after the end of the Terror. By a vote of 3,011,007 to 1,562 the exhausted French people, for whom the term *republic* had become a smear word, eagerly embraced the constitution that guaranteed Napoleon's autocracy — a constitution that contained neither a declaration of rights nor any mention of freedom. Though the people refused to repudiate the Revolution that had liberated them from the Old Regime, they were ready, commented Tocqueville, to give up the "freedom" that the Revolution had promised but never delivered, in order to have the tranquility and security necessary to enjoy the other things that the Revolution had brought about. The people who had loved freedom in 1789, Tocqueville concluded, no longer loved it in 1799.

One of Napoleon's first masterstrokes in his quest for absolute domination was to muzzle the newspapers of France. Newspapers, it was decreed in January 1800, that published anything "contrary to the respect due to the social pact, the sovereignty of the people, the glory of the Army" or that published any invectives against the government and its allies would be closed. Out of seventy-three newspapers in the Paris region alone, sixty were closed down. Even the ladies' fashion magazine, the *Journal des Dames et des Modes,* after expressing a few feminist ideas about the repression of women, was forced to abandon such positions. No newspapers ever protested. "The press, the only tocsin of a nation," Jefferson would sadly remark in 1802, "is compleatly silenced there."

Napoleon established his own official propaganda organ, *Le Moniteur,* for which he occasionally wrote articles. By 1811, Paris had only four newspapers left. By the end of the empire, in 1814, the situation of the press was worse than it had been in 1788, before the Revolution.

Napoleon's more potent version of the Federalists' Sedition Act was as successful as it was ruthless. He would brook no dissent, no criticism, no opposition as he embarked on building an astonishingly efficient, centralized, and enduring administrative machine. Parliamentary government became a mere rubber stamp. Virtually all important decisions — national and local — were made by Napoleon and his small group of advisers. Government officials throughout France, in every province and prefecture, were chosen in Paris, never elected by the people. And finally, to secure his power, Napoleon created a harsh Ministry of Police — only the Hapsburg monarchy had such an intense system of police and surveillance, commented historian Louis Bergeron.

Still, as the inheritor of the Revolution, Napoleon knew he had to give some lip service to the idea of the sovereignty of the people. But how? The trick, commented Tocqueville, was to govern in the name of the people but without the people. And so, in another masterstroke of democratic despotism, Napoleon substituted plebiscites for elections. Citizens were not called upon to cast an informed vote or make a political choice between different candidates. On the contrary, their role was reduced to voting "yes" or "no" in referenda, expressing global confidence in one man. Indeed, the guiding principle of the constitution, according to one of its architects, Emmanuel Sieyès, was that "authority must come from above and confidence from below." Napoleon forged his own synthesis of despotism and democracy, one that suited his grandiosity as well as the political passivity of a majority of the French people. "My kind of politics," Napoleon explained, "is to govern people as the majority of them want to be governed. This is, I believe, the way to recognize the sovereignty of the people."

Napoleon was modernizing France, transforming French society, and bringing numerous benefits to the French, from equality of taxation to public education. But at a great cost. Political life in France was dead. People had become equal, Tocqueville later observed, because everyone had been reduced to the same level of servitude. "Wherever one looked," he remarked, "one only saw the colossal figure of the Emperor himself."

Just months after Washington's death and Napoleon's coup d'état, Federalists were accusing Jefferson of being the "man of the choice of France." Federalist newspapers branded him the "Jacobin First Consul" and warned that the Constitution might "fall a sacrifice to Jacobinism." Jefferson countered with warnings of his own, alerting his followers that General Hamilton, the American "Buonaparte, surrounded by his comrades in arms, may step in to give us political salvation in his way." John Adams concurred with Jefferson. Hamilton, who was born on the Caribbean island of Nevis, came from a "Speck more obscure than Corsica," Adams wrote, and was "as ambitious as Bonaparte." For his part, Hamilton believed that it was Aaron Burr who wanted "to reform the government *à la Buonaparte*." Hamilton did not exempt other Republicans from the Napoleonic contagion: they were all mischievous, determined to make "a revolution after the manner of Bonaparte." Napoleons here, there, everywhere.

What would become of political life in America without the security ensured by the nation's father? Would it devolve into a Napoleonic tyranny? "When WASHINGTON lived," editorialized the *Pennsylvania Gazette*, "we had one common mind — one common head — one common heart — we were united — we were safe." "When shall we see a Washington?" Federalist Uriah Tracy asked. "Not till we get to Heaven" was his answer.

Would the United States, seeking to protect itself from Jefferson and his wild Jacobins, now take refuge in monarchy, as John Adams had once predicted? "I am clear," he had written, "that America must resort to [monarchical institutions] as an asylum against discord, seditions and civil war." Would neo-Napoleonic Federalists, also believing in authority from above and confidence from below, continue to hound Republicans, arrest their editors and supporters, convict them, and toss them in jail? Just weeks before Washington died, Hamilton had sternly demanded "new ramparts" to surround the Constitution and even tougher laws "for restraining and punishing incendiary and seditious practices."

Another Federalist, too, admired the Napoleonic brand of order. William Vans Murray, a friend of John Quincy Adams and one of President Adams's envoys to France, met Bonaparte in Paris and showered him with praise. "Friends of order and rational liberty," Murray told Bonaparte in his halting French, had "rejoiced" after the 18th of Brumaire. In 1800, Federalists and Brumairians could indeed meet, as historians Elkins and McKitrick pointed out, on "common ideological ground." Their common intolerance for opposition did not augur well for American democracy.

Or might Washington's death have a liberating effect? Might there take place, as Jefferson would predict, a "resuscitation" of the republican spirit in the country? Perhaps, without a Washington, there might be a resurgence of democratic energy. Federalism, after all, had relied more on the celebrity of leaders like Washington and Hamilton than on building and nourishing grass-roots support among the people. At the memorial service for the general in New York City, the head of the Tammany Society had sported the Revolutionary, republican symbol, the Cap of Liberty, but wore it "veiled in crape." In other words, Washington yes, Federalism no.

Perhaps reminders of Napoleon's autocracy would strengthen Republicans' commitment to individual liberties, self-government, checks and balances, and the principle of the legitimacy of opposition. Madison believed that Napoleon's military usurpation would provide an indelible lesson for Americans. "A stronger one," Madison wrote early in 1800, "was perhaps never given, nor to a Country more in a situation to profit by it."

Disillusioned by the fate of the Revolution in France and by the ascent of Napoleon, Jefferson could perceive nothing in Bonaparte that "bespeaks a luminous view of the organization of rational government." But he could reassure Americans that they had nothing to fear from despotism in France. The "character and situation" of Americans, he noted two months after the 18th of Brumaire, "are materially different from the French, and that whatever may be the fate of republicanism there, we are able to preserve it inviolate here." Eagerly divorcing himself from his old French allies and friends, Jefferson underscored that "our vessel is moored at such a distance, that should theirs blow up, ours is still safe."

As the election of 1800 approached, as prosecutions of Republican newspaper editors continued and even increased, as Federalists and Republicans all warned that Napoleonic clones were hiding in their enemies' ranks, it was not certain that rational, tolerant government in the United States would prevail.

Was the American "vessel" really moored at such a safe distance from the failure of the revolutionary experiment in France? Was the United States so immune from the repression choking France in 1800? Or might America be prey to a different malady? Were the tumult and conflict arising from political parties destroying the fabric of American society, as many people feared?

"The jealousies, the hatred, and the rancorous and malignant passions" of the Philadelphia political scene in 1797 disgusted Thomas Jefferson. Another twelve months in Philadelphia did not soften his stand. "Politics and party hatreds destroy the happiness of every being here," he wrote. "They seem, like salamanders, to consider fire as their element."

Federalists, too, felt the sting of party antagonism. Thomas Pinckney, Adams's running mate in 1796, deemed party the cause of "political rancour & malevolence." "Opposition to the government," complained Hamilton in 1799, "has acquired more system than formerly." Party strife was giving the American national character "an odious aspect in the eyes of many foreigners," reported John Quincy Adams, the ambassador to Berlin, to his mother in 1799. As for his father, even decades later the former president would continue to view parties as corrupt and destructive, "prone to every Species of Fraud and Violence, and Usurpation." Parties and factions, Adams fumed in a letter to Jefferson, thwarted any attempt at good legislation. Politicians opposed good bills, he wrote, just for the perverse pleasure of blocking them.

Many of the delegates to the Constitutional Convention had given deep thought to the question of how to block the creation of political parties. Madison knew well that factions would always exist. But, he wrote in *Federalist* No. 10, the extended sphere of the republic itself and the great variety of parties and interests that it contained would make it very unlikely that a majority would be able to coalesce into a faction and carry out "schemes of oppression." Still, the Framers wanted to be prepared for the worst. Through staggered elections, fragmented constituencies, the separation of power among the branches of government, and the division of powers between nation and states, they sought to break the thrust of any possible popular majority. By fragmenting power, the Framers hoped to promote — or compel — compromise; citizens and politicians would simply devote themselves to the public good. The last thing the Framers wanted was a government run by organized, adversarial, ideological parties striving to capture control of the government.

Socially disruptive, politically malignant, potentially conspiratorial and subversive, could anything be worse than political parties?

Yes. The absence of political parties.

Though still deeply ambivalent and conflicted about adversarial party politics, Americans — Federalists no less than Republicans — began to grasp the truth that nothing is more important to a vital self-governing polity than the engagement of citizens over controversial issues in public life. Although Jefferson regretted "political dissension" and clung to the idea that it was a "great evil," he nevertheless recognized that it was not as pernicious as "the lethargy of despotism."

When tumult is absent from a polity, Machiavelli lucidly perceived in 1513, when everyone in a state is tranquil, "we can be sure that it is not a republic." Some Americans were beginning to agree with the Florentine. Benjamin Franklin discerned the creative tension inherent in political conflict in 1786. Parties, he wrote, "will exist wherever there is liberty; and perhaps may help to preserve it. By the collision of different sentiments, sparks of truth are struck out, and political light is obtained." Parties were "so many blessings to the citizens," stated the Boston *American Herald* in 1790. They "are blasts, to keep alive the political fire; by them knowledge is disseminated through the states." Five years later, the New York *Argus* editorialized that parties were essential to keep alive citizens' engagement in self-government, "for when investigation ceases, the people become uninterested at elections [and] ignorantly rivet their own chains." Continued calm was symptomatic only of "THE QUIET OF SUBMISSION," commented the Boston *Independent Chronicle.*

Three hundred years after Machiavelli, some Americans understood his wisdom. In a society bereft of freedom, "the people sleep soundly in their chains," Fisher Ames declared in his eulogy for Washington. The fact that Washington had excoriated the spirit of party did not inhibit Ames from striking a new note. "Where there is no liberty," he remarked, people "may be exempt from party . . . . Liberty, with all its parties and agitations, is more desirable than slavery."

Jefferson took a slightly different tack, underscoring the need for citizens to take principled stands along party lines. Whereas Washington had passionately urged members of his cabinet to try to find a "middle course," Jefferson embraced partisanship. When substantive ideological differences divided citizens, he wrote in 1795, "I hold it as honorable to take a firm and decided part, and as *immoral* to pursue a *middle line,* as between the *parties* of Honest men and Rogues, into which every country is divided."

In his Farewell Address, Washington had stressed the theme of unity: Americans' freedom and security depended on the unity of the government and the unity of the people themselves. In his mind, the greatest threat to liberty was disunity. But what if the opposite were true? What if an acceptance of certain forms of disunity — adversarial parties — encouraged freedom and diversity? What if it was ideological unity — that inevitably excludes dissenters — that menaces freedom?

Indeed, despite the personal rancor arising from political antagonisms, despite the severed friendships, the suspicions, and accusations, despite the potential harm wreaked by conflict and fanaticism, many Americans had begun to discern something positive, something crucial, in adversarial party politics: citizens energized by issues, participating in self-government, taking their rights and responsibilities seriously, gave life and blood to their political culture.

It was no easy task for Americans to overcome the long-standing antipathy for political factions and create a party system. The challenge was all the more daunting since there was no theory of party. The evolution of parties in the United States was shaped far more by events and circumstances than by design.

One of those circumstances was the desperation of Republicans to oust Federalists from power. The losses that Republicans suffered in 1796 and in the midterm elections of 1798 only sparked them to try harder. Ever since Jefferson had resigned from Washington's cabinet in 1793, Republicans had been excluded from the executive branch. Now they wanted back in.

The political game had no established rules or blueprints, but Republicans nevertheless seized the initiative. Their only possible strategy was to become a majority party — and that meant an inclusive party with wide popular appeal, a party that cut across class and sectional lines, a party open to all (though not to women, blacks, and Native Americans). But how? By organizing, organizing, organizing: using the press, churning out articles attacking Federalist policies, planning strategy, promoting popular candidates for office, presenting a unified front in public, and forging a coalition of merchants, landowners, slave owners, professionals, small tradesmen, mechanics, seamen, and laborers, all growing in loyalty to their party, its ideas, and its leaders.

Republicans would try to become a majority party, if not, as they hoped, the *only* party, by courting average voters, by appealing to their hearts and minds, by offering them an emotional platform of fury at the Sedition Act, outrage at the Jay Treaty, principled objections to a standing army, and support for states' rights. There was an enticing smorgasbord of other goodies, too, for voters to choose from: Anglophobia, hostility to taxes, support for a frugal and simple government, distrust of bankers and speculators, a fairer distribution of wealth and property, and espousal of the aspirations of ordinary citizens — aspirations for social and economic equality and also esteem. It was crucial, Republicans agreed, to "bring our arguments home to their *feelings*."

Federalists were not without their own agenda for change — nor were they without a desire to win elections. Alexander Hamilton wrote in 1799 that he wanted to see changes made in American society, especially changes that would "promote the popularity of the Government" and confound its Republican enemies. But the proposals he enumerated in coolly impersonal terms mostly concerned improvements to the military and to the country's infrastructure — increasing military and naval forces, creating a military academy, building roads and canals, extending the judiciary, and encouraging agriculture and the arts. In an untimely move, Hamilton appended to his list of improvements additional punitive laws for "restraining and punishing incendiary and seditious practices."

Just a few months before he died, Washington had advised his Federalist colleagues that to win elections and defeat Republicans they needed clear principles and big ideas. "If principles instead of men are not the steady pursuit of the Federalists," he wrote, "their cause will soon be at an end." But despite Hamilton's agenda of practical ameliorations and his modern economic policies, his ideas were not big enough.

Many people seemed to be clamoring for something else, something more — a capitalist society, no doubt, but a classless one; a society, in the words of historian Joyce Appleby, that was more generous and emancipating. Republicans were awakening in ordinary Americans new desires, new needs, new emotions, tweaking them to be dissatisfied rather than content with the social order and the status quo. The Republican game plan called for average citizens to discover their voices and forge a new electorate — informed, active, pressing for its rights, demanding more material prosperity, assertively disputing the entitlement of the privileged few to rule, and mistrusting rather than deferring to authority.

Republicans were offering voters a vision of a society in which all Americans were invited to the table — and to the debate. All voices — responsible, irresponsible, wild, vociferous, idealistic, witty, venomous — would be heard. Jefferson had always favored the full exchange of ideas. In Paris in 1787, he learned about the secrecy rule adopted at the Philadelphia Constitutional Convention and was virtually alone among the Founding Fathers in criticizing that policy. There had been no point, he stressed, in the delegates' "tying up the tongues of their members"; on the contrary, their decision to impose silence only reflected "their ignorance of the value of public discussion." Jefferson wanted to hear plain talk from plain men.

This was how the new game of party politics would be played. And Republicans would master the rules and strategy by simultaneously trying to shape public opinion and heed it. "A free government," editorialized the Baltimore *Daily Intelligencer*, "must be obtained by continued expression of the public will."

Would it be an unruly game? Of course. All opinions should stand "undisturbed," Jefferson would later declare. Would public opinion ever err? Certainly. But all that was required, a sanguine Jefferson believed, was that reason be "left free to combat" error. Public opinion was the "real sovereign," Madison had written in 1791, categorically announcing that it "must be obeyed by the government." Ultimately, public opinion would evolve into a force far more potent than the illusory idea of the "public good" that was supposed to have been discerned and voiced by members of the ruling elite. "In the end," wrote historian Gordon Wood, public opinion "became America's 19th-century popular substitute for the elitist intellectual leadership of the Revolutionary generation."

While Republicans, casting caution, experience, and history aside, were electrified by experiment, upheaval, and change, by the prospect of more democracy, Federalists were more attuned to experience than to experiment.

They were more cautious, and perhaps understandably so. They could point to many historical examples of republics and democracy run amok. They wanted, above all else, order and stability, insisting that order depended on respect for authority. They preferred a passive to an active electorate; they distrusted public opinion and refused to pander to their inferiors.

"I have a pious and a philosophical resignation to the voice of the people," wrote John Adams in 1796, adding that the people's voice "is the voice of God." But was it reverence and acceptance of public opinion that he was really expressing — or dread? Public opinion, Adams allowed, was worthy of the consideration of the ruling elite — but it was also, he and other Federalists feared, something unstable, ill-informed, and potentially disruptive and damaging to the young republic. The situation could be especially critical, Adams's nephew William Smith Shaw pointed out, when the government allowed public opinion "to be misled and corrupted by the lowest miscreants of society, who have talents to invent falsehood."

Alexander Hamilton was even more categorical in his dismissal of public opinion. The maxim that the voice of the people was the voice of God, he had announced to the Philadelphia convention in 1787, "is not true in fact." "The people are turbulent and changing," he contended, "they seldom judge or determine right."

To acknowledge, absorb, and respond to the opinions and concerns of ordinary people would have contradicted the essence of the Federalist vision of their own excellent leadership, their confidence in their own wisdom and superiority. Appealing to the public, pandering to their inferiors would have made a mockery of their belief in their ability to govern well in the interest of all. They refused to engage in a "mawkish and vulgar courting of popular favor," as one conservative would later put it.

Unable to discern any inherent wisdom or even common sense in public opinion, Federalists lamented its ascendancy. "The instability and fluctuation of public opinion (the basis of our boasted Government)," wrote Federalist Daniel Dewey of Williamstown, Massachusetts, to his friend Theodore Sedgwick in 1800, "is enough to make any man of reflection heartily sick of such a state of things." Thus Federalists encouraged their leaders to be confident and resolute enough to see beyond transitory, volatile public opinion. "Popular gales sometimes blow hard, but they don't blow long," Senator George Cabot judged. "The man who has the courage to face them will at last *out*face them." Leadership for Federalists meant leadership from the top down. Able to discern the public good, the elite would guide society; they would publish and communicate their ideas for other rational and educated men like themselves; those ideas would eventually trickle down the social ladder; the less privileged and less educated would prudently place their trust — and their votes — in their leaders, and follow.

"It is essential," George Washington had noted in his Farewell Address, "that public opinion should be enlightened." But since it was not always enlightened, Washington explained, he would refuse to heed it, especially on "great occasions," when a decision of momentous national importance was imminent. The "real voice" of the people could only be ascertained, he wrote, "after time has been given for cool and deliberate reflection." When would Federalists bow to public opinion? That was not clear. Perhaps when it affirmed their views, when people concurred with the "truths" that their leaders had already discovered. In short, Federalists believed in government of the people and for the people, but not by the people.

So, while Republicans were creating and mastering the new game of party politics, Federalists were doing "nothing to give a proper direction to the public mind," grumbled Secretary of War James McHenry. Instead of creating a vital, popular press, instead of organizing in Congress as well as at the grass roots, instead of articulating party principles that struck at their adversaries' weaknesses, Federalists said and did little.

Few grass-roots rank-and-file Federalist political associations were organized; little effort was made to engage masses of voters in the party. Even while appealing for the votes of ordinary Americans, Federalists advertised their faith in the political eminence of the well-born, condemned expressions of disrespect for authority, and voiced their reservations about public opinion.

Republican opposition was becoming "more open and more enterprising in its projects," Hamilton wrote in 1799, but he devised no coherent plan for countering it. As the election of 1800 approached, Federalists were without a campaign strategy. When it was too late, Hamilton scolded his friends for having "neglected the cultivation of popular favor."

Federalists had fought for too long, commented Tocqueville, against the tide of their times.

7

The War of Words

A MERICAN GOVERNMENT HAD METAMORPHOSED into a "pure unadulterated logocracy," observed the writer Washington Irving in the beginning of the nineteenth century: it was a "government of words." Run neither by democrats, aristocrats, monocrats, nor plutocrats, the country seemed controlled by a new breed: logocrats. These were political gladiators who hurled, fired, spat, and spewed words. The buzzing, squalling, and clattering of thousands of bees, peacocks, parrots, and baboons, commented Irving, was "nothing compared to the wild uproar and war of words" raging throughout the American logocracy. A "chattering epidemick" had infected the whole population, permeating "every city, every village, every temple." The "fire and energy" of argument eclipsed the "polite phrases" of the English language, which itself seemed enervated by the verbal conflict. In his mind's eye, Irving saw a scowling "fiend of contention" crouching on the bosom of society, impairing social intercourse, disturbing the conviviality of the family table. The victors of elections enjoyed a brief honeymoon period, after which citizens ferociously resumed the battle, always eager to "abuse, calumniate, and trample [their elected leaders] under foot, in compliance with immemorial custom."

"Words are things, and things of mighty influence," pronounced lawyer-politician Daniel Webster. Pennsylvania polemicist Nathaniel Chapman concurred that "eloquence is power." Words indeed were powerful and consequential — they swayed minds, provoked actions, moved the public, shaped events, and changed the course of history.

And they could win elections. As the election of 1800 approached, language heated up, nourishing and animating an already adversarial political culture. Violence of opinion, venomous name calling, remarked a visitor from France, François de La Rochefoucauld-Liancourt, "infects the most respectable, as well as the meanest of men." At the end of the election year, Fisher Ames would suddenly come to realize that a war had just been fought — with words. Words were weapons, he said, recognizing that even "names & appearances are in party warfare arms & ammunitions."

Had words been transformed into formidable arms — or, on the contrary, had they lost their meaning, as Rufus King believed, and become so many empty shells, devoid of content? King pointed to certain code words — *liberty, love of country, Federalism, Republicanism, democracy, Jacobin, glory, philosophy*, and *honor* — that were mouthed by everyone and used with precision by no one. "The abuse of words," he concluded, "is as pernicious as the abuse of things." Another critic of political propaganda agreed, contending that Republicans possessed a cache of all-purpose "sounds" that they hauled out on all occasions. Words like *British influence, standing army, direct taxes, funding system, expensive navy*, and *aristocracy* served to arouse and mislead the people. John Adams, too, protested against the abuse of words to "signify any thing, every thing, and nothing." He urged the creation of a precise political language that was "governed more by reason, and less by sounds."

But words were far more than empty terms and catch phrases and even more than weapons honed to distort, manipulate, abuse, and deceive. After all, *logos* in Greek means "reason" as well as "word." Words — the democratic medium par excellence, free, open to all, the principal means by which rational human beings can construct a community around themselves — had become the building blocks of a modern nation. With language — immaterial, ephemeral *words* — Americans of all classes, backgrounds, and persuasions were creating a vital, participatory, egalitarian political culture, a national community, fresh visions of the American future, and an adversarial party system.

Political discourse was being democratized — as more people began to take part in political groups and discussions, as politicians sought to reach and sway more voters. Gentlemen-politicians might try to cling to their educated style of political writing, filling their essays and pamphlets with "inside" personal references, Latin quotations, and esoteric allusions to classical texts, but an aggressive, polemical style was taking over, as average citizens, continuing the American tradition of a lively working-class pamphlet and debate culture, insisted that they, too, were logocrats. Just as Thomas Paine had ignited the spirit of revolution in 1776 with his best-selling, simply written *Common Sense,* ordinary people would demonstrate, also with simple language and words, the depth of their involvement in self-government. It was impossible for a dozen Americans to sit together without quarreling about politics, a visitor from England remarked.

Republicans, and some Federalists too, were pushing journalism and political propaganda in new directions, spreading their party messages, praising or condemning the status quo, lambasting the ruling elite or the democratic rabble. Editorials, letters to the editor, eye-catching typography, bold headlines, articles reprinted from other papers, poems, eyewitness accounts, personal stories of political conversions, were all making newspapers more varied and appealing. A great many Americans read the Bible, one observer noted, but "all the people read a newspaper." By the 1780s, historian Jackson Turner Main noted, newspapers could be found in all parts of the country, and probably most people could read them if they wished.

In 1790, the country had about one hundred newspapers; by 1800, the number had more than doubled. When the federal government moved to Philadelphia in 1791, Benny Bache, the editor of the *Aurora,* had complained that, in addition to the sorry absence of duels, murders, accidents, and suicides, there were "no party disputes to raise the printer's drooping spirits." But by the year 1800, there was a surfeit of party disputes, and newspapers were transporting them to all corners of the country. Despite the sedition prosecutions — or perhaps also because of them — almost all of the nation's newspapers were aggressively partisan.

The Sedition Act had backfired. Two Republican newspapers — the *Time Piece* and the New York *Journal* — had collapsed (Freneau's *National Gazette* had died a premature death in 1793), but new Republican newspapers were springing up at the grass roots all over the country, from New Hampshire to North Carolina and beyond, openly trumpeting their party loyalty with names like *Herald of Liberty, Tree of Liberty, Genius of Liberty, Rights of Man,* and *Republican Atlas.* There were now two-thirds more Republican newspapers than before the Sedition Act, historian Jeffrey Pasley estimated. Their editors, who were usually also printers, functioned, as Pasley remarked, as their parties' "principal spokesman, supplier of ideology, and enforcer of party discipline" as well as chief strategist and manager. One editor, Meriwether Jones, founder of the *Richmond Examiner,* described his approach. Rather than boring the people with tired political *principles,* he wrote, it would be more effective "to bring our arguments home to their *feelings.* I am sorry to speak thus ill of the *sovereign people,* but they really have become very mercenary, and of consequence, opposed to war expenses. Let peace & economy then be our constant theme."

It was just as unlikely for a newspaper to be politically neutral, declared Alexander Martin, the editor of the Baltimore *American and Daily Advertiser,* as it was for a clergyman to preach "*Christianity* in the morning, and *Paganism* in the evening." Indeed, only political cowards, Martin held, strived for impartiality. There was too much at stake, "in the contest of liberty against slavery," he remarked, for an editor to attempt neutrality. Other editors, too, scornfully rejected the idea of an "equal attachment" to republicanism and aristocracy. "A despicable impartiality I disclaim," wrote editor Samuel Morse of Danbury, Connecticut. "I have a heart and I have a country." In a letter to Jefferson, Morse assured the vice president that he would do everything in his power "to promote your election." The most potent newspaper articles quickly spread across the country through an informal network of Republican newspapers, with the most partisan of them, the Philadelphia *Aurora,* serving as a kind of "reservoir" supplying the others with continuous political replenishment. Creative and innovative Republican newspaper editors had entered — and aroused — party warfare, declaring open season on "aristocracy," positioning themselves on the front lines.

And people were reading. In the 1790s, the sale of printed matter — books, pamphlets, handbills, periodicals, posters, broadsides — also multiplied. In New York City alone, there were twenty booksellers. A visitor from France, the Duke de La Rochefoucauld-Liancourt, remarked that even in the remotest corners of Massachusetts, "not a house is to be found, where a newspaper is not read." The literary talent of the nation was being consumed by newspapers, an English visitor commented, remarking on Americans' insatiable appetite for political news and commentary. In the cities on the eastern seaboard, people joined subscription libraries; lingered in reading rooms; patronized circulating libraries. The runaway best-seller in 1800 was Mason Weems's *Life and Memorable Actions of George Washington.* People were searching for the nation's history in Weems's biography — and shaping their future in newspapers.

Republicans were constructing a startling and novel message with a handful of simple words: *people, happiness, enjoyment, democracy, change.* The phrases were tailored to their presidential candidate, Thomas Jefferson. Gone was the reluctance to run that had slowed Jefferson down in 1796. Eager to oppose not only Adams but also financial speculators and the tribe of old "Tories," this time Jefferson was in the fight for real. His message was egalitarian, inclusive, forward-looking, designed to appeal to a broad audience of voters.

Who was Thomas Jefferson? Not a condescending "father" who expected deference and offered top-down leadership, but a friend who would work as an equal alongside others. The Friend of the *People!* Already in March 1797, when a Philadelphia artillery company welcomed Jefferson to Philadelphia as the new vice president, their flag bore the words "JEFFERSON THE FRIEND OF THE PEOPLE." In May 1800, at a meeting of the True Republican Society of Philadelphia, Jefferson was toasted as "the *friend and favorite of the people* — may the next election declare him the pilot of our political bark, that she may be conducted into the haven of peace and security." The *Richmond Argus* reported that Republicans had "embraced the rights of the people; not the arrogant pretensions, or usurpations of individuals."

And what did the "people" want from their friend? The New Jersey *Centinel of Freedom* promised voters that Mr. Jefferson would "lay open to you a field of *enjoyment,* which the concentrated efforts of a sordid aristocracy has been endeavoring to deprive you of." The Philadelphia *Aurora* evoked a new golden age of freedom, tolerance, and felicity: "Under the administration of so good and honest a man as Mr. Jefferson, men of every faith and clime will be *happy.* His whole life and all his writings prove that he is no bigot." In their Fourth of July toasts — which served as informal party platforms for local gatherings and which were often published — members of the Tammany Society of New York wished for the downfall of "the slaves of monarchy, and all who oppose the freedom and *happiness* of the human race." Jefferson would be elected, predicted the *Aurora,* and "preside over a free people, who require only his presidency to make them *happy."*

But people yearned for even more than happiness: they hungered, too, for equality. Feeding people's resentment of the social elite, Jefferson offered a vision of a classless society and an end to the politics of deference. The Virginian "perceives no grade in society, no partial distinctions," announced the *Vermont Gazette.* He "considers the people as the source of all power and the peculiar guardians of their own rights."

A longtime believer in the superiority of independent "yeomen" (they were the "children of God," he had written), Jefferson naturally attracted small farmers and planters in the North and South. He was a "friend and patron of agriculture," trumpeted the *Albany Register,* whereas his Federalist opponents comprised a "mushroom race of speculators." The Philadelphia *Aurora* urged voters to cast their ballots for Republican candidates, because "most of them are farmers, the occupation of all others that leads most to virtue." And in South Carolina, the Charleston *City Gazette* argued that Federalists were oppressing farmers with a direct land tax while they exempted the "monied interest" from the burdens of capitalism. Federalist foreign policy, noted the *Richmond Examiner,* by prohibiting commerce with France, had hurt southern tobacco planters. Federalists had snatched "money from the pocket of the Virginia planter" while enriching "the British merchant!"

Northern workers were also drawn to Jefferson. Artisans, mechanics, small merchants, captivated by a Virginia country squire and slave owner? Jefferson proved adept at creating a bond with ordinary people, more adept than his northern Federalist adversaries. Class and economic self-interest trumped geography. The real interests of the people, Republicans contended, were antithetical to those of their elitist leaders. Federalists wished only to "bask in the sunshine of monarchy and reap the appropriate fruits of aristocracy," jeered the Boston *Independent Chronicle.* The radical Republican William Manning sought to awaken "the Many" to the manipulations of "the Few." The elite "Few," Manning wrote in *The Key to Liberty,* tried to convince the "Many" of the goodness of their government and the wisdom of their policies. But if the Many understood their own interest better, Manning concluded, they "would never admit a Tory to be so much as a hog constable in town."

Republicans also appealed to immigrants. The Newark *Centinel of Freedom* printed a letter, written in Dutch, from a reader who, on behalf of the "Dutch inhabitants" of Bergen County, bestowed praise on Jefferson. Federalists were anti-Irish, charged the *Aurora;* and citizens, writing to the *Aurora* and the Charleston *City Gazette,* accused Federalists of being anti-Semitic.

Some Republicans stressed that Jefferson, the author of the Declaration of Independence, represented what was best in the American past. "If we want to return to the best days of Washington's presidency, let us elect Jefferson who was his principal minister in those days." But most often Jefferson was associated not with nostalgia for the past but with ardent hopes for the future. "My theory has always been," he would write in 1817, summing up his life's philosophy, "that if we are to dream, the flatteries of hope are as cheap, and pleasanter than the gloom of despair." This was the mentality that many Americans found irresistible. Jefferson seemed to possess the voice of a youthful, courageous, forward-looking spirit that was calling people away from a weary senescent order.

Republicans mocked Federalists, who darkly cautioned Americans not "to risque a change," who equated change with disorder, chaos, and immorality. Federalists had outlived their usefulness, declared the *Vermont Gazette,* portraying them as "stamped with all the babyhood imbecility of old age, tottering upon the brink of the grave." "A parallytic stroke now awaits them," predicted that newspaper. People were witnessing "the last struggles of a dying faction."

"Is it not high time for a CHANGE?" Republicans roared in their political pamphlets. "Take Your Choice!" blared the headline of the *Aurora* in October 1800, casting the two parties as polar opposites. Voters went on to read two parallel columns printed below, one entitled "Things As They Have Been" and the other "Things As They Will Be." What had Federalists produced during their time in office? "The Nation in arms without a foe, and divided without a cause." What kind of future would Republicans offer? "The Nation at peace with the world and united in itself." Blithely dismissing the very real threat of war that French aggression posed, Republicans promised "unity, peace and concord produced by republican measures and equal laws" and announced their ultimate goal: "Good government without the aid of priestcraft, or religious politics, and Justice administered without political intolerance."

The *Vermont Gazette* offered more specifics about what Republicans did *not* want in a prayer called "The Republican LITANY":

> From a burial place for American nobility
>   Good Lord deliver us.
> From a direct tax
>   Good Lord deliver us.
> From Jay's treaty . . . and from a war with the French Republic.
>   Good Lord deliver us.
> From all old Tories; from aristocrats
>   Good Lord deliver us.
> From heavy taxes, expensive salaries
>   Good Lord deliver us.
> From the alien act; from the sedition act, and from all other evil acts
>   Good Lord deliver us.

Some Republicans, like Thomas Cooper, attacked Federalist economic and trade policies in minute detail. In his 1798 pamphlet *Political Arithmetic,* Cooper protested that the interests of the whole nation — ordinary citizens and consumers — were being "sacrificed to serve a few bold mercantile speculators." The sudden wealth of commercial speculators, he pointed out, "introduces ostentation, luxury and pride, and manners out of harmony with republican principles." Moreover, the burden of taxes, he reminded his readers, did not fall on merchants and importers. Who pays taxes? he demanded. "The consumer, the farmer, the mechanic, the labourer, they and *they alone* pay." If the United States persisted in following Federalist economic policies, he warned, "sooner or later, war taxes, debts, and despotism are inevitable." Cooper advocated a large, progressive program of public works and public education: "Improve your roads, clear your rivers, cut your canals, erect your bridges, facilitate intercourses, establish schools and colleges, diffuse knowledge of all kinds."

Jefferson himself wrote virtually nothing for the press (though Mason Weems, looking for another best-seller after his *Life of Washington,* sold copies of Jefferson's *Notes on the State of Virginia*). He made no campaign speeches or appearances. Nor did he respond to Federalist attacks on him, "for while I would be engaged with one," he explained, "they would publish twenty new ones." But from behind the scenes he was pulling the strings, exerting control over his party, articulating a clear set of policies — frugal government, reduced national debt, smaller national defense, freedom of religion, press, and speech.

For political propaganda, he relied on the pens of his friends, frequently asking them to write letters to the editors or political pamphlets. "The engine is the press," Jefferson observed to Madison early in 1799. "Let me pray and beseech you to set apart a certain portion of every post day to write what may be proper for the public." The *Virginia Report* that Madison submitted to the Virginia House of Delegates in January 1800 served as a powerful election tool, sounding a "great and universal alarm" that Federalist policies, like the Alien and Sedition Acts, would "either destroy our free system of government, or prepare a convulsion that might prove equally fatal to it." Republican newspapers, too, feverishly poured out articles, "litanies," poems, and letters, often reprinted from other Republican papers. When a pamphlet caught Jefferson's eye, he made sure it received wide circulation, sending, for example, eight dozen copies of Cooper's *Political Arithmetic* to the chairman of the Virginia Republican state committee. He even thought that polemicist James Callender's interminable screed, *The Prospect Before Us*, would be helpful to the cause. In 1799 he passed political tracts along to Governor Monroe, urging him to try to persuade lukewarm Federalists to join Republican ranks. "It would be useless to give them to persons already sound," Jefferson wrote, adding a foxlike word of caution: "Do not let my name be connected with the business."

Federalists were asleep on the job, John Nicholas complained to Alexander Hamilton. Unlike the enterprising Republicans, they "seldom republish from each other," he noted. Whenever Republicans "get hold of anything however trivial in reality, they make it ring through all their papers from one end of the continent to the other." But Federalists seemed immobilized.

They were still playing by the old rules, though the nature of the game had changed. The Republicans' energetic, emotional outreach to voters did not galvanize Federalists to respond in kind. On the contrary, fretted Oliver Wolcott, "the papers on our side are filled with toasts and nonsensical paragraphs, attributing wisdom and firmness to the president, while at the same time all confidence is destroyed by the skillful attacks of a vindictive and intelligent opposition." But Wolcott himself was ambivalent about whether newspapers should even discuss public affairs; such public discussion, he sniffed, might be "improper."

Fisher Ames, too, criticized the passivity of his allies; they were "shaken by every prospect of labour or hazard," unable to match the "zeal and ardor" of the Jacobins. The Federalists' spirit, he wrote, "after flaming brightly, soon sleeps in its embers; but the jacobins, like salamanders, can breathe only in fire." His political friends, Ames allowed, possessed a sense of duty to defend their principles, but "sober duty" was a feeble antagonist against the passion of the Republicans, "dry leaves against the whirlwind."

Would Federalists — men who believed that they spoke for the common good and incarnated the dignity of the government — resort to language and tactics they had always disdained? Would they stoop to dirty their hands? Gentlemen of the old school, Federalist Samuel Goodrich explained, "did not mingle with the mass: they might be suspected of electioneering," which would have been "too degrading for them." Fisher Ames also counseled his friends to take the high road. Unlike the Jacobins, who were "formidable in lies and cunning," Ames wrote, "we cannot and will not resort to lies."

There had been too much delay. Federalists must "sound the tocsin about Jefferson," one Adams supporter urged. Tocsin, indeed. Even though Federalists wanted to take the high road, their words soon took on a desperate tone, for their fear and dread of Jefferson were real: they passionately believed that their property, economic security, and well-being were at stake. Alarmed Federalists in Delaware declared that Jefferson, with his "weakness of nerves, want of fortitude and total imbecility of character," would single-handedly destroy American moderation, prosperity, and morality.

Jefferson's very being was chaotic! "Born with a restless and ambitious soul," one letter writer to the *Gazette of the United States* noted in August 1800, Jefferson "delight[s] to roam in the storm of anarchy and confusion." Another writer discerned the outward signs of Jefferson's affinity for turmoil in Monticello, in its perpetual state of redesign and reconstruction. Mr. Jefferson had "never yet been able to agree to a fixed form or shape for anything," the author contended, informing readers that "one day the parlour is in front, the next day in the rear of the building" and that Jefferson had recently begun to tear down the second story of the building.

In Jefferson's architectural designs, Federalists discerned the symptoms of a dangerous philosophical frame of mind. He was a man who liked to "theorize about government," the *Connecticut Courant* charged. His love for experiment and his disdain for experience proved that he was, as one pamphleteer held, "a *philosophe* in the modern French sense of the word."

Jefferson's French connection was the smoking gun. The Virginian was "the man of the choice of France," wrote one pamphleteer, adding that "this is a strong reason why he should not be the choice of America." Republicans constituted a fifth column of Jacobins, determined to undermine if not destroy American institutions and society with violence imported directly from France, according to a pamphlet entitled *A Short Address to the Voters of Delaware.* "Let these men get into power, put the reins of government into their hands, and what security have you against the occurrence of the scenes which have rendered France a cemetery, and moistened her soil with the tears and blood of her inhabitants?"

Federalists also got mileage out of a letter that Jefferson had written to his Italian friend Philip Mazzei in 1796, in which he complained about Federalist leaders, scornfully calling them "timid men who prefer the calm of despotism to the boisterous sea of liberty." Mazzei leaked the letter to the press in Italy, after which it was picked up in Paris and then in the United States in May 1797. Here was a gold mine. Virginia Federalists blasted Jefferson for equating "the free, peaceful, and flourishing condition of the United States under the guidance of WASHINGTON" with the "calm of despotism." "Shall we then embark" with Jefferson, the author of one pamphlet asked, on "the tempestuous sea of liberty?"

On another subject, too, Jefferson walked on thin ice: slavery. Not that Federalists were proposing liberty and equality for all, but they did relish calling attention to Republican hypocrisy.

Citizens in Connecticut would not stoop "to learn the principles of liberty from the slave-holders of Virginia," editorialized the *Connecticut Courant.* A reader wrote back, agreeing that "We want no Southern lights in these parts. We have northern lights." When the state of Virginia "appears as the advocate of liberty and equality, and the enemy of aristocracy," Rhode Island Federalists wrote in a political pamphlet, "we may be excused if we doubt her sincerity." The *Newark Gazette* wondered what Mr. Jefferson had meant when he wrote that the only chosen people of God are the labourers in the earth. "Now as the *only labourers in the earth of Virginia* are the Black People," the *Gazette* noted, "we hope in the future the friends of Mr. Jefferson will be more explicit." While northern Federalists attacked Jefferson for hypocrisy on slavery, southern Federalists attacked him for undermining it, arguing that he held "opinions unfriendly to the property, which forms the efficient labor of a great part of the southern states."

But eclipsing ambiguous references to slavery and warnings about imminent tempests and French chaos was the Federalists' favorite theme: Jefferson's scorn for religion. Several times a month during the fall of 1800, the *Gazette of the United States* printed the same portentous announcement:

THE GRAND QUESTION STATED

At the present solemn and momentous epoch, the only question
to be asked by every American, laying his hand on his heart, is
"Shall I continue in allegiance to
GOD — AND A RELIGIOUS PRESIDENT;
or impiously declare for
Jefferson — and no god!!!"

Federalists delighted in branding Jefferson an atheist, a deist, and a generally diabolical, immoral creature. The Virginian seemed "never to have known the meaning of the term, *religion*," editorialized the *Connecticut Courant*. No one knew "whether Mr. Jefferson believes in the heathen mythology or, in the alcoran [Koran]; whether he is a Jew or a Christian; whether he believes in one God, or in many; or in none at all." "My eyes have been opened," wrote a former Republican to the *Gazette of the United States*, recounting his "political conversion" after having read about Jefferson's immorality and lack of religion. Now the reborn Federalist could not "get through half a paragraph [of the *Aurora*] without being almost choked."

Jefferson's deep commitment to religious tolerance did not help matters for Republicans. His remark in his *Notes on the State of Virginia* — that "it does me no injury for my neighbor to say there are twenty gods, or no god. It neither picks my pocket nor breaks my leg," a remark that subversively reduced divine revelation to a matter of opinion — was interpreted by two New York ministers, William Linn and John Mitchell Mason, as proof of his contempt for religion. In a political pamphlet, Linn recounted the story of Jefferson's once passing in front of a church in need of repair and, in response to his companion's remark that the building seemed neglected, saying, "It is good enough for him that was born in a manger." Such words, Linn asserted, could only have been spoken by a man who was "a deadly foe to His name and His cause." Jefferson had even disputed the Bible's timeline and had dared to suggest that young students study the history of Greece and Rome instead of the Bible! The Virginian's words, Mason railed, expressed "the morality of devils." "What is a man who makes not even a *profession* of Christianity?" demanded another pamphleteer. "What *is* he, what *can he be,* but a decided, a hardened infidel?"

Would this relentless stream of charges move sufficiently large numbers of voters to the Federalist camp? Perhaps not. Republicans condemned the Federalists' "theological inquisition," calmly asking, "Is it not sufficient that a man is a good citizen?" John Beckley, Jefferson's enterprising defender and pamphleteer, instructed all "fanatics, bigots, and religious hypocrites" to learn from Jefferson's long record of tolerance. In Pennsylvania, Republican committees portrayed Jefferson as fighting for "the equal Brotherhood of the Moravian, the Mennonist, and the Dunker." Jefferson "does not think that a catholic should be banished for believing in transubstantiation," wrote New Jersey Republicans, "or a jew, for believing in the God of Abraham, Isaac, and Jacob." The *National Intelligencer* editorialized that "religion ought to be kept distinct from politics." And the Newburgh, New York, newspaper, *Rights of Man,* held that only Republicans were true Christians, for only they were concerned with the welfare of all.

Even Federalists harbored doubts about the effectiveness of their strategy, acknowledging in private that Washington and Hamilton were no more pious than Jefferson. "Jeff is pretty fiercely attacked in different parts of the Continent on the ground of his religious principles," wrote a gloomy Robert Troup in the early fall of 1800. "It is not probable, however, that all that has been, or will be, written on this subject will deprive Jeff of a single vote." As for Adams, he was reported to have expressed "indignation" at the charge that Jefferson was irreligious: "What does that have to do with the public?" Adams supposedly said, insisting that Jefferson was a good patriot, citizen, and father. Indeed, Adams worried that his party's tactics were backfiring: Federalists had managed to "shuffle the cards into the hands of the jacobin leaders."

But Federalists were doing more than negative campaigning; they were also focusing their publicity on their own sage leadership, demonstrated ability, and long experience. For this, they would have to address voters' reason. "The democrats court the passions, prejudices, and feelings. The federalists address the *public understanding*," explained the *Gazette of the United States*, proud to be "devoted to higher and more salutary purposes than to . . . prophane babblings and the crudities of discontented democrats and unlettered men. We are perfectly weary of Chimney-sweeper politicians, and Scavenger Statesmen." Republicans indulged in deception, Federalists proclaimed, while they, the nation's best leaders, spoke only the truth.

As Federalists embarked on making the case for their own proven leadership, they could not refrain from portraying a stratified society in which they occupied the top ranks. In their eyes, American society was divided into three classes of citizens: there was, first, the Federalist elite; second, their enlightened followers; and third, the ignorant rabble, which included, according to the *Gazette of the United States,* "infidels — bankrupts . . . the lazy — the intemperate — the vicious and ignorant of this country." Republicans, too, belonged and appealed to the rabble and were on display in all their vulgarity, immorality, and ignorance at their political meetings. In August 1800, "An Observer," writing to the *Gazette of the United States,* reported on a meeting of the Philadelphia Democratic Society, commenting on the malapropisms, colloquialisms, confused parliamentary motions, and hiccups of the participants, who were "the very *refuse and filth* of society." He ridiculed their "ignorance and stupidity, as well as the self importance of these miserable wretches." The one Negro in attendance was identified as "Citizen Sambo." Another Republican event was attended by "fools" and "drunkards," the *New York Gazette* reported. "Treasonable sentiments were uttered, blasphemous toasts given, and smutty songs encored."

Federalists charged that Republicans, in their quest for popularity and votes, were pandering to the lowest element in society. In his "Ode to Popularity," one Federalist poet depicted Republicans as "Chemists" who, serving their idol "Popularity," transformed the dregs of society into "heroes."

> In truth and justice thou [Popularity] hast no delight
> Virtue thou dost not know by sight
> But as the Chemist by his skill
> From dross and dregs a spirit can distil
> Lo from the prisons or the stews,
> Bullies, blasphemers, cheats and Jews,
> Shall turn to heroes, if they served thy views.

The problem was that Federalists, while defending their record and praising the enlightenment of their followers, had boxed themselves into portraying a large fraction of politically active citizens as rabble and refuse, "dross and dregs," so many selfish, ignorant, uneducated fools and drunkards. By so doing, they were distancing and isolating themselves even more from the voting public, cementing an image in the public imagination of Federalists as arrogant, prejudiced, uninterested in the lives, needs, and aspirations of average Americans. "There is nothing said in defence of the government," confided the typically arrogant Oliver Wolcott to a friend, "which is understood by the people."

The vision of the future that Federalists offered voters was their own continuance in office. And yet, it was not an irrelevant vision. Federalists had provided the nation with outstanding leadership that had always seemed to address intelligently and prudently the long-term needs of the country. Men like Adams, Jay, Wolcott, and Marshall could effectively run on their records, stressing the stability and prosperity of the nation that Washington and his disciples had created.

Citizens could do no better, Federalists insisted, than to judge their leaders on the basis of their experience, performance, and character. Why should voters try to scrutinize and examine the intricacies of politics and policy for themselves? The issues dividing Federalists and Republicans were complex, one Federalist author in Rhode Island reasoned. "If time ever permitted, how few could find the leisure or the patience to pursue the voluminous enquiry," he observed. But fortunately there was "a shorter mode of deciding between the two classes of candidates," and that mode was simply "to choose the best men." But who were the "best men"? For the author of this "Candid Address" to

Rhode Island voters, the answer was clear. "They are men of property, and of landed property, who must stand or fall with their country." The *Connecticut Courant* took a similar tack, assuring Connecticut citizens that Federalist leaders are "men who are firm and honest, men who love the state, and its old manners and customs, men who think that peace, order, morals and religion, are necessary to make a flourishing and happy country." The *Washington Federalist* admiringly portrayed John Adams as "bred in the old school of politics, his principles . . . founded on the experience of ages." It was back to square one.

Federalists were making the ultimate conservative argument: leadership by wealthy, landed, virtuous, and experienced men who understood the critical importance of *conserving* the achievements and values of the past and maintaining the status quo. It was essential, they contended, to preserve the masterpiece of the founders, certainly not to alter or topple what they had so brilliantly fashioned. "This is the 12th year of our government," they reasoned, "and it has been in the *same hands*, and is it not as free and republican as it was the first year?"

Change and innovation had become the irrational, unreasonable, foolhardy option. "In times less critical and turbulent, we might indulge our love of novelty," Rhode Island Federalists contended, "by making experiments on the administration of our government." But such actions were not timely, they cautioned: "A false step at this time may never be retrieved."

Why, then, would any sane, rational person want to make fundamental changes in a system that worked so well? Who were these Republicans who refused allegiance and scorned submission to the fathers? What was their real grievance against American government? Would citizens be safer, happier, more prosperous, in Republican hands?

And so, in the spring, summer, and fall of 1800, the American press presented Americans with the inventions of the logocrats — happiness, enjoyment, aristocrats, deism, Jacobins, caution, order, experience. Voters would soon choose between two antithetical platforms — and languages.

8

Storms in the Atmosphere

I LIKE A LITTLE REBELLION NOW AND THEN," an insouciant Jefferson had written to John Adams in 1787, upon learning about Daniel Shays and his band of rebels in western Massachusetts. "It is like a storm in the Atmosphere," he added. But when slaves revolted in Virginia in the late summer of 1800, Jefferson expressed no enthusiasm for rebellions or storms.

During that summer of political turbulence, Virginia slaves could sense that the climate was one of ferment, contention, and latent violence. There were rumors that Federalists might refuse to hand over power to Republicans if Republicans won the election and that the conflict might lead to civil war. In May, the *Fredericksburg Herald* predicted an "ultimate appeal to arms by the two great parties." Meanwhile, Republicans had been spouting ideas about more equality and less deference to elites, about a fairer distribution of wealth. Did some slaves think that such talk applied to them?

In the last years of the eighteenth century, some Virginia slaves had already tasted freedom, more than they would be permitted in later decades. In the 1790s, many slave owners gave their human property leave from work on Saturday afternoons and all day on Sundays. On their days off, slaves could travel and visit relatives and friends on other plantations. Some slave owners, without enough work for their slaves to perform, let them work for others, some even permitting their slaves to contract themselves out. The owners would take a portion of the money earned by slaves, who then could keep the rest. Skilled artisans in Virginia were in such short supply, historian Douglas Egerton noted, that skilled slaves could choose among potential employers, going so far as to check out their credentials and their treatment of employees.

Working side by side with whites, these slaves had a taste of freedom — and money in their pockets. And they had the opportunity to see free blacks, people of their own color, living out of bondage. By the end of the century, such emancipated people made up nearly 10 percent of Virginia's black population, provoking Governor Monroe to write that the "publick danger proceeding from [free black] persons is daily encreasing." Although Federalists retained political control in Richmond, so torn by political combat was that city and so relaxed in its attitudes toward slavery that one Philadelphia newspaper referred to "Sans-culotte *Richmond,* the metropolis of *Negro-land.*"

One slave who lived in what Egerton termed this "twilight world between slavery and freedom" was named Gabriel; his owners, Thomas Prosser and his son Thomas Henry Prosser, ran a plantation six miles north of Richmond. Gabriel was an unusual slave: over six feet tall, twenty-four years old, able to read, trained as a smith, and permitted by his owner to hire himself out. But Gabriel was also a slave with a temper who had been in trouble with the law. In 1799 he tried to steal a pig, got into a scuffle with the pig's white owner, and bit his ear off. He was jailed, branded on his hand, and released for the crime of attacking a white man — then jailed a second time for the same crime. After that experience he started thinking about liberty and how to seize it.

He and another slave named Jack Ditcher hatched an idea for a slave revolt, recruiting other slaves and some free men to join them. According to their plan, the men, who would be armed with knives, swords fashioned from scythes, and a few guns, would gather at the plantation blacksmith shop, kill the plantation owner, and move on to Richmond, where they would be joined by more men, perhaps as many as a thousand. There they would set fires, occupy the treasury building, take Governor Monroe hostage, and use Monroe and other hostages to bargain for their freedom. Easy enough.

Throughout the spring and sultry summer of 1800, Gabriel recruited men for his conspiracy, keeping lists of the recruits' names. Two white men also joined the group. One was French. Charles Quersey, who had arrived in America with Rochambeau and the French navy to fight in the American Revolution, decided, after Yorktown, to remain in the United States. The other, Alexander Beddenhurst, was also European and a veteran of the War of Independence. Because Gabriel seemed to conceive the revolt along class lines as well as along racial lines — the enemy being the wealthy merchant class and not just whites in general — he was confident that poor white workers would join the revolt.

That spring rumors about a slave revolt reached Governor Monroe. In a letter to Jefferson he mentioned hearing about "a negro insurrection," but decided to take no action. In mid-August the mayor of Richmond informed Monroe of still more rumors of a revolt, but again the governor felt that no action was warranted.

What inspired the revolt? Perhaps it was the slave rebellion that had taken place in 1793, on the Caribbean island of Saint Domingue. There, slaves led by Toussaint Louverture turned against their French colonial masters and took over the colony. The following year, in 1794, the French revolutionary government abolished slavery and, in 1797, named Louverture general-in-chief and commander of the island. The new Dominguan constitution had even been reprinted in Republican newspapers in Virginia.

Perhaps Gabriel had come in contact with slaves who had left Saint Domingue with their fleeing owners. Monroe was indeed wary of their presence in Virginia and wrote that "it is our duty to be on our guard to prevent any mischief" resulting from the presence in Virginia of slaves from Saint Domingue. Jefferson, too, was alarmed that the "leven" from the French colony might cause "combustion" if it were "introduced among us." Congressman Robert Goodloe Harper warned that Toussaint was preparing to invade the southern states from Saint Domingue "with an army of blacks." And other Federalists claimed that "Jefferson would call upon France . . . [to] invade the country."

Perhaps the revolt was inspired by antislavery writings. Jefferson had written about the gradual emancipation of slaves, proposing that all children born of slave parents after 1800 be educated, emancipated at twenty-one, and deported to some foreign colony; in 1796, St. George Tucker had also composed a detailed plan for the abolition of slavery, imagining emancipated blacks becoming a landless agricultural working class, permitted to stay in the United States. Years earlier, Jefferson's tutor, George Wythe, who served on the Virginia Court of Chancery, had argued that it was the slave owner's responsibility to prove that he could own another human being, and not the duty of the slave to prove himself free.

Attitudes toward slavery seemed to be changing. An antislavery activist received an honorary degree from William and Mary College in

1785. A few years later an antislavery society in Manchester, Virginia, decried the "outrageous violation of one of the most essential rights of human nature." And abolition societies were initiating "freedom suits" and succeeding in liberating small numbers of slaves. By 1796, historian Egerton remarked, thirty such suits were pending in Virginia courts. "Cracks in the system were everywhere," Egerton concluded.

Through those cracks Gabriel must have seen a glimmer of light.

The night of the revolt, August 30, finally arrived. That same evening a drenching rainstorm hit the Richmond area. What would the slaves do? Try to reach Richmond? Turn back? The storm had made the bridge to Richmond impassable, and Gabriel feared that the conspirators would not be able to join him. Confusion. Uncertainty. A decision was made to postpone the uprising to the following night. But in the meantime, a few slaves talked.

They revealed the plot to their master, Mosby Sheppard. Others talked too. Sheppard immediately informed Governor Monroe that slaves in his county were going to kill their masters, move to Richmond, set fire to the city, and seize arms. The news reached Gabriel that "the insurrection had blown" and that patrols were on their way. The next day, six slaves were captured and jailed; Gabriel and his friend Jack Ditcher were denounced, a reward of $300 placed on their heads. They and others fled.

Now Monroe took swift action, calling out the militia and stationing some guards at the arsenal and magazines. Within hours, Richmond resembled a city under siege. The rebels, who came from several different Virginia counties as well as from Richmond, were hunted down. "This alarm has kept me much occupied," Monroe wrote to Madison on September 9. On that same day, he called up two more militia units to be stationed in and around the city.

In mid-September, trials began: the jailed men were tried and condemned to hang. Some implicated others, who were then caught. Others refused to cooperate: "I beg, as a favour," one man asked, "that I may be immediately led to execution. I know that you have pre-determined to shed my blood, why then all this mockery of a trial?"

"The plot has been entirely exploded," the *Virginia Gazette* assured its nervous readers, adding that the whole scheme was "shallow" and that, even had it been carried out, it would have required "but little resistance" to quash. "Thirty or forty of the party have been arrested and confined in jail for trial," reported the *Fredericksburg Herald*. Throughout September more arrests, more trials, more hangings, more graves.

"It is unquestionably the most serious and formidable conspiracy we have ever known of the kind," Monroe wrote to Jefferson. Ten men had been condemned and executed, "and there are at least twenty, perhaps 40 more to be tried, of whose guilt no doubt is entertained." How many more men would be put to death? Monroe was not sure "whether mercy or severity is the better policy in this case," but he believed that "when there is cause for doubt it is best to incline to the former." Still, what was Jefferson's opinion?

Monroe's question troubled Jefferson. Here was a complex being: an admirer of revolution; a theorist of radical change; a man who believed in freedom and equality; a slave owner who insisted on order, discipline, and obedience; a candidate in the middle of a campaign for the nation's highest office. Was he also a compassionate being? A humanitarian? "Where to stay the hand of the executioner," he wrote Monroe, "is an important question. There is a strong sentiment that there has been hanging enough. The other states and the world at large will forever condemn us if we indulge a principle of revenge." But either unwilling to make an unambiguous recommendation or aware of the possible political consequences of doing so, he added, "I hazard these thoughts for your own consideration only, as I should be unwilling to be quoted in the case." Monroe decided to urge the council to be merciful and pardon the men awaiting trial.

On September 23, Gabriel was captured in Norfolk and transferred to Richmond. There he refused to speak. Realizing that Gabriel had "made up his mind to die," Monroe permitted the law to take its course: Gabriel was convicted and sentenced to death. The judge agreed to Gabriel's request that the execution be delayed for three days so that he could die with two of his co-conspirators, his "brothers." Perhaps the judge hoped that Gabriel would reveal more information about the conspiracy. Two days later, Jack Ditcher, Gabriel's second man, turned himself in. Twenty-seven men in all would be hanged.

For the Republican governor of Virginia, it was crucial, during that election season, to suppress information about the participation, in the conspiracy, of white men, and especially of a white Frenchman. "If white men were engaged in it," Monroe reassured the lieutenant-governor of South Carolina, "it is a fact of which we have no proof." Republicans were not about to give political ammunition to Federalists, who were already screaming that Jefferson would soon call upon his French allies to invade the United States. When the names of Quersey and Beddenhurst finally came to light, the revelation did little damage. The editor of the *Aurora* dismissed the story of a Frenchman allied with Gabriel as a "good joke."

But Republicans in Virginia still had to deflect Federalist accusations of hypocrisy: the men who spoke of opening the gates of American democracy to some people were slamming them shut to others. On October 1, 1800, the *Gazette of the United States* minced no words. It was the Republicans themselves, along with "their eagerness and anxiety to propagate the doctrines of liberty and equality which their practice and principles so flagrantly belied," who had incited the slaves to revolt. Republicans had "whett[ed] the knife that would surely and infallibly sooner or later, cut their own *throats*."

"We are truly to be pitied," confessed a dejected Jefferson in late September, conflicted about the death sentences meted out to the slave rebels. The Virginian who, in that same letter, swore "eternal hostility against every form of tyranny over the mind of man" could not bring himself to swear hostility to tyranny over black people's bodies and souls.

"The gallows are in full operation," wrote Robert Troup to Rufus King in early October. "In Virginia they are beginning to feel the happy effects of liberty and equality," he added, pleased that the hypocrisy of the Republican devotees of freedom and equality was at last exposed to glaring light. Republicans like Jefferson and Monroe had made wrenching compromises with their consciences. And yet, Federalists had little time to gloat. Their party was in deep disarray.

Troup was not optimistic about Federalist prospects in the upcoming presidential election. "My good friend," he bemoaned in that same letter to King, "I cannot describe to you how broken and scattered your federal friends are! At present we have no rallying point; and no mortal can divine where or when we shall again collect our strength!" John Jay agreed: Federalists were fatally disunited. "Unfortunately, there is too little unanimity in many points," he wrote, "and the want of it exposes us to the hazard of many evils."

Republicans, who had closed ranks around Jefferson and Burr, could only smile at the stories of internal disputes among Federalists. The more divisions, the more poison injected and spread among them, the better. Tucked away in his exquisite mountaintop retreat, seeing his opponents divided into two camps, the "pure Monocrats" and the "Anglo-monocrats," Jefferson urged Republicans to do "nothing which may hoop them together."

Far from hooping together, Federalists were busy declaring war against one another. President Adams seemed to have turned against his fellow Federalists; Federalists had taken to attacking the ineptitude, unreliability, and impulsiveness of their president; Alexander Hamilton was busily plotting a way to elect to the presidency Charles Cotesworth Pinckney, the Federalist vice-presidential candidate. George Cabot also wanted to see Pinckney elected president but suspected that Jefferson and Adams had made a secret deal to elevate Jefferson to the presidency and demote Adams to the vice-presidency. So much faction and intrigue were bubbling up among Federalists that Fisher Ames reported to King that there had never been "a more singular and mysterious state of parties. The plot of an old Spanish play is not more complicated with underplot. I scarcely trust myself with the attempt to unfold it."

That June, President Adams had been slowly traveling home to spend the summer in Massachusetts, stopping in different states along the way to address the people. In Virginia and in Maryland, enthusiastic crowds welcomed him, and the *Gazette of the United States* described "the very affectionate reception and respectable addresses which have everywhere met our venerable and vigilant President." But in Newark, New Jersey, Federalists had arranged no receptions for him. People saw the president walking inconspicuously in the streets like a private citizen. It was even reported that he stopped to "to drink punch with Democrats, and to talk of things ordinary and local."

Back home in Quincy, Adams complained that Massachusetts Federalist leaders did not call on him. Something was cooking. In July, the president startled his old friends and supporters. In Boston's Faneuil Hall, Adams toasted two radical patriots, John Hancock and Samuel Adams. Adams praising his political adversaries? What was he up to?

"His language is bitter even to outrage and swearing and calling names," Fisher Ames reported. Strangely, the target of Adams's boiling temper was not the "Jacobins" but rather the ultra-conservative members of his own party. "He inveighs against the British faction and the Essex Junto like one possessed," Ames wrote. And just as telling, he was acting "as if he did not hate nor dread Jefferson."

What was Adams's game? Ames wondered. Was he trying to curry favor with Republicans? Perhaps. To distance himself from Federalist conservatives, to court moderates? Perhaps. And perhaps when Republicans realized that Adams and the conservative Federalist clique had turned against each other, Ames mused, Republicans might embrace Adams as their own! And perhaps, Ames continued, it would be to the advantage of Republicans to support Adams, for that support would ensure the "division & discomfiture" of their Federalist adversaries. And maybe this new realignment would please Jefferson, who might prefer once again to be vice president "without any responsibility." His head full of plots and counterplots, Ames concluded that "no affair can be more involved, in doubt or more dependent on intrigue, caprice or accident" than the present political situation.

Who had launched the first attack missiles in the war between Adams and his own party? Federalists when they pushed for war with France and termed Adams's pursuit of peace with France "disgusting"? Or Adams when, just after Federalists caucused in the spring of 1800 and nominated Adams and Pinckney as their presidential and vice-presidential candidates, he decided to fire both James McHenry, his secretary of war, and Timothy Pickering, his secretary of state, convinced that both men were more loyal to Hamilton than to himself?

Federalists now furiously turned against Mr. Adams. McHenry railed that Adams was "actually insane." Ames branded him a "creature of impulse or freakish humor." According to Representative James Bayard of Delaware, Adams was "liable to gusts of passion little short of frenzy, which drive him beyond the control of any rational reflection." And Robert Troup saw the president as governed by "fits and starts."

For Federalists, who were in no mood for peace with France or friendly relations with Jefferson and his Republicans, Adams served well as an all-purpose scapegoat. He even resembled Jefferson, they grumbled. Like the Virginian, the president too possessed "a strong revolutionary taint of mind," Ames remarked. The discharged Pickering claimed that Adams's decision to dismiss him had been made "in concert" with Jefferson and that the two had become allies. Governor Jay of New York was virtually alone among Federalists in approving

Adams's peace mission to France and in praising his "attachment to the dictates of honour and good faith."

For Alexander Hamilton, it was a busy spring and summer. Though practicing law in New York, defending a man in a notorious murder case, and traveling through New England on a military inspection trip before being demobilized in June, he remained engaged in national politics. Indeed, his Federalist friends made sure that he received detailed reports of Adams's intemperate comments about him. Hamilton heard how Adams had lashed out at him, attacking him as the leader of the "pro-British faction" and, going even further, branding him "a bastard and as much an alien as Gallatin." As if he were itching for a duel, Hamilton fired off a brusque letter to Adams, demanding — in the language typically used before a challenge to a duel — that Adams avow or disavow the words that had been attributed to him. Adams never responded. (Years later he would intriguingly assert that "General Hamilton never wrote or spoke at the bar, or elsewhere in public, without a bit of opium in his mouth.") For his part, President Adams was disgusted with the whole scene. The insolence of the Federalists and the "unreasonable conduct of the jacobins," he wrote, "make me too indifferent to whatever can happen." But Hamilton was not so indifferent.

Adams and Hamilton had a history — and recently it had been filled with bad blood. Especially after the death of Hamilton's cherished "Aegis," George Washington, Hamilton lashed out at the man who for him incarnated the anti-Washington, John Adams. Only three weeks after Washington's death, Hamilton sneered at Adams's "perverseness and capriciousness," and at his policies, which were "the effect of momentary impulse." Could Hamilton explain why Adams was behaving so irrationally and arbitrarily? He suggested that the cause lay in Washington's absence. "The irreparable loss of an inestimable man," he wrote to King, "removes a control which was felt, and was very salutary." Washington could no longer guide and calm Adams, but, more important, he could not guide and calm Hamilton. The two Federalists hated each other so much that both admitted preferring the democrat Jefferson to the other.

It was open war between them. The party be damned.

"My mind is made up," Hamilton calmly informed Theodore Sedgwick that spring. "I will never more be responsible for [Adams] by my direct support, even though the consequences should be the election of

Jefferson. If we must have an enemy at the head of the government, let it be one whom we can oppose, and for whom we are not responsible." If the party supported Adams, thereby sacrificing its principles and its cause to "a weak and perverse man," Hamilton concluded, "I withdraw from the party."

All summer Hamilton seethed at the thought of a second term for Adams. By August he described himself to Wolcott as being "in a very *belligerent* humour," determined to express his hostility directly and forthrightly to Adams, in a manner "suited to the *plain dealing* of my character."

Then he dropped his bombshell.

"I have serious thoughts," Hamilton wrote to Wolcott, "of giving to the *public* my opinions respecting Mr. Adams." His plan was to reveal those opinions in a signed letter to a friend, a letter that would be leaked to Federalist leaders. Hamilton claimed that this was the "most *authentic* way of conveying the information."

Plain dealing? Authentic? Belligerent? What was Hamilton really saying? That he alone had the courage to speak the truth and uphold Federalist principles, come what may? That he would not shrink from confrontation, whatever the price? Perhaps he was desperate, sensing that he was no longer the principal leader among Federalists. Or had his political instincts simply failed him? Arrogant, impetuous, and self-destructive, he had made up his mind to fracture the Federalist party by publicly denouncing its leader in the middle of a presidential campaign against a unified and hungry opposition party.

Now Hamilton's Adams-bashing, vitriol-spewing Federalist allies wanted to rein him in. Although they nodded in agreement with his antipathy for Adams, in an about-face, they switched to arguing in favor of prudence, urging Hamilton to put party first. "We must vote for [Adams], I suppose," wrote James Bayard to Hamilton, "and therefore cannot safely say to every one what we think of him." Such a public letter would only increase the divisions among Federalists, Oliver Wolcott pointed out, concluding that "the publication ought to be suppressed." George Cabot cautioned Hamilton that a letter attacking Adams would only backfire, injuring Hamilton more than Adams. "It will be converted to a new proof that you are a *dangerous man*."

Fisher Ames took a different, more tortuous approach. While believing that Adams's reelection would be "very inauspicious" for the nation, he held that Federalists could announce that while they opposed

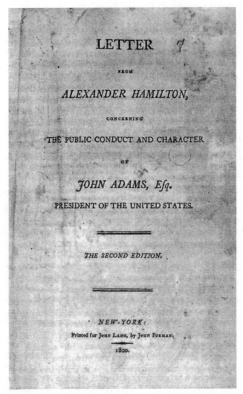

LETTER

FROM

ALEXANDER HAMILTON,

CONCERNING

THE PUBLIC CONDUCT AND CHARACTER

OF

JOHN ADAMS, Efq.

PRESIDENT OF THE UNITED STATES.

THE SECOND EDITION.

NEW-YORK:

Printed for JOHN LANG, by JOHN FURMAN,

1800.

Hamilton's 53-page pamphlet, "Letter from Alexander
Hamilton Concerning the Public Conduct and
Character of John Adams," 1800.

Adams they nevertheless would stand united behind him. "Where is
the inconsistency of saying," Ames wrote with an excess of subtlety,
"President Adams has not our approbation of some of his measures,
nor do we desire his re-election, but many federalists do, and the only
chance to prevent the triumph of the Jacobins, is to unite and vote . . .
for the two candidates. . . . Where is the absurdity or inconsistency of
this language?"

But, his mind made up, Hamilton plunged ahead, belligerency tri-
umphing over reason. His 53-page opus, "Letter from Alexander Hamilton Concerning the Public Conduct and Character of John Adams,"
came out in October 1800. The pamphlet, Hamilton insisted, was written for the eyes only of Federalist leaders, not for the general public.
Could this proven master of Realpolitik have been so naïve as to think

that a letter written and circulated by him would not become public property? Or had he made a calculated decision, betting that his act of guerrilla warfare would swing electoral votes to Charles Cotesworth Pinckney and away from Adams, thereby giving Pinckney the top spot? Four years earlier, during the election of 1796, he had similarly hoped to swing votes away from Adams to Thomas Pinckney, the cousin of C. C. Pinckney. Same strategy, same antipathy for Adams, only the first names of the South Carolina cousins were different.

In the fall of 1800, Hamilton's "Letter" fell into the hands of Aaron Burr, who leaked it to the press. The *Aurora* and the *New London Bee* immediately published extracts. At that point Hamilton reportedly authorized publication of the whole pamphlet. On page after page, Hamilton had catalogued Adams's vices, from "disgusting egotism" to "vanity without bounds," predicting that the government "might totter, if not fall, under . . . [Adams's] future auspices." Bizarrely he concluded his screed with a call to Federalists not to oppose Adams's election: "To refrain from a decided opposition to Mr. Adams' re-election has been reluctantly sanctioned by my judgment; which has been not a little perplexed between the unqualified conviction of his unfitness for the station contemplated, and a sense of the great importance of cultivating harmony among the supporters of the government."

Republicans could barely contain their glee. What more irresistible spectacle than Federalists destroying one another? Not even Republicans had lashed out at the president with such venom. Indeed, wasn't Hamilton's ruthless, malicious dissection of Adams an act of sedition? One man thought so.

Thomas Cooper had recently been released from prison for criticizing President Adams. Now he audaciously proposed that Hamilton too be prosecuted under the Sedition Act. His aim, he explained, was to try an "experiment" — an experiment through which Americans would discover "whether *Republicanism* is to be the victim of a law, which *Aristocracy* can break through with impunity." The *Aurora* congratulated Cooper on his move. It was high time, the *Aurora* insisted, for the Federalist party to swallow to the very dregs the cup they had administered to others. No Federalist prosecutor or judge responded to Cooper's demands. The result of his experiment was plain for all to see. Only Republicans would be prosecuted and thrown in jail for attacking the president. "The experiment I wished to make," Cooper later wrote, "was worth making."

Strangely, neither Federalists like Ames, Wolcott, and Cabot, with their tangled scenarios of the unpredictable Adams bonding with conspiratorial Republicans, nor Adams with his brash, ill-considered attacks on members of his own party, nor Hamilton with his insolent public letter denouncing his party's presidential candidate, had clear political vision. Indeed, Hamilton, the most brilliant of economic policymakers, political operator par excellence, utterly failed when confronted with the paramount goal of a politician: winning elections. Preoccupied with their fears, fantasies, and hatreds, their resentments and frustrations, none of these men was lucid or realistic enough to perceive that the task at hand was to overcome their elitist views, develop a rapport with their followers, and solidify a base in the electorate loyal to Federalists. Had they been pragmatic politicians, they would have sought to rise above personal rancor and vendettas and build a strong, unified party with a clear message. On the contrary, some Federalists held the outlandish belief that their very disunity was somehow emblematic of the moral high ground, for they disparaged Republicans, who acted, in the words of Federalist Theophilus Parsons, "with a union to be expected only from men in whom no moral principles exist."

Despite such a claim to the high ground, Federalists predictably turned against Hamilton. "I am *bound* to tell you," George Cabot scolded, "that you are accused by respectable men of egotism; and some very worthy and sensible men say you have exhibited the same vanity in your book which you charge as a dangerous quality and great weakness in Mr. Adams." Federalist Noah Webster went further. In his own public "Letter to General Hamilton," he accused the New Yorker of dividing Federalists and ensuring Jefferson's victory. Robert Troup reported to Rufus King that every member of their circle of friends condemned Hamilton's letter.

From a safe distance, a cool James Madison surveyed the ravages of the Federalists' internecine warfare. Hamilton had deeply wounded himself, but he had also performed a service, contributing "not a little to overthrow [Adams] staggering as he before was in the public esteem."

In the middle of an election in which the stakes could not have been higher for the infant republic, Federalists had staged a remarkable play for Americans to watch. It had all the elements of classical theater: heroic personages with gigantic egos, colliding, clashing, and betraying one another; ambition, jealousy, and vanity spinning out of control; passions overriding reason; anger and frustration skirting the edge of violence; and in the background, from the heavens, the specter of the wise father, George Washington, gazing down sadly on his reckless children as they battle with one another. And the audience? The spectators, like those of classical theater, feel terror and pity, as they behold the Federalists' singular performance of their own fall and destruction.

What could be more illogical — and ironic — than Federalists busily attacking their leader's "freakish humor" while simultaneously throwing Republicans like Thomas Cooper in jail for doing the same — or less? And yet, during the critical campaign months of the spring and summer of 1800, the number of prosecutions under the Sedition Act climbed and reached its apogee.

Inasmuch as the favorite pastime of the High Federalists was defamation of John Adams, their motive in prosecuting Republican editors and publishers could hardly have been a need to protect him from criticism and slander. How then did they justify prosecutions for sedition? Madison had astutely pointed out that "fetters imposed on liberty at home" usually result from real or imagined dangers from abroad. True enough. But in this case alarm about a possible war with France had subsided; foreign relations seemed calm; and thus the original rationale for the Alien and Sedition Acts could not be summoned. Still, during a volatile election season, what better way to defeat Republicans at the polls than to hammer away at them with impunity in Federalist newspapers while arresting and jailing them for publishing their own political opinions?

For his part, Thomas Jefferson viewed the sedition prosecutions as part of the Federalists' panicked reaction to their imminent downfall. "Our opponents perceive the decay of their power," he remarked to his daughter in the spring of 1800, adding that they were "trying to pass laws to keep themselves in power." Indeed, Thomas Cooper of Northumberland County, Pennsylvania, he added, had just been found guilty of violating the Sedition Act — the same Thomas Cooper who, a few months later, would seek to turn the table on Alexander Hamilton. Since June 1798, Cooper had been criticizing the administration in his book *Political Arithmetic* and in articles written while he was editor of the *Sunbury and Northumberland Gazette* for several months in 1799.

But only in April 1800, in the middle of all the state election campaigns, was he indicted and tried for a handbill scornful of Adams.

One of Cooper's most dogged pursuers was none other than Secretary of State Timothy Pickering — the same Pickering who, just days after Cooper's sentencing, would personally blast President Adams for having no "moral sense" and for being "capable of base, dishonorable, and dishonest conduct in the administration of public affairs." But Adams, too, had favored the prosecution of Cooper. "A meaner, a more artful, or a more malicious libel has not appeared," the president wrote to his secretary of state. "I have no doubt it is a libel against the whole government, and as such ought to be prosecuted."

At the trial, prosecutor William Rawle argued that Cooper's criticism of the president was "in error" and that errors led to "insurrection." Apparently Federalists were now equating opposition with insurrection. In his defense, Cooper stood up for freedom of speech and attacked the idea that the president was "infallible." Had it become a crime, he asked, to say that the president might be mistaken? He defended his handbill, point by point, and then noted that the judges at the trial and the marshal who selected the jury were political appointees of the very same president whose conduct he had criticized.

Replying to Cooper, Rawle got straight to the point: public policy was too complicated for ordinary citizens, and Cooper had no right to "raise surmises and suspicions" about the president's judgment. Going even further, he declared that Cooper's attempt to defend himself amounted to more seditious behavior. Associate Supreme Court Justice Samuel Chase, in his charge to the jury, did not hide his opinion that Cooper was guilty. Before sentencing, he candidly admitted the political nature of the trial, underscoring that there were two parties in the country and that Cooper had taken the side of the party against the government. He then sentenced Cooper to six months in prison and a $400 fine — but if the Republican party tried to pay his fine, he added, he would increase the fine to $2,000.

The Sedition Act constituted the "palpable and alarming infraction of the constitution," James Madison wrote in January 1800, at the beginning of that election year. Madison had just returned to the Virginia state legislature after his years of retirement in Montpelier. Almost fifty years old, dressed in silk stockings and black breeches, wearing "powder," he gave an impression of "sternness," commented an acquaintance. Madison had reason to be grave.

In January 1800, on behalf of the Virginia state assembly, he had composed a long, scathing protest against the Alien and Sedition Acts. The Sedition Act especially, Madison insisted, subverted the democratic system, for it was designed to coerce public opinion and undermine the ability of voters to make informed choices. It was a law "leveled against that right of freely examining public characters and measures, and of free communication among the people thereon." If the American press, during the War of Independence, had been forbidden from bringing "the constituted agents into contempt or disrepute," he observed, the United States would still be "groaning under a foreign yoke," so many "miserable colonies." "To the press alone," Madison declared, do "the United States owe much of the lights which conducted them to the rank of a free and independent nation."

That same month, James Callender published a book entitled *The Prospect Before Us*, assailing President Adams for being a "man who has deserted and reversed all his principles" and asserting that Adams intended to marry his son to the daughter of George III and create his own dynasty. Voters had a choice, he contended, "between Adams, war and beggary, and Jefferson, peace and competency." The slim book went on sale in Philadelphia bookstores, and Callender even sent a personal copy to President Adams himself. A horrified Abigail Adams gasped at its "abuse and scandal." If Jefferson and the Republicans won, she exclaimed, it would mean "the sacrifice of all that Good men hold dear and sacred."

Callender, who had come to the United States in 1793 from Scotland, was a notorious political journalist and pamphleteer, wielding a pen from which spilled as much venom as ink: in one pamphlet he charged Alexander Hamilton with adultery (indeed, Hamilton had publicly confessed to an affair with Maria Reynolds and had exposed her husband's attempt to blackmail him) but also unfairly accused him of corrupt financial dealings.

At first, Callender lived in Philadelphia, where he assisted Benjamin Franklin Bache and William Duane in editing the *Aurora*. But after Bache was arrested for sedition, Callender fled to Virginia, where the judicial system seemed more favorable to Republicans. In Richmond he wrote for the *Examiner*, his articles reprinted in the nation's leading Republican newspapers. Callender delighted in jeering at Adams; the president was not only a "repulsive pedant," but he was also a "hideous hermaphroditical character which has neither the force and firmness of a man, nor the gentleness and sensibility of a woman."

Claiming that the mission of the *Examiner* was to "oppose and vilify" the federal government and to "dissolve" the union, Pickering demanded that the federal district attorney scrutinize the newspaper for seditious material. Callender was indicted in late May 1800 and quickly arrested.

Virginians rallied to Callender's side; after all, twice the state legislature of Virginia had protested against the Sedition Act. "I think it essentially just and necessary that Callender should be substantially defended," Jefferson wrote to James Monroe. Monroe and Jefferson vowed to raise money for Callender's defense. Three defense lawyers also contributed their services: Philip Norborne Nicholas, the attorney general of Virginia, William Wirt, the clerk of the House of Delegates, and George Hay, Governor Monroe's son-in-law.

The trial began in June 1800, the first sedition trial to take place in Virginia. On the opening day, the *Virginia Gazette* reported that the courtroom "was thronged with spectators from every quarter."

As in all the other sedition trials, one of the fundamental principles of justice was turned upside down: the government did not have to prove that the allegedly seditious statements made by the defendant were false and injurious; instead the accused had to disprove the charges against him. One witness for Callender, John Taylor of Caroline, intended to justify Callender's charge that Adams was "a professed aristocrat" by relating statements that Adams had personally made to him, but Justice Chase ruled the evidence inadmissible. "It would deceive and mislead the jury," he decided. Defense counsel George Hay protested so effectively that the judge requested that the prosecutor admit the evidence, but the prosecutor refused to budge. Finally, when the judge refused to let defense lawyers argue against the constitutionality of the Sedition Act, Hay and the other lawyers closed their notebooks and withdrew from the case. Now Callender had no defense counsel.

After deliberating for two hours, the jury found Callender guilty. Before pronouncing the sentence, Justice Chase announced that no rational man could believe President Adams capable of "atrocious crimes" and went on to suggest that Callender had committed a crime against the people themselves, for the implication of his pamphlet, the judge reasoned, was that only "depraved and wicked" citizens would have voted for President Adams. The sentence was nine months in jail and a fine.

But the prosecution and trial would soon backfire. A pamphlet containing a transcript of the court proceedings was published, and Callender's writings circulated even more widely. From prison, Callender kept up his attacks on Federalists, now denouncing Justice Chase in addition to President Adams. "The insolence and abuse of liberty," he wrote from prison, "are preferable to the grovelling decorum, and the funereal silence of despotism." While in jail he published a second volume of *The Prospect Before Us*, another scorching attack on Adams, who was "super-eminently entitled not only to the laughter, but likewise to the curses of mankind." Callender would be the last person sentenced under the Sedition Act to be freed from jail.

Charles Holt, the editor of the *New London Bee*, also became a target of the Federalists' prosecution. "Are our young officers and soldiers to learn virtue from General Hamilton?" wrote Holt. "Or like their generals are they to be found in the bed of adultery?" More opposed to the idea of a standing army than to Hamilton's adultery, Holt urged Connecticut citizens to rethink sending their sons off to join an army. Holt was indicted for sedition in September 1799; his trial took place in April 1800. In its prosecution the government argued that Holt had brought the government into "contempt and disrepute" and that, moreover, the United States did not in fact have a standing army but only a "provisional" one. The defense argued that the sedition law was unconstitutional.

On April 12, 1800, a jury pronounced Holt guilty; he was sentenced to three months in prison and fined $200. After the sentencing, the New York *American Citizen* pointed out that "it would require a connoisseur in law terms to tell why the word *standing* is more seditious and libellous than the word *provisional*." Holt went to jail, his newspaper temporarily closed. The *Bee* would not die, Holt informed his subscribers, but "only SLUMBER." After his release from jail, Holt once again took up publishing the *Bee* and attacking the Sedition Act.

William Duane, the editor of the *Aurora*, had been prosecuted under the Sedition Act in 1798 and again in 1799, but those cases against him had been dropped. In the middle of the election of 1800, would Federalists permit his influential newspaper to continue spewing out its anti-Federalist propaganda? "If the *Aurora* is not blown up," one Federalist senator was reported to have said, "Jefferson will be elected in defiance of everything."

A new case against William Duane would be brought as a consequence of the Ross bill. In February 1800, in reaction to stalemates and disputes in several states as to how presidential electors would be chosen, Federalist senator James Ross of Pennsylvania introduced a bill in the United States Senate to establish a "Grand Committee of Thirteen" to act as a kind of super electoral college. This committee, composed of six members from the Senate and six from the House (both dominated by Federalists) plus the chief justice of the Supreme Court (also a Federalist), would meet in secret and decide which electoral votes to count and which to discard as illegal. The "Grand Committee" would thus possess the ultimate responsibility for deciding who would be president. They would report to the nation on March 1, and there would be no appeal from their decision. The principal author of the Constitution, James Madison, was alarmed at this "licentiousness in constructive perversions of the Constitution," for it appeared to him that the election of the president might be decided, not according to the Constitution but instead by the machinations of the legislature.

Three Republican senators leaked the text of the Ross proposal to Duane's *Aurora*, which published it in February 1800. Then the fireworks began.

Furious that this most partisan — and unconstitutional — of proposals had been made public, Federalists searched for a way to punish Duane. Senator Uriah Tracy of Connecticut proposed a five-man "committee on privilege" to examine whether Duane had impugned the Senate and breached its privileges. Tracy demanded not a judicial prosecution of Duane but rather his immediate punishment by the Senate itself, thereby depriving him of his constitutional right to a trial by jury. He also demanded that the senators who leaked the material to Duane be expelled from the Senate.

Nothing in the Constitution, exclaimed a Republican senator from South Carolina, gave the Senate the right to bring charges against an individual or to imprison him. So political and so arbitrary was Tracy's "committee on privilege" that it had the merit of making the Sedition Act appear moderate if not constitutional. But Tracy's motion went forward, and, in March 1800, the committee declared that Duane's article had constituted a "high breach of the privileges" of the Senate, thereby finding Duane guilty without a hearing.

Then the committee on privilege ordered him to appear on March 24 to defend his "false, defamatory, scandalous and malicious" assertions. The Senate clerk was to read the charges against Duane, and Vice President Jefferson, presiding over the Senate, was supposed to ask if he had anything to say. After the Senate's deliberations, Jefferson would announce the sentence.

But Duane had another plan in mind.

Uncowed and undaunted, he insisted that "no terror — no force — no menace — no fear" would make him betray the Constitution or collaborate with those who sought to undermine it. The Senate procedure, he asserted, made a mockery of the numerous constitutional provisions for the protection of the accused. He informed Jefferson of a scheme that he and two lawyer friends of his, Alexander James Dallas and Thomas Cooper, had just hatched. They would ascertain the limits that the Senate intended to impose on Duane's defense counsel so that the lawyers could publicly object to those restrictions and refuse to serve as counsel, thus giving Duane a solid reason for refusing to participate in the Senate proceedings.

And so, on March 24, Duane appeared in the Senate as ordered, but only to request that he be represented by counsel. The Senate agreed but announced that severe limits would be placed on Duane's lawyers. Duane was then ordered to appear before the Senate on March 26. On March 25, Duane officially asked Dallas and Cooper to serve as his counsel, explaining to them the constraints the Senate would place on them. Right on cue, the two lawyers refused to serve as Duane's counsel. "I will not degrade myself by submitting to appear before the senate," Cooper exclaimed, "with *their gag in my mouth.*" Cooper himself would be jailed for sedition that May, his six-month sentence in part a result of his having helped Duane.

Deprived of legal counsel, Duane presented Jefferson, the president of the Senate, with the entire official correspondence, informing him that he would not appear before the Senate — and then published the correspondence in the *Aurora.* When Duane did not show up at the Senate proceedings on March 26, the Senate declared him guilty of contempt and issued an arrest warrant, signed meekly by Jefferson. Duane went into hiding. But articles condemning the Federalists continued to pour out from his hiding place.

Federalists had still not had their fill of persecuting William Duane.

Although the Ross bill had been defeated in the Senate while Duane was in hiding, Federalists now asked President Adams to bring yet another suit against Duane for publishing the text of the Ross bill. Adams agreed. In October Duane was indicted, but his case was postponed several times until it was finally dropped in 1801, months after the sedition law expired.

"The three most active and most notorious foreign emissaries, Cooper, Duane and Callender have all at last been punished for their audacious attempts to involve the United States in one scene of confusion and blood," applauded the *Gazette of the United States* in June 1800. During the most heated months of the presidential campaign, leading Federalists in all three branches of government had enthusiastically called for and willingly participated in political trials. They attacked the Republican press, plotting and laboring to muzzle the opposition, bringing suits against editors and writers of every important Republican newspaper.

For his part, Jefferson believed that the tide of public opinion was set strongly against the proceedings in the Senate. But Federalist hard-liners were blind and deaf. "Firm to their purposes regardless of public opinion, and more disposed to coerce than to court it," Jefferson wrote to Madison that May, Federalists had remained intransigent in their support of the Ross bill. Madison, too, believed that the sedition trials would ultimately harm rather than aid Federalists. The kind of spirit that the Senate displayed in its prosecution of Duane, Madison remarked to Jefferson, "cannot fail I think to aid the progress of reflection and change among the people. In this view our public malady may work its own cure." Cooper, Callender, Holt, and Duane indeed continued their attacks on the administration, exposing the political nature of their trials and turning public opinion against the Federalists.

The prosecutions caused the defendants great personal hardship, but the trials supplied Republicans with a vast arsenal of political weapons in the middle of the election year. Newspapers, thundered the Frankfort (Ky.) *Palladium,* should "BE NOT INTIMIDATED . . . *by any terrors,* from publishing with the utmost freedom. . . . The true source of our sufferings has been our timidity." A writer in the *Augusta Herald* pronounced President Adams guilty of having supported the Sedition Act when he knew it was unconstitutional. Why was Adams's conduct shielded from criticism, demanded one candidate running for elector in Maryland, when Jefferson's character was exposed to the extremes of slander?

Although Federalists assailed Republicans for being "Jacobins," it was they who resembled the Jacobins of France, turning against their own leader, conducting political trials, attempting to purge members of Congress, outlawing opposition, and punishing and imprisoning their political adversaries. Fortunately none of these political trials ended, as they did in France, in a death sentence. The guillotine remained light years away. Still, borrowing the hollow, illogical maxims of the French Jacobins, Justice Chase declared that the publication of "calumny" would reduce "virtue to the level of vice." A licentious press, he insisted, was the "bane of freedom and the peril of Society."

9

On the Campaign Trail

POLITICS ARE SUCH A TORMENT," wrote Jefferson to his daughter Martha in February 1800, "that I would advise every one I love not to mix with them." His attachment to the world, he told his other daughter Maria, was "daily wearing off." The sole enjoyment offered by Philadelphia was socializing with scientists and thinkers, "of whom there is a valuable society here." But despite his old themes of revulsion for political discord and weariness in public life, Jefferson the cool-headed politico was already deeply engrossed in analyzing Republican prospects in the up-coming presidential election. Again and again, he went down the list of states one by one, carefully assessing the chances of Federalists and Republicans.

The subject was "indelicate," he admitted to Madison, and yet he plunged ahead in his calculations. North Carolina and Maryland were divided; New Jersey looked good for Republicans; the number of Republicans in Massachusetts, New Hampshire, and Connecticut was becoming "respectable." "I can say nothing," he told Madison, about Rhode Island and Vermont. What would happen in Pennsylvania was uncertain. Surveying the electoral landscape, he concluded that New York might well be the linchpin. In late April, voters there would go to the polls to elect representatives to the state assembly who would choose New York's 12 electors to the Electoral College. Those early results, Jefferson believed, would influence trends in other states. "So much depends" on New York, Madison agreed. The two friends also understood that the election in New York State hinged on the outcome of the vote in New York City.

Jefferson's allies in New York were supremely optimistic. Aaron Burr and Edward Livingston entertained "no doubt of the event of that election," Jefferson reported to Madison. And yet, he himself was more cautious. "We must make great allowance," he wrote, "for their sanguine views." A win in New York would give Republicans a great psychological boost, but the presidential election was still in its early stages: it would be a long year of campaigning, even by modern standards.

The political situation in New York had been recently evolving. In 1796, John Adams had received the votes of all twelve of New York's electors. Why had Republicans made no inroads in New York? Jefferson had wondered in the spring of 1797. On the one hand, he was convinced that people in the eastern states were "unquestionably republicans"; on the other hand, he felt that those same people had been hoodwinked into voting for Federalists. If only they could understand that they had been "duped into the support of measures calculated to sap the very foundations of republicanism." But would New Yorkers see the light? "We might still hope for salvation, and that it would come, as of old, from the east. But will that region ever awake to the true state of things?" Jefferson asked. "These are painful & doubtful questions."

By 1799, Republicans had made slight advances in New York. The state legislature was still Federalist, though in 1800 Republicans had a small advantage in upstate New York. But would the vote in New York City and the adjacent farm areas be strong enough to change the make-up of the new state legislature?

In January 1800, Aaron Burr — the leader of New York Republicans and a vice-presidential hopeful — had visited Jefferson in Philadelphia. Burr's ebullient confidence about the outlook for Republicans in New York was contagious. "At present there would be no doubt of our carrying our ticket there," Jefferson boasted to Monroe after Burr's visit. "Nor," he added, "does there seem to be time for any events arising to change that disposition."

But in March, Jefferson's nerves got the better of him, and he could not mask his apprehension. He even feared that Republicans might do worse than they had in 1796. He did not yet realize that Aaron Burr held the key to New York.

Burr was convinced that he could turn the situation around. He had already made important changes within the Republican Party in New

York, creating a veritable political machine. Understanding that it was not enough for Republicans to rely on the logocrats, he organized the party, energized its leaders, and recruited rank-and-file members to do innumerable political chores. Federalists confessed to being awe-struck by what Burr had accomplished. "By his arts & intrigues," Robert Troup wrote, Burr has "done a great deal towards revolutionizing the State." Federalist influence in the upstate New York counties, Troup grieved, had been "cut up."

Presidential electors in New York would be chosen by the state Assembly. For his part, Burr would have preferred districtwide elections instead, but Federalists opposed that plan. Even so, Burr was determined to turn the situation to his advantage. He had a master plan. As a member of the nominating committee, he decided that the key to victory was to present New Yorkers with a dazzling slate of Republican candidates for the state Assembly. Voters' eyes would light up when they saw the names of illustrious Revolutionary heroes on the ballot. They would undoubtedly cast their votes for men of courage, integrity, and experience, men in whom they could place their trust. His dream list included six-term governor of New York George Clinton; General Horatio Gates, the "hero of Saratoga"; John Broome, president of the New York Insurance Company; Samuel Osgood, ex-postmaster general of the United States; and Judge Brockholst Livingston.

Unfortunately, most of these men were reluctant at best to be nominated, and Clinton, Gates, and Livingston declared that they would refuse to serve. Governor Clinton was the most recalcitrant — he had served enough time in government, he felt. Nor did Clinton hold Mr. Jefferson in high esteem. The Virginian, in his eyes, was a "trimmer who would change with the times and bend to circumstances for purposes of personal promotion." And then Albany was so dreary! The prospect of several months in that provincial town demoralized all potential candidates. Burr himself had taken a dislike for the place. "Amusement from Albany!" he scoffed. "I eat breakfast and dinner & go to bed and attend court — this is the history of my life here."

But Burr negotiated, wheedled, persuaded — and got exactly the list of candidates he wanted, including Clinton, Gates, and Livingston. Next, he made a sly decision. He would keep his roster of stellar names a secret until after Alexander Hamilton, the leader of the New York Federalists, announced the Federalist slate.

Where did the Feds stand? They were "as usual supine till the eve of the election," one Federalist bemoaned. Federalists could not swallow the idea of organizing and electioneering. Just when Republicans were mastering the art of dirtying their hands, Federalists decided that they wanted to keep theirs clean. Eleven of the thirteen Federalist representatives in the New York Assembly refused to run again. Prominent merchants and lawyers disdained the idea of spending three months of the year in Albany. It seemed "next to an impossibility," Robert Troup admitted, to get "men of influence to serve."

The news trickled out from Hamilton's Federalist caucus that Federalists had selected for their slate two grocers, a shoemaker, a baker, a mason, a ship chandler, and a potter. It was an ironic moment, inasmuch as Republicans claimed to represent ordinary citizens while Federalists insisted that their distinguished partisans possessed a commitment to public service. But for his part, Burr could only gloat. Seizing the list of Federalist names, he "read it over with great gravity," an observer recalled, "folded it up, put it in his pocket, and . . . said, 'Now I have him [Hamilton] all hollow.'"

Two days later, on April 17, Republicans made public their own sparkling slate. All was "Joy & Enthusiasm," a delighted Republican reported. "Never have I observed such a union of sentiment; so much zeal and so general a determination to be active," said another Republican. "We have labored hard but the reward is great," wrote a satisfied Edward Livingston to Jefferson, adding that "there is a most auspicious gloom on the countenances of every tory and placeman."

Burr's success, his friend Matthew Davis later suggested, was due to his talent for "intrigue and management." He was more dreaded by his political opponents, Davis added, than any other Republican in the state. He was simply one of the most skillful, effective, aggressive political operatives and campaign managers of his time. And yet, Burr had hardly been bred to be a rough-and-tumble politico.

The son of a distinguished father who had been president of the College of New Jersey, later called Princeton, and the grandson of Jonathan Edwards, the most famous theologian and moralist in eighteenth-century America, the young man served in the revolutionary army as a "gentleman volunteer" and afterwards became a very able lawyer, occasionally appearing in the same courtroom with Hamilton. Neither man was tall; Burr was five feet six inches, Hamilton an inch taller. While Hamilton's style was "flowing and rapturous," a fellow lawyer recalled, Burr, with his piercing black eyes, was simply "terse and convincing."

Burr was elected to the New York State Assembly, appointed attorney general for the state, and then chosen United States senator, allying himself most of the time with Republicans. And yet Burr left little evidence of his political convictions or principles. Politics, he once wrote, was simply for "fun and honor & profit." He felt at home in the hard-nosed world of political gamesmanship. And more than anything, the slick New Yorker loved winning.

After successfully putting together the New York Republican slate, Burr faced a formidable array of challenges: how to engage voters, raise funds, mobilize the committees in each of the seven city wards, and get people to the polls. He and his lieutenants — Matthew Davis, John Swartwout, William Peter van Ness, Theodorus Bailey, and others — identified eligible voters in the city, compiling a list consisting of two-thirds of the city's free adult males, including free blacks. They found out which voters were the most enthusiastic Republicans, which ones might work for the party or make a financial contribution, or both. And they made sure that door-to-door canvassers visited all voters.

Colonel Burr "kept open house for nearly two months," wrote one aide. Day and night "refreshments were on the table and mattresses for temporary repose in the rooms. Reports were hourly received from sub-committees, and in short, no means left unemployed." "If we carry this election," a party member said in March 1800, "it may be ascribed principally to Colo. Burr's management and perseverance."

Politics had come a long way from 1788. Then James Madison had written to George Washington to express his "extreme distaste" for "any step which might seem to denote a solicitude" for office. That same year, Federalist Jonathan Jackson had demanded limitations on people's participation in politics, going so far as to propose a stringent ban against the solicitation of votes.

But in 1799, Federalists like Fisher Ames could only marvel at the ability of Republicans to organize and campaign. "Every threshing floor," he wrote, "every husking, every party work on a house-frame or raising a building, the very funerals are infected with bawlers or whisperers against government." Republicans were hungry for victory and would persevere until it was theirs. It was plain to Ames that if Republicans failed to win a majority, they would simply try again the following year, "never despairing of their final success."

Finally stirred to action, Federalists decided to fight back. With the election only weeks away, Hamilton geared himself for battle. He seemed to appear everywhere at once. The General "is seen in the street hurrying this way, and darting that," reported the *General Advertiser*. Federalist newspapers also jumped into the fray, attacking Jefferson and the Republican Party. A few days before voting began, a writer in the New York *Spectator* warned that if Jefferson should win the presidential election, the whole financial system of the nation would tumble into ruin. The Virginian sought nothing but "mischief." The *Daily Advertiser* hammered Burr. How could a gentleman "stoop so low as to visit every corner in search of voters?"

But Republicans were hopeful. On the eve of the election, the Republican *American Citizen* reminded voters to cast their ballots for the Republican slate, for Horatio Gates and others, the "HEROES who fought and bled for your cause." Giving an inadvertent boost to the Republican cause, a British cruiser arrived in New York with captured American merchantmen, fueling resentment against English depredations and Federalist proclamations of amity for Great Britain. Newspapers on both sides urged voters to cast their ballots for the party ticket, not for favorite individual candidates.

At last, on April 29, the polls opened, and the three-day voting period began. The *New York Gazette* reported that all manner of carriages, chairs, and wagons were taking elderly Republican voters to the polls. And out of nowhere German-speaking operatives appeared, urging German-Americans to go to the polls. Riding around the city on a white horse, Hamilton roused Federalist voters; he speechified at each polling place, passionately denouncing the Republican menace. When Burr and Hamilton occasionally crossed paths at the polls, they debated the issues in front of the crowds, behaving, one contemporary observer reported, as "accomplished and courtly gentlemen."

The final push was on. An exhausted Robert Troup worked day and night. Never had he witnessed such exertions on either side before. "I have not eaten dinner for three days," he wrote, "and have been constantly upon my legs from 7 in the morning till 7 in the afternoon." For ten straight hours, on the last day of voting, Burr posted himself at the polls in the seventh ward; when the polls closed at sunset on May 1, he assigned guards to supervise the counting of votes.

Poll workers quickly tallied the ballots; the results were announced the following day. Federalists had run strong in the wards where houses were large and addresses fashionable, but Republicans had won the city. They carried all thirteen seats in the New York City area, giving them a majority in the state Assembly and ensuring that in the Electoral College all 12 of New York's electoral votes would go for Jefferson.

Burr had engineered a spectacular coup. "The victory is complete," he crowed. "We have beat you by superior Management," he bragged to a dejected foe. Burr must have been the chosen intermediary of the gods, Commodore James Nicholson marveled. The election has been conducted and brought to its conclusion in "so miraculous a manner," he wrote, that he could only explain it as "the intervention of a Supreme Power" with Burr acting as the "agent" of God. Burr's leadership qualities, he waxed, exceeded all possible words. No reward could be too great for the master of the New York Republican political machine. "He deserves any thing and every thing of his country." A little more than a week later, Republicans caucused in Congress Hall and nominated Jefferson and Burr to run in the presidential election. Burr received his reward.

"The Goddess of Liberty has put to flight the demon of Aristocracy," the *Orange Patrol* of Goshen, New York, announced. Voters had "spurned the infamous menaces, and still more infamous promises of the Aristocrats. . . . They obtained a glorious, honorable, and complete VICTORY. Huzza for Liberty — Huzza for the Constitution — Huzza for Jefferson!" It was also a win for political parties and the principle of opposition. "In a free country let no man be afraid or ashamed to avow that he belongs to a party," editorialized the *Albany Register,* explaining that only through well-organized parties, "cemented by the union of sound principles," was it possible to oppose those in power.

When the news of the New York election results reached the Senate in Philadelphia, the hubbub was so loud that senators decided to adjourn. Learning of his victory, Vice President Jefferson paid a call on President Adams, who congratulated him on his win, voicing the hope that their friendship would not be affected. But another Federalist was less sanguine: the New York election results left Alexander Hamilton stunned.

"Hamilton exhibits a figure of rage and despair," one contemporary observer wrote. Rage was an understatement. Less than a week after the election results were known, an infuriated, defiant Hamilton wrote to the governor of New York, John Jay, proposing a startling plan to circumvent the new Republican state legislature and prevent it from choosing presidential electors. Given the "extraordinary nature of the crisis," Hamilton wrote in a soon-to-be famous letter, it would not do to be "overscrupulous" about adhering to conventional principles.

Hamilton frantically implored Jay to help him prevent "an *Atheist* in Religion and a *Fanatic* in politics from getting possession of the helm." It was no time, he cried, for "scruples of delicacy and propriety" or for "a strict adherence to ordinary rules." In the face of so great an evil and in the name of "the great cause of social order," Hamilton urged Jay quickly to call back into session the outgoing state legislature, still dominated by Federalists, and ram through a new plan for choosing electors by popular vote in districts — a plan, he wrote, that would ensure a Federalist victory. Ironically, Republicans had long wanted the choice of electors to be determined directly by voters in their districts rather than by the legislature, but Federalists had defeated their proposal. Now that the state legislature would be controlled by Republicans, Federalists proposed voting by districts.

"The reasonable part of the world will, I believe, approve it," Hamilton blithely wrote. Jay, moreover, should be forthright with the legislature, Hamilton advised, and openly explain to legislators that, unless they intervened, the executive authority would be transferred to hands "hostile to the system." No time ought to be lost, Hamilton warned. That same day, Hamilton's father-in-law, General Philip Schuyler, seconded Hamilton's proposal with a letter of his own to Jay, acknowledging that such an extralegal act might cause some "embarrassment," but that it was nevertheless entirely justified as the only way to save a nation from the disasters that would inevitably result from the "mis-rule" of Thomas Jefferson.

Both sides had played the game by the rules and in good faith, but now the losing side wanted to change those rules. Unwilling to accept the orderly outcome of a fair, democratic election and the predictable consequences of organized opposition to Federalist power, Hamilton demanded that the governor of an important state circumvent legal voting procedures and prevent the transfer of power to the opposition. Why did Hamilton demand such arrant manipulation? Why did he repudiate his own *Federalist* No. 68, in which he had assured his readers that the Electoral College afforded a "moral certainty" that only a man of outstanding talent and integrity would be elected president? Sheer panic. Panic at the prospect of handing the reins of power to Jeffersonian Republicans. The ends justified the means. Hamilton's breathtaking letter to Jay was intercepted and leaked to a Republican newspaper for all to read.

Jay kept his head. Though a staunch Federalist, he refused to manipulate established procedures for the sake of party politics. Upon receiving the letter, he scrawled across it, "Proposing a measure for party purposes, which I think it would not become me to adopt."

And in the other fifteen states? The Constitution directed each state to determine its own method for selecting presidential electors. The only uniform rule was that on December 3, those electors would meet and cast their ballots in their respective states — not in one place, which could theoretically lend itself, as Hamilton had noted in *Federalist* No. 68, to "heats and ferments." But heats, ferments, and cabals there would be, for party politicians throughout the country were trying to do everything in their power to make last-minute changes in their states' procedures for choosing electors. If their states had districtwide elections, they sought safer statewide winner-take-all elections or the appointment of electors by the state legislature. If their states had statewide elections, they demanded districtwide elections. The only criterion was political advantage. The name of the game was opportunism.

After the Republican victory in New York, Federalists in neighboring New Jersey mobilized themselves to prevent another Republican victory. They had an unusual tool in that state: women could vote. Unmarried females in New Jersey who were property owners and who paid taxes were entitled to vote — at least before that privilege was taken away in 1807. Some historians estimate that as many as ten thousand women may have been eligible to vote, though probably fewer than one hundred voted in any one election, not a critical voting bloc. Still, given the allegiance of the upper class to the Federalist party, those one hundred women of wealth and property would have overwhelmingly voted Federalist. When election results came in, New Jersey Federalists celebrated: New Jersey had elected a Federalist-dominated state legislature that would appoint seven electors prepared to vote for Adams and Pinckney.

Maryland had a different method for choosing electors: it was one of the five states in which electors were chosen directly by the people and in which the most open campaigning took place. Wherever people gathered, one observer remarked, "at a horse race — a cock-fight — or a Methodist quarterly meeting," all state and national candidates would campaign. But still there was an attempt to manipulate the rules of the game. The election for the Electoral College was scheduled to take place on the *second* Monday of October, whereas legislative elections were scheduled to take place on the *first* Monday in October. In those legislative elections, Federalists aggressively campaigned on the promise to transfer immediately the choice of electors to the state legislature, thereby canceling the popular election that was scheduled to occur the following week. But, in a stunning admission of their political opportunism, they added that the change in election rules would apply only to the election of 1800, after which the state would return to the old method of popular election of electors. "We deem it a sacred duty," they explained, "to pursue every proper and constitutional measure to elect John Adams president of the United States." Ultimately their brazen tactic failed, and Maryland's 10 electoral votes would be divided between Jefferson and Adams.

The stakes were higher in Virginia, for that most populous state had 21 electoral votes. In Republican Virginia, Federalists had made some inroads in 1799, alerting Republicans that they would have to fight hard to stay in control. John Adams had garnered 1 electoral vote in Virginia in 1796, part of the 3-vote margin that gave him the presidential election that year. It was clear that every electoral vote counted, and Virginia Republicans were determined to prevent Adams from getting even one vote in their state. The Republican senator from South Carolina urged his friend James Madison to lead an effort in the Virginia legislature to change the way presidential electors were chosen: the plan was to switch from choosing electors by districts to a statewide election for a general slate of electors — winner take all. A single statewide election for a general ticket would ensure that all of Virginia's electoral votes would be cast for Jefferson. When Federalists bitterly complained about the Republican tactic, the Virginia *Argus* countered that the "same game" was being played in New England and that, moreover, "it is necessary to fight an adversary at his own weapons." With backing from Jefferson — who had once candidly acknowledged that without voting by district, "the minority is entirely unrepresented" — Madison's proposal eventually passed by a small margin in time for the election of 1800. "This is no time for qualms," the South Carolinian had counseled Madison. Nor was it time for high-minded discussions of democracy, popular sovereignty, and minority representation. So fixated on victory were Republicans that not even the father of the Constitution was above political opportunism.

Virginia Republicans then got down to work: they needed an efficient, well-oiled political machine. They put together a central state committee as well as county committees that would all push for the Republican ticket. And they needed strong candidates. The state party constructed a slate of impressive leaders with illustrious, recognizable names: state senator James Madison, state chancellor George Wythe, General Joseph Jones, Edmund Pendleton, Creed Taylor, Thomas Read, Sr. It was not as easy for Virginia Federalists to find eminent men to run: they even ended up trying to usurp the tag "Republican" by presenting a slate called "The American Republican Ticket."

Ultimately Republicans won all 21 of Virginia's electoral votes and elected to the U.S. House of Representatives eighteen Republicans and one Federalist. "Virginia is sold," wrote one disappointed Federalist, "and past salvation."

In Massachusetts, the situation was different. There Federalists felt securely entrenched. The political culture in the Bay State had long been based on the idea that the "reputable class" would "keep the people steady," educating them in proper restraint and subordination. Although Massachusetts was briefly shaken by Shays's Rebellion in 1786, habits of deference lingered, and the state's politicians — Sedgwicks, Cabots, Dwights, Sargents, Lowells, and Lymans — continued to bask in the knowledge that the people accepted their "virtuous" leadership. It would be an uphill struggle for Republicans even to make their platform known in a state where the ruling elite disdained electioneering, campaigning, and soliciting votes. One member of the Massachusetts old guard had even proposed, in the late 1780s, that any candidate found guilty of canvassing for votes should be deprived of all political privileges for life. One young Massachusetts Federalist remarked that in his town "not a man had been spoken to about candidates" before the election of 1800. And in parts of New England, as historian David Fischer points out, some old school leaders used colored ballots to deprive their "dependents" of the protection of a secret ballot.

Since everyone in Massachusetts was assumed to be a Federalist, party lines were not clearly drawn, and party labels were interchangeable: some of the same men appeared on both Federalist and Republican lists. All politicians in Massachusetts "call themselves Republicans," the *Gazette* observed, "and most say they are Federalists." In the race for governor in 1800, both candidates — Caleb Strong and Elbridge Gerry — ran as centrists who supported Adams. In 1800 Gerry — who would later serve as vice president under Madison — was a consensus man who rejected the notion of political conflict, which he believed threatened the gains of the American Revolution. He saw himself as a conciliator, supporting a "unity" ticket of Adams and Jefferson. The re-election of those two great men, he asserted, would "unite their parties, both of which are true friends to this country."

But even in Federalist-dominated Massachusetts, Federalists were unwilling to take any chances. They feared that if the state continued to choose presidential electors in districtwide elections, Republicans might win in two districts. Since Virginia had just given up district-wide elections, Massachusetts Federalists proposed doing the same — switching from districtwide elections to the selection of electors by the state legislature. It was essential, one Federalist congressman insisted, to "guard against *one* antifederal vote from Massachusetts; for one vote may turn the election." At stake, editorialized the Boston *Columbian Centinel*, was the "principle of self-preservation." Massachusetts voters elected a state legislature that would cast all 16 of its electoral votes for Adams and Pinckney, although they simultaneously sent seven Feder-alists and seven Republicans to represent them in Washington.

In Pennsylvania, too, Federalists decided to play tough. Before the election of 1796, they had pushed through a change in the method for choosing electors, giving voters a choice between two general slates, winner take all. Republicans had opposed the plan, but when it passed, they organized an impressive network of Republican committees in each county, township, and ward and also succeeded in putting up a slate of distinguished men. They made the most of a situation they hadn't chosen: in the election of 1796, Jefferson won 14 electoral votes, Burr 13, Thomas Pinckney 2, and John Adams 1.

As the election of 1800 approached, Federalists were dead set against letting Republicans win another statewide winner-take-all victory. And so they proposed a change in the election law they had supported in 1796, while Republicans fought to keep it. The tables had turned. But with Federalists in control of the state senate and Republicans in con-trol of the state assembly, the debate went on for a year in the two houses with no conclusion. Nothing could be done until a new state legislature was elected in October 1800. Even then the new legislature would take weeks to decide on a compromise measure. In the meantime, Pennsylvania was deadlocked.

On December 5, with news slow to trickle in from all the states, Jefferson gave his son-in-law Thomas Mann Randolph a rundown of the electoral situation. Setting aside Pennsylvania, Rhode Island, and South Carolina, the Federalists seemed to have 53 votes and Republicans 58. Pennsylvania appeared unlikely to emerge in time from its impasse; both parties thought they would win in Rhode Island. "The issue of the election hangs on S. Carolina," he concluded.

A few days later, Jefferson learned that Federalists had won all 4 of Rhode Island's electoral votes and that Maryland was split, with each party winning 5 electoral votes. Was Pennsylvania still deadlocked? What was happening in South Carolina?

"We have never been so pestered with politics as we are at this day," one South Carolinian had written at the beginning of the political season in October. Political intrigue and tactics could hardly have been more complex than they were in South Carolina. Charles Cotesworth Pinckney, Adams's running mate, was a South Carolinian; Federalists hoped that he would help tip the balance for them there — the most Federalist of all the southern states. Hamilton, for his part, hoped that electors in South Carolina would vote for Pinckney and Jefferson, giving Pinckney enough votes to outrun Adams in the nation.

Republicans had an angle of their own. Another South Carolinian by the name of Charles Pinckney, the second cousin of Charles Cotesworth Pinckney and an ally of Jefferson, was working frantically against his cousin to swing the state's 8 electoral votes to Jefferson and Burr. "I have incessantly laboured to carry this Election here and to sprinkle all the southern states with pamphlets and essays and everything I thought would promote the common cause," he wrote. Pinckney could reassure South Carolinians that the Republicans represented the most practical option: they offered the best protection for the institution of slavery, the most reliable promise of markets for southern agricultural products, and the strongest support for the interests of settlers — not Indians — on the move west. But what could Pinckney do about Federalist control of Charleston or about obvious electoral shenanigans? "It is said several Hundred more Voted than paid taxes," Pinckney reported to Jefferson in mid-October, adding that "*the Lame, Crippled, diseased and blind were either led, lifted, or brought in Car-*

riages to the Poll." Republicans won only four of Charleston's fifteen seats in the state legislature, and even the most decided Republicans, Pinckney wrote, "began to despair."

To push for a Republican win, Pinckney, a United States senator, journeyed to the state capital in Columbia in late November — first to try to set aside the Charleston election, and then, when that tactic failed, to try to sway undecided legislators by promising patronage appointments from the new president. He had one week to operate. Republicans had a slim majority, but some of them nevertheless supported C. C. Pinckney, the native son. It was rumored that Federalists were willing to compromise on a joint slate for Jefferson and Pinckney, but it was also rumored that Pinckney objected to being on the same ticket with Jefferson. And one Republican wrote to Burr from Columbia that he was trying to prevent the compromise that the Federalists wanted. Still, compromise was in the air. The hectic week was filled with caucuses, compromise proposals, meetings, and maneuvering. On the eve of the final vote, Republicans abruptly cancelled a last meeting when they learned that Federalists were planning to send several speakers to try to weaken their commitment to Jefferson and Burr.

"All depends on the vote of South Carolina," Oliver Wolcott wrote from Massachusetts, noting that both parties "claimed and expected" a victory in that state. Federalists spread rumors that they would carry South Carolina, dashing Republicans' hopes. One Federalist editor announced that "the non-election of (Citizen) Jefferson is now certain." The Electoral College deadline of December 3 was approaching.

On December 1, there was finally news from Pennsylvania: a compromise had been reached by the newly elected legislature in Pennsylvania that gave Republicans 8 electoral votes and Federalists 7 — a net gain of 1 electoral vote for Republicans. But neither Jefferson nor Adams had a clear-cut majority.

On December 2, on the eve of voting in the Electoral College, at the very last hour, South Carolina pledged all 8 delegates to Jefferson and Burr. C. C. Pinckney had not even carried his own state of South Carolina.

"The Election is just finished and we have, thanks to Heaven's Goodness, carried it," wrote a jubilant Charles Pinckney to Jefferson. "As there were no hopes from Philadelphia," he noted, "it depended upon our State entirely to secure Your Election." A few months later, Jefferson penned a reminder to himself to "adopt C. Pinkney's nominations" for patronage appointments in South Carolina and named the helpful Pinckney minister to Spain. "I was turned out by the votes of South Carolina, not fairly obtained," John Adams would later carp.

The *National Intelligencer* announced the "SPLENDID INTELLIGENCE" that Republicans had carried South Carolina. "Our Country is yet safe," Philip Freneau exulted. "I know not what I am writing I am so rejoiced."

10

Showdown

MY HEALTH STILL SUFFERS from several complaints," James Madison wrote to Thomas Jefferson during the winter of 1800–1801. Though only fifty years old, a somber Madison feared that any more changes in his health "are not likely to be for the better." He was concerned, too, about his elderly father's declining state. Jefferson had hoped that his friend would join him in Washington, but Madison decided to remain at home with wife Dolley and his father. He would not come to Washington until officially summoned by the new president to appear "on the political Theatre." When his father passed away, Madison was at his side. "Yesterday morning, rather suddenly, though very gently," he wrote Jefferson, "the flame of life went out."

Life — and death — had not stopped during the election of 1800.

James Monroe had not slept for days when his infant son, his "beloved babe," died in September. "An unhappy event has occurr'd which has overwhelmed us with grief," he wrote to James Madison. "I cannot give you an idea of the effect this event has produc'd on my family, or of my own affliction in being a partner and spectator of the scene."

John Adams was spending the winter heartbroken and depressed after a double loss, the death of his alcoholic son Charles in late November and his electoral defeat in December. Meanwhile, in Albany, Aaron Burr was happily discussing plans for the wedding of his pretty eighteen-year-old daughter, Theodosia. Endings and beginnings.

And the presidential front-runner? Thomas Jefferson had just harvested a bountiful wheat crop before making his way to Washington in late November, stopping in Montpelier to discuss possible cabinet appointments with Madison. Jefferson's six-month stay in Virginia had been disturbed only by reports of his own death. While remaining in touch with his friends about the various state elections, he had tried to keep his political involvement to a minimum, spending most of his time caring for his estate and working on a manual on parliamentary procedure. But it was time for him to move to the federal city.

Jefferson took up residence in "Messrs Conrad and McMunn's Apartments" on the south side of Capitol Hill, the best of the eleven or so boarding houses in town. He had a parlor and a reception room in addition to his bedroom. Along with two dozen other Republican politicos, he took his meals at a common table. Were it not for the presence of two women, quipped Albert Gallatin, the table "would look like a refectory of monks." Federalists snickered that the men constituted the "Jacobin knot." Political lines were sharply drawn in the new capital; whereas Adams and Jefferson had lived in the same boarding house in Philadelphia in 1797, none of the major boarding houses in Washington contained members of the opposite party.

The "embryo capital," as one man called it, was a work in progress, like America's experiment with democracy. It was taking shape thanks to the efforts of President Washington and Secretary of State Jefferson. In 1790, they had agreed that the seat of government would be a ten-square-mile district on the eastern side of the Potomac. The French architect and engineer Major Pierre Charles L'Enfant drew up majestic plans for the new city. Jefferson decreed height limitations on all buildings, none of which, he decided, would be built in wood.

Now Jefferson could look down the swampy road called Pennsylvania Avenue that cut through the morass separating the Capitol from the unfinished executive mansion, where John and Abigail Adams were living in less than comfort. Washington could boast of having only one tailor, one shoemaker, one printer, a grocery shop, a small dry-goods store, a pamphlet and stationery shop, and also a wharf, "graced," said Gallatin, "by not a single vessel." Gouverneur Morris cheerfully remarked that the capital offered great advantages "as a future residence." One unenthusiastic French visitor called Washington a "city without houses and Georgetown a city without streets." Unaccustomed to life on the frontier, the Spanish minister complained that his elaborate gilded coach got stuck in the mud and snow. The exiled wives and daughters of the congressmen and senators longed for their own homes and for the civilized surroundings of Philadelphia.

But Jefferson was there strictly for business.

Republicans had won big in the congressional elections of 1800. Their fighting words had hit their target, while the Federalists' smear campaign against Jefferson had boomeranged. Voters had just awarded a 65–41 majority to Republicans in the House of Representatives — a significant change from the previous House, elected in 1798, in which Federalists had enjoyed a 63–43 majority. In the Senate, too, Republicans won a five-seat majority.

Above all, the Jefferson-Burr ticket had come in first. "The republicans have triumphed," the *National Intelligencer* rejoiced. "The people are on their side." In the *Vermont Gazette,* a banner headline, emblazoned across the front page, trumpeted that "the new Election of JEFFERSON and BURR is *Truly Glorious.*" The Georgetown *Cabinet* exulted that Americans were "A Seditious People!" The political configuration in the country had dramatically shifted. Majorities in both houses of Congress along with a win in the presidential race gave Republicans an unambiguous mandate for change.

Still, some Federalists found grounds for questioning the election results. The *Connecticut Courant* pointed to the contradictions implicit in the three-fifths rule (which included three-fifths of the number of slaves in the total population count of a state), asking whether free men or slaves had voted for Jefferson and Burr. "The absurd policy of representing the negroes of the southern states, who are no better entitled to representation than cattle and horses, will probably elevate to the presidential chair, two citizens . . . about to ride into the TEMPLE OF LIBERTY, upon the *shoulders of slaves.*" The *Courant's* implication — that if slaves had not had three-fifths representation in Congress, Adams would have won in the Electoral College, perhaps by a vote of 63 to 61 — was, according to late-twentieth-century political historians, probably correct. And if emancipated blacks had enjoyed voting rights, for which party would they have voted? Some evidence — from records in North Carolina where free blacks could vote — suggests that they would probably have voted Federalist.

For Federalists, it was time for second-guessing. Had Hamilton's attacks on Adams cost Federalists the victory? Adams thought so. "The federal party has been so imprudently managed, as well as so discordantly composed," he scolded, "that the overthrow of the party is no wonder." No party, Adams wrote, had ever "so vainly overrated its own influence and popularity, as ours." The only pleasure that he could derive from the whole fiasco was Hamilton's discomfiture. "Mr. Hamilton has carried his eggs to a fine market," Adams gloated. "The very two men of all the world that he was most jealous of are now placed over him." Fifteen years later, Adams would still hold Hamilton accountable for what he called "the revolution of 1801." Had the New Yorker supported him, that revolution simply "would not have happened."

But perhaps the Adams-Hamilton split had not caused the party's defeat. Adams had received 100 percent of the New England vote, while Jefferson had received 85 percent of the South's total vote. There seemed to be a sharp geographical divide in the country as well as an ideological one.

As for Republicans, they were not yet in a mood to celebrate. Jefferson had come in first, but he and Burr appeared to have received an equal number of electoral votes.

On December 15, the results of the Electoral College vote still uncertain, Jefferson wrote an upbeat letter to Burr that nevertheless betrayed his anxiety. He reported that South Carolina electors would probably withhold 1 vote from Burr and that Tennessee might too. "Yet," he added, "no one pretends to know these things of a certainty." The task of ensuring that at least 1 vote would be withheld from Burr had been, he admitted, "badly managed" and "left to hazard." He also passed on to Burr the rumor that in the event of a tie, the "high-flying Federalists" were already plotting a way to prevent the House of Representatives from deciding the election; their plan was to let the presidency "devolve" on a president pro tempore of the Senate whom they would name — a plan that Jefferson knew he could thwart as vice president and president of the Senate. Merely by always being present to preside over the Senate, he could make the selection of a president pro tempore impossible. Jefferson then went on to congratulate Burr on winning the vice-presidency, thereby making it clear that he expected Burr to accept second place. He also mentioned that he regretted not being able to appoint him to an important cabinet post instead. Seeking to fill his administration with men of talent, integrity, famous names, and proven dispositions, men who would "at once inspire unbounded confidence in the public mind," he claimed that the loss of Burr left a "chasm" in his arrangements.

Was Jefferson sincere in this letter? Why did he mention the possibility of appointing Burr to a cabinet position when he knew that Burr had most likely won the vice-presidency? Was it a tactic to flatter the New Yorker? Was it an attempt to feel him out and see what his reaction to a possible tie might be? Or did he think that Burr might come in third in the race, after Adams, and be available for a cabinet post as a consolation prize? Burr's close friend and future biographer Matthew Davis felt that Jefferson's letter contained "the *sincerity* of a refined Jesuit."

Burr responded diplomatically, his ambition piqued. "I will cheerfully abandon the office of V[ice] P[resident] if it shall be thought that I can be more useful in any Active station," he replied, eager to appear cooperative. "In short," he concluded, "my whole time and attention shall be unceasingly employed to render your administration grateful and honorable to our country and to yourself — To this I am impelled, as well by the highest sense of duty as by the most devoted personal attachment."

As for a possible tied vote, Burr spared no words in reassuring Jefferson that he would yield to him and accept the vice-presidency "out of the highest sense of duty" and "the most devoted personal attachment." Neither he nor his friends would "think of diverting a single vote" from Jefferson. Foreseeing that Federalists might try to enlist him in their efforts against Jefferson, Burr stated categorically that "the federal party can entertain no wish for such an exchange." Although six months earlier Burr had admitted that he placed "no confidence" in the Virginians and that they were not to be trusted, now his promises seemed genuine, and Jefferson accepted them at face value, dismissing for the moment the possibility that Burr might be playing a double game.

To others, too, Burr insisted that he would bow to Jefferson. "It is highly improbable that I shall have an equal number of votes with Mr. Jefferson," he told General Samuel Smith, the Republican representative from Maryland, "but if such should be the result, every man who knows me ought to know that *I would utterly disclaim all competition*."

Burr talked like a team player. But would the master opportunist really fall into line?

Jefferson's hopes for a clean victory collapsed on December 19. On that day the news came out — not yet official but, in Jefferson's opinion, "tolerable well ascertained" — that he and Burr had each received 73 electoral votes while Adams had won 65 votes and Pinckney 64. The grim turn of events, he reported to James Madison, was producing "great dismay and gloom" among Republicans, while at the same time it ignited "exultation" among the Federalists.

For the nation, the news was, on the one hand, good. The voting figures in the Electoral College proved that not only did two adversarial parties exist, but that members of those parties were disciplined and voted with their parties. In the 1796 election, votes had been scattered among thirteen candidates — Adams, Jefferson, Pinckney, Burr, Samuel Adams, Oliver Ellsworth, George Clinton, John Jay, George Washington, Charles Cotesworth Pinckney, and others. But in 1800, electors voted for the four principals (with John Jay receiving 1 lone vote cast by a Federalist, a guarantee that there would be no tie between Adams and Pinckney). Could anyone seriously conclude that political parties did not yet exist in America? "What a glorious revolution in the situation of parties!!!" one Kentuckian wrote to his brother in Connecticut, rejoicing that the Republican "faction" had metamorphosed into the majority. John Adams himself voiced awe at the strength of party. "How mighty a power is the spirit of party!" he wrote. "How decisive and unanimous it is!"

On the other hand, party unity and discipline had created a constitutional crisis — a tie in the Electoral College. That November Madison had assured his friends that Burr would lose a few votes in Virginia, giving Jefferson the top spot. But electors must have been confused or conflicted about the necessity of withholding votes from Burr. Perhaps they sought to avoid offending the New Yorker, who had been miffed in 1796 that southern Republicans had not supported him; he had received only 30 electoral votes compared to Jefferson's 68. In addition, Republicans may have been eager to reward the stellar work he had done in the New York election — and stay on the wily Burr's good side, too. In any case, they neglected to agree on a clear voting strategy in the Electoral College. The odd Electoral College voting system that, in

1796, had given the country a president and a vice president from opposing parties now, in 1800, produced a tie between the two candidates from the same party.

Alexander Hamilton had described the Electoral College as a kind of screening method for choosing the chief executive. In *Federalist* No. 68, he portrayed the Electoral College as "a small number of persons, selected by their fellow-citizens," who would be "most likely to possess the information and discernment" to make an intelligent choice and install a man of "ability and virtue" in the presidency. Fortunately, the Electoral College had not functioned as a screen but rather as a reflection of the wills of the two parties and, at least to some extent, the will of the people. But the combination of its poor design and the error Republicans had made in their voting strategy was about to precipitate high political drama.

With the Electoral College deadlocked, the choice, according to the Constitution, would be made in the House of Representatives, in which each state delegation would cast 1 single vote for one of the two men who had received an equal number of electoral votes — no matter that Virginia had almost a million people and Delaware and Rhode Island, just over fifty thousand each. There were sixteen states; the winner would need a total of nine votes. The body that would decide the election would not be the newly elected House controlled by Republicans, but instead the lame-duck House controlled by Federalists.

While eight state delegations could be counted on to support Jefferson, the situation was unclear in the six states that were Federalist and in the two states that were divided. The House could not begin voting until February 11.

And so, in mid-December, a tense waiting — and maneuvering — period began.

Back in November, Madison had expressed the fear that there might be a tie. But even though the worst-case scenario he could imagine was the decision going to the House of Representatives, he expressed confidence that "the candidates would certainly I think be arranged properly, even on the recommendation of the secondary one." In other words, Burr would behave like a gentleman and yield to Jefferson.

Many citizens agreed with Madison. "The electors intended Mr. Jefferson to be President, and Mr. Burr to be Vice-President," wrote "An American" to the *National Intelligencer.* "The spirit of the constitution requires the will of the people to be executed." But was the situation so clear-cut? "We have involved ourselves in great embarrassment by voting uniformly for Burr," Madison's friend John Francis Mercer bemoaned. Desperate Federalists would "leave no effort unattempted" to thwart the Republicans, and, he added, "I fear they will succeed."

For the first time in months, Federalists saw light. The deadlock was theirs to exploit, manipulate, prolong. The stalemate provided them with precious time to organize, plan, conspire. All bets were off.

On December 19, Gouverneur Morris, the junior senator from New York, passed on the news to Alexander Hamilton about the Federalists' plan to block an election in the House and give the presidency to one of their own; indeed, Morris reported, they had even begun to "cast about for the person." Such a ploy to obstruct a democratic election "appeared to me a *wild Measure*," Morris scoffed, explaining that he had "endeavored to dissuade those gentlemen" from their ill-conceived plan. What mattered, Morris underscored, was the principle of majority rule. "Since it was evidently the intention of our fellow citizens to make Mr. Jefferson their President," he calmly observed, "it seems proper to fulfill that intention. . . . The anti-federal party is, beyond question, the most numerous at present" and hence, he concluded, entitled to its victory.

Federalists were engaged in a dangerous sport, Hamilton agreed. "The game of preventing an election & leaving the Executive power in the hands of a future President of the Senate," he said, "would be for obvious reasons a most dangerous and unbecoming policy." Caleb Strong, the newly elected Federalist governor of Massachusetts, shared their view. Many citizens might not be happy with the election of Jefferson, he recognized, and yet those citizens must "reflect, that, in republicks, the opinion of the majority must prevail; and that obedience to the laws, and respect for constitutional authority are essential to the character of good citizens." No textbook writer on American government could have said it better.

But the following week, Jefferson learned that the Federalist plot to deny him the presidency was moving forward. "The Feds appeared determined to pass a bill giving the government to Mr. Jay . . . or to Marshall," he briefed Madison. Madison read Jefferson's letter with horror, appalled that Federalists meant to "strangle the election of the people and smuggle into the Chief Magistracy the creature of a faction." Were Federalists, the very men who had fought for the Constitution and who formed the "virtuous" ruling elite, now ready to turn the concept of civic virtue upside down? "It would seem that every individual member who has any standing or stake in society," Madison exclaimed, "or any portion of virtue or sober understanding, must revolt at the tendency of such a maneuver." But how should Republicans respond? Madison's mind raced from scenario to scenario. Should they acquiesce in the Federalist "suspension or usurpation of Executive authority" until the next congressional session in December 1801? Or should Jefferson and Burr call for a special session of Congress? Finally he concluded that it was simply best to hope that nine states in the House of Representatives would reach a "proper decision."

While Morris, Hamilton, Strong, and others were simply resigned to choosing "among Rotten Apples," other Federalists, bent on barring Jefferson from the executive mansion, cried for action. For James Bayard, Delaware's one representative in Congress, it was nothing less than a matter of the life of the republic. "There would be really cause to fear," he wrote, "that the government would not survive the course of moral & political experiments to which it would be subjected in the hands of Mr. Jefferson." Other Federalists, too, worried about the safety of their property. "Stocks have fallen," Fisher Ames anxiously informed a friend, "and rich men have begun to find out that they ought to bestir themselves."

During the tumultuous month of December, another play was being performed in the federal city, starring the ghost of George Washington. That winter, representatives debated the construction of an appropriate monument to the "indispensable man," who had died exactly twelve months earlier. Such a monument would "place his remains in the centre of the capitol," one writer noted in the National Intelligencer, "in the heart and bosom of the nation, where its laws are discussed and agreed to." Some representatives argued in favor of a mausoleum for the president's remains — "a structure well calculated to resist the ravages of time." Others wanted to erect an equestrian statue that would inspire the beholder with "lively emotions." Some saw no purpose in yet another likeness of the president, while others deplored the banality of a pyramid-shaped heap of stones. No structure, announced one representative, could ever be "commensurate to the object." And a "Distant Subscriber" to the National Intelligencer recommended a monument of paper, proposing that "a superb edition of one or two thousand copies" of all of Washington's public writings "be distributed and deposited in every public library in the United States, in Europe, and every other part of the civilized world."

Evenly divided between a monument and a statue, members of Congress could not decide to appropriate money for either one. And so the session ended in indecision, like the presidential election itself.

That winter, Federalist politicians in Washington decided to play a high-risk game of cards, and the wild card was named Aaron Burr.

"It is fashionable with feds to declare in favor of Mr. Burr," Federalist Joseph Hale informed Rufus King. Federalists pounced on a new strategy. They would support Aaron Burr, the dapper, unprincipled candidate from New York. Here was the chance, one Federalist told Hamilton, to sow "the seeds of a mortal division" among Republicans and simultaneously frustrate the ascension of the "ambitious" state of Virginia, all without voiding a democratic election. Ideologically, Burr seemed the safer choice.

The idea of supporting Burr as a way to block Jefferson's ascension had been on the minds of some Federalists since the summer. If they couldn't win the election, wouldn't they do well to turn the election from Jefferson to Burr? George Cabot had asked Hamilton that August. Whereas Jefferson was motivated by a dangerous admiration for Jacobin theories, Cabot explained, Burr was "actuated by ordinary ambition." Burr "may be satisfied by power & property," Cabot noted, but Jefferson "must see the roots of our Society pulled up & a new course of cultivation substituted." "It is granted that [Burr] is ambitious," the Boston *Centinel* blithely noted, "but he is no hypocrite." That was certainly true. Burr had never claimed to believe in anything grander or larger than himself. The reasons for supporting Burr, admitted Theodore Sedgwick, "are of a *negative* nature." Burr was "*not* a Democrat . . . *not* an enthusiastic theorist . . . *not* under the direction of Virginian Jacobins . . . *not* a declared infidel." He was selfish, pronounced Sedgwick, transforming unfettered self-interest into a virtue. That "very selfishness," Sedgwick believed, would prevent Burr from harming the economic interests of the Federalists, whereas Jefferson "would begin by democratizing the people and throwing everything into their hands."

And, Federalists told one another, they might be able to have Burr in their pocket. The New Yorker appeared willing "to consider the federalists as his friends," Delaware representative James Bayard wrote to Hamilton, "and to accept the office of president as their gift. I take it for granted that Mr. Burr would not only gladly accept the office, but will neglect no means in his power to secure it." The ultimate backroom deal: the ambitious candidate of one party, betraying his friends and associates, makes a secret agreement with the leaders of the party opposite. Federalists would "buy" Burr, and Republican ideologues like Jefferson would find themselves locked out of power. "Burr or no President," remarked New Yorker William Cooper, was "the order of the day."

Could Federalists have confidence in Burr? "It is much safer to trust a knave than a fool," remarked one Connecticut Federalist. But was Burr even interested? He was not showing his cards. From Albany, where he was spending the winter, attending to his duties in the New York State Assembly, he professed loyalty to his running mate and party, exclaiming that any Federalist coup would be met "by a resort to the sword." People "would dishonor my Views and insult my feelings," he remonstrated in a letter to Republican representative Samuel Smith, "by harbouring a suspicion that I could submit to be instrumental in counteracting the Wishes & expectations of the U.S." But when Burr penned that letter, on December 16, he was still under the impression that Jefferson had won the election. Two weeks later, he would sing a different tune.

A certain "Gentleman," Burr informed Smith on December 29, had asked him to state categorically that, if chosen president by the House, he would "engage to resign." Burr refused outright. The request itself, he said, was an insult, "unnecessary, unreasonable and impertinent." "I have . . . made no reply," he informed Smith. "If I had made any I should have told that as at present advised, I should not." In other words, Burr would not make a public pledge to withdraw from the race for president.

A few days after mailing that letter — but before Smith received it — Burr and Smith arranged to meet in Philadelphia. Accounts of their conversation were leaked to newspapers, and the *New York Gazette* reported that Mr. Burr had insinuated that he felt as competent to exercise the presidential functions as Mr. Jefferson. Dejected, Smith left Philadelphia. He had expected Burr to give him authority to announce that he would not serve if elected by the House. But Burr had agreed to no such thing. All Smith could do now was try to convince Burr that

Republicans had to hang together. "The feds will attempt to disunite us," he wrote to Burr. "We must not believe any thing that comes from them, we must be on our guards." Not only were Republicans standing firm for Jefferson, he stressed, but they all retained faith in Burr's loyalty. "Again let me intreat you to believe," Smith concluded, "that your Friends express the highest confidence in you — Disregard every report to the contrary."

But would Burr stay on board? A Federalist attorney from New York, David Ogden, claimed to have met with Burr. Burr denied ever having spoken to "a Mr. O," but Delaware Federalist James Bayard informed Hamilton that "persons friendly to Mr. Burr" had made it "distinctly understood" that Burr was willing to consider the Federalists "as his friends."

Had Burr decided to collaborate with the Feds? Hearsay — if not hard evidence — was mounting.

In late December, South Carolina Federalist Robert Goodloe Harper, one of the congressional "desperadoes" most opposed to Jefferson, had written to Burr, conspiratorially urging him to "keep the game perfectly in your hands" and cautioning him to leave no paper trail. "Do not answer this letter," Harper counseled, "or any other that may be written to you by a Federalist man, nor write to any of that party." On January 11, Smith reported to Burr that Ogden had tried to persuade New York and New Jersey Republicans to switch their votes to Burr. Five days later, Burr wrote again to Samuel Smith, repeating his promise of December 16 not to stand in Jefferson's way. The story was very complicated, Burr suggested, adding that he had no time to enter into details that "would take reams of paper and years of time." On January 13, Hamilton informed Gouverneur Morris that, although Federalists had indeed made overtures to Burr, Burr had declined to give any "assurances" to the Feds. Was Burr simply following Harper's advice?

Whatever may have been transpiring between Burr and the Federalists, Burr and Jefferson were falling all over themselves, emotively reassuring each other of loyalty and respect. Jefferson implored Burr to discount a letter, attributed to Jefferson, containing "highly injurious" remarks about Burr. "I affirm it solemnly to be a forgery," he swore. Jefferson was clearly on edge. "With the common trash of slander I should not think of troubling you," Jefferson explained, "but the forgery of one's handwriting is too imposing to be neglected." And ten days later, Burr beseeched Jefferson to pay no attention to the "most malignant Spirit of slander" and to the tales that were "calculated to disturb our harmony," exhorting the vice president to accept his "very great Respect & Esteem."

While the rumors passed from mouth to mouth, some Republicans caucused, pledging to one another that they would not give up Jefferson. Bravely Republicans tried to maintain a united front, closing ranks, even defending Burr. "No man placed in his situation could have acted with more propriety," noted Nathaniel Macon, who would soon be the new speaker in the Republican-dominated House of Representatives. Burr had repudiated the "feudalists," Elbridge Gerry wrote to Jefferson, assuring him that Burr wanted nothing to do with the "perfidy and enmity to this country" of the Federalists. But people reported that Madison blamed Burr, his fellow Princeton alumnus, for the turn of events. America would be *"degraded,"* the Virginian wrote, "by the attempt to elect Burr President." More than two decades later, Madison would reveal that he had always believed that Burr was responsible for the tie in the Electoral College, the source of the whole crisis. The electors of either New York or Virginia, Madison believed, had been given false information by Burr or by one of his agents indicating that the other state would withhold votes from Burr. Because of this strategem, neither state withheld votes from Burr, giving him and Jefferson an equal number of votes.

And what did Jefferson himself *really* think? Burr's "conduct has been honorable and decisive," he wrote to his daughter in January. But in 1807, Jefferson would admit that he had never believed that Burr was "an honest, frank-dealing man, but considered him as a crooked gun, or other perverted machine, whose aim or stroke you could never be sure of."

What game was the New Yorker playing? "Burr is a cunning man," wrote Federalist Uriah Tracy. "If he cannot outwit all the Jeffersonians, I do not know the man."

Burr "is bankrupt beyond redemption," wrote Alexander Hamilton, wracked by the deepest personal loathing and contempt for his fellow New Yorker and future slayer. No one was more objectionable to Hamilton than Aaron Burr. Not only was he "a voluptuary in the extreme," but his aim was *"permanent power* and with it *wealth."* He possessed "no principle, public or private," Hamilton railed. "As to his theory," he jeered, "no mortal can tell what it is." Burr was simply the "most unfit man in the U.S. for the office of President."

Enraged that more and more Federalists were joining the Burr bandwagon, frustrated that he was helpless to stop them, over and over again Hamilton lashed out at Burr. Firing off angry letters in every direction at once, Hamilton alerted his allies not to trust the corrupt, amoral New Yorker. Even if Burr made promises to them, "he will laugh in his sleeve when he makes them and he will break them the first moment it may serve his purpose." Burr was merely using the Federalists "as the *tools* of his aggrandisement," he warned. "Adieu to the Federal Troy if they once introduce this Grecian horse into their citadel."

In a lengthy letter to James Bayard, Hamilton attempted a dispassionate comparison of the two presidential front-runners, outlining their defects and qualities. Although he considered Jefferson "crafty," "not very mindful of truth," and "a contemptible hypocrite" whose politics were "tinctured with fanaticism," he felt that ultimately Jefferson warranted "the expectation of a temporizing rather than a violent system." Burr, on the other hand, was a man of "*extreme & irregular ambition*," "more cunning than wise," and "inferior in real ability to Jefferson."

Improbably, Hamilton disclaimed any personal antipathy for Burr, insisting that "with Burr I have always been personally well." "If there be a man in the world I ought to hate," he continued, "it is Jefferson." But the paramount criterion of "the public good" led him to prefer Jefferson over Burr. Even the good of the Federalist Party pointed to Jefferson. Federalists, Hamilton cautioned, should not make themselves complicit in the corrupt administration of Aaron Burr. On the contrary, there should be a clear distinction between those in the administration and those in the opposition. "If Jefferson is president, the whole responsibility of bad measures will rest with the anti-federalists. If Burr is made so by the federalists," he reasoned, "the whole responsibility will rest with them," and Federalists would have to "answer for all the evils of his bad conduct." Compromised by Burr, Federalists would inevitably disintegrate into "a disorganized and contemptible party." "Depend upon it, men never played a more foolish game than will do the federalists, if they support Burr," Hamilton wrote to Gouverneur Morris.

But was Hamilton still a credible witness? His attacks on President Adams had diminished his prestige, and he no longer enjoyed the protection of George Washington. Hamilton was "*radically deficient* in discretion," Robert Troup admitted, branding him "an unfit head of the party." Hamilton himself, Troup noted, had "declared that his influence with the federal party was wholly gone." For his part, Hamilton wanted nothing whatsoever to do with a party that supported Aaron Burr. "I shall be obliged to consider myself as an isolated man," he said. "It will be impossible for me to reconcile with my notions of *honor* or policy . . . a Party which . . . will have degraded itself & the country."

In the winter of 1800–1801, no one could predict the outcome of the election. Support for Burr among Federalists, Sedgwick observed in late January, "has been increasing until it has become nearly unanimous." "What will be the plans of the Federalists?" a bewildered Albert Gallatin, the prominent Swiss-born Republican representative from Pennsylvania, wrote to his wife in mid-January. "Will they usurp the Presidential powers? . . . I see some danger in the fate of the election." Would Federalists elect Burr? Would they call for new elections? Would they force a stalemate and then hand power over to one of their own? Would any Federalist be "bold enough to place himself in front as an usurper"? Would there be civil war? Resistance? "Shall we submit?" Gallatin wondered. "And if we do not submit, in what manner shall we act ourselves?"

Politicians found themselves entangled in a web of plots, deception, promises, ambitions, and secret deals. The unfinished city of Washington provided them with neither relief nor escape from the political cauldron. "A few, indeed, drink, and some gamble," a lonely Gallatin wrote to his wife, "but the majority drink naught but politics, and by not mixing with men of different or more moderate activities they inflame one another."

"Rumors are various, and intrigues great," observed Gouverneur Morris in early February.

And where did President John Adams, the loser in the presidential contest, stand in the crisis? The electoral defeat had deeply disappointed Adams, who was in mourning for his son Charles, his thoughts sadly focused on the young man "who was once the delight of my Eyes and a darling of my heart." The president was sinking into "a state of deep dejection," his friends whispered. "His feelings are not to be envied."

A few months earlier, in the spring of 1800, on the day it became clear that Jefferson had won all the electors in New York, the Virginian had asked to meet with the president. "Well," Adams said to his vice president, "I understand that you are to beat me in this contest." "Mr. Adams," replied Jefferson, "this is no personal contest between you and me. Two systems of principles on the subject of government divide our fellow citizens into two parties. With one of these you concur, and I with the other. . . . Were we both to die to-day, to-morrow two other names would be in the place of ours." The president promised to be a "faithful subject" if Jefferson should win the election and expressed the hope that the matter would not "affect our personal dispositions."

Now, in the cold winter months of 1800–1801, after Jefferson learned that Federalists wanted to circumvent his electoral victory, he crossed paths with President Adams on Pennsylvania Avenue. During their brief conversation, Jefferson voiced alarm at the "incalculable consequences" of the Federalists' plan to support Burr or to let the presidency devolve upon a president of the Senate. But brushing him off, Adams vehemently said, "Sir, the event of the election is within your own power" and went on to enumerate the political promises and concessions that Jefferson would have to make to Federalists in order to gain their support. "I will not come into the government by capitulation," Jefferson hotly replied. "I will not enter on it, but in perfect freedom to follow the dictates of my own judgment." "Then," said Adams, "things must take their course." It was one of the last face-to-face meetings the two old friends would ever have.

Still, Burr's improbable rise "like a balloon, filled with inflammable air," left Adams in dismay. There was so much talent among both Federalists and Republicans that Adams was pained to witness the ascension of someone he considered utterly devoid of integrity. "Mr. Burr's good fortune," the president wrote, "surpasses all ordinary rules, and exceeds that of Bonaparte." But even worse was the encouragement to party intrigue and corruption. "What course is it we steer and to what harbor are we bound," Adams sighed, admitting, "I am wholly at a loss."

But as the crisis dragged on through the winter months, Adams seemed to stand aside, aloof, unwilling to intervene. Why, he demanded, would the Federalists' circumvention of an election constitute more of a "political convulsion" than the election of Jefferson or Burr? "The President would be as legal in one case as in either of the others,"

Adams wrote, "and the people as well satisfied." Adams, Madison caustically observed, had "infinitely sunk in the estimation of all parties." When, later that winter, Adams called a special session of the Senate for March 4, anxious Republicans wondered if the president had more up his sleeve than confirmation of the new president's cabinet appointments. As Jefferson's term as vice president expired, was Adams setting the stage for the election of a Federalist president pro tempore of the lame-duck Senate who would become the interim chief executive?

All was "dead calm" in the nation, the *New England Palladium* improbably reported in January, in the midst of all the commotion. The *Palladium* claimed that Republicans were disappointed that Federalists conducted themselves with "propriety and dignity" and that there were "no tumults, no harangues, no associations, no missions to distant parts of the country."

Dead calm? That same day, the *Gazette of the United States* warned that only "bold resistance" could save the country "from the horrors and devastations of a civil war."

On January 20, in the snow-covered town of Washington, there were suddenly flames. A fire spread through the building housing the Treasury Department. Citizens — including President Adams himself — rushed out in the cold to put out the fire, passing buckets of water. That past November, a fire had broken out in the offices of the War Department. Had the fire been deliberately set? people still wondered. Now, after the second fire, the *Aurora* screamed that it was a case of arson, claiming that one witness saw "former Treasury Secretary Oliver Wolcott removing trunks of materials from the Treasury Department while the fire rages!" Was the fire a cover-up to hide Federalist support for slave rebellions, as some southern Republicans believed, or had it been set, as the *Aurora* charged, to destroy proof of Federalist mismanagement and misappropriations of funds? The Federalist secretary of the treasury, Samuel Dexter, "has been rather unfortunate in fire works," the *Aurora* dryly editorialized.

Fear and frenzy were reaching their zenith. The *Salem Federalist* predicted that when the "Philosopher" (Jefferson) gets into the presidential chair, he will "declare himself permanent!" Would there be violence, too? One Federalist was quoted proposing that "every democrat should be put to death in order to secure the government in the former hands." There were reports in mid-December and again in early January that threats had been made on Jefferson's life.

Several times in January the *Aurora* reported that Federalists intended to send the marines to Washington to install their own government. Perhaps led by Hamilton, these Federalists supposedly planned to seize forts, arsenals, stores, and arms to retain power, a Pennsylvania Republican told Jefferson, warning that the judiciary was on the Federalist side. Governors Monroe of Virginia and McKean of Pennsylvania threatened that their states would secede if Jefferson's election were impeded. To keep informed hour by hour of developments in Washington, Monroe set up his own system of couriers riding back and forth between Richmond and Washington.

Panic and paranoia gripped Republicans and Federalists alike, highlighting the distrust and the ideological abyss between them. In mid-January, amidst fears of civil war, the stability and future of the constitutional system in doubt, Federalists in the House of Representatives, in a bizarre, untimely move, decided to debate the renewal of the Sedition Act. "How could the rights of the people require a liberty to utter falsehoods?" demanded conservative Federalist Samuel Dana of Connecticut. "How could it be right to do wrong?"

The confusion in Washington baffled even the cool Gouverneur Morris. "You, who are temperate in drinking," he wrote to Hamilton, "have never perhaps noticed the awkward situation of a man, who continues sober after the company are drunk."

Jefferson awakens to see snowflakes falling outside his window. "This is the morning of the election by the H of R.," he writes to a friend on Wednesday, February 11, minutes before leaving his lodgings. The odds appear in his favor, and yet, he comments soberly, "the defects of our Constitution under circumstances like the present, appear very great."

From their rooming houses in the federal city, senators, representatives, and the vice president trudge through the snow to the Capitol, shielding their faces from the biting wind. One Republican representative, the ailing Joseph Nicholson of Maryland, is carried two miles on a cot, against the advice of his doctors. His vote in his divided state delegation is crucial. The wife of congressman Craik of Maryland threatens to divorce him if he doesn't vote for Jefferson.

In the new Capitol, only one wing of which — the Senate — had been completed, Vice President Thomas Jefferson stands before the joint session of Congress in the high-ceilinged, elegant chamber. He reads out loud for the first time the official tally of the vote in the Electoral College. Senators file out, leaving representatives to resolve the electoral tie. The members of the House of Representatives decide to work around the clock, taking as many votes as necessary, determined not to adjourn or to discuss any other business until the presidential election is decided. The sole choice now seems to be between Jefferson and Burr. But a critical deadline looms: Adams's term will expire on March 4. If they cannot break their deadlock, there will be a constitutional crisis.

At one o'clock, balloting begins. Eight states call out their votes for Jefferson: New York, New Jersey, Pennsylvania, Virginia, North Carolina, Kentucky, Georgia, and Tennessee. Six states cast ballots for Burr: New Hampshire, Massachusetts, Rhode Island, Connecticut, Delaware, and South Carolina. The delegations from two states, Vermont and Maryland, are divided and do not vote. Neither candidate can muster the 9 votes needed to win.

A second ballot is taken. Same result.

A third round. Same result.

Three more ballots immediately follow. No one yields. Intransigence on both sides. Representatives break for an hour. They vote eight more times. No change. Another break.

At nine o'clock balloting is still going on. The sickly Representative Nicholson lies on his cot in the committee-room, nursed by his wife, who helps him write out his votes. Equipped with pillows and nightcaps, representatives prepare to spend the night. Beds as well as meals are sent to the House, one witness notes, for the "accommodation of those whom age or debility disabled from enduring such a long protracted sitting." Wrapped in their greatcoats and shawls, stretched out on beds, sprawled on the floor, hunched over in their seats, they try to doze. "If our opponents will not take Burr," writes Connecticut Federalist Roger Griswold to his wife that evening, "they shall take nobody."

At one o'clock in the morning, members are awakened to vote again. Nothing has changed.

At two o'clock, as snow continues to fall outside, another vote is taken. No change. At two-thirty in the morning, representatives rouse themselves again to cast yet another ballot. When the sky begins to lighten, they vote for the twenty-seventh time. No one has budged.

Messengers scurry back and forth from the Capitol to the office of the *National Intelligencer*, bringing the results of each ballot. That night, writes the wife of the editor of the *Intelligencer*, "I never lay down or closed my eyes. As the hour drew near its close, my heart would almost audibly beat and I was seized with a tremour that almost disabled me from opening the door for the expected messenger."

The next day, Thursday, February 12, representatives vote once more. Deadlock. The *Washington Federalist* reports on the tense situation, "the happiness of five millions of people awfully suspended in the balance!"

On Friday, February 13, two more votes are taken. In vain. Between votes, representatives eat, drink, sleep, and mull over the results of the last ballot, comparing their reactions, some discussing their hopes that at least one vote will change, others gloomily anticipating the consequences of the stalemate. "I have not closed my eyes for thirty-six hours," writes John Dawson to James Madison. "We are resolved never to yield."

Riders traveling day and night carry news from Jefferson to Governor Monroe in Richmond. Rumors spread that if the deadlock persists, Secretary of State John Marshall will be named president. "If the union could be broken," Monroe writes, "that would do it." Both he and Governor McKean are making arrangements to mobilize their state militias should there be a usurpation. On February 11, Monroe learns that 22,000 Republicans in Pennsylvania are "prepared to take up arms in the event of extremities." He worries that Federalists in Virginia may try to disarm the state militia. Did Jefferson, McKean, and Monroe know that in 1799 Alexander Hamilton, then commander of the American army, had seriously proposed sending troops to Virginia to "put Virginia to the Test of resistance"? On February 12, a Virginia congressman advises Monroe to consider measures "to guard against a situation truly awful." Steps are taken to secure the federal arsenal in New London, Virginia, and to prevent any removal of weapons. Some Republicans urge Monroe to convene the state legislature, in case emergency legislation is required to prevent a Federalist coup. "If anything requires decision on our part," Monroe responds on February 12, "be assured it will not be wanting." Reports filter into Washington that citizens in Philadelphia have seized the public arms. "By all means, preserve the city quiet," writes a worried Gallatin to a friend in Pennsylvania. Soon after he discovers that the rumor was false.

The crisis is "momentous," hollers the *Washington Federalist*. But if it comes to violence, the 70,000-member well-armed militia of Massachusetts, that paper contends, will easily quash the untrained men of Virginia and Pennsylvania, carrying "cornstalks instead of muskets." Fifteen hundred men from Maryland are said to be preparing to travel to Washington on the fourth of March, reports Gallatin, "for the purpose of putting to death the usurping pretended President."

"Nothing new to-day," Gallatin writes on Saturday, February 14. "Three ballots, making in all 33, result the same."

Federalists hold several caucuses. They acknowledge that "nothing but desperate measures remain" in order to block Jefferson. But will they go that far? "We broke up each time," one representative reports, "in confusion and discord." Representatives decide to postpone more balloting until Monday at noon.

Sunday, February 15: a pause in the action.

"The scene passing here," Jefferson somberly writes to his daughter on that day of rest, "makes me pant to be away from it, to fly from the circle of cabal, intrigue and hatred, to one where all is love and peace." The courtesy and civility that make social life both possible and pleasurable seem to be collapsing, undoing "the whole labor of our lives." On Sunday too, Jefferson describes for James Monroe the political standoff: "Four days of balloting have produced not a single change of a vote," he writes. People are saying that there might be a change, but the usually optimistic Jefferson is skeptical: "I know of no foundation for this belief." Federalists, he notes, tried to pass a law giving the executive power to one of their own, but Republicans announced "openly and firmly" that the "middle States would *arm*, & that no such usurpation, even for a single day, should be submitted to." If force is required, so be it. He would not object to the election of Burr, for that would be constitutional, but he repeats that he would stand for no "usurpation."

The specter of a "convention" to reorganize and amend the government is raised by Republicans, Jefferson also reports to Monroe. Federalists are "completely alarmed" by the word *convention*, for it evokes the violence and terror of the Revolution in France. Given the "present democratical spirit of America," writes Jefferson to Monroe, the idea of a convention gives Federalists "the horrors," for they fear losing some of their "favorite morsels of the constitution."

On Sunday too, Pennsylvania lawyer Alexander Dallas observes that any Federalist attempt to give the presidency to a Federalist officer of the government "will irritate and inflame the calmest and coolest among us." Even Federalists are alarmed, he remarks. Those of "property and character here are terrified and disgusted."

"Rest assured that *we* will not yield," writes Gallatin. Deadlock.

That week, Federalist James Bayard has enjoyed the distinction of being the single most powerful man in the Congress, for he alone, as Delaware's only representative, bears the entire responsibility for casting Delaware's 1 vote. He is a strong supporter of Burr. Can he be persuaded to switch to Jefferson? It is rumored that Bayard wants assurances from the Virginian, promises that he will retain some Federalists in his administration, that he will continue to support Federalist credit policies as well as maintain a navy.

Republican Samuel Smith decides to take matters into his own hands. He meets first with Jefferson and then with Bayard. He feels Jefferson out on several issues and then reports to Bayard that Jefferson would do nothing to change certain key Federalist policies or remove certain men. Later Smith explains that Jefferson did not have "the remotest idea of my object" and had no knowledge that Smith was acting as a go-between with Bayard. "I was satisfied in my own mind that [Jefferson's] conduct . . . would be so and so," Smith writes. "But I certainly never did tell [Bayard] that I had any authority from Mr. Jefferson to communicate anything to him." On February 15, Jefferson gives his own account of the story: he was approached by people wanting to "obtain terms & promises from me," he tells Monroe. Would he agree to follow Federalist policies in exchange for their votes? "I have declared to them unequivocally," he asserts, "that I would not receive the government on capitulation, that I would not go into it with my hands tied." Burr hears rumors that Jefferson has "compromized" with the Federalists. His own ambiguous conduct notwithstanding, he comments, in an act of exquisite chutzpah, that the stories have "excited some anxiety" among New York Republicans.

What really transpired? Smith met with Jefferson and then met with Bayard, and . . . Bayard, swallowing hard, decided not to oppose Jefferson, admitting that if he continues to support Burr, it will only be "at the expense of the Constitution." Later on, he explains that he wanted to preserve not only the Constitution but also the people's choice: "*I was chiefly influenced by the current of public sentiment,* which I thought it neither safe nor politic to counteract." Or did he believe that Jefferson had agreed to Federalist terms? On Saturday, February 14, Bayard tells a few people that on Monday he will vote for Jefferson.

Monday morning: Federalists caucus. Bayard announces that he will cast his vote for Jefferson. "Deserter!" one man shouts. "The clamor," Bayard will later recall, "was prodigious, the reproaches vehement." Consternation. Confusion. The meeting breaks up, some Federalists proclaiming that they will "go without a constitution & take the risk of civil war" rather than vote for "such a wretch as Jefferson." Federalists succeed in prevailing upon Bayard to give them more time: letters from Burr are expected. Perhaps it is not too late to strike a deal.

The House votes again. "We have balloted for the 34th time," writes Gallatin to a friend, "and the result is still the same."

The letters from Burr finally arrive: Federalists' hopes are quashed. Burr "explicitly resigns his pretentions," writes a dejected Theodore Sedgwick to his son, concluding, "The Gigg is, therefore, up."

That same day, the *Gazette of the United States* charges that the "bold and imperious partisans of Mr. Jefferson" are planning to march on Washington and "dethrone" any usurper. "Are they then ripe for civil war," asks the *Gazette,* "and ready to imbrue their hands in kindred blood?" The *National Intelligencer* warns of violence and urges calm. "During that period of deep suspense, which may be yet to come," the *Intelligencer* editorializes, "it behooves the people of the United States to manifest that spirit of dignified and commanding fortitude. . . . It is right that public opinion should express itself. Let it then be expressed with respectful firmness from one end of the union to the other. Let the representatives of the people know the will of the people, and *they will obey.*"

On Tuesday, February 17, at noon, another vote, the thirty-fifth. Deadlock.

Federalists caucus again. They are weary; the mood is tense and grim. The Federalist members of the divided delegations of the states of Vermont and Maryland suddenly decide to abstain in their state votes, permitting those two states to cast their ballots for Jefferson. They realize that, merely by abstaining, they are determining the course of American history. Incidentally, Bayard is spared the embarrassment of casting his vote for Jefferson. About that final bargain, Bayard would later write that "the step was not taken until it was admitted on all hands that we must risk the Constitution and a civil war or take Mr. Jefferson." He would also confide to John Adams that his state of Delaware, the smallest in the union, depended on the Constitution for its "political existence."

At one o'clock, a few minutes after the Federalist caucus, another vote, the thirty-sixth. Maryland votes for Jefferson. "Spitting Matt" Lyon of Vermont, who languished for four months in jail for sedition, proudly announces the vote of the Green Mountain state. South Carolina casts a blank ballot, and, to the jeers and hoots of some of his Federalist colleagues, James Bayard too casts a blank. The tie is broken. Jefferson wins ten states. In the end, four New England states stick with Burr; not one Federalist member of the House of Representatives casts a vote for Jefferson.

The Virginian is victorious. "The storm we have passed through," he announces to Lafayette, "proves our vessel indestructible."

Sixteen cannon are fired in the Jeffersonian stronghold of Baltimore. Across the country, explosions of joy: parades, balls, bonfires, barbecues, and feasts, with toasts to the Constitution, to freedom of the press, and to the "tree of Liberty moistened by the tears of Aristocracy." In Philadelphia, the bells of Christ Church are rung wildly, provoking Abigail Adams to object to the ringing of the bells for "an infidel." "Nothing could then equal the general joy which our citizens expressed. Huzzas echo through the City until morning," the *National Intelligencer* reports the following day. "The voice of the People has prevailed and Thomas Jefferson is declared by the Representatives of the People to be duly elected President of the United States." The *Gazette of the United States* relays "alarming intelligence" that "four democrats burst their sides with laughing; twenty-seven huzzaed till they were seized by the lock-jaw til their mouths wide open; and three hundred are now drunk beyond the hope of recovery. Gin and Whiskey are said to have risen in price, 50 per cent." And a would-be poet publishes his own opus:

> Now roar the cannon, loud the halo! sounds,
> The public joy can scarce be kept in bounds;
> Each patriot hails the tidings from afar,

Of peace returning and the death of war;
For JEFFERSON's elected chief of state
To guide the helm and check the lewd debate;
Protect his country from each threat'ning harm,
"Ride in the whirlwind and direct the storm!"

"The defeat of the Federalists in the elections of 1800," one political scientist would later observe, "represented the first occasion in modern politics in which an incumbent political party suffered an electoral defeat and *simply turned over power* to its opponents." *Simply* turned over power? Hardly. Much would be made in later years of the astonishing, peaceful shift in power. Astonishing, yes. Peaceful? No.

Republicans had triumphed, achieving a singular victory. The Federalists were the villains of the drama — and yet, they were also the heroes.

Despite their paralyzing fears of Jefferson's Frenchified politics, despite their profound antipathy for his democratic principles and ideals, despite their incendiary language, anti-Republican pamphlets and articles, and their eight years of raving against the wild-eyed visionary and atheist, despite the rumors of civil war, despite their schemes to block Jefferson, despite the intense strain on the constitutional consensus, Federalists did not persist in prolonging the deadlock — as they might have — until after the expiration of Adams's term and then try to appoint one of their allies. After months of plotting, they ultimately permitted the orderly, constitutional transfer of power and followed to the letter the procedures outlined in the Constitution.

It might all have turned out differently had it not been for Hamilton's loathing for Burr, Burr's indecision, Jefferson's steely determination to claim his victory, the restraint of leaders of both parties, and perhaps, most important, the wait-and-see attitude of citizens around the country, who, despite the mounting tension, looked to Washington for a decision before taking matters — and arms — into their own hands.

Verbal aggression did not explode, as it typically does, into physical violence. Unlike in France, on neither the Federalist nor the Republican side was there a slide into extremism. Although the potential for disruption had been real, no secession took place, no coup d'état, no attempts to change the Constitution, no military confrontations, no assassinations. Two years earlier, when they passed the Sedition Act, it had been the Federalists' intention to suppress opposition. But now willingly — if reluctantly — they handed over power to their political adversaries. Indeed, they were the first political incumbents in modern history to do so, setting a luminous example that virtually no future revolutionaries would choose to emulate.

What was their motivation? Was it political pragmatism? The realization that Republicans had captured not only the executive branch but both houses of Congress, and that Federalists could not have governed without some kind of mandate? Was it also the comforting, compensatory knowledge that die-hard Federalists in New England still wielded undisputed political control in their states? Or was it, as James Madison believed, the absence of a standing army that helped make the peaceful transition a reality? "What a lesson to America and the world," he rejoiced a week after Jefferson's victory, "is given by the efficacy of the public will when there is no army to be turned against it." Or might it also have been a question of class? The realization that most Federalists and Republicans, though they often spoke as if they belonged to two separate nations, were largely gentlemen of the same nation and same social class who shared the same past, the same privileged status, the same memories of courageous rebellion and war, the same commitment to the Constitution and to the principles of life, liberty, and the pursuit of happiness? "Presidents, Secretaries, Generals and Ministers — myself among them, may be removed," commented a sage Rufus King in London, "still the machine will move on!" Even Jefferson's Maryland foe, Robert Goodloe Harper, had had a change of heart. "Because he is President," Harper wrote, "I shall be one of the last to oppose, thwart, or embarrass his administration."

The Constitution had survived a major political crisis, its validity unquestioned; the Bill of Rights had been wounded by the Sedition Act but could recover; and now there was a party system — well, almost. And the precedent had been established — even though it would not be followed for years — that opposing parties, both equally legitimate, would alternately govern.

Orderly party conflict had at least partially replaced the aspiration for political consensus. In his Farewell Address, Washington had memorably branded parties "potent engines, by which cunning, ambitious and unprincipled men will be enabled to *subvert* the Power of the People, and to usurp for themselves the reins of Government." But the opposite proved to be true, for parties were a means of *restoring* power to the people. Through party politics, a majority of citizens could find their voice and recapture power. Despite Abigail Adams's dyspeptic judgment that "party spirit is blind, malevolent, uncandid, ungenerous, unjust and unforgiving," despite the founders' fears that factions and parties would *weaken* the polity, this early creation of organized opposition *strengthened* the young republic. How? By according legitimacy to dissent. The nation was sufficiently unified in citizens' commitment to the Constitution to permit organized opposition to the party in power. The world of government and the world of adversarial party politics had become one. Ultimately the election of 1800 demonstrated that the essence — and the durability — of democratic politics reside in conflict. Great political parties, defined by a political faith, organized around significant ideas and not around individuals, may disturb and shake up a society, commented the great Tocqueville, but, he added, they may also save it.

"The Revolution of 1776 is now, and for the first time, *arrived at its completion*," cheered the *Aurora* the day after Jefferson's triumph. "Till now the Republicans have indeed beaten the slaves of monarchy in the field of battle, and driven the troops of the King of Great Britain from the shores of our country; but the *secret enemies of the American Revolution* — her internal, insidious, and indefatigable foes, have never till now been completely discomfited. This is the true period of the triumph of Republican principle."

The *Aurora* had it dead wrong. The American Revolution had "arrived at its completion" not because Republicans had "completely discomfited" the nation's "internal, insidious, and indefatigable foes," but rather because those "foes" had survived, had been willing to hand over power and become the "opposition." Neither side had crushed the other.

And on another point, too, the *Aurora* had it dead wrong. The Federalists were in no way the "secret enemies of the American Revolution." On the contrary, it was they who had taken the lead in drafting the Constitution and creating a strong, united, and prosperous nation. Praising the Federalist period, Tocqueville called it "one of the luckiest circumstances" in American history. The democratization that would occur under Jefferson, Tocqueville felt, would have happened sooner or later. But he credited the Federalists with founding the stable institutions that permitted the young republic to "face without ill consequences the rapid development of the very doctrines they had opposed."

In February 1801, the "fathers" of American society, the virtuous few whom citizens, for decades, had trusted and to whom they had deferred, demonstrated that they were resilient enough to accept political defeat, transfer power to their political enemies, and wait — patiently playing the part of the loyal opposition — for the next election. A free two-party system, especially one in which all citizens would eventually come to enjoy the right to vote, would take away any moral right to revolution. Revolution in America would henceforth be politically superfluous. If there was to be a democratic revolution, it could take place at the polls.

At the threshold of a new century, this was why the American Revolution was finally complete.

11

March 4, 1801

MARCH 4, 1801. Thirty people sat down to breakfast at the communal dining table in Conrad & McMunn's Boarding House in Washington. The president-elect, Thomas Jefferson, took his usual place. Wouldn't he like to sit at the head of the table, near the fire? someone asked. No, he politely responded, not informing his interlocutor that displays of rank bored him.

Jefferson's calculated disregard for ceremony, his elimination of Washington's and Adams's formal "levees," horrified some European — and American — observers. The new president, unlike the magisterial Washington, was trampling upon "all our received notions of propriety and etiquette," objected one very proper Englishman, accusing Jefferson of seeking to flatter "the low passions of a mere newspaper-taught rabble." The British chargé, Edward Thornton, commented that Mr. Jefferson refused "to admit the smallest distinction, that may separate him from the mass of his fellow citizens." And Anthony Merry, the Envoy Extraordinary and Minister Plenipotentiary of His Britannic Majesty, attired in full uniform to present his diplomatic credentials, was reduced to sputtering in disbelief when Jefferson received him in casual morning dress and slippers.

Nothing could have pleased Jefferson more than eliminating symbols of status from manners. Washington had perspicaciously sought to surround the new office of the presidency with dignity and ritual, but Jefferson felt that the time had come to loosen that stylized protocol and democratize the office. No less aware than Washington of the importance of image in government, Jefferson wished to send out the message, as he rode around the new capital on a horse instead of in a magnificent coach-and-six, that Republican leaders were no different from ordinary men. "In social circles all are *equal*," he wrote, noting that in those circles, "the same equality exists among ladies as among gentlemen." He called this the principle of "pêle mêle." Indeed, even at the president's dinner parties, guests would be seated at a round table that did not lend itself to distinctions of social hierarchy. Though these were small gestures rather than grand political pronouncements, Jefferson nevertheless was determined to steer the nation away from what he termed the "arrogance of precedence in society" and toward new, more democratic patterns of behavior.

Those patterns of behavior would apply to government, too. The new president insisted that he was conscious of "no difference between writing to the highest or lowest being on earth." As for his philosophy of administration, he remarked, a few months into his presidency, that "forms should yield to whatever should facilitate business." Standing for practical simplicity, informality, and equality, he perceived "no mysteries" in public administration. "Common sense and honest intentions," he said, were all that was required.

After breakfast, the fifty-seven-year-old Virginian left for the Capitol, preceded by Virginia militiamen from Alexandria with drawn swords, a company of artillery and one of infantry, and behind him a motley crowd of dignitaries, Republican congressmen, and two members of Adams's cabinet. They headed toward the north wing of the still unfinished Capitol.

Four years earlier, at his own inauguration, President Adams had arrived in an elegant European-style coach drawn by six horses. Now, no pomp — and no John Adams. Loath to witness the momentous transfer of power from his own party to the party opposite, Adams had abruptly skipped town before dawn, refusing to be present at the inauguration of his old friend and successor.

George Washington, always impeccable in his use of symbol and gesture to create a foundation of legitimacy for the new republic, had attended Adams's inauguration. But Adams discerned little value in nourishing that potential tradition. Or perhaps the self-protective former president attached more importance to the care of his own open wounds. "Sensible, moderate men of both parties," commented the *Massachusetts Spy,* "would have been pleased had he tarried until after the installation of his successor. It certainly would have had a good effect." Adams had been "sufficiently humbled," James Bayard granted, "to be allowed to be absent." Or did Albert Gallatin know better? "You can have no idea of the meanness, indecency, almost insanity, of his conduct, specially of late," Gallatin wrote to his wife. For the next two hundred years, almost no other sitting president would fail to attend his successor's inauguration.

To most observers, Adams had made a hasty, undiplomatic departure — as ungraceful as his "midnight appointments." During his last weeks in office, he had rushed to fill judicial slots — dozens of them, including some lifetime appointments — with loyal Federalists. John Marshall became chief justice; John Lowell, chief judge of the District of Massachusetts; Harrison Gray Otis, district attorney; Oliver Wolcott, judge in the Second Circuit. The appointments themselves were not made at midnight, but the Senate had remained in session until 9:00 P.M. on Adams's last day in office, confirming his nominations, while the president worked late into the night, fixing his signature on dozens of commissions.

After March 4, Republicans would control two branches of government, and Adams was determined to prevent them from controlling the third, the federal judiciary. "In the future administration of our country," he had written to John Jay, offering him the chief justiceship, "the firmest security we can have against the effects of visionary schemes or fluctuating theories, will be in a solid judiciary." Jay had turned the job down, but Marshall accepted it. "I shall endeavor in the new office," he pointedly promised Adams, "not to disappoint my friends."

Adams had saddled the new president with a judiciary composed of his most ardent political foes. "Instead of smoothing the path for his successor," a shocked Madison remarked, "he plays into the hands of those who are endeavoring to strew it with as many difficulties as possible." It was simply "common justice," Jefferson later wrote to Abigail Adams, "to leave a successor free to act by instruments of his own choice." Adams's "midnight" appointments, he wrote, were "indecent." Just like his improper early morning retreat from Washington.

The morning of Jefferson's inauguration, bells rang out in Philadelphia, Baltimore, New York, and even in conservative Boston. As Jefferson mounted the steps of the Capitol in Washington, cannon boomed.

He headed toward the Senate. Hundreds of people, chattering excitedly, had already jammed into the chamber. They all wanted to be present at the ceremony that one witness called "one of the most interesting scenes a free people can ever witness." While changes in administration in virtually every other government and every other age, commented Margaret Bayard Smith, the wife of the editor of the *National Intelligencer,* "have most generally been epochs of confusion, villainy and bloodshed, in this our happy country [they] take place without any species of distraction, or disorder." Mrs. Smith was right in her assessment. When power shifted in a European government, it was often accompanied by turmoil and violence — from assassination to coup d'état to revolution. From the 1790s to the 1870s, a power shift in France would mean the entire transformation of the government: monarchy to republic, republic to directorate, directorate to empire, empire back to monarchy. But here was a peaceful transfer of power from one party to another, while the same constitutional government remained intact and strong.

In the Senate chamber, Vice President Burr, sworn in that morning, greeted the president-elect. Chief Justice Marshall, Jefferson's old Virginia adversary, was in a sour mood. That very morning, he had gloomily remarked that Republicans were divided into two groups, "speculative theorists & absolute terrorists," allowing that Jefferson probably did not fall into the latter camp. Marshall proceeded to administer the oath of office.

Then Jefferson turned to face the crowd. Leaning forward in their seats, people strained to hear him, for he delivered his address "in so low a tone," one observer noted, "that few heard it." But the *National Intelligencer* had scored a coup in publishing the speech ahead of time, familiarizing the president's listeners with his remarks. Even so, his message was subtle and complex.

He spoke the words softly, and yet those almost inaudible sounds heralded a new century and a new political epoch. He was bidding adieu to the old backward-looking world of wise fathers who regarded history as a repository of knowledge, authority, and guidance. There were no "principles, institutions, or systems of education," John Adams had said to a group of young men in 1798, "more fit than those you have received from your ancestors." But Jefferson promised that in his administration there would be no reverence for the past. "This whole chapter in the history of man is new," he would write two weeks after his inauguration. He would show no tolerance for those who "look backwards, not forwards, for improvement." What then would be new in his own speech?

"The will of the majority is in all cases to prevail," Jefferson declared. That simple sentence was a revolution in itself, for it stripped the old elites of their political prestige and instead invested authority in the people — mutable, unruly, self-interested, but also alive, rational, and sovereign. He was proposing nothing less than a new philosophical basis for American government. It was a philosophy of "naked" majority rule, diametrically opposed to checks and balances, to the majority-pulverizing Constitution, to all the old eighteenth-century fears of the "tyranny" of the majority, and the long-standing distrust of the "people" when they organized themselves into a national bloc or party, a crowd or a mob. He could not have disagreed more with John Adams. "Checks and Ballances, Jefferson," Adams would admonish him years later, "however you and your Party may have ridiculed them, are our only Security."

But in Jefferson's mind, first and foremost came the principle of majority rule, the fundamental law of a democratic republic. There would always be "absolute acquiescence in the decisions of the majority," he told the crowd, though adding two memorable provisos: that the will of the majority must be "reasonable" in order to be "rightful," and that the "minority possess their equal rights, which equal law must protect."

Jefferson's message was not only about majority rule. Rather it wove together majoritarianism and the ideal of national unity. Turning to the tormented election that had just taken place, he called it a "contest of opinion," one that "strangers" from abroad, men unused to thinking and writing freely, might well find "imposing." And yet, as divisive as those differences of opinion were, Jefferson held, there was a strong, deep, and unifying national consensus that transcended them. "Every difference of opinion is not a difference of principle," he explained. "We have called by different names brethren of the same principle."

Jefferson's meaning was clear — writing no fewer than three drafts of the speech, he had chosen his words with extreme care. On questions of political ideology and political *opinion*, Americans had been and continued to be divided. But on fundamental *principles* — a universal, bedrock commitment to constitutional republican government and to federal union — they were "brethren." Partisan politics neither challenged nor threatened the basic constitutional consensus, America's social contract. "We are all federalists, we are all republicans," the new president intoned, referring not to the two political parties but rather to Americans' shared bond of core constitutional beliefs — their commitment to a republican form of government and their preference for a federal bond among the states — that constituted their underlying national identity. Two years earlier he had similarly written that "both parties claim to be federalists and republicans, and I believe with truth as to the great mass of them." In no way was Jefferson advocating accommodation with his Federalist adversaries. "His statement was more a political platitude," noted historian Joseph Ellis, "than an ideological concession."

"All will unite in common efforts for the common good," Jefferson continued in his Inaugural Address. Was he suggesting that his own majority would be so broad and inclusive as to bring over moderate Federalists to the Republican camp and create an invincible coalition behind his administration? Did he expect that a middle-of-the-road Republican Party would ultimately absorb all Americans? Was he equating his Republican majority with the entire nation? Did he feel that the Republican Party could define for all, even in its own partisan way, the "common good"?

Yes to all of the above.

The differences between Republicans and moderate Federalists, Jefferson implied, were not significant. All could find a political home in the Republican Party. Indeed, "patriotic" Federalists had already come over to the Republicans and had, as he remarked to a friend, "separated from their congressional leaders." Jefferson was convinced that those centrist Federalists would remain "consolidated with us, if no intemperate measures on our part revolt them again." Just days after his inauguration, he would write that "nothing shall be spared on my part to *obliterate the traces of party* and consolidate the nation, if it can be done without abandonment of principle." In short, "party spirit" would not be necessary; harmony could reign and friendships could resume — provided that everyone came around to undiluted Republican principles.

A week before his inauguration, Jefferson had informed James Madison that, during the final moments of the election, Federalist moderates had begun "most anxiously" to wish for a Republican administration and would even consider it "a child of their own." Those middle-of-the-road Federalists, he predicted, "will cement & form one mass with us, & by these means harmony & union be restored." One unified, harmonious mass? A fraternal nation with no traces of party? Was Jefferson encouraging the creation of a free and open party system or setting the stage for a restrictive "one party democracy"? Do his words suggest that he steadfastly believed in nonviolent, political conflict — or in an apocryphal reign of unity, friendship, and harmony? Which strategy did Jefferson believe would guarantee America's political future? He did not say. The notions of a permanent opposition and of two equally potent and legitimate political parties had not yet come of age.

Standing in the Senate well, Jefferson proceeded to reassure his audience that American government would continue in its present form. Despite Federalists' fears of the Jacobin from Monticello, he would make no drastic changes. Americans, he acknowledged, had created "the strongest government on earth." It had "so far kept us free and firm." But even as he implicitly praised the legacy of the Federalists, he took a final swipe at those Anglophile fans of monarchy among them. Turning against his opponents the very words they had used against him, he accused them of harboring "the *theoretic* and *visionary*" fear that republican government in America might be too weak to survive. "Sometimes it is said that man can not be trusted with the government of himself," Jefferson remarked. "Can he, then, be trusted with the government of others? Or have we found angels in the forms of kings to govern him?" Jefferson was casting himself as a pragmatic leader: the real theorists, he implied, were the Federalist monocrats.

"Let us then, fellow citizens," he urged his listeners, "unite with one heart & one mind; let us restore to social intercourse that harmony & affection, without which Liberty, & even Life itself, are but dreary things. . . ." This was Jefferson's recipe for his own presidential leadership: conciliation and national unity, yes, but on Republican terms. Two weeks later he would clarify his meaning, explaining that, while he would try for "a steady line of *conciliation*," he would do so only "without yielding a single republican principle." The basis for the harmony and affection he yearned for would be an acceptance of Republican values.

Jefferson had high aspirations for his administration, but he also possessed a melancholy awareness of his own human frailties and the pitfalls that inevitably lay ahead. "I shall often go wrong," he acknowledged toward the end of his speech, "through defect of judgment."

And, as a man with decades of experience in the political arena, he realistically foresaw that he would not "retire from this station with the reputation and the favor" that had brought him into it. Readily admitting that he was no George Washington, he harbored no pretension, he told his listeners, "to that high confidence you reposed in our first and greatest revolutionary character, whose preeminent services had entitled him to the first place in his country's love." Washington's successor, the absent John Adams, went unmentioned.

After the inaugural ceremony, a few federal gentlemen who had lingered out of "curiosity" to attend the inaugural paid their respects to the president and the vice president. They were received, a relieved James Bayard informed Hamilton, "with very decent respect." "The speech in political substance," conceded Bayard, was "better than *we* expected." Hamilton too expressed relief, finding in Jefferson's address "virtually a candid retraction of past misapprehensions, and a pledge to the community, that the new president will not lend himself to dangerous innovations, but in essential points will tread in the steps of his predecessors."

The speech convinced many that Jefferson would aim at harmony and compromise. "You have opened a new era," Benjamin Rush wrote to Jefferson right after the inauguration, delighted with his friend's success. People were experiencing a fresh sense of brotherhood, he noted. Old friends, who had been separated for many years by party names, now "shook hands with each other." Everywhere citizens were speaking in the "highest terms" of Jefferson's talk. It had been a triumph.

Fears vanished. The storm had passed. "We are all tranquil, as they say at Paris, after a Revolution," wrote George Cabot to Rufus King.

But a skeptical chief justice, quietly sitting just feet away from Jefferson as he softly delivered his address, had listened more carefully. As if reading between the lines, Marshall grasped the implications of the president's partisan message. Jefferson's speech, he wrote later that day, seemed obliging, and yet, he decided, "it is strongly characteristic of the general cast of his political theory." A hard-nosed Fisher Ames, too, dismissed Republicans' "smooth promises, and a tinsel called conciliation." Jefferson, he lucidly warned, sought only to attract Federalist deserters and thin Federalist ranks. Indeed, whereas John Adams — idealistically and naively — had rejected the idea that a president had to be a party leader as well as a national leader, President Jefferson, despite his appeasing language, already understood the importance — even the necessity — of party leadership.

Many Federalists felt stung by Jefferson's victory. In a town near Philadelphia, on the eve of the inauguration, one "aristocrat" removed the clapper from a church bell, determined to prevent any triumphant ringing the following day. In New Jersey, a Federalist who had begun building a new house several months earlier declared that he would not complete the dwelling until Federalists returned to power. For the next twenty years, the building would stand unoccupied. And in Boston a newspaper ran an epitaph within a black border:

YESTERDAY EXPIRED
Deeply regretted by MILLIONS of grateful Americans
And by *all* GOOD men,
The FEDERAL ADMINISTRATION.

12

The New Politics

MY DEAR FRIEND, this farce of life contains nothing, which should put us out of humor," Gouverneur Morris wrote to Robert Livingston days after Jefferson's victory. But there was more to Morris's thinking than this world-weary approach to politics and life. Now that Federalists were out of power, he also had a clear grasp of the essential contribution that the "loyal opposition" can make to democratic government. "*Nil desperandum,*" he coolly wrote to Rufus King. "Let the chair of office be filled by whomsoever it may, opposition will act as an outward conscience, and prevent the abuse of power."

Fisher Ames, too, had seriously meditated on the positive role that an opposition Federalist Party should henceforth play — at least until the next presidential election. The opposition, he wrote, should be "a champion who never flinches, a watchman who never sleeps." He advised Federalists to exploit to the fullest their new role of shadow government that offered a compelling alternative agenda to that of the party in power. "We must make it manifest that we act on principle," he wrote, "and that we are deeply alarmed for the public good; that we are identified with the public." A unified and energized opposition, he went on, would, by its very criticism of the administration, produce a more responsive and responsible government. "We should, I am sanguine enough to believe, throw upon our antagonists the burdens of supporting and vindicating government, and enjoy their late advantages of finding fault, which popular prejudice is ever prone to listen to.

We should soon stand on high ground, and be ready to resume the reins of government with advantage."

Resume the reins of government. Ames articulated the essence of democratic government: an organized and ideologically unified majority, after winning elections, captures control of the national government, governs the nation, and attempts to carry out its agenda. At the next election, the opposition party has the chance to "resume the reins of government." "A party can never be too high to fall," wrote Republican Alexander Dallas in the spring of 1801, "and we find a party can never be too low to rise." Americans now understood that politics — and politicians — are perpetually in flux. Majorities are liquid, everchanging. As politicians reason, urge, implore, expostulate, cajole, threaten, and harangue, coalitions fluctuate and change, demonstrating that politics is the art of persuasion, not annihilation. "We are not dead yet," said one Federalist three days after Jefferson's inauguration. The *Gazette of the United States,* too, accepted its new status as organ of the opposition. "Mr. Jefferson, whose politics and whose promotion we have been accustomed to oppose, we are now bound to respect and obey. If we must oppose, we shall endeavour to oppose with the *honorable weapons of warriors, and not with the poisoned daggers of cowards and assassins.*"

But would Federalists be able to mount an effective opposition? Would they be skillful warriors, adapting to the times, broadening their message and their political base?

Just weeks after the first issue of the New York *Evening Post,* a newspaper that was Hamilton's brainchild, rolled off the press, Hamilton began writing a series of articles for it. The articles, entitled "The Examination," ran from December 17, 1801, until April 8, 1802. In minute detail, he dissected and criticized Republican policies on war, immigration, taxes, banking, and the judiciary. Jefferson's political, social, and economic ideas, Hamilton believed, were so egregious that he diagnosed something more virulent and threatening than mere political and intellectual differences of opinion. Jefferson's ill-conceived policies, Hamilton insisted, could be traced directly to "the culpable desire of gaining or securing popularity at an immediate expense of public utility." "*Good patriots must at all events please the people,*" he sarcastically remarked.

Still clinging to Federalist elitism and to "the collected wisdom" of the Federalist founders, disparaging "LITTLE POLITICIANS" and

their nefarious "schemes of innovation," Hamilton, in a singularly untimely move, took on the ascendancy of public opinion. "Those whose
patriotism is of the OLD SCHOOL," he explained, "would rather risk incurring the displeasure of the people, by speaking unpalatable truths,
than betray their interests by fostering their prejudices." Hamilton fully
expected old school Federalists like himself to continue to argue for the
proven, principled leadership of the elite few while refusing to be influenced by the "*impure tide*" of popular opinion.

History was on the Federalist side, Hamilton was convinced. Sooner
or later the people would see the light. They "will open their eyes and
see the precipice on which they stand!" They would turn to men with
solid records of distinguished public service. People would no longer
have any use for Republicans, those "wretched impostors, who, with
honeyed lips and guileful hearts are luring them to destruction!"

But a few months later, rethinking his position, Hamilton made an
about-face, suddenly scorning Federalists who unrealistically believed
that the people would eventually return them to office. "Among federalists old errors are not cured," he wrote. Federalists continued to
dream that power would return to their hands, and that people would
"repose a permanent confidence in good men. Risum teneatis? [Can
you restrain your laughter?]" What strategy, then, was Hamilton proposing — sticking to principle or bending to public opinion? He did
not say. Perhaps, in light of the ascendancy of the "people," there was
no viable opposition strategy, and Hamilton would gracefully bow out
of a life of public service. "What can I do better than withdraw from
the scene?" he said glumly.

Fisher Ames, too, was torn. "It is perfectly proper to be taught by
one's enemy," he noted, appearing eager to master modern political
tactics in the Republican school. If the new political game required
pandering, so be it. "We must study popular opinion and accommo-
date measures to what it is," he wrote. But Ames's notion of what constituted the courting of popular favor revealed a certain gap in his
understanding of the times. "We must speak," he proposed, "in the
name and with the voice of the good and the wise, the lovers of liberty
and the owners of property." The wise owners of property? Really?
Alas, his nostalgia for the authority of the wealthy elite and his con-
flation of liberty and property signaled no fresh start, no grasp of the
sea change that Jefferson and the Republican Party had set in motion.
Exhausted by the irresolvable tensions of the Federalist predicament,

Ames lurched back and forth between hope and gloom. "Weary and disgusted myself," he wrote in the summer of 1801, "despairing, as well I may, of any good effect from my single efforts, I now claim the quiet repose which, like a fool, I have so long refused to enjoy." In the political life of his country, Ames found himself "an outside passenger."

Federalist newspapers offered advice, but that advice, too, was contradictory. "Our defeat has taught us more than we should have learnt from a thousand victories," the *Gazette of the United States* earnestly declared, exhorting Federalists to perform their duty and prevent the "ruin of their country." And yet the *Gazette*, not unlike Hamilton and Ames, expressed a certain weariness, a certain resignation. "The efforts of patriots cannot control the fate of their country," the *Gazette* held, suggesting that Federalists would be hard pressed to "prevail against the league which forever exists, between ambition, corruption and ignorance." Should Federalists fight? wait? hope? or . . .

They were confused, apathetic, adrift. Federalists were "palsied," John Quincy Adams diagnosed. Dipping into more exotic imagery, the *New England Palladium* declared that "Federalism sits like a Turk benumbed with opium," adding that "the Federalists want zeal, want plan, want union — they will soon want a hiding place."

In part, Federalists blamed their overwhelming defeat on a lack of leadership. In the past they had owed their political successes to the reputation, charisma, and ability of a few outstanding men. But the great Washington had died; Hamilton had compromised himself by sabotaging Adams; Adams had left office after failing to lead his party. "The party committed suicide," wrote a frustrated Adams, and "indicted me for the murder." In the post-Washington world, no one leader stood out; the brothers were orphaned. Where to find the father who could salvage what was left of their party, inspire and guide them? The party had no "rallying point," bemoaned Robert Troup. "What destinies await us must be left to that Supreme Governor who directs all things according to his sovereign pleasure." The "Supreme Governor": another formula for docility, inactivity, resignation. Rudderless, without inspiration, Federalists were playing a hand with no trump cards.

But perhaps it was not just the absence of a savior that was to blame. Perhaps the trouble went deeper. Perhaps the trend toward democracy spelled the deterioration of stable, rational government. Denouncing the "tyranny of what is called the people," Fisher Ames asserted that the country had become "too democratic for liberty." The object of democracy was "to destroy every trace of civilization in the world," declared Theodore Dwight, the editor of the *Connecticut Courant,* in a Fourth of July oration in 1801. In a democratic land, there appeared to be no role for men of honor and integrity to play. "Reason, common sense, talents and virtue, cannot stand before democracy," the New York *Spectator* sadly editorialized. "Like a restless flood it sweeps all away." John Adams, too, bemoaned the fate of "democratical" governments. "Oh my Country," he wailed, "how I mourn over thy follies and vices, thine ignorance and imbecillity, thy contempt of Wisdom and Virtue and overweening admiration of fools and knaves! the never failing effects of *democracy!*" And at a New York dinner party, Alexander Hamilton replied to the expression of a democratic sentiment by hitting the table and snapping, "Your people, sir, — your people is a great *beast!*"

The specter of democracy caused Gouverneur Morris also to despair of his country's future. "When the people have been long enough drunk, they will get sober," he wrote in 1803, "but while the frolic lasts, to reason with them is useless." For him, the democratic festivities had already gone on for too long. The only hope, he wrote two years later, was to "*compel* a reluctant people to choose a wise and virtuous administration." Compel them? Just what did the former United States senator — who had spoken so wisely about the role of opposition in government — now have in mind? Perhaps it was just as well for him to leave politics altogether. That year this delegate to the Constitutional Convention in 1787, minister to France, and United States senator decided that "few men or things are worth one anxious thought." Echoing Voltaire, he poignantly asked, "What remains but to cultivate quietly my farm?"

Sounding very much like the displaced aristocracy of Revolutionary France, Federalists persisted in digging their own graves, disparaging the people, ridiculing their ignorance, shuddering at the power of the mob. When would Federalists realize that it was too late to revile democracy, that they could not win elections by directing their disappointment and frustration, their anxiety and their bewilderment, their venom and their wit, against the people? Federalism had been "completely and irrevocably abandoned and rejected by the popular voice," admitted John Quincy Adams, trying to convince his friends that, in its old form, "it never can and never will be revived." But would old guard

Federalists accept his judgment and work to renew and recreate their party?

Some tried. A small number of Federalist leaders gathered in Washington in 1802 at a meeting convoked by Hamilton, but they agreed on little. Hamilton also drew up a plan for a nationwide "Christian Constitutional Society," in which members would pay annual dues and work for the election of "fit" men to office, but this scheme, too, failed. Gouverneur Morris proposed a network of political committees, headquartered in New York, but his efforts led nowhere.

Disoriented and confused by the new politics, the old guard were ready to go down with their ship. "I never will surrender my principles to the opinions of any man," declared one Federalist candidate from North Carolina, "and I wish no man to vote for me, who is not willing to leave me free to pursue the good of my Country according to the best of my judgment." The candidate, William Davie, predictably went down in defeat. If the public no longer allowed them to lead exemplary lives of public service, these distinguished men would accept exemplary deaths — and political martyrdom. "To be counted one of [Washington's] disciples and suffer death for adhering to his principles," exclaimed Massachusetts conservative Rufus Putnam, *"what an honour!"* The duty of every Federalist, wrote Vermont congressman Daniel Buck after the election of 1800, was simply "to retire from office." A dejected Massachusetts man concluded that "Federalists may as well go home."

Federalists indeed were forced to go home. In Pennsylvania, they scarcely dared to name a candidate to oppose Governor McKean's reelection in 1802. The same year, in many districts of New York, no Federalists could be found to run for Congress. In the spring of 1804, looking for a strong candidate to run for governor of New York, Federalists would back a man who was running as an Independent but who, nevertheless, appealed to some of the most conservative Federalists. Although that man had already served as vice president of the United States, in the race for governor, he went down in defeat. His name was Aaron Burr.

Unable to mount an offensive, Federalists braced themselves for a tidal wave from the boisterous sea of liberty. Would anything be left standing after Jefferson's wild schemes? "Every minutia is to be changed," complained Roger Griswold of Connecticut. "When Mr. Adams was

President, the door of the president's House opened to the East. Mr. Jefferson has closed that door and opened a new door to the West."

In reality, the new president, aided by his secretary, Meriwether Lewis, and a staff consisting of a steward, a chef, and a few servants, worked quietly and diligently in his office in the southwest corner of the main floor of the executive mansion. Modeled on Leinster House in Dublin, it was the first public building erected in the new capital. The president's office had a desk, many large and small tables, and a press for making copies of his letters. Beyond was his antechamber, which he called his sitting room, as well as a well-furnished oval drawing room, two dining rooms, and a library. Upstairs were his bedroom, dressing room, guest rooms, and an oval ladies' drawing room. When the Madisons left after a long visit in the spring, Jefferson commented that he and Lewis felt like two mice in a church.

In appearance and demeanor, Jefferson did not strike observers as a crazed, irresponsible, or extremist politician. "He is tall in stature and rather spare in flesh," one friend wrote of him at the time. "His dress and manners are very plain; he is grave, or rather sedate, but without any tincture of pomp, ostentation, or pride, and occasionally can smile, and both hear and relate humorous stories as well as any other man of social feelings." His lively dinner parties bore no resemblance to the grave, funereal dinners that Washington had given. At Jefferson's table, usually set for twelve, diplomats, scientists, representatives, and senators feasted on French delicacies as they discussed philosophy, history, inventions, beasts, and birds as well as politics. Jefferson possessed, one guest remarked, "true politeness, which places his guests perfectly at their ease." His acquaintances knew of his interest in French and Italian architecture, his prodigious spending for fine European furniture, his French chef, his aristocratic taste for the best wines. "His instincts were those of a liberal European nobleman," commented historian Henry Adams. Indeed, some Federalists could almost mistake Jefferson for another patrician, one of their own.

But the Federalists' fears were genuine: Jefferson's visionary ideas, his ebullient writings about the "people," his admiration for revolution in France, his role in the Virginia and Kentucky Resolutions affirming states' rights — all that shook them to the core. He and his party now controlled the executive branch of government as well as both houses of Congress. The founders had designed the Constitution's checks and balances essentially to prevent citizens from establishing political par-

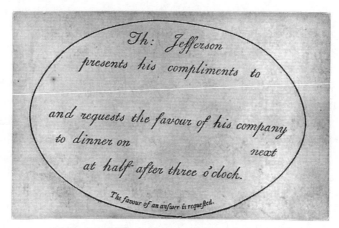

Thomas Jefferson's invitation to dinner, no date.

ties and to restrain a popular majority, but now the representatives of such a majority wielded power in Washington. Republicans had carte blanche to demolish all that the Federalists had crafted so carefully, so thoughtfully, so intelligently.

And Jefferson was ferociously partisan. Despite his earlier preaching about unity and harmony and his deep ambivalence about political parties, he sought no conciliation with the High Federalists, the "royalists or priests" in the opposition. On the contrary, he hoped for their complete disintegration. Whereas both Morris and Ames had insightfully discerned a positive role for Federalists as the "loyal opposition," Jefferson wanted only Republican hegemony.

Failing to grasp the important contribution that an opposition party can make in a government, he hoped for nothing more than to watch Federalism "sink . . . into an abyss from which there shall be no resurrection for it." Even the name of that party aroused his loathing. The label "Federalist," he sneered, had "become so scouted that no party can rise under it." "I wish nothing but their eternal hatred," he lashed out at his foes, not unlike his combative successor Franklin Delano Roosevelt, who would announce, in 1936, that his enemies "are unanimous in their hate for me, and I welcome their hatred!" Were another presidential election to take place at the end of his second year in office, Jefferson believed, the "federal candidate would not get the vote of a single elector in the U.S." It would not be long before the whole nation would be "consolidated" in Republican principles, he wrote in 1803.

And yet, Jefferson promised that, however "unequivocal in principle" he would be as the national political leader, "the right of opinion shall suffer no invasion from me." In his Inaugural Address, he had taken on the Sedition Act, underscoring that "errors of opinion" should be "tolerated where reason is left free to combat it." The paramount right of the people was "to think freely and to speak and to write what they think." Indeed, he considered his support of freedom of the press a mark of Republican respect for the intelligence of average Americans, which he contrasted with the Federalist stratagem of overawing Americans into deference and acquiescence. Whereas Federalists sought to "dazzle" the minds of citizens with "pomp, splendor, or forms," Republicans would show "real respect" for their reason and encourage "the habit of bringing everything to the test of common sense."

But is it true that, as president, Jefferson would take no measures to repress the opposition? The Sedition Act itself had expired at the end of Adams's term of office and was not renewed at the start of Jefferson's presidency. But although the new president pardoned the Republican victims of the act who were still languishing in jail, Jefferson's own record in tolerating opposition would not be unblemished. As president, not unlike Adams, he was so incensed by his critics that he occasionally proposed legal action against them in state courts. State legislatures, Jefferson wrote in 1804, retained the power to suppress "the overwhelming torrent of slander" that was undermining all truth and virtue in America. While he opposed the right of Congress to control the press, "we have ever asserted the right of the states, and their exclusive right to do so." Convinced that slander and lies in the "tory presses" of Pennsylvania were discrediting the principle of freedom of the press, Jefferson proposed to Governor McKean "a few prosecutions of the most prominent offenders" as a way to restore "integrity" to the press. It should not be a "general prosecution for that would look like a persecution," he cautioned McKean. Jefferson's forays into the suppression of criticism, well documented by historian Leonard Levy, demonstrate that respect for opposition was a lesson that would take decades to be absorbed and integrated into the political culture.

And yet, despite Jefferson's uneven record regarding freedom of the press and despite his grip on executive and legislative power, the sky did not fall, as Federalists had hysterically predicted. On the contrary, to retain and to increase his majority, the president's policies had to be moderate. The "majority" itself was not governing; rather, a responsible, moderate party representing the majority stood at the helm.

Above all, Jefferson claimed to want a small, frugal, efficient government. "The path we have to pursue is so quiet," he wrote during his first year in office, "that we have nothing scarcely to propose to our Legislature." The sign of a healthy polity, in his eyes, was a "noiseless course." "If we can prevent the government from wasting the labor of the people, under the pretense of taking care of them," he wrote, "they must become happy." The Federalists, Jefferson contended, had raised not only enough money but too much money, and he was determined to spend less and "bring the government to a simple and economical course." Discovering myriad expenses in the Adams administration, he delighted, he told James Monroe, in "lopping them down silently." He also worked to reduce the national debt of $112 million, lower federal spending by a third, eliminate almost all domestic taxes, shrink the civil service, and, he boasted, "reduce the army and navy to what is barely necessary."

Meanwhile, the nation was growing. The population had increased from 4 million in 1790 to about 5.3 million in 1800. Though most Americans lived in rural areas, with only about 6 percent of the people living in towns or cities, the cities were nevertheless expanding. In 1775 there had been 40,000 people in Philadelphia and 25,000 in New York. But by 1800, both cities had more than 100,000 residents. The economy was similarly expanding. Federalists could take at least some comfort in seeing that Jefferson did nothing to dismantle Hamilton's Bank of the United States. On the contrary, his secretary of the treasury, Albert Gallatin, added new branches to the bank and continued to keep most federal funds in it. "It mortifies me," Jefferson wrote, "to be strengthening principles which I deem radically vicious." Though he would not be able to undo Hamilton's financial system, he would nevertheless open up that system, making it more inclusive. Whereas there were 3 banks in the United States in 1790, 25 new banks opened in 1800, and by 1810 there were 327.

Like the president's dining table, the economy would become — at least in the early nineteenth century — less hospitable to hierarchy. Small businessmen and entrepreneurs could seek credit, not just for the grand projects that the Bank of the United States continued to support, but also for a variety of commercial, industrial, and agricultural ventures. Instead of the centralized, planned economic growth that

Hamilton had envisaged, unregulated private enterprise, for good or for ill, became the order of the day, as the United States developed a diversified economy. "We must now place the manufacturer by the side of the agriculturist," Jefferson would assert in 1816, in the wake of the War of 1812 and the failure of his embargo. He had not given up his preference for the cultivation of the land; that was still the best "nursery" for self-government and equal rights, he believed. But he recognized that the world had become a more dangerous place and that the United States had to become self-sufficient: "to be independent for the comforts of life," he wrote, "we must fabricate them ourselves." Indeed, people who were against domestic manufacturing, he commented, "must be for reducing us either to dependence on that foreign nation or to be clothed in skins and to live like wild beasts in dens and caverns . . . . Manufactures are now as necessary to our independence as to our comfort."

In the domain of manufacturing and industry, Jefferson, as historian Peter Onuf reminds us, was opposed to the exercise of federal power, but in certain other areas, Jefferson went further toward "consolidation" and national control than had Hamilton. While Washington's secretary of the treasury had been reluctant to go so far as to recommend a national plan for internal improvements — roads and canals — Jefferson and Gallatin embarked on a wide-ranging program for additions to the national infrastructure, from canals in New York State to a road leading to Ohio. Under Jefferson, writes historian John Larson, "the federal government took bolder steps toward a national system of internal improvements than Hamilton ever had dared."

But did Republicans have another hidden agenda, too? Did they secretly hope to shrink the federal government, reducing it to the kind of weak government the country had experienced under the Articles of Confederation? In 1798, Jefferson and Madison had taken strong positions in the Kentucky and Virginia Resolutions on the right of states to declare federal legislation unconstitutional; three years later, in his Inaugural Address Jefferson had asserted that state governments were "the most competent administrations for our domestic concerns and the surest bulwarks against antirepublican tendencies."

Would Jefferson, Madison, and their Republican allies now seek to undermine an effective central government by asserting states' rights? Or would they remain committed to a truly national vision? The answer is not unambiguous. On the one hand, it can be argued that Madison and Jefferson's defense of states' rights had been their *means* in attacking Federalist policies, especially the unconstitutional Sedition Act; states' rights were not their *end*. "The means were taken seriously," historian Lance Banning wrote, "but they were never held among the absolutes." Jefferson and Madison "never sought, as their essential end, to hold the federal government within the narrowest of bounds. . . . To judge them only on the basis of their loyalty to strict construction and states' rights is to apply a standard they had never held." Indeed, the argument for state sovereignty was a technique that could be mobilized to defend a variety of different interests: Federalist Timothy Pickering called for New England states to nullify Jefferson's embargo; and under the banner of state sovereignty, abolitionists in Massachusetts like Horace Mann, Charles Beecher, and others would defend their right to disobey the Fugitive Slave Act in the 1850s.

On the other hand, Madison had long been opposed to "consolidation." In 1791, when he argued against a "gradual consolidation of the states into one government," in 1799 when he insisted that state governments "must always be a powerful barrier against dangerous encroachments" of the federal government, and in 1800 when he held that the last resort against federal encroachments was not the judiciary (which might "concur" with the other branches of government in usurping power) but rather the states, Madison consistently conceived of the federal government as a compact of the states, underscoring that the ultimate sovereignty lay, not in the Constitution, but in the "people over constitutions." And although Madison did not believe that a single state had the right to withdraw from the compact, he did accept the idea, as Banning notes, that the sovereign people retained the natural right of revolution.

Were Madison and Jefferson, then, seriously bent on promoting the authority and autonomy of the states? No, concludes Banning. "The strategy of 1798," he writes, "was not developed for the sake of states as states, but for the sake of the republican and liberal ideals that were the essence of the Revolution." It is a subtle point: the two Virginians would be content with the subordination of the states to the national government so long as that government remained favorable to Republican ideals, that is, limited federal power, individual liberty, and southern agrarian values.

But even if Jefferson had no burning desire to radically shrink the national government, some "Old Republicans" in Virginia certainly did. Led by John Randolph, Edmund Pendleton, John Taylor of Caroline, and Wilson Cary Nicholas, these "Old Republicans" fervently believed that the Federalist "danger" was not yet over and demanded — unsuccessfully — a series of constitutional amendments limiting the power of the president and the national government. Loyal to Jefferson, whom they were loath to condemn, they targeted Madison instead (after all, they noted, he had authored *The Federalist*) and later, in the presidential election of 1808, would support Monroe instead of Jefferson's secretary of state. For these antinationalists and others, the Virginia and Kentucky Resolutions, whatever Jefferson and Madison's intentions were, would become, in the words of historian Garry Wills, "the basic document of anti-governmentalism in America . . . a sacred text to the South as it took the road toward the Civil War."

Jefferson's earlier foray into anti-governmentalism notwithstanding, as president he would keep the promise he made in his Inaugural Address: to preserve "the General Government in its whole constitutional vigor." Jefferson was no enemy to the power of the executive, Hamilton had suspected during the stalemate of January 1801. The Virginian, he wrote, favored "a large construction of the Executive authority." As president, Jefferson would prove Hamilton's judgment correct. His most vigorous undertaking during his first term was the Louisiana Purchase. It was a brilliant, far-sighted decision.

Through New Orleans, Jefferson noted, "the produce of three-eighths of our territory must pass to market." After Spain ceded Louisiana back to France in 1801, Jefferson's paramount goal was to purchase New Orleans and guarantee for Americans free navigation on the Mississippi. He instructed his minister in France, Robert Livingston, to try to purchase only West Florida and the port of New Orleans. The president advised Livingston to conduct negotiations with painstaking tact and diplomacy. "We wish to remain well with France," Jefferson underscored, counseling his ambassador to wear a mask of easy good will. "We had better give to all our communications with them a very mild, complaisant and even friendly complexion," he wrote, adding that nothing was "important enough to risk a breach of peace." Jefferson also realized that it would be pointless to play a risky game of brinkmanship with Napoleon. "An American contending by stratagem against those exercised in it from their cradle," he wrote to his secretary of state James Madison, "would undoubtedly be outwitted by them."

But in early 1803, after Napoleon lost more than 24,000 troops in

Haiti, he impulsively decided to rid himself of his newly reacquired colony of Louisiana. His foreign minister, Talleyrand, approached Livingston. What would Livingston "give for the whole"? Talleyrand asked. It would take longer to draw up the final documents than it had to negotiate the sale — $15 million for 565 million acres. Neither diplomatic finesse nor timing nor persistence clinched the deal: it was mainly good luck. But it would take all Jefferson's political skill to get the agreement through Congress.

To his closest advisers the president confided his understanding that the Constitution had not given the government the necessary authority to acquire and incorporate new territory into the union. Though toying with the impractical idea of a constitutional amendment, he could only justify the treaty to himself and to his confidants as an extraordinary action. He trusted that Americans would realize that, although the treaty lay "beyond the Constitution," it was so beneficial to the interest of the nation that there was no choice for Congress but to move purposefully forward, "casting behind them *metaphysical subtleties.*"

When word arrived from France that Napoleon had second thoughts about the treaty, Jefferson realized that Congress had to pass it with all dispatch. "The less we say about constitutional difficulties respecting Louisiana the better," he wrote to Madison, adding that "what is necessary for surmounting them must be done sub silentio."

Several years later, after much reflection, Jefferson remarked that "a strict observance of the written laws is doubtless one of the high duties of a good citizen, but it is not the highest." Citizens' paramount obligation was not to the *letter* of the law but rather to the *meaning* of the law, that is, the protection of life, liberty, and property. It would be absurd, he concluded, to sacrifice "the end to the means." In other words, the Constitution was made for American citizens, not American citizens for the Constitution. Although Jefferson was an idealistic theorist — of revolution, of republican government, of a bill of rights — pragmatism would trump visionary dreams in his administration. "What is practical must often control what is pure theory," he wrote in 1802, adding that "the habits of the governed determine in a great degree what is practical." In the case of the Louisiana Purchase, that pragmatism called for the acquisition of vast territory and was justified by Jefferson's broad popular mandate, if not by the Constitution or by the Supreme Court. Indeed, while focused on the relatively insignificant question of John Adams's "midnight" appointment of William Mar-

The Louisiana Purchase by H. C. Whorf. James Monroe, Robert Livingston, and Talleyrand sign the cession agreement, April 30, 1803. In the medallions on the top left and right are Jefferson and Napoleon.

bury as justice of the peace, the Supreme Court ignored and relegated to the executive and legislative branches the most important constitutional event of 1803.

A few Federalists objected to the purchase. The new territory was "a great waste, a wilderness unpeeled with any beings except wolves and wandering Indians," wrote one man in the *Columbian Centinel,* with a breathtaking lack of foresight. Hamilton, hostile to the idea of a westward-looking agrarian empire, muttered that the western region was "not valuable to the United States for settlement," though he allowed that it was "essential to the peace and prosperity" of the nation and would open a "free and valuable market to our commercial states."

But for some Federalists, reservations about the purchase went beyond mere grumbling: they worried — not unrealistically — that incorporation of new western states into the union would undermine the already waning influence of Federalist New England while simultaneously increasing the domain of bondage. "Let those who wish for the increase of slaves," wrote David Humphreys, the former minister to Spain, "rejoice in this new nursery for them." While Jeffersonians celebrated the new political and commercial ties between East and West and smiled, as Garry Wills suggests, at a vast potential market for the domestic slave trade, Federalists opposed to the Louisiana Purchase accurately predicted the widening of fissures between North and South. The Massachusetts legislature even proposed a constitutional amendment removing the three-fifths clause from the Constitution.

But Timothy Pickering, now senator from Massachusetts and one of only five senators to vote against the purchase, went even further. Looking for a way to combat both the political influence of Virginia and the likely spread of slavery into the Louisiana territory, he proposed to a few ultra-conservative friends that the five New England states along with New York and New Jersey secede from the union and form a northern confederacy. "Without a separation, can those States ever rid themselves of negro Presidents and negro Congresses?" he asked Rufus King. Party leaders like George Cabot and Fisher Ames urged Pickering not even to discuss secession. Cabot perceived that Pickering's scheme would only undermine even more the Federalists' already weak standing in the public mind. Such a venture, he warned, "would be fatal to its advocates as public men." Imagining that secession would revive Federalism, Pickering had instead dealt another blow to his faltering party.

While the explosive issue of slavery loomed overhead, the Louisiana Purchase nevertheless represented an unparalleled bargain: the United States had bought 828,000 square miles and doubled the size of its territory. The new land extended west of the Mississippi all the way to the Rockies. The treaty ensured the realization of Jefferson's heady dream of enough land "for our descendants to the thousandth and thousandth generation." So vast was the new domain that its boundaries were unknown. No one was certain if Florida and Texas were included, but that was a minor detail. Lewis and Clark would set out in 1804 to discover the extent of the new territory.

For the president, the great benefit of the treaty was not so much the fulfillment of his agrarian dream and the transformation of the United States into a truly continental nation but rather the bolstering of American security. He had succeeded in eliminating foreign powers from most of the continent and in ensuring free navigation on the Mississippi. Though he hoped that the United States would ultimately absorb all the new territory, he declined to express certainty about it. "Whether we remain in one confederacy, or form into Atlantic and

Mississippi confederacies," he wrote in 1804, "I believe not very important to the happiness of either part." The safety and preservation of the nation, not its size, were his top priorities. The United States, protected and strengthened by the bulwark of the purchase, could become, Jefferson said, "an empire of liberty."

On the broad question of circumventing the letter of the Constitution for an overriding goal, Jefferson had marched in step with Federalists. Like them, he was using his political capital to build a powerful nation. Indeed, some Federalists pounced on Jefferson's inconsistency. If the Federalists had dared to propose such a treaty, remarked Senator William Plumer, Republicans would have branded them monarchists. The Louisiana Purchase was "an assumption of implied power" greater than all those in the years of the Washington and Adams administrations put together, remarked John Quincy Adams. Federalists who were opposed to the Louisiana Purchase, historian Peter Onuf acutely observed, "embraced strict construction at precisely the point Jefferson abandoned it." Federalists would also protest against Jefferson's "Embargo Act" of 1807 prohibiting all commerce with foreign nations. The man who, in 1787, had insisted that he was "not a friend to a very energetic government" and who, in 1798, had defended states' rights, proved to be the most energetic of national leaders, using all the power of his office to enlarge, protect, and preserve the union.

The passage of the Louisiana treaty — by a vote of 24 to 7 — was more than a political masterstroke; it was also a display of Jefferson's skillful, vigorous presidential leadership buttressed by his usual exquisite, deferential courtesy. At every step Jefferson wined and dined, consulted and wheedled, persuaded and charmed the men who constituted the government. From France, where he had been negotiating the purchase, Livingston sent a revealing portrait of the different kind of leadership exerted on the other side of the ocean. "There never was a Government in which less could be done by negotiation than here. There is no people, no Legislature, no counselors. One man is everything. He seldom asks advice, and never hears it unasked."

Unlike Napoleon, Jefferson was not a ruler but a democratic leader who counted on followers and allies. He was adept at outlining his goals with clarity, convincing the public to accept his programs, building support for his most sweeping and controversial measures, tolerating differences of opinion, and knowing when to retreat before incurring political damage. And most unusual, he possessed the ability to speak in moral terms while simultaneously acting on the basis of Realpolitik and national self-interest.

The foundation for his leadership lay in party solidarity. Indeed, Jefferson is ranked by political scientists as the foremost party leader of the nineteenth century. Though many of the features of modern congressional parties — such as elections for party leaders and whips — did not yet exist, Jefferson nevertheless exploited every ounce of his skill and influence to control the congressional agenda, to dominate the Republican caucus in the House, to cast himself as leader of the party, to engage his followers, to create party loyalty, and to exert leadership in Washington and beyond. He also relied on the leadership of his own cabinet, on the talent of men like Madison and Gallatin. "There never arose," he later said about his harmonious administration, "an instance of an unpleasant thought or word between the members." Whether center stage or in the wings, Jefferson was fully in control. "Behind the curtain, [Jefferson] directs the measures he wishes to have adopted," one man reported, "while in each house a majority of puppets move as he touches the wire." Few other presidents, remarked Jefferson's biographer Dumas Malone, would be "as successful in getting through Congress the measures he favored."

Jefferson saw himself not only as a partisan party leader but also as a party builder. Whereas Madison's original blueprint for checks and balances centered around foiling and splintering any majority, Jefferson's notion of majoritarian party politics depended on creating a continually expanding majority, broadening its base, and including ever more voters — however poor or uncultured they might be. In other words, his twin beliefs in the *lex majoris partis* and in an inclusive democracy nourished and fed off each other, resulting in a hard-nosed electoral strategy. As a party leader, his paramount goal was party victory, and the vehicle was expansion of the political arena and inclusion: getting more warm bodies — old voters, new voters — to the polls and defeating the opposition soundly.

Jefferson's majoritarian strategy was not only about including old and new voters: it was also about including nonvoters. Indeed, his majority depended, as historian Garry Wills emphasizes, on his retaining the representation of three-fifths of the nonvoting slave population — in other words, on retaining the votes of the South — and, since property qualifications severely limited the suffrage in Virginia, especially the votes of slaveholders. And yet, in Jefferson's mind, the South was less the stronghold of slavery than that of Republicanism. The Northeast, he wrote to his friend Elbridge Gerry, had "drunk deeper of the delusion" of Federalism and was "therefore slower in recovering from it." Nor was Jefferson opposed to the expatriation of some freed black slaves from Virginia, even though that might decrease his political base. While he expressed reservations about Governor Monroe's plan for a colony of blacks in the western territory, he was open to sending them to the Caribbean instead. "Nature," he wrote Monroe, "seems to have formed these islands to become the receptacle of the blacks transplanted into this hemisphere." Such an expatriation scheme posed some problems, but they were, he wrote, "overweighed by the *humanity* of the measures proposed."

While working to increase his majority, would the president seek to exclude Federalists from the federal bureaucracy and from the judiciary? Would he sweep them out of office and give judicial and ministerial plums to his own supporters? Here Jefferson walked a fine line, especially in the wake of his inaugural message of harmony and reconciliation. Removing Federalists en masse from office would only heighten party conflict, harden partisan lines, and alienate potential converts to Republicanism. Indeed, even before inauguration day, Federalist Timothy Pickering predicted that the new president would not remove his opponents from office; "yet when *vacancies* happen," Pickering wrote, "no doubt he will fill them with his friends; and the hopes of office will add to their number." Pickering's prediction was correct: Jefferson's friend and ally John Beckley also advised him to make changes in men "so as *gradually*, but certainly and effectively, to place the executive administration in the hands of decided republicans." At least for the moment Federalists were relieved, as Robert Troup remarked to Rufus King, that Jefferson was not going to "carry his displacing system to an extreme." King's own job as minister to Great Britain, Troup happily reported, appeared secure.

Ever hopeful of bringing moderate Federalists into the Republican camp, Jefferson decided to remove few Federalists from office — other than some customs officials who had worked under the secretary of the treasury, some marshals alleged to have packed juries, a group of "attornies & marshals removed for high federalism," and the infamous Supreme Court Justice Samuel Chase, whom Jefferson tried unsuccessfully to oust. The repeal of Adams's Judiciary Act of February 1801 (which created sixteen circuit courts along with new judgeships, attorneys, marshals, and clerks) and the Supreme Court's refusal to intervene on behalf of William Marbury permitted Jefferson to withhold the commissions of many of the justices of the peace appointed by Adams. Natural attrition, Jefferson was confident, would sooner or later take care of the rest.

But when openings did occur, Jefferson had no intention of being an equal opportunity employer. During the Adams administration, Jefferson remembered, ninety-nine out of a hundred offices were filled exclusively by members of the "federal sect." Indeed, on the foreheads of Republicans, Federalists discerned "the mark on Cain" and, Jefferson remarked, they swiftly exiled them from public trusts. That virtually total exclusion of Republicans from the last administration called for "prompter correctives" than death or resignation. "Does it violate [Federalists'] *equal rights,* to assert some rights in the *majority* also?" Jefferson demanded. "Is it *political intolerance* to claim a proportionate share in the direction of the public affairs?" Jefferson wanted no members of "the noisy band of royalists" in his government.

Patronage was a troublesome burden. No other aspect of the presidency weighed as heavily on him as did these "appointments & disappointments." Solicitations for office made up the "most painful" part of his duties, he confessed. Whereas "the ordinary affairs of a nation offer little difficulty to a person of any experience," he noted, "the gift of office is the dreadful burden which oppresses him." The day might come, Jefferson said, "when the only questions concerning a candidate shall be, is he honest? is he capable? is he faithful to the Constitution?" But in the meantime, a man's beliefs and party affiliation would secure him a position in the government — or exclude him from it. The president displayed all the mettle of a tough party boss while mouthing congenial words of conciliation.

But what about including women in the government? Gallatin made the audacious suggestion that a few women might be recruited for some minor positions in the treasury department. "The appointment of a woman to office," Jefferson stonily replied, "is an innovation for which the public is not prepared, nor am I."

Jefferson's dual gift for partisan politics and peacemaking was challenged by one man: his vice president, Aaron Burr.

Jefferson faced the vexing choice of helping Burr consolidate his political base in New York through patronage appointments or shutting him out of the loop. He sensed that Burr was an operator, "always at market," and that little was more important to him than patronage. Making connections, creating loyalties, and expecting payback: this was the essence of politics for Burr. At first, Jefferson took him into consideration when making appointments in New York State, naming Burr's ally John Swartwout a federal marshal and Edward Livingston district attorney. But little by little the president started heeding the advice of Burr's New York rival, Governor George Clinton, boosting Clinton's allies rather than Burr's. The man Burr wanted most to reward was his political aide Matthew Davis. "Davis is too important to be trifled with," Burr warned Gallatin, urging him to intervene on Davis's behalf. But not even Davis's unusual trip to Monticello and face-to-face meeting with the president helped his case. Jefferson decided not to act, unperturbed by the idea of a public break with his vice president.

In December 1803, a proposal was made in Congress for the Twelfth Amendment to the Constitution, distinguishing the election of the president from that of the vice president and making impossible another tie between two candidates of the same party. It was a signal not lost on Burr. A master of hardball politics, he deduced that he would be dropped from the presidential ticket. A few weeks later, in late January, he asked for a private meeting with Jefferson. Conceding that he had lost much of his support in New York, especially that of the important Clinton and Livingston families, he told the president that he felt it would be in the best interest of the Republican Party for him not to run again as vice president. But, he asked, wouldn't Jefferson bestow on him "some mark of favor," an ambassadorship perhaps, or an endorsement in another political race, some outward sign that he had not lost the president's confidence? Jefferson was coolly noncommittal, noting in his diary, immediately after his meeting with Burr, that Burr's conduct had always "inspired me with distrust. I habitually cautioned Mr. Madison against trusting him too much."

That spring, Burr decided to run for governor of New York. The field was open. George Clinton, the longtime governor of the state, had decided not to run again; instead he would run as Jefferson's vice president. But New York Republicans, shunning Burr, chose Morgan Lewis for their candidate. Burr would have to run as an Independent. He had the support of some Federalists, like Timothy Pickering, who hoped that Burr might join them in their separatist plot while also helping them breathe new life into Federalism in New York. But not all New York Federalists would welcome Burr. Enter Alexander Hamilton.

The antipathy between Hamilton and Burr went back to 1789, when Burr defeated Hamilton's father-in-law, Philip Schuyler, for a Senate seat from New York. Over the next decade, the mutual hostility only intensified — in the early 1790s, when Burr opposed Hamilton's economic policies and Hamilton forcefully blocked Burr's appointment as minister to France, and during the presidential election of 1800, when Hamilton found himself forced to support Jefferson, whom he only disliked, over Burr, whom he loathed. During Burr's campaign for governor of New York, Hamilton could no longer restrain himself from advertising his contempt for him.

By June 1804, Burr had had enough. His political isolation in Jefferson's administration, the Twelfth Amendment, his exile from the upcoming presidential race, Jefferson's refusal to offer some sign of support, Hamilton's smear campaign against him, his defeat for the governorship in late April: all descended upon him at once like the waves of a rising tide, submerging him in anger, pushing him headlong into a series of strange, desperate acts.

Six weeks after losing the race for governor, he wrote a curt letter to Hamilton, demanding that Hamilton affirm or deny having made libelous comments about him to a certain Dr. Charles Cooper. He enclosed a letter that Cooper had published in the *Albany Register,* containing the sentence "I could detail to you a still more despicable opinion which General HAMILTON has expressed of Mr. BURR."

What were Hamilton's options? Four years earlier, in 1800, he had written a brusque note to President Adams, demanding to know if Adams had made certain accusations against him. Adams never responded. Hamilton, too, considered the possibility of not responding to Burr; since Burr could point to no specific insult, Hamilton could have ignored his vague accusation. And yet, he decided to enter into an agonizing correspondence with his rival.

Hamilton's response to Burr was both supercilious and tortured. "I have maturely reflected on the subject of your letter," he replied, claiming that it was impossible for him to make an avowal or disavowal. Why? Evidently Cooper's language was too vague to permit either one. Giving free rein to his talent for literary exegesis, he judged that "the phrase 'still more despicable' admits of infinite shades, from very light to very dark. How am I to judge of the degree intended?" He stood ready to avow or disavow only precise words that could be attributed to him. He hoped that Burr would accept his point. "If not, I can only regret the circumstance, and must abide the consequence." His unyielding stance recalls his overheated reaction to a minor contretemps with General Washington in 1781, a miscommunication that the prickly twenty-six-year-old Hamilton magnified into a parting of the ways. "I am importuned," he had written then, "to listen to a reconciliation: but my resolution is unalterable."

Nor would Burr retreat. Hamilton's response neither satisfied nor placated him. "*Political opposition* can never absolve Gentlemen from the necessity of a rigid adherence to the *laws of honor* and the rules of decorum," Burr informed his nemesis. Although many men recognized such "laws of honor," one can only smile at Burr's idea of a "rigid adherence" to them, for he had never rigidly — or even flexibly — adhered to any principles in his life. But more important, while perceiving that their quarrel ultimately concerned "political opposition," Burr placed greater importance on the supposedly higher and more compelling values of honor and "decorum."

Hamilton, too, perceived that the dispute was fundamentally political. "I am conscious of no *ill*-will to Col Burr, distinct from political opposition, which, as I trust, has proceeded from pure and upright motives." Why then should he consider apologizing? "I have not censured him on light grounds," he wrote, adding that he "had strong reasons for what I may have said."

Both men explicitly stated that their dispute was political. And yet neither one looked for a political solution to a political problem. On the contrary, they both preferred an alternative, symbolic way to act out and resolve their long-standing quarrel. Burr issued a challenge to duel. Hamilton accepted it. Now nothing could stop the murderous, ritualistic dance.

Duels were "Gothic and absurd," Thomas Paine said. They were "barbarous and lawless" as well as "absurd and immoral," protested Thomas Jefferson when his own son-in-law was considering fighting a duel. How could the "murderous Practice of dueling" still be in "vogue"? an astonished Benjamin Franklin had wondered in 1784. In the Age of Enlightenment, how could so many men, he asked, continue to tolerate this medieval vestige, based on the irrational belief that "Providence would in every instance favour Truth and Right with Victory?"

Many states had stringent laws against dueling. In 1779, the governor of Virginia, Thomas Jefferson, ordered that anyone who committed murder in a duel be hanged and the estates of both duelers forfeited. A Massachusetts statute stipulated that the corpse of a dueler be delivered to a surgeon to be dissected and anatomized. But despite a variety of penalties, from whipping to dissection, not only did the practice of dueling become more and more prevalent — "scarce a mail arrives," commented one writer in a New Hampshire newspaper in 1800, "that but brings accounts of one or more [duels]" — but it became particularly popular among politicians. Often they would attempt to exploit the duel to influence public opinion, as historian Joanne B. Freeman points out. Sometimes they would find the duel useful to defend their honor, prove their worth, or perhaps rejuvenate a languishing career. Still, the idea of dueling was repugnant to many. "My character is not within their power," Jefferson would write about the political zealots who fought for honor. "It is in the hands of my fellow citizens at large." The only verdict on his honor and character that mattered, he explained, was the political verdict of "the republican mass of our country." In 1803, a resolution prohibiting duelers from holding any office in the national government was defeated in the House of Representatives. The struggle did not end there. No man should vote for a dueler, declared Lyman Beecher in his *Remedy for Duelling*, grasping the abyss separating the primitive performance of the duel from the conduct of modern politics. But the duelers dueled on.

Just two and a half years before the Hamilton-Burr duel, in November 1801, Hamilton's oldest son Philip had been killed in a duel. "The highest as well as the eldest hope of my family," he desolately wrote to Benjamin Rush, "has been taken from me." On the day Philip Hamilton died, the New York *Evening Post*, founded by Alexander Hamilton, announced his death, decrying the "horrid custom" of dueling and pleading for strong legislation to· end this barbarous "fashion." But from Philip's father there was nothing but silence on the matter of the duel. Indeed, though Hamilton had written in 1779 that "we do not now live in the days of chivalry," he seemed oddly drawn to this feudal ritual, although he was more experienced in issuing challenges to duels than in actually fighting them. All in all, he was involved in eleven affairs of honor. Still, in 1795, while defending the Jay Treaty, Hamilton had crisply written that "true honor is a rational thing." Stressing the value of moderation, he had insisted that "it is consistent with honor to preceed rupture by negociation." But on the eve of his duel with Burr, while claiming that he "abhorr[ed] the practice of Duelling," he abjured moderation and restraint, confessing that "what men of the world denominate honor impressed on me a peculiar necessity not to decline the call."

The duel was an anachronistic relic of the feudal age. Then, an elite class of warrior-knights, the protectors and defenders of their society, centered their lives around a code of "honor" shared only with members of their own class, a rigorous standard of behavior that distinguished them from all other members of the community. The duel was the dramatic centerpiece of their world: through the duel, aristocrats staged and publicly displayed their difference and superiority. As far as the adjudication of their grievances was concerned, the two combatants preferred the arbitrariness of the duel's outcome to a rational system of justice. The key to understanding America, maintained the political theorist Louis Hartz, was the fact that it had no feudal past, but America's duelers apparently sought to inject just such a dose of feudalism into American society. In the eighteenth century, as in the Middle Ages, commented historian Douglass Adair, "honor" was "elitist, for small male in-groups" and "ethically reactionary."

The duel wildly contradicted the essence of the modern, mobile society that the United States was becoming under Thomas Jefferson. A country that seeks to promote commerce, economic growth, and prosperity for its citizens requires a predictable and rational environment, one that is buttressed by a legal system that applies equally to all; it cannot tolerate private, class-bound codes of justice or a legal system based on chance. In a modern society, the ultimate reward for people's efforts is tangible wealth. What, after all, could be more unproductive and antimodern than the lethal, implacable pursuit of honor? "What is honor?" asked Shakespeare's Falstaff. "A word. What is that word honor? air."

The duel also contradicted the meaning of politics in general (an arena for persuasion and negotiation) and party politics in particular (a channel for nonviolent conflict). Politics, after all, is largely the art of the deal, not the art of the duel. But both Hamilton and Burr were sufficiently negative about party politics, alienated from their old allies, and pessimistic about their chances of returning to power that they turned their backs on politics and parties, on the channels they offer for the nonviolent expression — and resolution — of political conflict, and on the party politician's code of "sportsmanlike decency." Or perhaps it was the weakness itself of that incipient party system — the decline of the Federalists as a vital opposition party and Burr's alienation from the Republican Party — that left the two New Yorkers adrift, free to turn to violence, the ultimate antipolitical response.

At the dawn of the new century, Alexander Hamilton, forty-nine years old, one of the architects of the Constitution, secretary of the treasury, and general in the army, and Aaron Burr, forty-eight years old, lawyer, senator, vice president of the United States, and gubernatorial candidate, in a breathtaking, backward step, abjured their political lives and bowed to the supreme value of the aristocratic, feudal world: *honor.*

On the eve of his duel with Burr, Hamilton strangely experienced pangs of guilt — not because of the primitive nature of the duel itself or because of the distress he was inflicting on his family, but rather because he felt that he might indeed have injured Burr's reputation. Even more strangely, he decided that he would not aim his first two shots at Burr, "thus giving a double opportunity to Col Burr *to pause and to reflect.*" Pause and reflect in the middle of a duel, heart pounding wildly, pistol in hand? An intriguing scenario. But he did not budge from that determination. "The scruples of a Christian," he told his wife, compelled him to expose his own life rather than to take the life of another. About the Christian ethos of repentance and pardon he said nothing. What could Hamilton now do but draw up his will and bid farewell to his wife, daughter, and three surviving sons — to whom he was bequeathing his considerable debt? "Adieu best of wives and best of Women," he wrote. "Embrace all my darling Children for me."

Turning their backs on the very world they and their generation of leaders had created, preferring the immutable rules of a bizarre feudal code to the rough-and-tumble world of political strife, renouncing their responsibilities to their nation and to their families, trading freedom of speech — the sine qua non of politics — for blood, Burr and Hamilton met on the dueling field in Weehawken, New Jersey, on the morning of July 11, 1804, to obey archaic and illegal rules, fire their pistols, and wound or blow out the other's brains.

The men counted off ten full paces. The gentleman in charge an-

The death of Alexander Hamilton on the dueling field
of Weehawken, New Jersey.

nounced the rules; the two men said that they were prepared. Hamilton stopped to put on his glasses. They took aim. The two pistols were discharged within a few seconds of each other, a witness reported. Hamilton instantly fell. Burr advanced a few steps toward Hamilton but then, without speaking, turned around and withdrew. Burr later said that smoke from Hamilton's pistol obscured his sight before he could fire. Had Hamilton really fired first? Did he aim at Burr or in the air? No one can know.

Burr's bullet penetrated Hamilton's right side, passing through his liver before shattering his lumbar vertebrae. "This is a mortal wound," he whispered before losing consciousness. When he awoke aboard the little barge transporting him back to New York, he said that he had lost all feeling in his lower extremities and asked that his wife be sent for. In New York, his friends tenderly placed him on a bed and sat with him, as he moaned from pain in his back. During the next day, his sufferings were "almost intolerable," his doctor reported. The French consul summoned French surgeons aboard a frigate in the harbor, but they too could only concur that it was a mortal wound. He was treated with laudanum but remained conscious until the end. "I have found, for some time past, that my life *must* be exposed to that man," Hamilton murmured on his deathbed, as if yielding to the implacable dictates of some cruel gods. Thirty-one hours after the duel, at two o'clock in the afternoon, Alexander Hamilton died. "His most determined Ennemies did not like to get rid of him, in that Way," John Adams said.

In his funeral oration, Gouverneur Morris portrayed Hamilton as a man of impeccable judgment, a role model for all. He exhorted his listeners to ask themselves, when in doubt as to what line of conduct to adopt, "Would Hamilton have done this thing?" About the practice of dueling, he said nothing, though he recommended that those in attendance do nothing to "offend the insulted majesty of the law." Hamilton's friend Matthew Clarkson offered a more insightful comment, remarking just days after the funeral that it took more courage to refuse a challenge than to accept one. "If we were truly brave," he told Gouverneur Morris, "we should not accept a challenge; but we are all *cowards.*" Indeed, as historian Joseph Ellis remarked, Burr and Hamilton, two self-proclaimed gentlemen, "shot each other in juvenile displays of their mutual insecurity." As for Jefferson, when his own son-in-law was about to fight a duel two years later, he wrote to the young man that risk taking was "the falsest of honour . . . a mere compound of crime & folly." In Jefferson's mind, feudal honor was no match for family values and his "tender anxieties" for his loved ones.

Hamilton was dead, but both men were losers. Across the Hudson River from New York, they had both performed the dramatic end of their lives of public service. Perhaps they had sensed that it was time for them to quit the political arena, for Burr had too little principle to survive in the new political world, and Hamilton had too much.

Burr considered himself a disciple of Lord Chesterfield, who summed up his philosophy in the maxim that "a gentleman is free to do whatever he pleases, so long as he does it with style" and "so long as no ill-will is intended." In politics, Burr followed Chesterfield's advice, creating no deep or lasting loyalties to Republican precepts or colleagues, playing a double game, betraying whomever he wished. In vain his contemporaries had searched for some underlying ideals or vision in his conduct, something more than ambition and egocentrism. As for his adherence to the so-called "laws of honor," Burr had wildly miscalculated the effect of a duel and a murder: he fled New York in disgrace, raving about "the persecutions which are practised against me."

Days after killing Hamilton, he surfaced for a romantic tryst in Philadelphia. "If any male friend of yours should be dying of ennui," a depraved Burr wrote to his daughter, as if he were a character in Laclos's prerevolutionary novel of aristocratic libertinage, *Les liaisons dangereuses*, "recommend him to engage in a duel and a courtship at the same time." The absence of any moral conscience was absolute.

While Burr had no principles, Hamilton had too many. "Our real Disease," he wrote on the very eve of his death, "is DEMOCRACY," underscoring his "growing distaste to politics." On that same evening, he feebly argued that he had to go through with the ritual violence and preserve his honor in order to retain "the ability to be in future useful [in] crises of our public affairs." But in truth, he realized all too painfully that there could be no useful role in America for an adversary of the people. In the new Jeffersonian era, his antidemocratic political convictions were offensive and obsolete. "General Hamilton *hated* republican government," Gouverneur Morris later commented in a lengthy examination of his friend's politics. How could a bitter foe of democracy, swimming against the democratic tide, deploring the absence of an aristocracy in America, scorning the populace, survive in an open and expanding political arena? "He never failed on every occasion," Morris admitted, "to advocate the excellence of, and avow his attachment to, monarchical government." He was "covetous of *glory*," Morris explained, adding that Hamilton "was too *proud* and too *virtuous* . . . [to] tolerate measures eventually fatal to liberty and *honor*." Glory, pride, virtue, honor: all the makings of a medieval knight. The manly values of "Pride, Strength and Courage," remarked John Adams insightfully, were not sufficient to create great leaders of character and intelligence for a free, rational, peaceful republic. "Another Hamilton, another Burr," Adams wrote in 1819, "might rend this mighty Fabric twain."

Hamilton had rejected the dynamic trends that were reshaping and redefining American politics. Did Aaron Burr's bullet kill him, or was he destroyed by his own anachronistic ideas? Perhaps, for the sake of his own reputation in history, he died at the right time and, in tune with his own elitist political beliefs, in a singularly undemocratic way.

"This American world was not made for me," Hamilton had confessed to Morris in 1802. Divorced from the Constitution of the United States, which he now termed "a frail and worthless fabric," alienated from his own society, longing to "withdraw from the Scene," in 1802 he had begun construction of a new house in northern Manhattan.

"A garden, you know," he wrote, "is a very useful refuge of a disappointed politician." But a garden refuge would prove insufficient. Already in 1780, Hamilton — then General Washington's twenty-five-year-old aide-de-camp, had described himself as "disgusted with everything in this world" and as "not fit for this terrestreal Country." "I have no other wish," he wrote, "than as soon as possible to make a brilliant exit." A quarter of a century later he finally made that exit.

13

Would the System Work?

Despite Hamilton's scorn for republican government and for the "frail and worthless" fabric of the Constitution, the system appeared to be working smoothly. Harmony was in; intrigue and murder were out.

Indeed, the election of 1804 had none of the spectacular drama of the election of 1800 or the infamous duel. Jefferson and George Clinton ran against Charles Cotesworth Pinckney and his running mate, Rufus King, garnering 162 electoral votes out of 176, winning every state except Connecticut and Delaware — which, Jefferson quipped, was "a mere county of England." For the second time, Pinckney lost his own state of South Carolina. In the new House of Representatives, Republicans won 116 seats out of 141, and in the Senate, there would be 27 Republicans and 7 Federalists. Americans were "almost melted into one," Jefferson cheered. Even Connecticut, he predicted, "will be with us in a short time." It had been a lopsided victory, but at least there had been a contest. Across the ocean, the French had just "elected" an emperor in a farcical national plebiscite, by a vote of 3,500,000 to 2,500. In December 1804, Napoleon Bonaparte, draped in ermine and scarlet velvet, ceremoniously placed a glittering crown on his own head, as Pope Pius VII morosely looked on.

Federalists had suffered disastrous setbacks, not the least of which was Hamilton's premature death. But they were not yet ready to also play dead. While the old guard preferred principle to victory, a new generation of young Federalists was willing to make the opposite bargain — and sacrifice principle for victory. Armed with the energy and optimism of young men, they set out to master the new rules of the political game and rejuvenate their party. No longer able to count on the fame of a Washington and a Hamilton, Federalists had to build and nourish grass-roots support. They began by organizing statewide committees, engaging in preelection door-to-door canvassing and get-out-the-vote campaigns, publishing and distributing their own political propaganda, and sponsoring Federalist newspapers to counter the energetic Republican press. While there were 260 newspapers in the nation in 1800, there would be 396 in 1810 and 582 in 1820. Young Federalists held political dinners and invited voters to barbecues; they speechified on national holidays and even at funerals; hundreds of "Washington Benevolent Societies" popped up across the country, more focused on politics than on charity.

Federalists did more than adopt Republican techniques for organization and propaganda: they pillaged their ideas, too. Federalist candidates would present themselves as friends of the people, as historian Alan Taylor noted, no longer as authoritarian fathers. They claimed that they, not the Republicans, were the real majoritarians: Republicans heeded the *mob*, but Federalists respected the *people*. If Jefferson demanded frugal government, so would they! If Republicans trumpeted self-interest and individualism to the detriment of the public good, they would do the same. In the wake of Jefferson's embargo of 1807, Federalists did an about-face, forgetting Hamiltonian economics and advocating instead laissez-faire economics and free trade, criticizing Jefferson's administration for claiming "to protect better the property of an individual than his own sense of personal interest." New England Federalists even borrowed the language of Jefferson and Madison's Virginia and Kentucky Resolutions to protest the embargo; in Connecticut some declared the embargo's enforcement act "not binding on the citizens of this state." If Republicans sang the praises of the independent yeoman of the soil, Federalists would follow suit, recycling themselves as agrarians. And if Republicans could get mileage out of Anglophobia, Federalists would play the same game. If the Sedition Act had cost them votes in 1800, now, in a 180-degree reversal, they championed freedom of the press. Hopeful that the worn theme of religion still had some tread left, they proclaimed themselves in favor of freedom of religion, attacking the atheistic Jefferson for subverting Christianity.

In their hunt for popular new issues, young Federalists came out for universal white male suffrage and an end to property qualifications and religious tests. Trying to expand their base, they appealed to new minorities, welcomed Irish voters, and embraced Jews — or exploited existing anti-Semitism, depending on the locality. In the North, they courted the black vote and spoke out against slavery. (However, when Federalists in the Massachusetts legislature came out in 1804 for a constitutional amendment repealing the three-fifths clause, it backfired. Republicans accused them of wanting to destroy the union.) And most intriguing, Federalists encouraged women — especially elite white women — to play an informal role in politics. Federalists seemed finally to have learned the lesson, as historian Alan Taylor remarked, that it was not sufficient to parade their genteel social superiority; they had to "enact publicly their friendship for the people."

A spirited young generation had revived its party and moved it to the center of the political spectrum. This was just how the system was supposed to work: parties would become moderate in order to attract a majority of voters. Two-party politics seemed to be back. And yet, what did Federalists now stand for? What alternative vision of government and society, what political and social nourishment, did they offer? Few people could tell. "Our two great parties have crossed over the valley," wrote the isolated John Adams toward the end of Jefferson's second term in office, "and taken possession of each other's mountain." Nor could a visitor from Europe in 1805 detect any substantive differences between Federalists and Republicans. "They equally lay claim to the title of Republicans," he wrote. As if to prove the point, Oliver Wolcott, the conservative secretary of the treasury under John Adams, startled his friends by converting to Republicanism in 1807.

But was Jefferson too successful as a leader? Was America becoming a one-party democracy? Jefferson neither offered thoughts about a healthy political arena, in which two parties oppose each other, nor reflected on the role of an opposition party as watchdog over minority rights. In his First Inaugural Address, he had praised majority rule while stressing that the "minority possess their equal rights." But what body, if not an opposition party, would defend minority rights ignored or trampled on by the majority? Indeed, in the absence of an effective opposition to act as a *political* check on the majority, there arose a *constitutional* check on the majority — in the form of the Supreme Court. The principle of judicial review of legislative and executive actions, established in 1803 in the case of *Marbury v. Madison,* would, over the next two centuries, thwart the will of the majority — at times, all too effectively and undemocratically.

In his Second Inaugural Address Jefferson articulated his vision of the American future, describing a harmonious land over which reigned not only a "union of sentiment" but also an "entire union of opinion." He predicted that Federalist holdouts would soon come to realize that Republicans "think as they think, and desire what they desire." Was this the ultimate aim of society, all citizens thinking alike, desiring the same things? Was the wish for unanimity so strong that Jefferson wanted to do away with political opposition? How could political vitality survive in a society smothered by an "entire union of opinion"?

Jefferson's Republican majority was irresistible — and it was reshaping the country economically as well as politically. The charters that his administration granted for new banks, the new forms of credit that were allowed, the repealing of taxes, the retirement of the national debt, the elimination of regulations on business, the ease with which small farmers could acquire land in the West, the opening up of the Louisiana territory to settlement — all this democratized wealth and opportunity, replacing privilege with competition, contributing to the creation of a dynamic economy and a more open, egalitarian society. And through his embargo, which prohibited American trade overseas for more than year, he kept the country out of the European wars and at peace — though at a high price, that of a severe economic depression. Perhaps the nation's first president might have agreed with Jefferson's policy. "Twenty years peace," Washington noted in 1796, combined with "our remote situation," would "enable us in a just cause, to bid *defiance* to any power on earth." One can easily mistake Jefferson's words, written at the end of his second term, for Washington's. "If we can keep at peace eight years longer, our income," he wrote, "will be adequate to any war . . . and our position and increasing strength put us *hors d'insulte* from any nation."

In the presidential election of 1808, James Madison ran against Federalist Charles Cotesworth Pinckney, who was trying for national office for the third time. Federalists capitalized on hostility to the embargo and picked up some support. Pinckney carried all of New England, except Vermont; this time Federalists could take some comfort in their 47 electoral votes to Madison's 122. But it was not to be the beginning of a new trend. Federalists, despite the efforts of their young Turks, could not overcome their crabbed, elitist ideology. While Republicans were becoming the party of entrepreneurs, bowing to ascendant capitalism, outmoded, elitist ideas continued to flow from the mouths of men like conservative Massachusetts congressman Samuel Lyman, who declared that "nothing is so unequal as equality," and Thomas Sinnickson, United States representative from New Jersey, who yearned for "those happy times in which there was a reciprocity of confidence between the *rulers* and the *ruled.*"

Gouverneur Morris, too, wanted to believe that a chastened people, hungry for the "wisdom and virtue" of the enlightened, judicious fathers, would ultimately return to the Federalist fold. "They will then listen to the voice, which, in the wantonness of prosperity, they despised." Finally, in 1812, no longer willing to pull his punches, Morris publicly attacked the "Ignorance and Presumption" of the "general mass," scornfully lashing out against their "false notions of their Power and Importance." His mean, contemptuous words stunned moderates like Rufus King and John Jay, who tried desperately to censor him. Before another one of Morris's incendiary talks, King proposed that he and Jay vet the speech first. The old guard were demonstrating "more integrity than address," sighed Noah Webster. How could they remain so blind to "the means by which all popular governments are to be managed?"

Slowly the old guard slipped away. John Jay and George Cabot retired to their estates. Charles Cotesworth Pinckney moved to an island off the Carolina coast. United States senator William Bingham of Pennsylvania, a believer in government by the "best" people, moved to England soon after Jefferson's election. The sickly Fisher Ames died in 1808, at the age of fifty.

Whether it was the old-school men sacrificing victory for principle or the young Turks sacrificing principle for victory, Federalists — despite some innovations and flexibility, such as receptiveness toward a role for women — could trumpet neither principle nor victory. Republicans, moreover, had some novel election tricks up their sleeves. In 1812, before the state senatorial election, Massachusetts governor Elbridge Gerry signed a law redistricting Essex County, the bastion of ultra-conservatives. The new district, resembling a salamander on the map, led a cartoonist of the times to invent the word *gerrymander.*

In the first decades of the new century, Federalists won few elections. In the presidential election of 1812 they nominated no candidate of their own but threw their support to New York lieutenant-governor

DeWitt Clinton, the Republican candidate who opposed the war with Great Britain that had been declared earlier that year. Madison won 128 electoral votes to Clinton's 89. Although Federalists doubled their strength in Congress that year and would still hold on to the state governments in Maryland, Connecticut, Delaware, and Massachusetts, they were nevertheless unable to mount a viable opposition.

In the election of 1816, they turned to the experienced and dignified Rufus King. Despite Madison's weak presidential leadership, despite the Federalists' opposition to the War of 1812, which had ended in an American defeat, and despite the New York *Evening Post*'s enthusiastic call for an all-out effort for King — "Come on then! shoulder-to-shoulder! heads up! charge!" — nothing helped. Federalists proved unable to capitalize on their own strengths and the Republicans' weaknesses. King won only 34 electoral votes to James Monroe's 183.

The convention that New England Federalists had held in Hartford in December 1815 — at which mostly moderate Federalists attacked the Republican administration and called for constitutional amendments to limit commercial embargoes and presidential power in general — was caricatured in the Republican press as an elitist, subversive, secessionist cabal. Giving a new twist to the old Anglomen-Gallomen rivalry, Jefferson now referred to the Federalists at the Hartford convention as "the Marats, the Dantons and Robespierres of Massachusetts," bent, in French mode, on "anarchising" the United States. The Federalists' attempt at concerted, responsible action only served to dig deeper Federalism's political grave. Hartford, commented historian James MacGregor Burns, was "a final convulsive effort, half protest, half death cry, of a movement slowly passing out of existence."

"The existence of parties is not necessary to free government," James Monroe wrote to Andrew Jackson, the popular military hero from Tennessee, in 1816, a few days after winning the presidency. Though many men, he noted, believed that free government could not exist without parties, that was not his opinion. Jackson agreed. "Now is the time to *exterminate* the monster called party spirit," he wrote. In his First Inaugural Address, Monroe — now in his late fifties, tall and erect, a man less philosophical than his friends Madison and Jefferson but esteemed for his good sense — announced that the American people "constitute one great *family* with a common interest," stressing that "*discord* does not belong to our system." Though he would prove to be a tough party man who appointed few Federalists to his government, Monroe would nevertheless insist that his job was not to be the head of a party "but of the nation itself." Could he not be both?

On June 1, three months after his inauguration, Monroe left with a small entourage on a Washington-like tour of New England. Just as Washington had hoped that, by touring New England in 1789, citizens would find in him a symbol of their new national unity, Monroe, too, wanted to give Americans the opportunity to express the new spirit of unity. Unlike Washington, Monroe wished to travel as a private citizen, paying his own expenses and shunning ceremony. But ceremony would not shun him.

Parades, accolades, odes, songs, and dinners were the steady fare. He reviewed troops, visited arsenals and fortifications, heard sermons, attended receptions. Traveling by steamboat and carriage, Monroe saw a different landscape from the one that Washington had viewed twenty-eight years earlier. Spending a week in New York, the president could glimpse Cornelius Vanderbilt's ferryboats dotting New York harbor, transporting passengers between Staten Island and Manhattan. By steamboat, he journeyed up the Hudson to West Point, the site that Washington had selected for the United States Military Academy, which opened in 1802. Moving on to Boston, he saw a busy port city adorned by fine buildings by Charles Bulfinch and a famous century-old lighthouse, the "Boston Light."

Boston was not only a city of ships and merchants; it was becoming a manufacturing, financial, and cultural center too. A few miles out of town, in Waltham, Monroe toured Francis Cabot Lowell's new textile mill, the first factory to contain power cotton spinning and weaving machinery under the same roof. Just a few months before Monroe's election, the first savings bank in the nation had been chartered in Boston. He attended a concert of the Haydn and Handel Oratorio Society and could also have heard a concert given by the first regular orchestra in the nation, the Boston Philharmonic Society. Perhaps someone presented him with a copy of a new literary magazine, the *North American Review,* edited by Jared Sparks. At Harvard, the president received an honorary Doctor of Laws degree, amid elaborate pomp.

Though Federalists were still a strong presence in Boston, the city's jubilant welcome for Monroe resembled a "love fest," in the words of his biographer Harry Ammon. "Bostonians who had not spoken to one another in years appeared side by side at private and public gatherings as though united in bonds of life-long friendship." Federalists and Republicans tried to outdo each other in honoring the fourth president from Virginia. Forty thousand people filled the streets near the Boston Common, where he would receive his official welcome; four thousand boys and girls — the boys in blue, the girls in white, all carrying a red or white rose — lined the final approach to the welcoming stand. Even ultra-Federalist and northern secessionist Timothy Pickering, one of Monroe's old adversaries, greeted him warmly. All who met the new president, said Abigail Adams, who had entertained Monroe at a dinner party in her home in Quincy, were enchanted by his "agreeable affability . . . unassuming manners . . . his polite attentions to all orders and ranks." Monroe was pleased, he wrote to Madison, to have given Federalists the opportunity to "get back in the great family of the union." Was a new era, devoid of party antagonisms, dawning?

The next election, in 1820, was uncontested. No Federalist candidate could be found to run against Monroe. But it was not because of the unanimity of approbation, explained disaffected Republican senator John Randolph of Virginia, but rather because of "the unanimity of indifference." Indeed, there was no vocal opposition party to awaken people to the burning issues of the day: economic depression, state bank closings, slowdown in foreign trade, slavery in the new state of Missouri. For the "general safety of the Republic," noted the *Ohio Monitor*, there was too much quiet in the land. Monroe captured every electoral vote but one.

Had political parties run their course? Had the myth of a national "family" and the desire for a unitary national identity delegitimized opposition to government? Had the emotional dream of harmony eclipsed a rational understanding of the need for party conflict and meaningful political debate in an open democracy? The organization of American government would soon approach "perfection," Monroe loftily proclaimed in his Second Inaugural Address. No higher degree of "order and harmony" was conceivable in human institutions, he maintained.

Perfection in a stagnant Shangri-la? "Sir, I do not believe in this harmony, this extinction of party spirit," exclaimed Republican Henry Clay, the Speaker of the House from Kentucky, interrupting Monroe's fantasy. "I do not believe that men have ceased to be men." As if to hammer home that point, one day Secretary of the Treasury William Crawford of Georgia grabbed his cane and prepared to strike the president because Monroe had hesitated to grant one of his requests. "You damned infernal old scoundrel!" Crawford shouted.

Years earlier, Jefferson had warned that, in the face of dwindling opposition from the outside, Republicans "would schismatize among themselves," their bloated party splintering into different factions. Indeed, after 1826, the Jeffersonian Republicans, no longer facing a viable opposition from the Federalists, split into the Jacksonian "Democratic Republicans" and the "National Republicans" who, by the mid-1830s, became the "Whigs." But even before those new parties surfaced, Jefferson's prediction of Republican schisms provided the scenario for the election of 1824. Five Republican candidates — the cane-wielding Crawford, Henry Clay, Secretary of State John Quincy Adams of Massachusetts, United States senator Andrew Jackson, and Secretary of War John Calhoun of South Carolina — ran against one another. The factions were personal rather than ideological, commented Martin Van Buren. People voted according to their own individual preferences or antipathies, which, he noted, "moved the bitter waters of political agitation to their lowest depths."

Making matters worse, elder statesman James Monroe threw his support to — no one. Calhoun quit the race to run for vice president; Crawford was ill and fell behind. Andrew Jackson won a plurality of both popular and electoral votes, but no candidate won a majority of votes in the Electoral College. And so, once again, the election was thrown into the House of Representatives. It was a time for making deals, and Clay made one with Adams. Adams won — and appointed Clay his secretary of state. Jackson turned down an offer to lead the war department. He would come back later for more.

If nothing else sealed the fate of the Federalists, it was the 1825 inauguration of John Quincy Adams, the son of Federalist John Adams, as a Republican president.

While Adams, in his Inaugural Address, repeated the stale, irrelevant mantra of "harmony of the nation," remarking to a visitor that his paramount goal was to "break up the remnant of old party distinctions," Jefferson was once again rethinking his ideas about unity and harmony. During his first term in the presidency, while expressing his belief that the Republican Party would ultimately absorb all right-thinking Americans, he had also simultaneously spoken out for the salutary effects of party. "A respectable minority is useful as censors," he had written — though he apparently wanted control over the make-up of that minority, for the Federalist minority in Congress, he noted, was too bitter, desperate, and furious to be "respectable." In 1817, he seemed to have renounced the idea of a useful minority party of "censors," rejoicing instead that the "complete suppression of party" had "sweetened society beyond imagination." Then, seven years later, reconsidering the consequences of one-party democracy, he made another about-face. "I am no believer in the amalgamation of parties nor do I consider it either desirable or useful to the public," he stated. "Tories are Tories still, by whatever name they may be called," he muttered about his age-old foes.

The Republican umbrella, Jefferson realized, would not be large enough to contain all political differences. There could be no escape from politics and parties. "The same political parties which now agitate the U.S. have existed thro' all time," he wrote to John Adams in 1813, explaining that "everyone takes his side in favor of the many, or of the few." While Adams responded that adversarial parties did little but misconstrue, misrepresent, ridicule, and insult each other's policies, thereby preventing any kinds of improvements to society, he skirted Jefferson's central point that ideological political conflict will always exist when people are free, when their "minds and mouths are not shut up by the gag of a despot." Whether the division was between elitists and democrats, between those in favor of a strong central government and those advocating states' rights, or, as Federalists preferred to put it, between "friends of order and its foes," Jefferson came to consider such principled political confrontations most salutary. "Take away this," he warned in 1825, "and some more dangerous principle of division will take its place." Jefferson perceived that division along the general — and traditional — lines of political ideology was less explosive than other more potentially explosive divisions, such as geography.

And yet, ultimately Jefferson could provide little intellectual help and guidance for future generations on the subject of a party system and the legitimacy of opposition — for always woven into his acceptance of parties was a simultaneous rejection of them. Never did he make a clear, ringing endorsement of the importance of opposition in government or give undiluted praise to the immense contribution of an adversarial party system in a democracy. Did this rabidly partisan leader even know himself whether he believed in no parties, one all-encompassing party, two equal parties, or one and a half parties — that is, one powerful party and a feeble opposition? Did he want his own party to absorb the opposition, annihilate them, fight them, or placate them? Perpetually revising his thoughts about opposition, unable to resolve his own contradictory feelings about party, he wanted it both ways: harmony and consensus one day, parties, opposition, and war against the Tories the next. But how can we fault him when, more than two centuries later, many Americans are still nostalgic for a politics of harmony and consensus, still drawn to politicians who earnestly talk about bipartisanship while misunderstanding the very essence of politics — which is conflict.

Would James Madison have better advice for the younger generation of political leaders entering the arena, vying for power? In 1819, while factions in the Republican Party were forming around sectional interests, Madison looked for an antidote to such potentially disruptive divisions. He remarked that political parties, far from dividing the country, could be useful in unifying it but only if they were national, their members spread out "in every part of the Country." In that case, he noted, "they strengthen the Union of the Whole, while they divide every part." But in a farsighted prediction of the political terrain before the Civil War, he observed that, "Should a State of parties arise, founded on geographical boundaries and other Physical & permanent distinctions, . . . what is to controul those great repulsive Masses from awful shocks against each other?"

Toward the end of his life, Madison was still meditating on government and politics. In 1833, three years before his death, he was a semi-invalid, suffering from painful rheumatism, usually confined to his home. But his mind and his memory, visitors remarked, were "perfectly sound." What were his thoughts as he viewed the political developments that had taken place over three decades?

Although he and his generation of political thinkers had feared an "overbearing," "unjust and interested" majority and had devised the system of checks and balances in order to protect the minority from "interested combinations of the majority," Madison had witnessed no tyranny, no extremism, no oppressive majority, no mobocracy or demagogues during several decades of constitutional federal government. To construct their majorities, presidents had had to appeal not only to loyal members of their own party but also to voters in the center, gaining their support with moderate policies. The will of the majority had been reasonable, and minorities had not been deprived of their political or legal rights. And yet the system of checks and balances that divided power and created conflicting, colliding majorities — in addition to the division of power between state and national governments — had often stalled the wheels of government.

After reflecting for almost half a century on the problem of stable government via checks and balances versus energetic government via majority rule, an older and wiser Madison — educated by practical experience as opposition leader and as president and by the flaws he came to perceive in what he had created in theory — came out for energetic government by the people, by the majority of citizens.

"The vital principle of republican government," he wrote in 1833, "is the *lex majoris partis,* the will of the majority." Refuting his own leitmotif in *Federalist* No. 10 — that is, his apprehension of an oppressive majority — Madison now argued passionately that "every friend to Republican Government ought to raise his voice against the sweeping denunciation of majority Government as the most tyrannical and intolerable of all governments." Indeed, criticism of majority government, he insisted, "strikes at the root of Republicanism." At the age of eightytwo, he demanded from government not fragmentation of power or even protection for minorities but rather protection for the majority and the assurance of their ability to wield power. Minorities, too, would of course be protected, but their rights would not outweigh the interests of the majority. It was clearly a greater injustice to frustrate a majority of citizens than to frustrate a minority of them.

And yet, although Madison came to embrace the concept of majority rule, and although he had remarked that "no free Country has ever been without parties, which are a natural offspring of Freedom," he did not follow the implications of those ideas to their logical conclusion. He did not explicitly state that the only way a majority could defeat his system of checks and balances and overcome the conflicting majorities created by that system was through a strong national party system. He never argued that only a disciplined national party, capable of winning presidential as well as congressional and senatorial elections, could capture the reins of government, unifying and mobilizing support for national policies and programs. On the contrary, Madison predicted that the numerical majority, though it had "justice on its side," could easily be thwarted by the "constitutional majority," which had, on its side, checks and balances, staggered elections for president, House, and Senate, and veto traps and other minority-empowering devices. And to this fundamental injustice he could offer no real remedy. For good or for ill, American government would henceforth operate, Madison realized, as a strange hybrid of checks and balances and majoritarian party politics. Although the two models would coexist for the next two centuries, together shaping American political life, the original Madisonian model of checks and balances — cast in a Constitution as enduring as stone — would always dominate the equation.

Without the help of Jefferson, Madison, or Monroe, two-party politics nevertheless managed to stage a comeback. A new breed of political organizer and strategist led the charge: men who held positive ideas about party and political conflict and believed that a *permanent* opposition was useful in democratic government, men like the amiable, calculating senator from New York, Martin Van Buren, who trumpeted party discipline and loyalty. For them, partisanship was not a dirty word. Unlike Jefferson, who once wrote that submitting one's opinions to the creed of any party was "the last degradation of a free and moral agent," a new generation of politicians praised dedication to the party cause. The ability to commit oneself to the principles of one's party, wrote an associate of Van Buren, was "as indispensable as any other *moral qualification.*"

Refusing to bow to hackneyed slogans about unity, the new professional politicians were convinced that the rhetoric of harmony and nonpartisanship merely masked the ruling elite's desire to impugn the opposition and stay in power. The "very discord" produced by competitive parties, Van Buren noted, "may in a government like ours, be conducive to the public good." Van Buren was in tune with political thinking in England: in 1826 the expression "His Majesty's Opposition" was used for the first time by John Hobhouse, arguing for a permanent opposition. The party opposite, he declared, constitutes "to all intents and purposes a branch of his Majesty's Government."

The return of a strong opposition party was also abetted by Andrew Jackson's steely determination to oust John Quincy Adams, the man who, he believed, had snatched from him the election of 1824. But it was more than a personal contest between two men: the outs wanted back in. The "outs" were westerners, southerners who resented the influence of the eastern elite, people angered by tariffs, small businessmen, mechanics, and farmers. More people, too, could participate directly in presidential elections; by 1828 electors in most states were chosen by popular election instead of by state legislatures. The task of Jackson and his allies was to get these people to the polls to vote for him. How could this be done, if not through party organization, local committees, state conventions, a plethora of new party newspapers, requests for contributions, and tireless campaigning? "Hickory Clubs" sprang up; men sporting hickory leaves in their hats flocked to "Grand Barbecues"; "hickory poles" were erected in towns. Party spirit was reborn.

What about ideas and platforms? Neither the Republican Party nor its offshoot had a very coherent political philosophy, but the Jackson–Van Buren coalition resuscitated the old Jeffersonian principles. Their "Democratic Republicans" stood for states' rights, small, frugal government, and popular rule. John Quincy Adams and allies like Henry Clay, campaigning under the name of the "National Republicans," emphasized strong central government, internal improvements such as roads and canals, and a host of new institutions, from a national university to a naval academy. Jacksonians assailed Adams for his "kingly pretensions" and touted their own man as the "candidate of the People," while Adams supporters praised their man's zeal for the common good and attacked Jackson as an adulterer, murderer, and traitor. People said that the contest was really between "one who can write and one who can fight," but the old battle between the "people" and the "aristocrats" seemed to be back. Jackson won big, capturing 56 percent of the popular vote and 178 electoral votes to Adams's 83. It was a double victory for a popular candidate and party machinery.

A vast and motley crowd of twenty thousand people watched their hero, Andrew Jackson, take the oath of office, and then poured into the executive mansion — trampling on chairs, fighting, smashing china and glasses — a "regular Saturnalia," one congressman said. The outsiders had scrambled in.

Antipartyism had retreated to the wings — from which it periodically emerges to this day — as a two-party system of government finally stepped to center stage. The "second party system" could begin its run. It had taken decades for a party system and the idea of a permanent opposition to be institutionalized, absorbed, and integrated into American political culture. Now the nation would be rescued from an antidemocratic one-party system, from uncontested elections, a multiplicity of factions, and from citizens' indifference to elections. Politicians who organized, campaigned, and courted the people were engaging ordinary Americans in politics — national and local. And the eventual by-product of that organizing and energizing would be the "mores" — the activity, the associations, the meetings, the participation in self-government, the self-confidence — that would so captivate Tocqueville when he visited America in 1831.

"As soon as you step onto American soil," Tocqueville marveled, "you find yourself in the middle of a kind of tumult." Everyone was attending meetings! One group was debating whether to build a new church; another deciding whom to elect as representative; still another considering what kinds of improvements to make in their township. Farmers left their fields to discuss the construction of a new road or a new school. Some citizens showed up at a meeting merely to declare their opposition to the government. And at another meeting citizens were passionately denouncing drunkenness, the source of all social evil. Even women went to meetings — perhaps to forget their household cares.

The political community that Tocqueville so admired comprised a rich array of associations and factions — clashing, cooperating, and creating ferment. "Freedom of association," he explained, "is not as threatening to public order as people suppose, and it is even probable that, after a certain period of instability, it actually strengthens the polity." Like Machiavelli, Tocqueville came to the sagacious conclusion that the guardian of freedom was tumult. The direct source of the tumult? Democracy itself. Democracy seemed to spread throughout the social body a restless activity, an overwhelming power, a civic energy impossible without it. How to organize the tumult? How to channel it productively? Through all manner of civic associations and through dynamic, responsible, democratically open political parties with *big* ideas.

American individualism worried Tocqueville. He feared that people's preoccupation with their own self-interest would tend to isolate them, making them social and political recluses, cutting them off from meaningful engagement in their communities. The solution to the problem of atomization? Political parties. "Whatever natural repugnance people might have to act in concert, they will always be ready to do so in the interest of a party." Indeed, he saw the energy emanating from political associations permeating all of society, fostering all kinds of civic associations, for, he realized, politics instills "the taste for associating with others; it makes people want to organize; and it teaches people, who are used to living and acting alone, the art of coming together." There was, he maintained, a "natural and even necessary" relationship between political parties and civic associations. He considered political parties "great free schools, where all citizens can come to learn the general theory of associations."

Returning home to France after his visit to the New World, Tocqueville found the differences between the two cultures stunning. "When one leaves a free country for another that is not free," he observed, "one is struck by an extraordinary perception: in the first, everything is activity and movement; in the latter, everything seems calm and immobile." In Restoration France, he saw a society composed of atomized individuals, powerless and excluded from self-government, unengaged in public affairs, focused only on the narrow sphere of their own private welfare, offering neither resistance nor opposition to government. He saw a people still reeling from their revolutionary interlude with liberty, wanting nothing more than to relax and retreat, far from liberty's storms and tempests.

Tocqueville was convinced that only by following the example of Americans and participating in all kinds of political and civic groups and associations could citizens preserve their freedom. Why were Europeans so wary of factions and associations? Possessing virtually no experience in participatory democracy or in freedom, Tocqueville remarked, they mistakenly confused political associations with conspiracies; they equated political opposition with war against government. They had simply not matured enough politically to understand that the object of the political game is not violence or conspiracy, but simply persuasion and change.

"My aim," Tocqueville wrote in *Democracy in America*, "has been to show, through the example of America, that laws and especially mores can permit a democratic people to remain free."

Epilogue

W ASHINGTON BELIEVED IN CONSENSUS, warning that party spirit was a "fire not to be quenched"; Adams governed without the support of his own party and sought to repress the opposition party; Hamilton sabotaged his own party's candidate. Not one of them discerned the path that American politics would take. It was Jefferson and Madison — despite their ambivalence about parties and their lack of any coherent theory of party — who intuitively understood that politicians and voters had to organize into a disciplined majority party in order to wield power in a system of checks and balances. The two friends proved to be effective opposition leaders who created the party structures, mechanics, and election strategies that would define American politics far into the future. They had even recognized — and exploited — the novel role that partisan newspaper editors would play in the clamorous political life of the country.

For the next two hundred years, as the names, principles, and fortunes of parties would change, elections would be discussed and fought in Jeffersonian terms: majority rule; public opinion; party platforms and goals; party organization, strength, and loyalty; grass-roots support; campaign planning; and clear and appealing visions of national purpose, explained and circulated by newspapers. Under Jefferson and Madison, radical, revolutionary ideas — equality, majority rule, self-interest, democracy — had entered the mainstream of American politics. The old style of elitist, deferential politics was gone for good.

The year 1800 had witnessed a revolution, Jefferson memorably remarked in 1819. It was, he wrote, "as real a revolution in the principles of our government as that of 1776 was in its form." It had not been fought "by the sword," he explained, but rather "by the rational and peaceable instrument of reform, the suffrage of the people." In other words, while the Revolutionary War had been a military confrontation, the revolutionary election of 1800 had been a nonviolent, "rational and peaceable" transfer of power by means of public opinion and orderly elections. The Constitution had permitted the people to declare their will by "dismissing functionaries of one principle," that is, Federalists, and electing Republican politicians representing a different principle.

Jefferson conceived his revolution in the astronomical sense of a *return* to the point of origin. He viewed it as the rediscovery of — and renewed commitment to — the bold ideas of freedom and equality of America's founding period and the limitless, dizzying hopes for the happiness of a new race of free (white) human beings. Federalists, attempting to transform the republic into an American version of an armed European nation-state, had steered her into the waves, "with a view to sink her," Jefferson wrote shortly after his inauguration. But his second American revolution of 1800, he confidently predicted, would "put her on her republican tack," and the American ship would "now show, by the beauty of her motion, the skill of her builders." The revolution of 1800 was thus for Jefferson a return to 1776. His revolution was also a return to a unitary national identity: just as John Jay, in *Federalist* No. 2, had portrayed all Americans as "one united people," Jefferson happily proclaimed in his First Inaugural Address that Americans had once again united "with *one* heart and *one* mind."

And yet the revolution of 1800 was more than the temporary defeat of the Federalists' vision of political "consolidation" and a powerful military-fiscal nation and more than the return to the ideal of a peaceful federal republic; it was also more than an imaginary return to a fictional, unitary Eden. It was a revolution in the modern — not the astronomical — sense: a *transformation*. From the revolution of 1800 emerged the principle of the legitimacy of opposition and the beginnings of the first American party system. For generations of Americans after Jefferson, the most enduring gift of the revolution of 1800 was not unity but conflict, not family but parties — the healthy, invaluable strife of competitive parties, the essential feature — the sine qua non — of democracy. Ironically, the one place where this particular revolution did not occur was Virginia. Jefferson's victory, as historian Richard Beeman remarked, "sounded the knell for the two-party system in Virginia" — so much so that V. O. Key, in his groundbreaking study of southern politics, described one-party Virginia as "a political museum piece."

The revolution of 1800 was also transformational because it proved to be a democratizing revolution — socially, economically, and politically. More average Americans — and not just wealthy squires and land speculators — could become property owners, as land, including that of the Louisiana Purchase, could be bought with lower down payments and in smaller, more attainable parcels. The minimum price for public land was lowered to $1.64 an acre, credit terms were made more liberal, and land could be paid for over a ten-year period. Jefferson's vision of a virtuous nation of independent small landowners almost came true. "Every industrious citizen of the United States has the power to become a freeholder," one early-nineteenth-century observer wrote. "The land being purely his own, there is no setting limits to his prosperity." The proliferation of banks permitted more middle-class entrepreneurs to receive credit and enter the capitalist arena.

The political landscape, too, was opening up. In 1800, only four out of sixteen states chose presidential electors through direct popular elections; by 1824, electors were chosen in popular elections in eighteen of the twenty-four states. Voter participation, which was high in 1800 — almost 70 percent in some states — continued its upward trend, especially where there was stiff ideological competition between Federalist and Republican candidates. One of the exceptions, again, was one-party Virginia, where by 1820 voter participation had plummeted to 3 percent of free adult white males.

In general, this democratizing revolution began the process of transforming the United States into a modern capitalist society and a more open and egalitarian society. Jefferson's mistrust of big business and antipathy for urban centers notwithstanding, his "politics of inclusion," in the words of historians Elkins and McKitrick, provided the "political opener" for the rise of middle-class capitalism in the United States. Fortunately, in this endeavor, Republicans faced few serious obstacles: the United States, unlike European nations, was not a country spoiled by wretched poverty, dominated by a privileged, hereditary caste, or riven by religious hatred. If there was any disfavored minority among voting white men — at least in some parts of the nation — it was the old elite, the rich, the propertied, the well-born. Indeed, in the early nineteenth century, those Federalist "fathers" found themselves exiled from positions of national leadership.

But what about other disfavored, dispossessed groups? "We are acting for all mankind," Jefferson had triumphantly written in 1802. And yet, for Jefferson and Madison and the succeeding generation of Republicans, democracy and majority rule referred to white males. Excluded from the majority — and even from the minority! — were women, the propertyless, masses of laborers, the illiterate, Indians, and especially blacks. Although the two Virginians rejected wealth and breeding as prerequisites for political participation and power, they did not reject gender and race.

As the country was moving forward toward democracy, in some ways it was simultaneously moving backward toward exclusion and inequality. Major improvements were being made in women's education, but women property owners in New Jersey, who had been permitted to vote in the election of 1800, were deprived of that right in 1807. Workers also suffered setbacks, especially when they tried to organize. In 1805, when members of a shoemakers union went on strike for higher wages, their leaders were arrested and found guilty of criminal conspiracy. Strikes would be considered conspiracies until 1842.

Although President Jefferson extolled Native Americans for their "ardent love of liberty and independence," he nevertheless exhorted them to renounce their "reverence for the custom of their ancestors" and instead adapt themselves to an agricultural way of life. His administration continued to purchase Indian lands and planned for the removal of Indians from the east side of the Mississippi to the west. "Instead of inviting Indians to come within our limits," Jefferson wrote, "our object is to tempt them to evacuate them." Indians in the Wisconsin area negotiated in 1804 the transfer of 5 million acres to the government, but Indians who resisted the advance of settlers onto their lands would find themselves crushed by the likes of Major General Andrew Jackson.

Blacks fared no better. While some states would count no slaves in their census, while New Jersey passed legislation in 1804 calling for the gradual emancipation of slaves in that state, and while the number of free blacks in the northern states had grown to 50,000 by 1810, other states tightened laws regulating slavery. The number of slaves in the country was increasing, and the domain of slavery was spreading steadily west. Though Jefferson signed legislation prohibiting the importation of any more slaves into the United States after 1808, his postmaster general, a Connecticut Republican, dismissed all free blacks who had been employed by the post office. Free blacks, who had enjoyed the right to vote in some states, were disenfranchised in Maryland in 1810 and in North Carolina in 1835. The "true" revolution of 1800, argues historian James Sidbury, would have accomplished more than saving the republic from "monarchical" Federalism: it would have meant the success of Gabriel's rebellion in Virginia.

On the issue of slavery, Jefferson walked a tightrope. Many of his statements about slavery are difficult to reconcile with one another. He professed to want to abolish slavery, and yet he bitterly opposed the intervention of the national government in limiting its expansion. The Missouri Compromise of 1820, prohibiting new slave states to be carved out of the Louisiana Purchase north of the line 36°30′, provoked his principled ire as well as his profound disappointment. He insisted that the compromise was "not a moral question, but one merely of power." In Jefferson's mind, the Missouri question was not really about slavery; it was about union. The threatened rejection of the new slave state of Missouri from a union based on the equality of all states would, he feared, mean the end of the American federation of self-governing republican states. He viewed the compromise as "a party trick" designed once again only to further the Federalist agenda by consolidating political parties along geographical lines and opening the door to the separation — of the North!

As for slavery in the new territories, not only did Jefferson insist that the compromise would do nothing to decrease the slave population, but he attacked it as counterproductive. By prohibiting slavery in certain states, the compromise, he was convinced, dispensed them of the burden of helping to find a solution to the problem of slavery; it aggravated the sectional division in the nation; and it accorded ominous power to the national government. Congress's next step, he worried, might even be to "declare that the condition of all men within the US. shall be that of freedom." Were sharp limitations on the power of the national government and the principle of the equality of the states more significant, more compelling for Jefferson than the inalienable rights of mankind and the opportunity to diminish — if not end — the abomination of slavery? Had he forgotten his criticism of the king for vetoing legislation in Virginia to end the slave trade? Had he forgotten his plea, in 1774, for the "rights of human nature" and his call, in 1782 in his *Notes on the State of Virginia*, for "total emancipation" along with his description of the master-slave relationship as a perpetual exercise of "the most unremitting despotism on the one part, and degrading submissions on the other"? Had he forgotten that he had wanted to exclude slavery entirely from the trans-Appalachian West in 1784? Did the property rights of slave owners now trump human rights? Did the constitutional claims of states outweigh the rights of individuals to life, liberty, and the pursuit of happiness? Was the Enlightenment over in Virginia? "This Missouri question," Secretary of State John Quincy Adams commented about southern politicians, "has betrayed the secret of their souls."

The leaders of the Virginia dynasty — Jefferson, Madison, Monroe — cherished liberty and equality and trumpeted the pursuit of happiness, but they were unwilling — or perhaps intellectually unable — to begin the process of creating institutions and programs to extend those principles to all Americans. Republicans touted their responsiveness to public opinion, but they remained unresponsive to the basic needs of the numerical majority of Americans — women and blacks combined. Hampered by their view of liberty as protection *against* government, by their old distrust of government and fear of "monarchical" power, Jeffersonians did not yet grasp that only *through* government could genuine equality and liberty be achieved "for all mankind" — though it must be said that Federalists and their successors, while more sensitive than Republicans to the suffering of blacks, less fearful of a mixing of the races, and more welcoming to a role for women in the polity, were unable to offer strong alternative proposals.

Jefferson was not blind to the need for solutions to the problem of slavery, and he came up with a plan: "My proposition would be," he wrote in 1820, "that the holders should give up all born after a certain day . . . that these should be placed under the guardianship of the State, and sent at a proper age to S. Domingo." It was a scheme as impractical as it was morally inadequate, certainly no better than his strained argument against the Missouri Compromise. Stumbling in the dark shadows of slavery, at a loss for a solution, Jefferson would ultimately abdicate any leadership of the problem, announcing his "abandonment of the subject." Still, neither he nor the other great Virginians of his generation would become the heroes of slavery's defenders.

Yet it might be said that still another revolution surreptitiously began in 1800, one that would slowly develop and explode sixty years later. When Jefferson and Madison drafted the Virginia and Kentucky Resolutions in 1798, their motives had been less to advocate states' rights than to attack the Sedition Act and reverse what they perceived as the "monarchical" trend in the national government. But advocates of states' rights would nevertheless exploit and distort the so-called principles of 1798. The idea that states could justly nullify federal laws, combined with the Republican victory in 1800, may have contributed to reversing, in the words of historian Paul Rahe, "the momentum leading toward a subordination of the states to the nation. . . . Republican leaders unwittingly restored to the states something of the supremacy which they had possessed under the Articles of Confederation. This would have been perilous under any circumstances; for a republic situated on an extended territory and divided by the question of slavery, it would be very nearly fatal."

The distrust of national power that Jefferson expressed in 1798 did not disappear from view; on the contrary, it was an integral part of his vision of the revolution of 1800. In 1819, when he memorably praised the "true principles of the revolution of 1800," he was writing to Virginia Chief Justice Spencer Roane, congratulating him on his newspaper essays attacking John Marshall's Supreme Court; Roane's excoriation of Court decisions and defense of states' rights, Jefferson commented, were faithful to the "revolution of 1800." Jefferson's resentment of national "consolidation," his fear of northern hegemony, and his insistence on states' rights would all buttress his opposition to the Missouri Compromise. In the wake of that controversy and of the other "rapid strides" that Jefferson saw the government making in its apparent mission to usurp "all the rights reserved to the States," the former activist president now objected bitterly to the national government's power. "It is but too evident," he wrote in 1825, that all three branches of the federal government "are in combination to strip their colleagues, the State authorities, of the powers reserved by them." Though the dissolution of the federal compact "must be the last resource," he contended that there might be no choice but secession if the sole alternative was "submission to a government without limitation of powers."

A decade later, Madison would spring to the defense of his late friend to deny that Jefferson had stood for states' rights. "The nullifiers who make the name of Mr. Jefferson the pedestal for their colossal heresy," he observed, "shut their eyes and lips, whenever his authority is ever so clearly and emphatically against them." It was "high time," Madison wrote, "that the claim to secede at will should be put down by the public opinion." For his part, Madison reaffirmed his faith in a strong national government, insisting that "the advice nearest to my heart and deepest in my convictions is that the Union of the States be cherished and perpetuated." But, by then, the cat had been let out of the bag. Or perhaps it would be more accurate to say that the revolution of 1800 let two cats out of the bag: one healthy cat would scamper toward a vital two-party system; the mangy one, called the "Spirit of '98," would slink toward the Civil War.

Jefferson had "caught a vision of a comprehensive Enlightenment ideal," observed historian Bernard Bailyn, "and strove to make it real, discovering as he did so the intractable dilemmas." The most critical of those dilemmas was his wish somehow to eliminate slavery without the impetus and authority of the national government. Ultimately it would take a startling new synthesis of Hamiltonian means — an activist, interventionist, powerful national government — to achieve Jefferson's enlightened ends — a tolerant, nonhierarchical, egalitarian democracy that promotes economic justice and the individual's ability to pursue happiness. Presidents Theodore Roosevelt, Franklin Roosevelt, and Lyndon Johnson would absorb and pass on that Hamiltonian-Jeffersonian lesson.

The intractable dilemmas nevertheless took their toll on the aging Jefferson, for he began to despair of the future of the union. He doubted that Americans were becoming more enlightened, more rational, more disposed to equality and emancipation. While approving a plan for emancipation and colonization offered by a northern friend in 1817, he remarked that "I have not perceived the growth of this disposition [toward emancipation] in the rising generation, of which I once had sanguine hopes." He had long glimpsed the latent tragedy in American history — "I tremble for my country when I reflect that God is just," he had written in his *Notes on Virginia,* commenting on the cruelty of slavery — and yet his mind was closed to the opportunity that the Missouri question presented for resolving the problem of slavery.

What had happened to the idealism, the utopian ideas of the men of his generation? Jefferson wondered. In the first decades of the nineteenth century, the country seemed overrun by business, religious revivalism, and anti-intellectualism. "All, all dead," he murmured in 1825, as he looked back on his old friends, distressed to find himself so very alone amidst a new generation "whom we know not, and who know not us."

And yet, the buoyant optimism that had always accompanied him as he sailed through the turbulence of his political life never completely abandoned him. In 1818, as he contemplated the continuation of the American experiment, he assured a friend that "our descendants will be as wise as we are." A few months before he died, he again remarked that the younger generation of Americans would take the country toward sounder principles than it had known. "I cannot live to see it," he wrote the day after Christmas 1825, fully at one with the spirit of rebirth and renewal. "My joy must only be that of anticipation."

"It is a good world on the whole," Jefferson wrote to his faithful correspondent, John Adams, in 1816. He was neither "disgusted" with the present, he insisted, nor "despairing of the future." "I steer my bark with Hope in the head, leaving Fear astern. My hopes indeed sometimes fail; but not oftener than the forebodings of the gloomy." Five years later, in another letter to Adams, he insisted that he did not believe that their "labors are lost. I shall not die without a hope that light and liberty are on steady advance." That unconquerable spirit was one of Jefferson's most invaluable contributions to American political life.

Neither he nor anyone else ever imagined the political catastrophe that the blight of slavery would produce only a few decades later. He would never know how the two-party system he had helped create would utterly fail to provide a compromise solution, how neither party would take a strong leadership role, how moderate reform on the issue of slavery would never materialize. He would never know that the South would turn to secession — the ultimate antipolitical, anticonstitutional response that he himself had toyed with — and how both sides, North and South, would turn to violence to resolve the political and moral crisis.

"The hour of emancipation" was advancing, Jefferson wrote in 1814, adding simply that it was "a leaf of our history not yet turned over." Twelve years later, in the last letter he ever wrote, he still looked expectantly to the future. "All eyes are opened, or opening," he wrote ten days before he died, "to the rights of man." The Enlightenment fire was not spent, and Jefferson's hope was not misplaced. His deep faith in the ideals of the Revolution and his forward-looking spirit — whatever his blind spots about slavery, race, and Virginia localism may have been — carried the country into the future, offering to all, for centuries to come, the inspiring vision of a freer, more democratic society, the legacy of a political culture energized by the creative conflict of opposing parties and opposing ideas, and the sunny anticipation of more leaves of our history to turn over, more new beginnings.

Notes

Acknowledgments

Index

Notes

1. On the Brink

page

1 *Connecticut Courant:* 20 September 1800, in James Roger Sharp, *American Politics in the Early Republic: The New Nation in Crisis* (New Haven: Yale University Press, 1993), 227.

1 **"a medicine necessary . . .":** Thomas Jefferson, *Writings,* ed. Merrill Peterson (New York: Library of America, 1984), 882.

1 **"fanatic":** Alexander Hamilton to John Jay, 7 May 1800, in *The Papers of Alexander Hamilton,* ed. Harold C. Syrett et al., 27 vols. (New York: Columbia University Press, 1976), 24:465.

1 **"great arch priest . . .":** Theophilus Parsons to John Jay, 5 May 1800, in *The Correspondence and Public Papers of John Jay,* ed. Henry P. Johnston, 4 vols. (New York: G. P. Putnam's Sons, 1893), 4:270.

1 **turn America upside down:** See Stanley Elkins and Eric McKitrick, *The Age of Federalism* (New York: Oxford University Press, 1993), 750.

1 **"the most serious and alarming evils . . .":** Daniel Dewey to Theodore Sedgwick, 8 December 1800, Massachusetts Historical Society.

2 **"fangs of Jefferson":** Hamilton to Sedgwick, 4 May 1800, in *Papers of Alexander Hamilton,* ed. Syrett, 24:453.

2 **anarchy and military despotism:** Carroll to Hamilton, 27 August 1800, in *Papers of Alexander Hamilton,* ed. Syrett, 25:94.

2 **"contempt for the Christian religion . . .":** Robert Troup to Rufus King, 2 October 1798, in *The Life and Correspondence of Rufus King,* ed. Charles King, 6 vols. (New York: G. P. Putnam's Sons, 1896), 2:432.

2 **Federalist press against Jefferson:** See Charles O. Lerche, Jr., "Jefferson and the Election of 1800: A Case Study in the Political Smear," *William and Mary Quarterly,* 3rd ser., 5, no. 4 (October 1948):470ff.

2 **"Do you believe . . ."; poison the minds . . . :** Charles Warren, *Odd Byways in*

American History (Cambridge: Harvard University Press, 1942), 128; see ch. 7, "Jefferson's Death Falsely Reported."

2 **"Shadows . . .":** Troup to King, 1 October 1800, in *Life and Correspondence of Rufus King*, ed. King, 3:315.

2 **"alarming and truly melancholy . . .":** *Baltimore American*, 30 June 1800, in Warren, *Odd Byways in American History*, 129.

2 **sudden manner:** Philadelphia *True American*, 1 July 1800, in Warren, *Odd Byways in American History*, 129.

2 **"the report of Mr. Jefferson's death . . .":** *Gazette of the United States*, 2 July 1800, in Warren, *Odd Byways in American History*, 130.

2 **"distressing information":** *American Daily Advertiser*, 4 July 1800, in Warren, *Odd Byways in American History*, 131.

3 **"Old Tories . . . winks of congratulations":** Philadelphia *Aurora*, 7 July 1800.

3 **"some compassionate being . . ."; "The asses of aristocracy . . .":** *Connecticut Courant*, 7 July 1800, in Warren, *Odd Byways in American History*, 131–32.

3 **"I have never enjoyed. . . .":** Jefferson to Dupont de Nemours, 26 July 1800, in *Correspondence Between Thomas Jefferson and Pierre Samuel Dupont de Nemours, 1798–1817*, ed. Dumas Malone, 1930, in Warren, *Odd Byways in American History*, 135.

3 **beloved estate he had so carefully planned:** Jefferson to William Hamilton, July 1800, in Jefferson, *Writings*, ed. Peterson, 1168.

3 **"passion" . . . "duty" . . . "torment":** Jefferson to Martha Jefferson Randolph, 11 February 1800, in *The Family Letters of Thomas Jefferson*, ed. Edwin Morris Betts and James Adam Bear, Jr. (Charlottesville: University Press of Virginia, 1986), 184; see also Jefferson to Harry Innes, in Paul Wilstach, *Jefferson and Monticello* (Garden City, N.Y.: Doubleday, Page and Company, 1925), 142.

4 **"calumnies . . .":** Jefferson to Samuel Smith, 22 August 1798, in *The Writings of Thomas Jefferson*, ed. Paul Leicester Ford, 10 vols. (New York: G. P. Putnam's Sons, 1896), 7:279.

4 **truth in advertisements:** Wilstach, *Jefferson and Monticello*, 150.

4 **"Is this the violent democrat . . .":** Margaret Bayard Smith, The *First Forty Years of Washington Society*, ed. Gaillard Hunt (New York: Charles Scribner's Sons, 1906), 5–6.

4 **little republic of St. Marino:** Charles Carroll of Carrollton to Hamilton, 18 April 1800, in *Papers of Alexander Hamilton*, ed. Syrett, 24:412.

4 **"the wise & good":** G. Cabot to R. King, 9 August 1800, in *Life and Correspondence of Rufus King*, ed. King, 3:292.

4 **"Obedience and submission . . .":** John Wilkes Kittera, "To the Electors of Lancaster County," *Baltimore Federal Gazette*, 18 August 1800, in David Hackett Fischer, *The Revolution of American Conservatism: The Federalist Party in the Era of Jeffersonian Democracy* (New York: Harper and Row, 1965), 341.

4 **"own the country . . .":** John Jay to William Wilberforce, 25 October 1810, *Correspondence and Public Papers of John Jay*, ed. Johnston, 4:336.

5 **"strident exclusivism":** Elkins and McKitrick, *Age of Federalism*, 27.

5 **"Our government is as free . . .":** "Short Address to the Voters of Delaware," 21 September 1800, in Noble Cunningham, "Election of 1800," in *History of American*

Presidential Elections, 1789–1968, ed. Arthur M. Schlesinger (New York: Chelsea House, 1971), 152.

5 **"those morals which protect our lives . . ."**: Cunningham, "Election of 1800," 124.

5 **"a few BOLD STROKES"**: 30 September 1800, "To the People of New Jersey," document adopted at Republican state convention in Princeton, in Cunningham, "Election of 1800," 135.

6 **they wished to establish a monarchy**: Gouverneur Morris to Rufus King, 4 June 1800, in *Life and Correspondence of Rufus King*, ed. King, 3:252.

6 **"utterly devoted . . ."**: 21 June 1800, in Sharp, *American Politics in the Early Republic*, 227.

6 **"secure to us forever . . ."**: James Monroe, 12 July 1800, in Sharp, *American Politics in the Early Republic*, 227.

7 **Electoral College**: See James MacGregor Burns and Susan Dunn, *George Washington* (New York: Times Books, 2004), ch. 3. See also Robert A. Dahl, *How Democratic Is the American Constitution?* (New Haven: Yale University Press, 2002), ch. 4, "Electing the President."

7 **"This is the day . . ."; "The calculations now . . ."**: Troup to King, 4 December 1800, in *Life and Correspondence of Rufus King*, ed. King, 3:340.

7 **"The storm . . ."**: Dumas Malone, *Jefferson and the Ordeal of Liberty* (Boston: Little Brown, 1962), 3:498.

7 **"badly managed"**: Jefferson to Burr, 15 December 1800, in *Writings of Thomas Jefferson*, ed. Ford, 7:467.

8 **"I never once asked . . . 4th of March"**: Jefferson to Burr, 15 December 1800, in *Writings of Thomas Jefferson*, ed. Ford, 7:467–68.

8 **"probable equality . . ."**: Jefferson to John Breckenridge, 18 December 1800, in *Writings of Thomas Jefferson*, ed. Ford, 7:469.

8 **"produced great dismay . . ."**: Jefferson to Madison, 19 December 1800, in *Writings of Thomas Jefferson*, ed. Ford, 7:470.

8 **"Rotten Apples"**: James Gunn to Hamilton, 18 December 1800, in *Papers of Alexander Hamilton*, ed. Syrett, 25:263.

8 **"men of desperate fortunes . . . dark valley of anarchy"**: *Gazette of the United States*, 10 January 1801, Reel 8.

8 **French invasion**: Lerche, "Jefferson and the Election of 1800," 480.

9 **"stretch"; openly declaring . . .**: Jefferson to Madison, 19 December 1800, in *Writings of Thomas Jefferson*, ed. Ford, 7:470; Sharp, *American Politics in the Early Republic*, 256–57.

9 **"reverse what has been . . ."; "abyss"**: Jefferson to John Breckinridge, 18 December 1800, in *Writings of Thomas Jefferson*, ed. Ford, 7:469.

9 **The "feds" intended to pass a bill . . .**: Jefferson to Madison, 26 December 1800, in *Writings of Thomas Jefferson*, ed. Ford, 7:483.

9 **"devolve" on the president**: Jefferson to Coxe, 31 December 1800, in *Writings of Thomas Jefferson*, ed. Ford, 7:475.

9 **"Degree of boldness . . ."**: Harry Ammon, *James Monroe: The Quest for National Identity* (New York: McGraw-Hill, 1971), 191.

9 **Republicans make transition difficult**: Malone, *Jefferson and the Ordeal of Liberty*, 3:499.

9 **"Ought we then . . .";** **"honors of our country":** Theodore Sedgwick to Hamilton, 10 January 1801, in *Papers of Alexander Hamilton,* ed. Syrett, 25:311.

10 **"Resistance must be . . .":** *Gazette of the United States,* 10 January 1801, Reel 8.

10 **"We are resolv'd . . .":** John Dawson to Madison, 12 February 1801, in *Papers of James Madison,* ed. William T. Hutchinson, William M. E. Rachal, Robert A. Rutland, C. F. Hobson, J. C. A. Stagg, David B. Mattern, et al., 17 vols. (Charlottesville: University Press of Virginia, 1962–91), 17:464.

10 **the start of another revolution . . . :** John Beckley to Albert Gallatin, 15 February 1801, in John James Beckley, *Justifying Jefferson: The Political Writings of John James Beckley* (Washington, D.C.: Library of Congress, 1995), 232.

10 **"If any man should be thus appointed . . .":** Gallatin to Henry Muhlenberg, 8 May 1848, in Henry Adams, *The Life of Albert Gallatin* [1879] (New York: Peter Smith, 1943), 249, italics added.

10 **middle states would arm . . . :** Jefferson to Monroe, 15 February 1801, in *Writings of Thomas Jefferson,* ed. Ford, 7:491.

10 **"sincere wish":** Jefferson to Mary Jefferson Eppes, 15 February 1801, in *Family Letters of Thomas Jefferson,* ed. Betts and Bear, 197.

10 **"There is nothing more common . . .":** Benjamin Rush, "Address to the People of the United States," 1786, in Jack N. Rakove, "From One Agenda to Another: The Condition of American Federalism, 1783–1787," in *The American Revolution: Its Character and Limits,* ed. Jack P. Greene (New York: New York University Press, 1987), 81–82.

12 **"Understand that the democrats . . .":** J. McHenry to Rufus King, 2 January 1801, in *Life and Correspondence of Rufus King,* ed. King, 3:363.

2. "If the people be governors, who shall be governed?"

14 **Madison's meeting with Washington:** Memorandum on Washington's Retirement, Substance of a Conversation with the President, 5 May 1792, in James Madison, *Writings,* ed. Jack N. Rakove (New York: Library of America, 1999), 519–21. See also Washington to Edmund Randolph, 26 August 1792, in *Writings of George Washington,* ed. Worthington Chauncey Ford, 14 vols. (New York: G. P. Putnam's Sons, 1889–93), 12:180.

14 **"The confidence of the whole union . . .":** Jefferson to Washington, 23 May 1792, in *Writings of Thomas Jefferson,* ed. Ford, 6:5.

14 **"The greatest evil . . . as unanimous as ever"; "relaxed":** Hamilton to Washington, 30 July–3 August 1792, in *Papers of Alexander Hamilton,* ed. Syrett, 12:137–39.

15 **"It was scarcely possible . . .":** Fisher Ames, Eulogy on Washington, 8 February 1800, in *Works of Fisher Ames,* ed. Seth Ames, 2 vols. (Boston: Little, Brown and Company, 1854), 2:77.

15 **"chagrin":** Washington to Henry Lee, 20 January 1793, in *Writings of George Washington,* ed. Ford, 12:256.

15 **"The liberties of America . . .":** John Adams to Abigail Adams, 17 June 1775, in Edmund C. Burnett, ed., *Letters of Members of the Continental Congress* (Washington, D.C.: Carnegie Institution of Washington, 1921), 1:131.

15 **"Father of his country":** Richard Brookhiser, *Founding Father: Rediscovering George Washington* (New York: The Free Press, 1996), 159.

15 **"I cannot describe . . ."**: Pierre-Etienne Duponceau, in Gilbert Chinard, ed., *George Washington as the French Knew Him* (Princeton: Princeton University Press, 1940), 14, italics added.

16 **"doubly entitle you . . ."**: Henry Knox to Washington, 19 March 1787, in John P. Kaminski and Jill Adair McCaughan, eds., *A Great and Good Man: George Washington in the Eyes of His Contemporaries* (Madison, Wisc.: Madison House, 1989), 74.

17 **"He looked oppressed . . ."**: *The Diaries of George Washington,* ed. Donald Jackson and Dorothy Twohig, 6 vols. (Charlottesville: University Press of Virginia, 1976), 5:484 n; on Washington's tours, see Burns and Dunn, *George Washington,* 58–61.

17 **roads, accommodations, church:** James Thomas Flexner, *George Washington and the New Nation, 1783–1793* (Boston: Little, Brown, 1970), 230–31.

18 **factories in Massachusetts and Connecticut:** *Diaries of George Washington,* ed. Jackson and Twohig, 5:470–85.

18 **"anything of an elegant appearance"; log houses; accommodations; dancing:** Flexner, *George Washington and the New Nation,* 287–89.

19 **"appears to be in a very improving state . . ."**: Washington to David Humphreys, 20 July 1791, in *Writings of George Washington,* ed. John C. Fitzpatrick, 39 vols. (Washington, D.C.: United States Printing Office, 1930–44), 31:318–19.

19 **"tend to elevate . . ."**: Barry Schwartz, *George Washington: The Making of an American Symbol* (New York: The Free Press, 1987), 88; Glenn Phelps, *George Washington and American Constitutionalism* (Lawrence: University Press of Kansas, 1993), 194.

19 **"the marks of respect . . ."**: Washington to Alexander Martin, 14 November 1791, in *Writings of George Washington,* ed. Fitzpatrick, 31:416.

19 **"I wish he had a Son"**: Anthony Wayne to Marquis de Lafayette, 4 July 1788, in Kaminski and McCaughan, *A Great and Good Man,* 98.

19 **"I have no child . . ."**: Draft of Washington's First Inaugural Address, 1788, in George Washington, *Writings,* ed. John Rhodehamel (New York: Library of America, 1997), 706.

20 **"Americans! he had no child . . ."**: Gouverneur Morris, *An Oration, Upon the Death of General Washington* (New York, 1800), 8.

20 **fatherly goodness and protection:** See Douglas Southall Freeman, *George Washington: A Biography,* 7 vols. (New York: Charles Scribner's Sons, 1951), 3:198.

20 **"the resentment of dutiful children . . ."**: Melvin Yazawa, *From Colonies to Commonwealth: Familial Ideology and the Beginnings of the American Republic* (Baltimore: Johns Hopkins University Press, 1985), 92.

20 **on the contrasts in Washington's character:** See Lawrence Friedman, *Inventors of the Promised Land* (New York: Alfred A. Knopf, 1975), ch. 2, "The Flawless American: The Invention of George Washington," 73ff.

20 **unity of people and government:** Farewell Address, 19 September 1796, in Washington, *Writings,* ed. Rhodehamel, 964.

20 **"sacramental center"**: Catherine Albanese, *Sons of the Fathers: The Civil Religion of the American Revolution* (Philadelphia: Temple University Press, 1976), 145.

20 **"rampart"**: John Adams, Inaugural Address, 4 March 1797, in *The Works of John Adams,* ed. Charles Francis Adams, 10 vols. (Boston: Little, Brown and Company, 1854), 9:108, italics added.

20 **"to raise Washington up anymore . . .":** Seth Willison, *The Agency of God* (Geneva, 1800), in Jay Fliegelman, *Prodigals and Pilgrims: The American Revolution Against Patriarchal Authority, 1750–1800* (Cambridge: Cambridge University Press, 1982), 221.

20 **object of a cult:** Adams, in Schwartz, *George Washington*, 22.

20 **"Instead of adoring . . .":** Adams to John Jebb, 10 September 1785, in *Works of John Adams*, ed. Adams, 9:540.

20 **"without appealing to their own reason . . .":** Jefferson to Archibald Stuart, 4 January 1797, in *Writings of Thomas Jefferson*, ed. Ford, 7:101.

21 **adoration of Washington:** *Boston Gazette*, 16 December 1793, in Eugene Perry Link, *Democratic-Republican Societies, 1790–1800* (New York: Octagon Books, 1973), 193–94.

21 **fathers:** See Michael Walzer, "On the Role of Symbolism in Political Thought," *Political Science Quarterly* 82, no. 2 (June 1967).

21 **defeat the hold that birth and wealth . . . :** Jefferson to Adams, 18 October 1813, in *The Adams-Jefferson Letters: The Complete Correspondence Between Thomas Jefferson and Abigail and John Adams*, ed. Lester J. Cappon, 2 vols. (Chapel Hill: University of North Carolina Press for the Institute of Early American History and Culture, 1959), 2:390.

21 **political leadership a consequence of social leadership:** Gordon S. Wood, "The Democratization of Mind in the American Revolution," in *Leadership in the American Revolution* (Washington, D.C.: Library of Congress, 1974), 62–89.

22 **leadership of Founding Fathers:** Ibid., 64–67.

22 **"without a marked subordination . . . rebellion":** John Adams to Thomas Adams, 17 October 1799, in Page Smith, *John Adams* (Garden City, N.Y.: Doubleday and Co., 1962), 2:1016–17, italics added.

22 **"true family authority":** John Adams to Thomas Adams, 17 October 1799, in Smith, *John Adams*, 2:1016–17, italics added. See also Adams, *Discourses on Davila*, in *Works of John Adams*, ed. Adams, ch. xiii, 6:274–81.

22 **"I always consider . . .":** Adams, Philadelphia *Aurora*, 29 March 1809, in John M. Murrin, "Escaping Perfidious Albion: Federalism, Fear of Aristocracy, and the Democratization of Corruption in Postrevolutionary America," in *Virtue, Corruption and Self-Interest*, ed. Richard K. Matthews (Bethlehem, Pa.: Lehigh University Press, 1994), 121.

22 **hierarchy and deference:** See Alan Taylor, "From Fathers to Friends of the People: Political Personae in the Early Republic," in *Federalists Reconsidered*, ed. Doron Ben-Atar and Barbara B. Oberg (Charlottesville: University Press of Virginia, 1998), 225–26; see also C. Bradley Thompson, *John Adams and the Spirit of Liberty* (Lawrence: University Press of Kansas, 1998), 165.

22 **"habitual state of deference":** Adams, *Discourses on Davila*, ch. viii.

23 **even in act of voting; not between rival programs:** Charles S. Sydnor, *Gentlemen Freeholders*, in Linda Kerber, *Federalists in Dissent* (Ithaca, N.Y.: Cornell University Press, 1970), 179 n; Rhys Isaac, *The Transformation of Virginia, 1740–1790* (Chapel Hill: University of North Carolina Press for the Institute of Early American History and Culture, 1982), 252.

23 **"If the people be governors . . .":** John Cotton, in James Morton Smith, *Freedom's*

Fetters: The Alien and Sedition Laws and American Civil Liberties (Ithaca, N.Y.: Cornell University Press, 1956), 10.

23 **"the rich, the few, the rulers":** Samuel Dana, *Essay on Political Society* (Philadelphia, 1800), 18.

23 **"canonized"; "traditionary reverence":** Jefferson to Adams, 28 October 1813, in *Adams-Jefferson Letters*, ed. Cappon, 2:389; Isaac, *Transformation of Virginia*, ch. 6, "Textures of Community: Mobility, Learning, Gentility, an Authority," 115–42.

23 **"constant respect":** Adams to Jefferson, 15 November 1813, in *Adams-Jefferson Letters*, ed. Cappon, 2:400, 402.

23 **virtue as prerequisite for leadership:** Gordon S. Wood, *The Radicalism of the American Revolution* (New York: Alfred A. Knopf, 1992), 105.

24 **virtuous leaders:** David H. Fischer, "The Myth of the Essex Junto," *William and Mary Quarterly*, 3rd ser., 21 (1966):202.

24 **"no Moral but their Interest":** Gouverneur Morris, *A Diary of the French Revolution*, ed. Beatrix Cary Davenport, 2 vols. (Boston: Houghton Mifflin, 1939), 1:61.

24 **"miracle of virtue":** Fisher Ames to Richard Peters, 14 December 1806, in *Works of Fisher Ames*, ed. Ames, 1:378.

24 **"We were accustomed . . .":** Devereaux Jarratt, "The Autobiography of Reverend Devereux Jarratt, 1732–1763," ed. Douglass Adair, *William and Mary Quarterly*, 3rd ser., 9, no. 3 (July 1952):361.

24 **the "meanest" among men in Pennsylvania:** J. R. Pole, *The Pursuit of Equality in American History*, rev. ed. (Berkeley: University of California Press, 1993), 136.

24 **"a mean, low, dirty envy . . .":** Charles Carroll, in Wood, *Radicalism of the American Revolution*, 145.

24 **"free-and-easy mechanic":** Ronald Formisano, *The Transformation of Political Culture: Massachusetts Parties, 1790s–1840s* (New York: Oxford University Press, 1983), 131.

24 **"aristocracy of virtue . . .":** Sedgwick to Rufus King, in Joyce Appleby, *Capitalism and a New Social Order* (New York: New York University Press, 1984), 15.

24 **William Henry Drayton:** Gordon S. Wood, *The American Revolution: A History* (New York: Modern Library, 2002), 51.

25 **disobedience of militia:** Wood, *Radicalism of the American Revolution*, 163.

25 **North Carolina Regulators; law and order:** Pole, *Pursuit of Equality*, 21–22.

25 **on St. Tammany:** James MacGregor Burns, *The Vineyard of Liberty* (New York: Vintage Books, 1983), 81–82.

25 **mobility in Virginia and Boston:** Jackson Turner Main, *The Social Structure of Revolutionary America* (Princeton: Princeton University Press, 1965), 170, 195.

25 **on flux and exchange:** See Alexis de Tocqueville, *De la Démocratie en Amérique* ed. J.-P. Mayer (Paris: Gallimard, 1951), Bk. 2, Pt. 3, ch. 5, "Relations between servant and master." Translations from the French are my own.

25 **George Mason at the convention:** 31 May 1787, in Max Farrand, ed., *Records of the Federal Convention of 1787*, 3 vols. (New Haven: Yale University Press, 1986), 1:48–49.

26 **poor within three generations:** Jefferson to Joseph Cabell, 14 January 1818, in *Writings of Thomas Jefferson*, ed. Ford, 10:100–101.

26 **"constant rotation":** Madison, 4 August 1822, in Marvin Meyers, ed., *The Mind of*

the Founder: Sources of the Political Thought of James Madison, rev. ed. (Hanover, N.H.: University Press of New England, 1981), 345.

26 **"run too much to sending their sons . . .":** John Rutherford, "Notes on the State of New Jersey," *N.J. Historical Society Proceedings,* 2nd ser., 1 (1867):81–82.

26 **"If those who know much are few . . .":** *Philadelphia General Advertiser,* 15 March 1792, in Donald H. Stewart, "Jeffersonian Journalism: Newspaper Propaganda and the Development of the Democratic-Republican Party, 1789–1801" (Ph.D. diss., Columbia University, 1950), 844.

26 **"it is the universal custom . . .":** William Manning, *The Key of Liberty* [1799], ed. Michael Merrill and Sean Wilentz (Cambridge: Harvard University Press, 1993), 138–39; Burns, *Vineyard of Liberty,* 144.

26 **"soul of a republic":** John Jay to Benjamin Rush, 24 March 1785, in *Correspondence and Public Papers of John Jay,* ed. Johnston, 3:139, 250.

26 **"lower class of citizens":** Letter to the Trustees of the Alexandria Academy, 17 December 1785, in *Writings of George Washington,* ed. Fitzpatrick, 28:357.

26 **national university:** Washington, Message of 7 December 1796, in Washington, *Writings,* ed. Rhodehamel, 982. See also Paul Rahe, *Republics Ancient and Modern,* vol. 3, *Inventions of Prudence: Constituting the American Regime* (Chapel Hill: University of North Carolina Press, 1992), 170–73.

27 **"convert men into republican machines . . . COMMERCE . . .":** Benjamin Rush, "Of the Mode of Education Proper in a Republic," in *Essays: Literary, Moral and Philosophical,* ed. Michael Meranze (Schenectady, N.Y.: Union College Press, 1988), 9, 7.

27 **William Findley:** Wood, *American Revolution,* 165–66.

27 **"by the exertion of each individual . . .":** Wood, *Radicalism of the American Revolution,* 296. See also John Patrick Diggins, *The Lost Soul of American Politics: Virtue, Self-Interest, and the Foundations of Liberalism* (New York: Basic Books, 1984), ch. 4, 100–130.

28 **"one great & equal body . . . whole Community":** Opinions of William Pinckney, 25 June 1787, in J. R. Pole, ed., *The Revolution in America: Documents and Commentaries* (Stanford: Stanford University Press, 1970), 563–65.

28 **Charles Pinckney:** Charles C. Tansill, ed., *Documents Illustrative of the Formation of the Union of the American States* (Washington, D.C.: Government Printing Office, 1927), 273.

28 **"well-bred, well-fed . . .":** Burns, *Vineyard of Liberty,* 33.

29 **pass the expressed interests and passions:** Ibid., 61.

29 **"Elections, my dear sir . . .":** Adams to Jefferson, 6 December 1787, in *Adams-Jefferson Letters,* ed. Cappon, 1:214.

29 **"a permanent barrier . . .":** Hamilton, Speech of 18 June 1787, in Cecelia Kenyon, "Alexander Hamilton, Rousseau of the Right," *Political Science Quarterly* 73, no. 2 (June 1958):163.

30 **"never was, and never will be . . .":** Gouverneur Morris, in Farrand, *Records of the Federal Convention of 1787,* 1:545.

30 **"guardian of the people . . ."; "appointed by the people":** Gouverneur Morris, 19 July 1787, in Farrand, *Records of the Federal Convention of 1787,* 2:42, 52.

30 **men in executive branch should receive no salaries; "no debate ensued":** Wood, *Radicalism of the American Revolution,* 291–92.

30 "humble sons . . .": Madison, *Federalist* No. 57.

30 "bulk of mankind . . . acquaintance and confidence": Madison to Edmund Randolph, 10 January 1788, in Madison, *Writings*, ed. Rakove, 191.

30 men who "possess most wisdom . . .": Madison, *Federalist* No. 57.

30 "enlightened statesmen . . .": Madison, *Federalist* No. 10.

30 "cool and deliberate": Madison, *Federalist* No. 63.

31 "a corrupt oppressive aristocracy": Mason Objects to Constitution, in Pole, *Revolution in America*, 195.

31 "the well born . . .": *Independent Gazetteer*, 7 February 1788.

31 "men of learning . . .": Amos Singletary, in Jonathan Elliot, ed., *The Debates in the Several State Conventions on the Adoption of the Federal Constitution*, 5 vols. (Philadelphia: J. B. Lippincott, 1937), 2:102.

31 "The great consider themselves. . .": Melancton Smith, in Cecelia Kenyon, *The Anti-Federalists* [1966] (Boston: Northeastern University Press, 1985), xlix–l, 385.

31 high turnover: Jack N. Rakove, "The Structure of Politics at the Accession of George Washington," in *Beyond Confederation: Origins of the Constitution and American National Identity*, ed. Richard Beeman, Stephen Botein, and Edward C. Carter II (Chapel Hill: University of North Carolina Press, 1987), 261–94.

32 "stupid . . . with force": James Madison, "Who Are the Best Keepers of the People's Liberties?", 22 December 1792, *National Gazette*, in Madison, *Writings*, ed. Rakove, 532–33.

32 "We both consider . . .": Jefferson to P. S. Dupont de Nemours, 24 April 1816, in Jefferson, *Writings*, ed. Peterson, 1386.

32 "hereditary and high-handed aristocracy": Jefferson, "Thoughts on Lotteries," February 1826, in *Writings of Thomas Jefferson*, ed. Ford, 10:370.

32 "not so well dressed . . ."; "the People's men": Jefferson to Benjamin Franklin, 13 August 1777, in *Papers of Thomas Jefferson*, ed. Julian Boyd, 30 vols. (Princeton: Princeton University Press, 1950–2003), 2:26.

33 "Those who advocated reformation . . .": Jefferson to Adams, 15 June 1813, in *Adams-Jefferson Letters*, ed. Cappon, 2:332.

34 on the theme of time: See J. G. A. Pocock, "Time, Institutions, and Action: An Essay on Traditions and Their Understanding," in *Politics, Language, and Time: Essays on Political Thought and History* (New York: Atheneum, 1971).

34 "eternal, unchangeable truth": Adams, Letters to John Taylor, letter 8, in *Works of John Adams*, ed. Adams, 6:464.

3. Farewell to Harmony

35 Dressed in velvet . . . : Burns, *Vineyard of Liberty*, 76.

35 departure from the truth: Washington to Henry Lee, 20 January 1793, in Washington, *Writings*, ed. Rhodehamel, 833.

35 republic in which "the light of truth and reason": "To the Members of the New Church in Baltimore," in Washington, *Writings*, ed. Rhodehamel, 834.

36 on Philadelphia: Burns, *Vineyard of Liberty*, 110–15.

37 "subject to the upbraidings . . .": Second Inaugural Address, 4 March 1793, in Washington, *Writings*, ed. Rhodehamel, 835.

37 **Gazette had welcomed Washington's reelection:** *National Gazette,* 10 October
    1792.

37 **"every species of royal pomp . . . funeral pyre for their liberties":** *National Ga-
    zette,* 2 March 1793, in James Thomas Flexner, *George Washington: Anguish and
    Farewell* (Boston: Little Brown, 1969), 15.

37 **"offspring of inequality . . .":** James Thomas Flexner, *Washington: The Indispens-
    able Man* (Boston: Little, Brown and Company, 1974), 275.

37 **"Tranquility reigns . . .":** Burns, *Vineyard of Liberty,* 93.

37 **"insidious":** Washington to Jefferson, 7 October 1793, in *Writings of George Wash-
    ington,* ed. Fitzpatrick, 33:113.

37 **destroying people's confidence:** Washington to Henry Lee, 21 July 1793, in *Writ-
    ings of George Washington,* ed. Fitzpatrick, 33:23.

37 **destroy the union:** Washington to Edmund Randolph, 26 August 1792, in *Writings
    of George Washington,* ed. Ford, 12:180.

38 **coach and four horses:** Marshall Smelser, "The Jacobin Phrenzy: The Menace of
    Monarchy, Plutocracy, and Anglophilia, 1789–1798," *Review of Politics* 21, no. 1
    (January 1959):245.

38 **"Ah thought I . . .":** *Aurora,* 29 January 1793, in Simon P. Newman, *Parades and the
    Politics of the Street: Festive Culture in the Early American Republic* (Philadelphia:
    University of Pennsylvania Press, 1997), 52.

38 **"the arrows of malevolence" . . . contempt and silence:** Washington to Henry
    Lee, 21 July 1793, in *Writings of George Washington,* ed. Fitzpatrick, 33:23–24.

38 **"Inveloped in the rags of royalty . . .":** Jefferson to Madison, 9 June 1793, in *Re-
    public of Letters,* ed. Smith, 2:782.

38 **"Gratitude no longer blinds . . .":** John Beckley, in Schwartz, *George Washington,* 65.

38 **coins:** John C. Miller, *The Federalist Era, 1789–1801* (New York: Harper and
    Brothers, 1960), 8.

38 **"almost idolatrous . . .":** John Page, in Newman, *Parades and Politics,* 56.

38 **"incompatible" . . . :** *Aurora,* 18 February 1793, in Newman, *Parades and Politics,*
    62.

38 **"frenchified zelots":** John Adams to Abigail Adams, 9 January 1794, in *Letters of
    John Adams, Addressed to His Wife,* ed. Charles Francis Adams (Boston: Charles C.
    Little and James Brown, 1841), 1:137.

38 **"Internal dissentions . . . torn asunder":** Washington to Jefferson, 23 August 1792,
    in Washington, *Writings,* ed. Rhodehamel, 817.

39 **"United we stand . . . existence hangs":** Patrick Henry to Jefferson, 10 September
    1785, in Daniel Sisson, *The American Revolution of 1800* (New York: Alfred A.
    Knopf, 1974), 45.

39 **"There is nothing which I dread . . .":** Adams to Jonathan Jackson, 2 October
    1780, in *Works of John Adams,* ed. Adams, 9:511.

39 **"If I could not go to heaven . . .":** Jefferson to Francis Hopkinson, 13 March 1789,
    in *Papers of Thomas Jefferson,* ed. Boyd, 14:650.

40 **Burke on men acting in concert with one another:** Edmund Burke, *Thoughts on
    the Cause of the Present Discontents* [1770], in *The Writings and Speeches of the
    Right Honourable Edmund Burke* (Boston: Little Brown, Beaconsfield Edition,
    1901), 1:529 and 533–34.

40 **"principles of concert . . . post-Revolutionary era":** Jackson Turner Main, *Politi-*

cal Parties Before the Constitution (Chapel Hill: The University of North Carolina Press for the Institute of Early American History and Culture, 1973), xviii–xix, 321, 363, 398–99.

40 **"the aggregate happiness . . .":** Washington to Moustier, 1 November 1786, in *Writings of George Washington*, ed. Fitzpatrick, 31:42.

40 **"diversified in local & smaller matters . . .":** Washington to Madison, 20 May 1792, in Washington, *Writings*, ed. Rhodehamel, 805.

40 **"Truth is a thing . . .":** John Taylor, *A Definition of Parties* [1794], in Noble E. Cunningham, Jr., *The Jeffersonian Republicans: The Formation of Party Organization, 1789–1801* (Chapel Hill: University of North Carolina Press for the Institute of Early American History and Culture, 1957), 75.

41 **"turbulent and changing"; "faithful to the national interest":** Hamilton, speech of 18 June 1787, in Kenyon, "Alexander Hamilton: Rousseau of the Right," 163.

41 **"would look down with contempt . . .":** Hamilton, Publius Letter, III, 16 November 1778, in *Papers of Alexander Hamilton*, ed. Syrett, 1:580–81.

41 **Washington's cabinet:** Jefferson to Destutt de Tracy, 26 January 1811, in *Writings of Thomas Jefferson*, ed. Ford, 9:307.

41 **"daily pitted in the cabinet . . .":** Jefferson to Dr. Walter Jones, 5 March 1810, in *Writings of Thomas Jefferson*, ed. Ford, 9:273.

42 **"without more charity . . . irritable charges":** Washington to Jefferson, 23 August 1792, in Washington, *Writings*, ed. Rhodehamel, 817.

42 **"internal obstructions . . . wounds which have been given":** Washington to Hamilton, 26 August 1792, in Washington, *Writings*, ed. Rhodehamel, 819–20.

42 **"to keep the machine together":** Washington to Edmund Randolph, 26 August 1792, in Washington, *Writings*, ed. Rhodehamel, 821.

42 **Jefferson's reply to Washington:** Jefferson to Washington, 9 September 1792, in Jefferson, *Writings*, ed. Peterson, 992–1001.

42 **"My farm, my family":** Peterson, *Thomas Jefferson and the New Nation*, 516.

42 **"If any prospect shall open . . .":** Hamilton to Washington, 9 September 1792, in *Papers of Alexander Hamilton*, ed. Syrett, 12:347–49.

43 **"sincere esteem and regard":** Washington to Jefferson, 18 October 1792, in Washington, *Writings*, ed. Rhodehamel, 826. See Richard B. Morris, "Washington and Hamilton: A Great Collaboration," *Proceedings of the American Philosophical Society* 102, no. 2 (April 1958):115.

43 **"good dispositions"; "suspicions unfounded":** Washington to Madison, 20 May 1792, in Washington, *Writings*, ed. Rhodehamel, 805.

43 **"What do you think I had best do?":** Washington to Madison, 9 August 1789, in *Writings of George Washington*, ed. Fitzpatrick, 30:375.

43 **"Ascribe it to friendship"; "Yours ever"; "affectionate regard":** Washington to Madison, 25 September 1789, 20 May 1792, in *Writings of George Washington*, ed. Fitzpatrick, 30:415, 32:49. See also Irving Brant, *James Madison: Father of the Constitution, 1787–1800* (Indianapolis, Ind.: Bobbs-Merrill Company, 1950), 3:285.

44 **"been cheated out of their honest dues . . .":** *Keene (New Hampshire) Recorder*, 26 February 1789, in Stewart, "Jeffersonian Journalism," 671.

44 **"endure seeing the pay . . .":** *New-York Packet*, 19 January 1790, citing a pamphlet from Philadelphia entitled *A Plea for the Poor Soldiers*, in Stewart, "Jeffersonian Journalism," 672.

44 **Esau:** Samuel Livermore, in Brant, *James Madison,* 3:295.

44 **speculation had once meant . . . :** Marcus Cunliffe, *George Washington: Man and Monument* (Boston: Little, Brown and Company, 1958), 34.

44 **"wrong, radically & morally . . .":** Madison to Edward Carrington, 14 March 1790, in *Papers of James Madison,* ed. Hobson and Rutland, 13:104.

44 **remorse:** Brant, *James Madison,* 3:297.

44 **nonfungible; Hamilton on public credit:** Paul Rahe, letter to the author; and Rahe, *Republics Ancient and Modern,* vol. 3, *Inventions of Prudence,* 118–19.

44 **moneyed class and government partners:** Hamilton to Robert Morris, 1780, in *Works of Alexander Hamilton,* Constitutional Edition, ed. Henry Cabot Lodge (New York: G. P. Putnam's Sons, 1903), 3:332.

45 **"He never meant for monied men . . .":** Lance Banning, *The Jeffersonian Persuasion: Evolution of Party Ideology* (Ithaca, N.Y.: Cornell University Press, 1978), 139.

45 **Madison wants government to aid ordinary citizens:** Brant, *James Madison,* 3:333.

45 **"Thank God":** Boston *Columbian Centinel,* 20 March 1790, in Stewart, "Jeffersonian Journalism," 65.

45 **"stupid":** John Adams to John Trumbull, April 1790, in Ralph Ketcham, *James Madison: A Biography* (Charlottesville: University Press of Virginia, 1990), 311.

45 **"insignificant leader":** Trumbull to Adams, 5 February 1791, in *Papers of Thomas Jefferson,* ed. Boyd, 20:445.

45 **"at the head of the discontented . . .":** Theodore Sedgwick to his wife, 4 March 1790, in Ketcham, *James Madison,* 311.

45 **wealth and power would shift:** Lance Banning, "The Problem of Power," in Greene, ed., *American Revolution,* 188.

46 **"scramble . . .":** Madison to Jefferson, 10 July 1791, in *Papers of James Madison,* ed. Rutland et al., 14:43.

46 **"I would wish the debt . . .":** Jefferson to Washington, 9 September 1792, in *Writings of Thomas Jefferson,* ed. Ford, 6:105.

46 **"he hated debt":** Edmund S. Morgan, "Slavery and Freedom: The American Paradox," *Journal of American History* 9, no. 1 (June 1972):7.

46 **temporarily cordial:** Jefferson to Hamilton, 24 January 1791, in *Papers of Thomas Jefferson,* ed. Boyd, 18:460, 563.

46 **"There are epochs . . .":** Hamilton to James Duane, 3 September 1780, in *Alexander Hamilton, Writings,* ed. Joanne B. Freeman (New York: Library of America, 2001), 86.

46 **Hamilton an inegalitarian:** See James MacGregor Burns, *Presidential Government* (Boston: Houghton, Mifflin, 1966), 21.

47 **"the right of the widows . . .":** *Columbian Centinel,* 24 February 1790, in Brant, *James Madison,* 3:299.

47 **"A soldier's pay . . .":** "On the rejection of Mr. Madison's motion," *Pennsylvania Gazette,* 24 March 1790, in Brant, *James Madison,* 3:299.

47 **"Not a sprig . . .":** Jefferson to his daughter, in James MacGregor Burns, *The Deadlock of Democracy* (Englewood Cliffs, N.J.: Prentice-Hall, 1963), 25.

47 **"sultry hot":** Jefferson to Martha Jefferson Randolph, 31 May 1791, in *Papers of Thomas Jefferson,* ed. Boyd, 20:464.

47 **"most beautiful water":** Jefferson to Martha Jefferson Randolph, 31 May 1791, in *Papers of Thomas Jefferson*, ed. Boyd, 20:463.

48 **"less infested with musketoes":** Jefferson's Journal of the Tour, in *Papers of Thomas Jefferson*, ed. Boyd, 20:455.

48 **free negro:** Ketcham, *James Madison*, 324.

48 **botanical excursion mere pretext:** John Hamilton, Editorial Note, in *Papers of Thomas Jefferson*, ed. Boyd, 20:437.

48 **historians agree with John Hamilton:** Samuel Eliot Morison and Henry Steele Commager, *The Growth of the American Republic* (New York: Oxford University Press, 1930), in *Papers of Thomas Jefferson*, ed. Boyd, 20:437, editorial note.

49 **Livingston helps Burr:** Elkins and McKitrick, *Age of Federalism*, 242.

49 **"Are the people in your quarter . . . god knows":** Jefferson to Robert Livingston, 4 February 1791, in *Papers of Thomas Jefferson*, ed. Boyd, 19:241.

49 **"Our delegates deceive . . .":** Livingston to Jefferson, 20 February 1791, in *Papers of Thomas Jefferson*, ed. Boyd, 19:296.

49 **"passionate courtship":** Robert Troup to Hamilton, 15 June 1791, in *Papers of Alexander Hamilton*, ed. Syrett, 8:478

49 **"scouted silently . . .":** Nathaniel Hazard to Hamilton, 25 November 1791, in *Papers of Alexander Hamilton*, ed. Syrett, 8:478 and 9:529–37.

49 **avoid certain Federalists:** See *Papers of Thomas Jefferson*, ed. Boyd, 20:444.

49 **"fund of political knowledge":** *Vermont Gazette*, 6 June 1791, in *Papers of Thomas Jefferson*, ed. Boyd, 20:441.

50 **"mutual influence . . .":** John Quincy Adams, in *Republic of Letters*, ed. Smith, 1:1–2.

50 **headaches:** Editorial Note, in *Papers of Thomas Jefferson*, ed. Boyd, 20:453.

50 **end of journey:** Ketcham, *James Madison*, 325; Brant, *James Madison*, 3:343.

50 **Jefferson sweetened offer:** Burns, *Deadlock of Democracy*, 29. See also Jeffrey Pasley, *"Tyranny of Printers": Newspaper Politics in the Early American Republic* (Charlottesville: University Press of Virginia, 2001), 65.

50 **"favored a conspiratorial interpretation . . .":** Banning, "Problem of Power," 119.

51 **"No government ought to be without . . .":** Jefferson to Washington, 9 September 1792, in *Writings of Thomas Jefferson*, ed. Ford, 6:106–8.

51 **newspapers:** Burns, *Vineyard of Liberty*, 90.

51 **"monolithically"; Dallas:** Pasley, *"Tyranny of Printers"*, 42, 45.

51 **essay on "Property":** "Property," *National Gazette*, 29 March 1792, in Madison, *Writings*, ed. Rakove, 515–17. On other aspects of Madison's political and economic agenda in the *National Gazette*, see Rahe, *Republics Ancient and Modern*, vol. 3, *Inventions of Prudence*, 61–62.

52 **buckles on shoes and "mutability of fashion":** "Fashion," *National Gazette*, 22 March 1792, in Madison, *Writings*, ed. Rakove, 513–15.

53 **"Parties":** *National Gazette*, 23 January 1792, in Madison, *Writings*, ed. Rakove, 504–5, italics added.

54 **"Candid State of Parties":** *National Gazette*, 26 September 1792, in Madison, *Writings*, ed. Rakove, 530–33. See also Madison, The Power of Commerce, in Meyers, *Mind of the Founder*, 221; Saul Cornell, *The Other Founders: Anti-Federalism and the Dissenting Tradition in America, 1788–1828* (Chapel Hill: University of

North Carolina Press for Omohundro Institute of Early American History and Culture, 1999), 166–68, 247–53.

55 **"Who Are the Best Keepers?":** *National Gazette,* 22 December 1792, in Madison, *Writings,* ed. Rakove, 532–34.

55 **institutionally split "between different bodies of men":** Madison, in Elliot, *Debates,* 5:242.

57 **two-party system did not yet exist:** See Formisano, *Transformation of Political Culture,* 28. See also Ronald Formisano, "The American Party Period Reconsidered," *Journal of American History* 86 (1999):93–120.

57 **statewide and local committees:** See Maude Howlett Woodfin, "Contemporary Opinion in Virginia of Thomas Jefferson," in *Essays in Honor of William E. Dodd,* ed. Avery Craven (Chicago: University of Chicago Press, 1935), 60.

57 **coalitions forming:** Cunningham, *Jeffersonian Republicans: Formation of Party Organization,* 22–23, 267–72. See also Elkins and McKitrick, *Age of Federalism,* 484.

57 **handbills and pamphlets:** Jeffrey L. Pasley, "1800 as a Revolution in Political Culture: Newspapers, Celebrations, Voting, and Democratization in the Early Republic," in *The Revolution of 1800: Democracy, Race, and the New Republic,* ed. James Horn, Jan Ellen Lewis, and Peter S. Onuf (Charlottesville: University Press of Virginia, 2002), 132–33.

57 **"coal-pit":** Fisher Ames to Minot, 30 November 1791, in *Works of Fisher Ames,* ed. Ames, 1:105.

57 **"regular, well-disciplined . . .":** Ames to George Richards Minot, 3 May 1792, in *Works of Fisher Ames,* ed. Ames, 1:118.

57 **"Prussian":** Ames to Thomas Dwight, January 1793, in *Works of Fisher Ames,* ed. Ames, 1:127.

58 **"plot thickens":** Hamilton to Adams, 25 June 1792, in *Works of John Adams,* ed. Adams, 8:514.

58 **"head of a faction . . . awaken your attention":** Hamilton to Edward Carrington, 26 May 1792, in *Papers of Alexander Hamilton,* ed. Syrett, 11:427–35.

58 **Whiskey Rebellion, farmers object to principle of tax:** Burns, *Vineyard of Liberty,* 97.

59 **"privileged order of men . . .":** "Franklin," *General Advertiser,* 22 August 1794, in Banning, *Jeffersonian Persuasion,* 228.

59 **"men of distinction":** George Clymer to Hamilton, 10 October 1792, in *Papers of Alexander Hamilton,* ed. Syrett, 12:541.

59 **"next storm":** Brant, *James Madison,* 3:416.

59 **"If the laws are to be so trampled on . . .":** Washington to Charles Mynn Thruston, 10 August 1794, in Washington, *Writings,* ed. Rhodehamel, 874.

59 **"armament . . . against people . . .":** Jefferson, *Anas,* Entry for 2 August 1793, in Burns, *Vineyard of Liberty,* 99.

59 **"self-created societies":** Washington, Sixth Annual Message to Congress, 19 November 1794, in *Writings of George Washington,* ed. Fitzpatrick, 34:29.

60 **"nefarious doctrines . . . shade of Night":** Washington to Burges Ball, 25 September 1794, in *Writings of George Washington,* ed. Fitzpatrick, 33:506.

60 **Philadelphia Democratic societies:** Albrecht Koschnick, "The Democratic Societies of Philadelphia," *William and Mary Quarterly,* 3rd ser., 58, no. 3 (July 2001):615–36.

60 "to exercise the right of speech . . .": *New London Bee,* 4 April 1798, in Link, *Democratic-Republican Societies,* 162.

60 merchants . . . newspaper publishers: Philip S. Foner, ed., *The Democratic-Republican Societies, 1790–1800: A Documentary Sourcebook of Constitutions, Declarations, Addresses, Resolutions, and Toasts* (Westport, Conn.: Greenwood Press, 1976), 8–9.

60 "charms of wealth": Tunis Wortman, 12 May 1796, in ibid., 9.

60 "safeguard": Ibid., 38.

60 clubs "absolutely necessary"; "what is every man's business . . .": Ibid., 3–4.

61 "the vapors of putrefying democracy": Ibid., 39.

61 "perverting the truth . . .": Cornell, *Other Founders,* 197.

63 "liberty in a feather-bed": Jefferson to Lafayette, 2 April 1790 in *Papers of Thomas Jefferson,* ed. Boyd, 16:293. On the French Revolution, see Susan Dunn, *Sister Revolutions: French Lightning, American Light* (New York: Faber and Faber, 1999), ch. 1.

63 "an Adam and an Eve": Jefferson to William Short, 3 January 1793, in *Papers of Thomas Jefferson,* ed. Boyd, 25:14.

63 "When will these savages . . .": Smith, *John Adams,* 2:785–86.

63 "horrid and disgusting scenes": Hamilton, *Americanus* No. 1, 31 January 1794.

64 Ames and Wolcott: Foner, ed., *Democratic-Republican Societies,* 23.

64 "pledge of friendship . . .": "American Cockade," *Massachusetts Mercury,* 10 July 1798, in Newman, *Parades and Politics,* 160.

64 "itinerant gang . . . *approach me not*": Morris U. Schappes, "Anti-Semitism and Reaction, 1795–1800," *Publication of the American Jewish Historical Society* 38 (December 1948), Part 2, 114.

64 "If by the word Shylock . . .": *Argus,* 19 December 1795, in ibid., 118. See also Pasley, "Tyranny of Printers," 170ff.

65 "No; you are too mild . . ."; pregnant women: William Cobbett, *A Bone to Gnaw for the Democrats* [1795] and *A Kick for a Bite* [1795], in Keith Arbour, "Benjamin Franklin as Weird Sister: William Cobbett and Philadelphia's Fears of Democracy," in Ben-Atar and Oberg, *Federalists Reconsidered,* 191, 193.

65 "self-created societies": Sixth Annual Message to Congress, 19 November 1794, in *Writings of George Washington,* ed. Fitzpatrick, 34:29.

65 "It is wonderful indeed": Jefferson to Madison, 28 December 1794, in *Writings of Thomas Jefferson,* ed. Ford, 6:516–17.

65 Senate's motion: Foner, ed., *Democratic-Republican Societies,* 31. See also Elkins and McKitrick, *Age of Federalism,* 485.

65 "Opinions . . . are not the objects . . .": House Address to the President, 27 November 1794, in *Papers of James Madison,* ed. Mason and Rutland, 15:391.

65 "attack made on the essential . . .": Madison to Jefferson, 21 December 1794, in *Papers of James Madison,* ed. Mason and Rutland, 15:419.

66 "greatest error . . .": James Madison to James Monroe, 4 December 1794, in *Papers of James Madison,* ed. Mason and Rutland, 15:406.

66 backfiring; "invigorated": Brant, *James Madison,* 3:419ff. Madison to Thomas Jefferson, 21 December 1794, in *Papers of James Madison,* ed. Mason and Rutland, 15:419.

66 "Is it for assembling . . .": *Journal,* 17 January 1795, in Foner, ed., *Democratic-Republican Societies,* 34.

66 **Were Americans to be muzzled . . . :** Boston *Independent Chronicle*, 11 December 1794, in Stewart, "Jeffersonian Journalism," 810.

66 **If the President and Congress aimed at voiding . . . :** Philadelphia *Aurora*, 27 December 1794, in Stewart, "Jeffersonian Journalism,", 813.

66 **"mobocrats":** Brant, *James Madison*, 3:419.

66 **"disagreeable pill":** Jefferson to Madison, 28 April 1793, in *Republic of Letters*, ed. Smith, 2:770.

67 **five thousand people in Philadelphia:** Link, *Democratic-Republican Societies*, 131–32.

67 **guillotine Jay:** See Smelser, "Jacobin Phrenzy," 253–54.

67 **"execrable":** Hamilton, in Gerald Stourzh, *Alexander Hamilton and the Idea of Republican Government* (Stanford: Stanford University Press, 1970), 266, n. 106.

67 **stones at Hamilton; challenges two men to duels:** Joanne Freeman, "Dueling as Politics: Reinterpreting the Burr-Hamilton Duel," *William and Mary Quarterly* 53, no. 2 (1996):307.

67 **Boston and New Hampshire:** Marshall Smelser, "The Federalist Period as an Age of Passion," *American Quarterly* 10, no. 4 (Winter 1958):398.

67 **"blindest partiality":** Madison to Robert Livingston, 10 August 1795, in *Papers of James Madison*, ed. Stagg and Mason, 16:47.

67 **"sentiment & voice" of the people in Virginia:** Madison to Robert Livingston, 10 August 1795, in *Papers of James Madison*, ed. Stagg and Mason, 16:47–48.

67 **"nothing more than a treaty . . .":** Jefferson to Edward Rutledge, 30 November 1795, in *Writings of Thomas Jefferson*, ed. Ford, 7:40.

67 **"demanding war against England . . .":** Adams to Williams Cunningham, 15 October 1808, in *Correspondence Between the Honorable John Adams . . . and William Cunningham, Esq.* (Boston, 1823), 34.

67 **"To deny that there has been a French influence . . .":** Adams to Dr. Benjamin Rush, 23 January 1809, in *Old Family Letters: Copied from the Originals for Alexander Biddle* (Philadelphia: J. P. Lippincott, 1892), 216.

68 **"not favorable to it":** Washington to Randolph, 22 July 1795, in *Writings of George Washington*, ed. Fitzpatrick, 34:244. See also Burns and Dunn, *George Washington*, ch. 7.

69 **"pale, withered . . .":** John Adams to Abigail Adams, 28 April 1796, in *Republic of Letters*, ed. Smith, 2:894.

69 **"supported his judgment . . .":** Jefferson to James Monroe, 12 June 1796, in *Writings of Thomas Jefferson*, ed. Ford, 7:80.

69 **"strength or dexterity . . .":** Madison to Jefferson, 1 May 1796, in *Papers of James Madison*, ed. Stagg and Mason, 16:343.

69 **"were left at full liberty":** Albert Gallatin, in Cunningham, *Jeffersonian Republicans: Formation of Party Organization*, 82.

69 **"No attempts":** Washington to John Hawkins Stone, 6 December 1795, in *Writings of George Washington*, ed. Fitzpatrick, 34:385.

70 **"childish comfort":** Fisher Ames to Dwight Foster, 4 January 1796, in *Works of Fisher Ames*, ed. Ames, 1:181.

70 **"I was no party man . . .":** Washington to Jefferson, 6 July 1796, in Washington, *Writings*, ed. Rhodehamel, 952.

70 **historians who analyzed voting patterns in Congress:** Gillis J. Harp, "Patrician

Partisans: New York in the House of Representative, 1789–1803," *Canadian Journal of History* 29 (December 1994):480–500; H. James Henderson, "Quantitative Approaches to Party Formation in the United States Congress: A Comment," *William and Mary Quarterly* 30 (1973):315ff.

70 **"Through what official interstice . . .":** Brant, *James Madison*, 3:431.

70 **"grossest and most insidious misrepresentations":** Washington to Jefferson, 6 July 1796, in Washington, *Writings*, ed. Rhodehamel, 952.

70 **"wound my reputation . . .":** Draft of Farewell Address, in Washington, *Writings*, ed. Rhodehamel, 946.

70 **"been guilty of a willful error":** Washington to David Humphreys, 12 June 1796, in *Writings of George Washington*, ed. Fitzpatrick, 35:91–92. See also Marshall Smelser, "George Washington and the Alien and Sedition Acts," *American Historical Review* 59, no. 2 (January 1954):327ff.

70 **"The trouble and perplexities":** Washington to John Jay, 8 May 1796, in *Writings of George Washington*, ed. Fitzpatrick, 35:37.

71 **"No consideration under heaven":** Washington to nephew Robert Lewis, in *Writings of George Washington*, ed. Fitzpatrick, 35:99.

71 **"an early example":** Washington, Farewell Address, First Draft, 15 May 1796, in Washington, *Writings*, ed. Rhodehamel, 941.

71 **"Hold the thing undecided . . .":** Hamilton to Washington, 5 July 1796, in *Papers of Alexander Hamilton*, ed. Syrett, 20:247.

72 **Farewell Address:** 19 September 1796, in Washington, *Writings*, ed. Rhodehamel, 969–70, italics added.

73 **"the king can do no wrong":** *Albany (N.Y.) Register*, 21 December 1795, in Stewart, "Jeffersonian Journalism," 795.

73 **Citizens had not only the privilege . . . :** Fredericktown (Md.) *Bartgis's Federal Gazette*, 14 April 1796, in Stewart, "Jeffersonian Journalism," 795.

73 **"The moment he retires"; "In the mean time, . . . patience":** Jefferson to James Monroe, 10 July 1796, in *Writings of Thomas Jefferson*, ed. Ford, 7:89, italics added.

4. Heir Apparent

74 **"I am heir apparent . . .":** John Adams to Abigail Adams, 20 January 1796, in *Letters of John Adams, Addressed to His Wife*, ed. Adams, 2:191.

74 **"pride and boast . . .":** Adams to Gerry, 20 February 1797, in Sharp, *American Politics in the Early Republic*, 160.

74 **"no more danger":** Adams to Abigail Adams, 15 February 1796, in Smith, *John Adams*, 2:884.

74 **"whether our system and union . . .":** Page Smith, "Election of 1796," in Schlesinger, *History of American Presidential Elections*, 69.

74 **"voluntary retreat":** Adams to Abigail Adams, 7 January 1796, in *Letters of John Adams, Addressed to His Wife*, ed. Adams, 2:189–90.

74 **"mode of becoming great . . .":** Adams to Abigail Adams, 14 January 1797, in *Letters of John Adams, Addressed to His Wife*, ed. Adams, 2:240.

75 **"I have no very ardent desire . . .":** Adams to Abigail Adams, 20 January 1796, in *Letters of John Adams, Addressed to His Wife*, ed. Adams, 2:191.

75 **"good patriot, statesman, and philosopher":** Smith, *John Adams*, 2:885.

75 **"silent spectator"**: Ibid., 2:885.

75 **"very indifferent"**: Adams, 5 May 1796, in ibid., 2:885.

75 **without a complaint, without the smallest dread . . . :** Adams to Abigail Adams, 15 February 1796, in *Letters of John Adams, Addressed to His Wife,* ed. Adams, 2:202.

75 **"fool"**: Adams to Abigail Adams, 9 April 1796, in *Letters of John Adams, Addressed to His Wife,* ed. Adams, 2:217.

75 **"murder all good men"**: Smith, *John Adams,* 2:885–86.

75 **"I don't know how I should live out of it"**: Adams to Abigail Adams, 10 February 1796, in *Letters of John Adams, Addressed to His Wife,* ed. Adams, 2:197.

75 **"government will go on"**: Adams to Abigail Adams, 15 February 1796, in *Letters of John Adams, Addressed to His Wife,* ed. Adams, 2:201.

76 **"endanger too much"**: Adams to Abigail Adams, 27 February 1796, Massachusetts. Historical Society.

76 **"detect my errors"**: Adams to Dr. Benjamin Rush, 31 August 1809, in *Old Family Letters,* ed. Biddle, 238.

76 **"I have never seen a Philadelphia paper . . ."**: Jefferson to Madison, 3 April 1794, in *Writings of Thomas Jefferson,* ed. Ford, 6:503.

76 **"Never let there be more . . ."**: Jefferson to Madison, 9 June 1793, in *Writings of Thomas Jefferson,* ed. Ford, 6:292.

76 **Jefferson in his Eden:** remark of the Duc de La Rochefoucauld-Liancourt, in Peterson, *Thomas Jefferson and the New Nation,* 520.

76 **seven miles:** Jefferson to Madison, 22 January 1797, in *Republic of Letters,* ed. Smith, 2:960.

76 **crop rotation; fruit trees; peas and clover:** Jefferson to John Taylor, 1 May 1794, in *Writings of Thomas Jefferson,* ed. Ford, 6:506; see also Jefferson to Madison, 15 May 1794, 6:511; Jefferson to Washington, 19 June 1796, 7:84.

76 **"essence of dung"**: Jefferson to George Washington, 14 May 1794, in *Writings of Thomas Jefferson,* ed. Ford, 6:509.

76 **nail manufacture:** Jefferson to Démeunier, 29 April 1795, in *Writings of Thomas Jefferson,* ed. Ford, 7:26.

76 **"I put off answering . . ."; "I return to farming . . ."**: Jefferson to Adams, 25 April 1794, in *Adams-Jefferson Letters,* ed. Cappon, 1:254.

76 **"Antediluvian patriarch"**: Jefferson to Edward Rutledge, 30 November 1795, in *Writings of Thomas Jefferson,* ed. Ford, 7:39.

77 **"No circumstances, my dear Sir"**: Jefferson to Edmund Randolph, 7 September 1794, in *Writings of Thomas Jefferson,* ed. Ford, 6:512.

77 **but a "passenger" in life:** Jefferson to Mann Page, 30 August 1795, in *Writings of Thomas Jefferson,* ed. Ford, 7:23.

77 **"If we are made in some degree . . . perpetual service"**: Jefferson to James Monroe, 20 May 1782, in Jefferson, *Writings,* ed. Peterson, 777–79.

77 **"having interdicted to myself . . ."**: Jefferson to Tench Coxe, 10 September 1795, in *Writings of Thomas Jefferson,* ed. Ford, 7:30.

77 **"Jefferson thinks by this step . . . Cromwell"**: John Adams to John Quincy Adams, 3 January 1794, in Joseph J. Ellis, *Founding Brothers: The Revolutionary Generation* (New York: Vintage Books, 2002), 171.

77 **"unambitious, unavaricious . . .":** Adams to Dr. Benjamin Rush, September 1807, in *Old Family Letters,* ed. Biddle, 163.

77 **"shameless corruption":** Jefferson to Edmund Randolph, 3 February 1794, in *Writings of Thomas Jefferson,* ed. Ford, 6:498.

78 **subscription to *Aurora:*** See Joseph J. Ellis, *American Sphinx: The Character of Thomas Jefferson* (New York: Alfred A. Knopf, 1996), 155–56.

78 **"at the helm":** Jefferson to Washington, 23 May 1792, in *Writings of Thomas Jefferson,* ed. Ford, 6:5.

78 **"justify wishing one . . .":** Jefferson to Madison, 28 December 1794, in *Writings of Thomas Jefferson,* ed. Ford, 6:519.

78 **"red clover":** Jefferson to James Madison, 27 April 1795, in *Writings of Thomas Jefferson,* ed. Ford, 7:10–11.

78 **"age of experiments":** Jefferson to Adams, 28 February 1796, in *Adams-Jefferson Letters,* ed. Cappon, 1:260.

78 **"mar the project":** Madison to James Monroe, 26 February 1796, in *Papers of James Madison,* ed. Stagg and Mason, 16:232.

78 **"dropping a hat":** Ames to Wolcott, 26 September 1796, in Smith, *John Adams,* 2:898.

78 **"I have not seen Jefferson":** Madison to Monroe, 29 September 1796, in *Papers of James Madison,* ed. Stagg and Mason, 16:404.

79 **"unprofitable conditions of Virginia estates":** Peterson, *Thomas Jefferson and the New Nation,* 544.

79 **"An Anglican monarchical aristocratical party . . .":** Jefferson to Philip Mazzei, April 24 1796, in Jefferson, *Writings,* ed. Peterson, 1037.

79 **"Southern interest":** Jefferson to Madison, 27 April 1795, in *Papers of James Madison,* ed. Stagg and Mason, 16:2 and n. 2. See also Sharp, *American Politics in the Early Republic,* 158–59.

79 **"There is a debt of service . . .":** Jefferson to Edward Rutledge, 27 December 1796, in *Writings of Thomas Jefferson,* ed. Ford, 7:94–95.

79 **"I do expect that your farm . . .":** Jefferson to Monroe, 8 February 1798, in *Writings of Thomas Jefferson,* ed. Ford, 7:198.

79 **"unfit for society . . . state of mind into which they get":** Jefferson to Maria Jefferson Eppes, 3 March 1802, in *Family Letters of Thomas Jefferson,* ed. Betts and Bear, 219.

80 **middle of Atlantic:** see Elkins and McKitrick, *Age of Federalism,* 515.

80 **"Virginianism":** George Cabot to Rufus King, 16 February 1799, in *Life and Correspondence of Rufus King,* ed. King, 2:543.

80 **"o-er turn" the Constitution:** Lemuel Hopkins, "The Guillotina" (Philadelphia, 1796), in Fischer, *Revolution of American Conservatism,* 289.

80 **"avowed friend . . .":** Handbill, 3 October 1796, in Malone, *Jefferson and the Ordeal of Liberty,* 283.

80 **"continued eulogium":** *General Advertiser,* October 1796, in Sharp, *American Politics in the Early Republic,* 153.

81 **Republican Committee of Pennsylvania circular:** R. R. Palmer, *The Age of Democratic Revolution: A Political History of Europe and America, 1760–1800* (Princeton: Princeton University Press, 1964), 2:534.

81 **"moral and political habits":** *Connecticut Courant,* in Sharp, *American Politics in the Early Republic,* 158.

81 **"Southern interest":** Jefferson to Madison, 27 April 1795, in *Writings of Thomas Jefferson,* ed. Ford, 7:10. James Roger Sharp discovered that the Ford edition of Jefferson's writings contains a crucial error. The original letter, in the James Madison Papers, in the Library of Congress, contains the word *Southern,* which Ford transcribed as "Republican." See Sharp, *American Politics in the Early Republic,* 311, n. 17. The correct form of the letter is quoted in Stephen G. Kurtz, *The Presidency of John Adams: The Collapse of Federalism 1795–1800* (Philadelphia: University of Pennsylvania Press, 1957), 91.

81 **people were being "abused and deceived":** Adams to Abigail Adams, in *Letters of John Adams, Addressed to His Wife,* ed. Adams, 2:216.

81 **Beckley:** See Cunningham, *Jeffersonian Republicans: Formation of Party Organization,* 102–6; see also Noble Cunningham, "John Beckley: An Early American Party Manager," *William and Mary Quarterly,* 3rd ser., 13 (1956):40–52.

82 **Pinckney-Jefferson ticket:** See Elkins and McKitrick, *Age of Federalism,* 527.

82 **poorly informed:** Kurtz, *Presidency of John Adams,* 92.

82 **public unaroused:** Elkins and McKitrick, *Age of Federalism,* 521.

82 **"license to innovate":** Jack N. Rakove, "The Political Presidency: Discovery and Invention," in Horn, Lewis, and Onuf, eds., *Revolution of 1800,* 50.

82 **"too headstrong . . .":** Madison to Jefferson, 5 December 1796, in *Papers of James Madison,* ed. Stagg and Mason, 16:422.

82 **"we [will] have Mr. Pinckney . . .":** Troup to King, 16 November 1797, in *Life and Correspondence of Rufus King,* ed. King, 2:110.

82 **"Julius Caesar":** Abigail Adams to John Adams, 31 December 1796, Massachusetts Historical Society.

82 **"as great a hypocrite . . .":** Abigail Adams, in Smith, *John Adams,* 2:908.

82 **"subtlety of your arch-friend":** Jefferson to Adams, 28 December 1796, in *Adams-Jefferson Letters,* ed. Cappon, 1:263.

83 **"opposite boxes":** Kurtz, *Presidency of John Adams,* 79.

83 **"solicit on my behalf . . .":** Jefferson to Madison, 17 December 1796, in *Papers of James Madison,* ed. Stagg and Mason, 16:431–32.

83 **"Jefferson was but a Boy . . .":** Adams to Dr. Benjamin Rush, 24 October 1809, in *Old Family Letters,* ed. Biddle, 246.

83 **"On principles of public respect" . . . corn and peas:** Jefferson to Edward Rutledge, 27 December 1796, in *Writings of Thomas Jefferson,* ed. Ford, 7:93–94.

83 **"stir a step":** *Letters of John Adams, Addressed to His Wife,* ed. Adams, 2:201.

84 **"insidious deception":** Theodore Sedgwick to Rufus King, 12 March 1797, in *Life and Correspondence of Rufus King,* ed. King, 2:156.

84 **"Such hypocrisy . . . formidable danger":** Ames to Thomas Dwight, 5 January 1797, in *Works of Fisher Ames,* ed. Ames, 1:213.

84 **"affecting zeal . . .":** Fisher Ames to Christopher Gore, 17 December 1796, in *Works of Fisher Ames,* ed. Ames, 1:211.

84 **"No one will congratulate you . . .":** Jefferson to Adams, 28 December 1796, in *Adams-Jefferson Letters,* ed. Cappon, 1:263.

84 **Hamilton's "machinations":** Jefferson to Elbridge Gerry, 13 May 1797, in *Writings of Thomas Jefferson,* ed. Ford, 7:120.

84 **"I do not believe Mr. Adams . . .":** Jefferson to James Madison, 22 January 1797, in *Writings of Thomas Jefferson,* ed. Ford, 7:109.

84 **"philosophical evenings . . .":** Jefferson to Benjamin Rush, 22 January 1797, in *Writings of Thomas Jefferson,* ed. Ford, 7:114.

84 **"with great friendship . . .":** Jefferson to James Madison, 22 January 1797, in *Writings of Thomas Jefferson,* ed. Ford, 7:107–8, italics added.

85 **"future elections . . . English constitution":** Jefferson to Madison, 1 January 1797, in *Republic of Letters,* ed. Smith, 2:953.

85 **Madison's reaction to Jefferson's letter to Adams:** Madison to Jefferson, 15 January 1797, in *Republic of Letters,* ed. Smith, 2:957.

85 **"of his friendship for me":** Adams to Abigail Adams, 3 January 1797, in Smith, *John Adams,* 2:909–10.

85 **"unshaken"; "wrong in politics":** Abigail Adams to John Adams, 15 January 1797, in Smith, *John Adams,* 2:904.

86 **would "act harmoniously . . .":** Robert M. S. McDonald, "Was There a Religious Revolution in 1800?" in Horn, Lewis, and Onuf, eds., *Revolution of 1800,* 180.

86 **"fraternizing":** Robert Troup to Rufus King, 28 January 1797, in *Life and Correspondence of Rufus King,* ed. King, 2:135.

86 **"serve readily under Mr. Adams":** Stephen Higginson to Hamilton, 12 January 1797, in *Papers of Alexander Hamilton,* ed. Syrett, 20:465–66.

86 **"The Lion & the Lamb . . . vigorous administration":** Hamilton to Rufus King, 15 February 1795, in *Papers of Alexander Hamilton,* ed. Syrett, 20:515–16, italics added.

86 **"Govt would find in party all the combination & energy . . . need of a clear Sighted guide":** Fisher Ames to Hamilton, 26 January 1797, in *Papers of Alexander Hamilton,* ed. Syrett, 20:488.

87 **"divided and crumbling":** Adams to Abigail Adams, 31 January 1797, Massachusetts Historical Society.

87 **Madison retires from politics:** Brant, *James Madison,* 4:12. See also Milton Lomask, *Aaron Burr: The Years from Princeton to Vice President* (New York: Farrar, Straus and Giroux, 1979), 162.

87 **"put our vessel":** Jefferson to James Madison, 1 January 1797, in *Writings of Thomas Jefferson,* ed. Ford, 7:98.

87 **"harmony":** Jefferson to James Madison, 30 January 1797, in *Writings of Thomas Jefferson,* ed. Ford, 7:115.

87 **"unattended and on foot"; "impossible to describe":** Theodore Sedgwick to Rufus King, 12 March 1797, in *Life and Correspondence of Rufus King,* ed. King, 2:259.

87 **"all grief for the loss . . .":** Adams to Abigail Adams, 9 March 1795, in *Letters of John Adams, Addressed to His Wife,* ed. Adams, 2:247.

87 **"talents and science" of Adams:** Smith, *John Adams,* 2:909.

88 **"spirit of party, spirit of intrigue . . . decent respect for Christianity":** John Adams's Inaugural Address, 4 March 1797, Appendix, Smith, "Election of 1796," in Schlesinger, *History of American Presidential Elections,* 94–98.

88 **"Nothing is more dreaded . . .":** John Adams to Benjamin Rush, 12 June 1812, in John A. Schutz and Douglass Adair, eds., *The Spur of Fame: Dialogues of John Ad-*

ams and Benjamin Rush, 1805–1813 (San Marino, Calif.: The Huntington Library 1966), 224.

88 **deferring to new president and vice president; people rush after Washington:** Flexner, *George Washington: Anguish and Farewell*, 4:333.

88 **nation's father was already grieving . . . :** Washington to Jonathan Trumbull, 3 March 1797, in *Writings of George Washington*, ed. Fitzpatrick, 35:412.

88 **"fortunate to get off . . . hold the bag":** Jefferson to Madison, 8 January 1797, in *Papers of James Madison*, ed. Stagg and Mason, 16:448.

88 **"Ay! I am fairly out . . .":** Adams to Abigail Adams, 5 March 1795, in *Letters of John Adams, Addressed to His Wife*, ed. Adams, 2:245.

88 **"never had "a more trying day":** Adams to Abigail Adams, 5 March 1797, in *Letters of John Adams, Addressed to His Wife*, ed. Adams, 2:244.

88 **"amiable light of friends":** *Aurora General Advertiser*, 11, 12, 14 March 1797, in Sharp, *American Politics in the Early Republic*, 162.

89 **"It carries conciliation and healing . . .":** Kerber, *Federalists in Dissent*, 195.

89 **"unanimity is . . .":** Edward Rutledge to John Rutledge, Jr., 9 June 1797, in ibid., 195, italics added.

89 **"democrats and jacobins . . .":** Adams to Wolcott, 4 October 1800, in *Works of John Adams*, ed. Adams, 9:87.

89 **"It is intolerance!":** "To the Printers of the *Boston Patriot*" [1809], Letter XVII, in *Works of John Adams*, ed. Adams, 9:303.

89 **"extreamly desirous of availing myself . . .":** Adams to Dr. Benjamin Rush, 23 August 1805, in *Old Family Letters*, ed. Biddle, 76.

89 **"profound gloom . . . name of Madison":** "To the Printers of the *Boston Patriot*," Letter XIII, in *Works of John Adams*, ed. Adams, 9:286.

89 **"violent Party Spirit":** Adams to Dr. Benjamin Rush, 23 August 1805, in *Old Family Letters*, ed. Biddle, 77.

89 **"Unless Mr. Madison will go . . .":** Hamilton to Washington, 25–31 January 1797, in *Papers of Alexander Hamilton*, ed. Syrett, 20:481.

89 **"deep and extensive roots":** "To the Printers of the *Boston Patriot*," Letter XIII, in *Works of John Adams*, ed. Adams, 9:286.

89 **"Jacobins are flattering . . .":** William Smith to Rufus King, 3 April 1797, in *Life and Correspondence of Rufus King*, ed. King, 2:167.

89 **foreign travel would harm his health:** See Jack N. Rakove, *James Madison and the Creation of the American Republic* (New York: HarperCollins, 1990), 124–25.

89 **"hot-headed executive":** Madison, in Rakove, *James Madison and the Creation of the American Republic*, 125.

90 **Madison would have refused to negotiate for Federalist administration:** See Elkins and McKitrick, *Age of Federalism*, 548.

90 **"unfit for office":** Adams to John Quincy Adams, in Peterson, *Thomas Jefferson and the New Nation*, 568–69. See also Adams to Uriah Forrest, 20 June 1797, in *Works of John Adams*, ed. Adams, 8:546–47.

90 **"We consulted very little"; "useless":** "To the Printers of the *Boston Patriot*," Letter XIII, in *Works of John Adams*, ed. Adams, 9:285.

90 **"smooth handle":** Jefferson to Paul Clay, in *Writings of Thomas Jefferson*, ed. Ford, 10:93, n.

90 **"never enter into dispute . . ."**: Jefferson to Thomas Jefferson Randolph, 24 November 1808, in *Writings of Thomas Jefferson,* ed. Ford, 11:78–83.

90 **"a few individuals of "no fixed system . . ."**: Jefferson to Burr, 17 June 1797, in *Writings of Thomas Jefferson,* ed. Ford, 7:145–46.

90 **"the very life and soul of the opposition"**: Theodore Sedgwick to Rufus King, 9 April 1798, in *Life and Correspondence of Rufus King,* ed. King, 2:311.

90 **"and all his colleagues . . ."**: Adams to Elbridge Gerry, 13 February 1797, in *Works of John Adams,* ed. Adams, 8:523.

90 **"I wish you were in a situation . . ."**: Pickering to Hamilton, 9 June 1798, in Hamilton, *Works,* ed. John C. Hamilton, 7 vols. (New York: J. F. Trow, Printer, 1850–51), 6:307.

91 **"I knew if I removed . . ."**: John Adams, 22 April 1812, in Stephen Skowronek, *The Politics Presidents Make: Leadership from John Adams to George Bush* (Cambridge: The Belknap Press of Harvard University Press, 1993), 66.

91 **"steer impartially . . ."**: *Anas,* in *Writings of Thomas Jefferson,* ed. Ford, 1:273.

91 **"shackled"**: Adams, "To the Printers of the *Boston Patriot"* [1809], Letter XVII, in *Works of John Adams,* ed. Adams, 9:301.

91 **"I had all the officers . . ."**: Adams to Dr. Benjamin Rush, 4 March 1809, in *Old Family Letters,* ed. Biddle, 219.

91 **"confident . . . and presumptuous"**: "To the Printers of the *Boston Patriot"* [1809], Letter XVII, in *Works of John Adams,* ed. Adams, 9:302.

91 **"capable of mediating between two infuriated Parties"**: Adams to Dr. Benjamin Rush, 25 July 1808, in *Old Family Letters,* ed. Biddle, 188.

91 **"abjured and abhorred . . ."**: Adams to Dr. Benjamin Rush, 23 March 1809, in *Old Family Letters,* ed. Biddle, 224.

91 **"Great is the guilt . . ."**: Adams to Abigail Adams, in David G. McCullough, *John Adams* (New York: Simon and Schuster, 2001), 474.

92 **"thunderstruck"**: McCullough, *John Adams,* 524.

92 **"remonstrate"**: "To the Printers of the *Boston Patriot,"* Letter V, in *Works of John Adams,* ed. Adams, 9:255.

92 **"babyish and womanly blubbering"**: Adams to Washington, 19 February 1799, in *Works of John Adams,* ed. Adams, 8:626.

92 **"Here lies John Adams . . ."**: Adams to James Lloyd, January 1815, in *Works of John Adams,* ed. Adams, 10:113.

92 **"get rid of Mr. Adams"**: Robert Troup to Rufus King, 6 November 1799, in *Life and Correspondence of Rufus King,* ed King, 3:141–42. See also Theodore Sedgwick to Rufus King, 15 November 1799, 3:146.

92 **"men of most importance . . ."**: Richard Stockton to Oliver Wolcott, 27 June 1800, in Oliver Wolcott, *Memoirs of the Administrations of Washington and John Adams,* edited from the papers of Oliver Wolcott by George Gibbs (New York: Printed for the Subscribers, 1846), 2:374.

92 **Adams reversed his administration's policies:** See Skowronek, *The Politics Presidents Make,* 68.

92 **Madison already intuited:** Madison to Jefferson, 15 January 1797, in *Republic of Letters,* ed. Smith, 2:957. See also Ralph Ketcham, *Presidents Above Party: The First*

American Presidency, 1789–1829 (Chapel Hill: University of North Carolina Press for the Institute of Early American History and Culture, 1984), 225.

93 **"We can never have a national President . . ."**: Adams to Richard Rush, 13 May 1821, in Adrienne Koch, ed., *The American Enlightenment* (New York: George Braziller, 1965), 231.

93 **two roles that complemented each other . . .** : Burns, *Presidential Government,* 326.

93 **"Legislative leadership is not possible . . ."**: John F. Kennedy, interview with the author, in Burns, *Deadlock of Democracy,* 338–39.

93 **"The machine has worked . . ."**: William Loughton Smith to Rufus King, 3 April 1797, in *Republic of Letters,* ed. Smith, 2:966.

93 **"in all free governments . . ."**: Washington to Jonathan Trumbull, 3 March 1797, in *Writings of George Washington,* ed. Fitzpatrick, 35:412.

5. Sedition

95 **"The mornings . . ."**: Abigail Adams to her sister, 25 June 1798, in *New Letters of Abigail Adams, 1788–1801,* ed. Stewart Mitchell (Boston: Houghton Mifflin, 1947), 196.

95 **"The extreem heat . . . bricks are so Hot"**: Abigail Adams to her sister, 3 July 1798, in *New Letters of Abigail Adams,* ed. Mitchell, 199.

95 **"nausious . . . Soar Throat"**: Abigail Adams, 23 June 1798, in *New Letters of Abigail Adams,* ed. Mitchell, 194.

95 **"again scourged . . ."**: William Bingham to Rufus King, 30 September 1798, in *Life and Correspondence of Rufus King,* ed. King, 2:426–27.

95 **"destroying angel"**: *Gazette of the United States,* 10 September 1800, Reel 8.

95 **"in every Direction . . ."**: William Bingham to Rufus King, 30 September 1798, in *Life and Correspondence of Rufus King,* ed. King, 2:426–27.

95 **"safety in flight . . ."**: Robert Troup to Rufus King, 2 October 1798, in *Life and Correspondence of Rufus King,* ed. King, 2:428–29.

95 **Poorer people . . .** : T. Pickering to Rufus King, 29 August 1798, in *Life and Correspondence of Rufus King,* ed. King, 2:403.

96 **"Some days last week . . ."; "All private business . . ."**: Troup to King, 2 October 1798, in *Life and Correspondence of Rufus King,* ed. King, 2:428–29.

96 **Fifteen hundred of Philadelphia's poorest . . .** : Oliver Wolcott to John Adams, 14 September 1798, in Smith, *John Adams,* 2:985.

96 **"The Physicians . . ."**: William Bingham to Rufus King, 30 September 1798, in *Life and Correspondence of Rufus King,* ed. King, 2:426–27.

96 **"found to baffle . . . violent fermentation"**: Troup to King, 2 October 1798, in *Life and Correspondence of Rufus King,* ed. King, 2:428–29.

96 **Congress passed bill empowering American war vessels . . .** : Smith, *John Adams,* 2:967.

97 **"Where is it possible for her to get ships . . ."**: Adams to Elbridge Gerry, 3 May 1797, in Elkins and McKitrick, *Age of Federalism,* 596.

97 **"unparalleled stupidity"**: Rakove, *James Madison and the Creation of the American Republic,* 125.

97 **"electrified all classes"**: Fisher Ames to Gore, 28 July 1798, in *Works of Fisher Ames,* ed. Ames, 1:238.

97 **"outrageous"**: George Washington to Alexander Hamilton, 27 May 1798, in *Writings of George Washington*, ed. Ford, 14:6–7.

97 **"deformities and horrors"**: Pickering to King, 27 June 1798, in *Life and Correspondence of Rufus King*, ed. King, 2:351.

97 **"too much afraid of measures . . ."**: Fisher Ames to Timothy Pickering, 4 June 1798, in *Works of Fisher Ames*, ed. Ames, 2:227.

97 **"A spirit of warm and high resentment"**: Troup to King, 3 June 1798, in *Life and Correspondence of Rufus King*, ed. King, 2:329–30.

97 **"If the French invade . . ."**: Troup to King, 10 June 1798, in *Life and Correspondence of Rufus King*, ed. King, 2:344.

98 **"Every day's delay . . ."**: Fisher Ames to Timothy Pickering, 4 June 1798, in *Works of Fisher Ames*, ed. Ames, 2:22.

98 **"Why, when we have the thing . . ."**: Abigail Adams to Mary Cranch, 9 June 1798, in McCullough, *John Adams*, 504.

98 **"I could not remain an unconcerned spectator"**: Washington to Lafayette, 25 December 1798, in *Writings of George Washington*, ed. Ford, 14:127.

98 **"irreparable"**: Washington to Adams, 25 September 1798, in *Writings of George Washington*, ed. Ford, 14:101–2.

98 **windowpanes**: Peter S. Onuf and Leonard J. Sadosky, *Jeffersonian America* (Malden, Mass.: Blackwell, 2002), 70.

98 **"Hamilton and a Party . . ."**: John Adams, Gerry's Minutes of a Conference with the President, 26 March 1799, in Elkins and McKitrick, *Age of Federalism*, 617.

98 **"We may have to enter . . . province of France"**: Hamilton to Washington, 19 May 1798, in *Papers of Alexander Hamilton*, ed. Syrett, 21:467.

99 **"Agents and Partizans"**: Washington to William Heth, 5 August 1798, in *Writings of George Washington*, ed. Fitzpatrick, 36:389. See also Smelser, "George Washington and the Alien and Sedition Acts," 330.

99 **"subvert the constitution . . . Grand Turk"**: Washington to Lafayette, 25 December 1798, in *Writings of George Washington*, ed. Ford, 14:123–24.

99 **"discontented"**: Washington to Bryan, Lord Fairfax, 20 January 1799, in *Writings of George Washington*, ed. Ford, 14:143.

99 **"injudicious"; "Embarrassing"**: Washington to William Vans Murray, 26 October 1799, in *Writings of George Washington*, ed. Ford, 14:215.

99 **"self-preservation"**: *Observations on the Alien and Sedition Acts* [1799] in Peter S. Onuf, *Jefferson's Empire: The Language of American Nationhood* (Charlottesville: University Press of Virginia, 2000), 101.

99 **"intimate acquaintance . . . human and divine"**: John Allen of Connecticut, in Leonard Levy, *Emergence of a Free Press* (New York: Oxford University Press, 1985), 299.

99 **Congregational church**: *Connecticut Courant*, 20 August 1798, in Newman, *Parades and Politics*, 162.

99 **butcher boys**: *Gazette of the United States*, 10 May 1798, in Newman, *Parades and Politics*, 162.

100 **"skulk through the streets . . ."**: *Boston Gazette*, 16 July 1798, in Newman, *Parades and Politics*, 162–63.

100 **Harvard College**: Alexander DeConde, *The Quasi-War: The Politics and Diplomacy of the Undeclared War with France, 1797–1801* (New York: Scribner, 1966), 86.

100 **march down Market Street:** Merrill D. Peterson, *Adams and Jefferson: A Revolutionary Dialogue* (Athens: University of Georgia Press, 1976), 76; David Waldstreicher, *In the Midst of Perpetual Fetes: The Making of American Nationalism, 1776–1820* (Chapel Hill: University of North Carolina Press for the Omohundro Institute of Early American History and Culture, 1997), 162–63.

100 **"dangerous and restless men":** "To the Inhabitants of Arlington and Sandgate, Vermont," 25 June 1788, in *Works of John Adams,* ed. Adams, 9:202.

100 **"We are now wonderfully popular":** Abigail Adams to Mary Cranch, 28 April 1798, in McCullough, *John Adams,* 500.

100 **"see the Bible cast into a bonfire . . .":** Levy, *Emergence of a Free Press,* 299.

100 **"war party"; "as a defense . . . evils may ensue":** Jefferson to Madison, 24 May 1798; Madison to Jefferson, 12 February 1798, in *Republic of Letters,* ed. Smith, 2: 1052, 1019.

100 **"unanimity":** Adams, Address to Both Houses of Congress, 19 March 1798, in *Works of John Adams,* ed. Adams, 9:157.

100 **"He that is not for us . . .":** Smith, *Freedom's Fetters,* 15.

101 **"possibility of internal disorders":** Hamilton to Harrison Gray Otis, 27 December 1798, in *Papers of Alexander Hamilton,* ed. Syrett, 22:394.

101 **"refractory . . .":** Hamilton to Theodore Sedgwick, 2 February 1799, in *Papers of Alexander Hamilton,* ed. Syrett, 22:453.

101 **"close connection":** Abigail Adams to her sister, 19 June 1798, in *New Letters of Abigail Adams,* ed. Mitchell, 193.

101 **"Whatever American opposes the administration . . .":** *Columbian Centinel,* 5 October 1798, in Levy, *Emergence of a Free Press,* 300, italics added.

101 **"paranoid style":** Richard Hofstadter, *The Paranoid Style in American Politics and Other Essays* (New York: Alfred A. Knopf, 1965), 3–4.

102 **Otis and Harper:** Richard Buel, Jr., *Securing the Revolution: Ideology in American Politics, 1789–1815* (Ithaca, N.Y.: Cornell University Press, 1972), 245.

102 **"the crackbrain could be convicted . . .":** Fisher Ames to Christopher Gore, 10 January 1795, in *Works of Fisher Ames,* ed. Ames, 1:161–62.

102 **"morbid excrescences . . .":** John Allen, in Fischer, *Revolution of American Conservatism,* 293.

102 **"How mischievous . . .":** James Lloyd, Address to the Citizens of Kent (Annapolis, 1794), in Fischer, *Revolution of American Conservatism,* 360.

102 **Ames wants to purge his own party of hypocrites:** Cornell, *Other Founders,* 231.

103 **"Democracy is a distemper . . .":** John Adams to Benjamin Rush, 6 February 1805, in Schutz and Adair, eds., *Spur of Fame,* 21.

103 **"were it left to me to decide . . .":** Jefferson to Edward Carrington, 16 January 1787, in Jefferson, *Writings,* ed. Peterson, 880.

103 **"If by the Liberty of the Press . . .":** Benjamin Franklin, "The Court of the Press," 12 September 1789, in Smith, *Freedom's Fetters,* 429.

103 **"a series of errors and crimes . . .":** James Tagg, *Benjamin Bache and the Philadelphia Aurora* (Philadelphia: University of Pennsylvania Press, 1991), 313.

103 **"Damn":** Robert A. Rutland, *The Newsmongers: Journalism in the Life of the Nation, 1690–1972* (New York: Dial Press, 1973), 70. See also Richard N. Rosenfeld, *American Aurora* (New York: St. Martin's Press, 1997), 28.

103 **"person without patriotism":** Buel, *Securing the Revolution,* 248.

103 **"old, bald . . .":** Smith, *John Adams*, 2:961.

103 **Republican newspapers:** Jeffrey L. Pasley, *"Tyranny of Printers"*, 117–18.

104 **Tocqueville on newspapers:** Tocqueville, *De la Démocratie en Amérique*, ed. Mayer, Bk. 1, Pt. 2, ch. 3, 191. All translations from the French are my own.

104 **freedom of the press and assembly the same:** Ibid., Bk. 1, Pt. 2, ch. 4, 195.

104 **"The censorial power . . .":** James Madison, House Address to the President, 27 November 1794, in *Papers of James Madison*, ed. Mason and Rutland, 15:391.

104 **"A licentious press . . .":** Smelser, "Jacobin Phrenzy," 463.

104 **"glorious opportunity . . .":** Theodore Sedgwick, 7 March 1798, in Smith, *Freedom's Fetters*, 21.

105 **"I believe faction and Jacobinism . . .":** Wolcott to Hamilton, 5 April 1798, in *Papers of Alexander Hamilton*, ed. Syrett, 21:397.

105 **"wrest it from them":** John Allen, in Smith, *Freedom's Fetters*, 117.

105 **constitutional consensus:** Richard Hofstadter, *The Idea of a Party System* (Berkeley: University of California Press, 1969), 4.

105 **"Gag-bill":** Smith, *Freedom's Fetters*, 110.

105 **"suppress the opinions . . .":** Buel, *Securing the Revolution*, 257.

105 **today's minority might become tomorrow's majority . . . :** *Washington Gazette*, 7 January 1797, in Stewart, "Jeffersonian Journalism," 848.

106 **"false facts":** Jefferson to Rabout de St. Etienne, 3 June 1789, in Jefferson, *Writings*, ed. Peterson, 956.

106 **obliged printers to bow . . . :** Philadelphia *Aurora*, 22 August 1798, in Stewart, "Jeffersonian Journalism," 880.

106 **"property" in their opinions:** "Property," *National Gazette*, 29 March 1792, in Madison, *Writings*, ed. Rakove, 515–17.

106 **"Truth has but one side . . .":** Fischer, *Revolution of American Conservatism*, 332.

106 **truth and opinion:** See Wood, "Democratization of Mind," 83.

106 **Dana; final bill strikes out injurious:** Smith, *Freedom's Fetters*, 125, 128.

107 **"their motives in any official transaction":** John Chester Miller, *Crisis in Freedom: The Alien and Sedition Acts* (Boston: Little, Brown, 1951), 67.

107 **"In any other Country . . .":** Abigail Adams to her sister, 19 June 1798, in *New Letters of Abigail Adams*, ed. Mitchell, 193.

107 **"meanest of cowards":** Ames to Gore, 18 December 1798, in *Works of Fisher Ames*, ed. Ames, 1:245.

107 **"useless" and "calculated . . .":** Smith, *Freedom's Fetters*, 151.

107 **"we might have hanged traitors . . .":** Theodore Sedgwick to Rufus King, 20 January 1799, in *Life and Correspondence of Rufus King*, ed. King, 2:515.

107 **on the stated purpose of the Sedition Act:** See Burns, *Vineyard of Liberty*, 126. See also Cornell, *Other Founders*, 230–41, 253–73.

107 **"Until lately . . .":** "To the officers and men of Colonel Romyen's Militia," 19 July 1798, in Smith, *Freedom's Fetters*, 152.

107 **Jefferson fled to Monticello:** Malone, *Jefferson and the Ordeal of Liberty*, 379.

108 **Boston Gazette motto; Massachusetts state constitution:** Smith, *Freedom's Fetters*, 252; *Works of John Adams*, ed. Adams, 4:227.

108 **antigovernment talk was seditious:** See Levy, *Emergence of a Free Press*, 202ff.

108 **"I cannot but be of the opinion":** John Adams, 7 August 1798, in Smith, *Freedom's Fetters*, 152.

108   **"be but one freeman . . .":** Boston *Independent Chronicle,* 7 June 1798, in Stewart, "Jeffersonian Journalism," 849.

108   **not one of Adams's primary concerns:** Elkins and McKitrick, *Age of Federalism,* 590.

108   **"helped to create the climate of opinion . . .":** Peterson, *Adams and Jefferson,* 80.

108   **"obloquy":** "To the Young Men of Boston," 22 May 1798, in *Works of John Adams,* ed. Adams, 9:194.

108   **itinerant Democratic speaker:** Smith, *Freedom's Fetters,* 262, 268.

108   **fulminated against William Rawle:** Adams to Pickering, 1 August 1799, in *Works of John Adams,* ed. Adams, 9:5.

108   **"hideous clamor":** "To the Printers of the *Boston Patriot"* [1809], Letters XIII and XII, in *Works of John Adams,* ed. Adams, 9:291, 278.

108   **"constitutional and salutary . . .":** Adams to Benjamin Rush, 25 December 1811, in Schutz and Adair, eds., *Spur of Fame,* 201.

108   **"A Proclamation":** 23 August 1775, in Smith, *Freedom's Fetters,* 427.

109   **"begin first with JEFFERSON . . .":** Philadelphia *Carey's United States Recorder,* 19 June 1798, in Stewart, "Jeffersonian Journalism," 876.

109   **"necessity of *purifying . . .":*** Harrison Gray Otis, in Smith, *Freedom's Fetters,* 106, italics added.

109   **"weight with the people"; restrict circular letters:** Robert Goodloe Harper, in ibid., 120, 122.

109   **"most ancient principles . . .":** Wolcott, *Memoirs,* ed. Gibbs, 2:84–85.

109   **"one party to oppress the other":** Gallatin, 10 July 1798, in Levy, *Emergence of a Free Press,* 298n. See also Smith, *Freedom's Fetters,* 143.

110   **printing presses under the imprimatur . . . :** Jefferson to Madison, 3 May 1798, in *Republic of Letters,* ed. Smith, 2:1045.

110   **all defendants Republican . . . :** Smelser, "Federalist Period," 412.

110   **"harmonizer of parties":** New York *Time Piece,* 13 July 1798, in Smith, *Freedom's Fetters,* 144.

110   **"at Constantinople or Philadelphia?":** *Aurora,* 29 June 1798, in Smith, *Freedom's Fetters,* 116.

110   **"tooth picks":** *Aurora,* 14 July 1798, in Smith, *Freedom's Fetters,* 144.

110   **"THINKING CLUB"; "Dumb waiters are provided":** Philadelphia *Carey's United States Recorder,* 12 July 1798, in Stewart, "Jeffersonian Journalism," 878.

110   **"as to shew they mean to pay . . .":** Jefferson to Madison, 7 June 1798, in *Republic of Letters,* ed. Smith, 2:1056–57.

110   **loud conversations, coughing, laughing:** Jefferson to Madison, 26 February 1799, in *Republic of Letters,* ed. Smith, 2:1100.

110   **"experiment on the American mind"; congressional acts:** Jefferson to Stephens Thompson Mason, 11 October 1798, in *Writings of Thomas Jefferson,* ed. Ford, 7:283, italics added.

110   **"the present republican system . . .":** Madison, Virginia Resolution, in Douglass Adair, *The Intellectual Origins of Jeffersonian Democracy,* ed. Mark E. Yellin (Lanham, Md.: Lexington Books, 2000), 4.

110   **"right of freely examining . . .":** "Report of 1800," in *Papers of James Madison,* ed. Mattern et al., 17:326. See Cornell, *Other Founders,* 242–43.

111 **"staggering under the sedition law":** Jefferson, 1802, in Cunningham, "Election of 1800," 114.

111 **"to nullify of their own authority":** Adrienne Koch and Harry Ammon, "The Virginia and Kentucky Resolutions: An Episode in Jefferson's and Madison's Defense of Civil Liberties," *William and Mary Quarterly*, 3rd ser., 5, no. 2 (April 1948):157.

111 **his "warm attachment . . . so much value":** Jefferson to Madison, 23 August 1799, in *Republic of Letters*, ed. Smith, 2:1119.

111 **"every spirit should be ready . . .":** Jefferson to William Munford, 18 June 1799, in Koch and Ammon, "Virginia and Kentucky Resolutions," 152.

111 **"conspiracy":** Hamilton to Sedgwick, 2 February 1799, in *Papers of Alexander Hamilton*, ed. Syrett, 22:452.

111 **Madison against unilateral state action:** Madison to Rev. — Adams, 1832, in *Writings of James Madison*, ed. Gaillard Hunt (New York: G. P. Putnam's Sons, 1910), 9:490. See also "Notes on Nullification," 1835, in *Writings of James Madison*, ed. Hunt, 9:580, 583.

111 **"necessarily drive these states into revolution . . .":** Drafts of the Kentucky Resolution of 1798, November 1798, in *Writings of Thomas Jefferson*, ed. Ford, 7:303, italics added. See James Madison, "Advice to My Country," October 1834, in Meyers, *Mind of the Founder*, 445. See also Rahe, *Republics Ancient and Modern*, vol. 3, *Inventions of Prudence*, 147–49, 150–51.

111 **"protestations against . . .":** Jefferson to Madison, 26 November 1799, in *Republic of Letters*, ed. Smith, 2:1122.

112 **southern sectionalism:** Sharp, *American Politics in the Early Republic*, 207.

112 **"Those who complain of legal provisions . . .":** Timothy Pickering, in John Chester Miller, *Crisis in Freedom*, 90.

113 **"there seems to be no bounds . . .":** Washington to Pickering, 4 August 1799, in *Writings of George Washington*, ed. Fitzpatrick, 37:322–24.

113 **father of public school system:** Sherman Williams, "Jedidiah Peck, the Father of the Public School System of the State of New York," N.Y. State Historical Association, *Quarterly Journal* 1 (1920):219–40.

114 **Peck's indictment; "triumphant processional":** Smith, *Freedom's Fetters*, 393–94.

114 ***New York Argus:*** 12 and 15 October 1799, 15 November 1799, in Smith, *Freedom's Fetters*, 272, 274.

115 **on Lyon and Griswold:** Aleine Austin, *Matthew Lyon: "New Man" of the Democratic Revolution, 1749–1822* (University Park: Pennsylvania State University Press, 1981), 96–100.

115 ***The Scourge of Aristocracy:*** 1 October 1798, in Smith, *Freedom's Fetters*, 227.

115 **"inculcating a proper submission . . .":** Philip Freneau, *Letters on Various Interesting and Important Subjects*, ed. Harry Hayden Clark (New York: Scholars' Facsimiles and Reprints, 1943), 13.

116 **on Bache, Baldwin, Cooper, Lyon, Haswell:** See Burns, *Vineyard of Liberty*, 126–33, 138ff. See also Smith, *Freedom's Fetters*, 257–70, 360–73.

116 **"expiring Aristocracy":** *Aurora*, 6 July 1798, in Smith, *Freedom's Fetters*, 108.

116 **"speaking Aristocracy":** Cotton Mather, *Magnalia Christi Americana* (Hartford, 1820), in Fischer, "Myth of the Essex Junto," 200.

116 **"How can the Congress . . ."**: Buel, *Securing the Revolution*, 245–46.

117 **"peculiar favorites"**: Norfolk *Epitome of the Times*, 16 February 1799, in Smith, *Freedom's Fetters*, 147.

117 **"In no case . . . ought the eyes . . . chosen their representatives"**: Madison, "Political Reflections," 23 February 1799, in *Papers of James Madison*, ed. Mattern et al., 17:238–39.

117 **"jewel"**: Patrick Henry, in Elliot, *Debates*, 3:45.

117 **"offspring . . . obey the established Government"**: Farewell Address, in Washington, *Writings*, ed. Rhodehamel, 968, italics added. See also Ketcham, *Presidents Above Party*, 93.

118 **"view that the government was master"**: Smith, *Freedom's Fetters*, 419.

118 **"The moderation, dignity . . . anarchy"**: "To the Inhabitants of the Town of Hartford, Connecticut," 10 May 1798, in *Works of John Adams*, ed. Adams, 9:192.

118 **"Reputation . . . is of as much importance . . ."**: "To the Students of New Jersey College," in *Works of John Adams*, ed. Adams, 9:205–7, italics added.

119 **"Let us not establish . . ."**: Hamilton to Wolcott, 29 June 1798, in *Papers of Alexander Hamilton*, ed. Syrett, 21:522.

119 **"We have broken the democratic fetters . . ."**: Robert Troup to Rufus King, 6 May 1799, in *Life and Correspondence of Rufus King*, ed. King, 3:14.

6. Life Without Father

121 **"The death of the General!"**: Henry Van Schaack to Theodore Sedgwick, 26 December 1799, in Fischer, *Revolution of American Conservatism*, 56.

121 **at the urging of Hamilton and his friends**: See *Works of John Adams*, ed. Adams, 9:45, editorial note.

121 **"Should you decline . . ."**: Gouverneur Morris to George Washington, 9 December 1799, in *The Life of Gouverneur Morris*, ed. Jared Sparks (Boston: Gray and Bowen, 1832), 3:123–24.

121 **"I am too far advanced . . ."**: Washington to Jonathan Trumbull, 30 August 1799, in *Writings of George Washington*, ed. Fitzpatrick, 37:349.

121 **"thoroughly convinced . . . in toto!"**: *Writings of George Washington*, ed. Fitzpatrick, 37:313.

122 **description of Washington's death and funeral**: See Flexner, *George Washington: Anguish and Farewell*, 456–62. See also John Alexander Carroll and Mary Wells Ashworth, *George Washington: First in Peace*, vol. 7 of Freeman, *George Washington*, 617–34.

123 **"The whole United States . . ."**: *Autobiography of Benjamin Rush*, 248, in Carroll and Ashworth, *George Washington: First in Peace*, 648.

123 **stroke**: Carroll and Ashworth, *George Washington: First in* Peace, 649.

124 **"our country mourns her father"; "I feel myself alone"**: 23 December 1799, in *Writings of George Washington*, ed. Ford, 14:263–64.

124 **"From a calamity . . ."**: Hamilton to Martha Washington, 12 January 1800, in *Papers of Alexander Hamilton*, ed. Syrett, 24:184.

124 **congressional decree of national mourning**: *Writings of George Washington*, ed. Ford, 14:265–66.

124 **accusations that his absence had been deliberate slight:** Malone, *Jefferson and the Ordeal of Liberty*, 442.

124 **orations printed and distributed:** Carroll and Ashworth, *George Washington, First in Peace*, 651.

124 **"almost an impossibility for ladies to be present . . .":** Newman, *Parades and Politics*, 69.

124 **"gods upon earth":** Catherine Albanese, *Sons of the Fathers*, 159.

124 **"every man looked round . . . constellations of the sky":** Fisher Ames, Eulogy on Washington, 8 February 1800, in *Works of Fisher Ames*, ed. Ames, 2:71.

125 **"I praise a man who never yielded . . .":** Louis de Fontanes, Funeral Oration for George Washington, 8 February 1800, in Chinard, *George Washington as the French Knew Him*, 129–38.

125 **"crowned Washington . . .":** J. Christopher Herold, *The Age of Napoleon* (Boston: Houghton Mifflin, 1963), 123.

126 **ready to give up the "freedom":** Alexis de Tocqueville, *L'Ancien Régime et la Révolution*, Part 2, *Fragments et notes*, ed. J.-P. Mayer (Paris: Gallimard, 1953), 2:289. All translations are my own.

126 **Napoleon and the press:** J. Godechot, "La presse sous le Consulat et l'Empire," in *Histoire générale de la presse française* (Paris: Presses Universitaires de France, 1969), 563.

126 **"press, the only tocsin . . .":** Jefferson to Thomas Cooper, 29 November 1802, in Jefferson, *Writings*, ed. Peterson, 1110.

126 **Napoleon and *Le Moniteur*:** Godechot, "La presse sous le Consulat et l'Empire," 557.

126 **Ministry of Police:** Louis Bergeron, *L'Episode Napoléonien*, vol. 4 of *Nouvelle histoire de la France contemporaine* (Paris: Seuil, 1972), 4:18.

126 **govern in the name of the people without the people:** Tocqueville, *L'Ancien Régime et la Révolution*, Part 2, *Fragments et notes*, ed. Mayer, 2:320.

127 **"My kind of politics . . .":** Bergeron, *L'Episode Napoléonien*, 7.

127 **same level of servitude:** Tocqueville, *L'Ancien Régime et la Révolution*, Part 2, *Fragments et notes*, ed. Mayer, 2:320.

127 **"wherever one looked . . .":** Ibid., 2:301.

127 **"man of the choice of France":** Address to the Citizens of South Carolina, in Lerche, "Jefferson and the Election of 1800," 485.

127 **"Jacobin First Consul":** *Virginia Gazette and General Advertiser*, 21 October 1800, reprinting editorial from the *Commercial Advertiser*, in Lerche, "Jefferson and the Election of 1800," 481 n.

127 **"sacrifice to Jacobinism":** 21 and 23 July 1800, *Connecticut Courant*, in Lerche, "Jefferson and the Election of 1800," 482.

127 **"Buonaparte, surrounded by his comrades in arms . . .":** Jefferson to Thomas Mann Randolph, 2 February 1800, in *Writings of Thomas Jefferson*, ed. Ford, 7:423.

127 **"as ambitious as Bonaparte":** Joseph J. Ellis, *Passionate Sage: The Character and Legacy of John Adams* (New York: W. W. Norton, 1993), 62.

127 **"reform the government à la Buonaparte":** Hamilton to James Bayard, 6 August 1800, in *Papers of Alexander Hamilton*, ed. Syrett, 25:58.

127 **"a revolution after the manner of Bonaparte"**: Hamilton to John Jay, 7 May 1800, in *Papers of Alexander Hamilton,* ed. Syrett, 24:465.

127 **"When Washington lived . . ."**: *Pennsylvania Gazette,* 8 January 1800, in Schwartz, *George Washington,* 81.

127 **"When shall we see a Washington?"**: Uriah Tracy to James McHenry, 19 October 1803, in Bernard C. Steiner, *The Life and Correspondence of James McHenry* (Cleveland: The Burrow Brothers Company, 1907), 522.

128 **"I am clear . . ."**: John Adams to Benjamin Rush, 9 June 1789, in Zoltan Haraszti, *John Adams and the Prophets of Progress* (Cambridge: Harvard University Press, 1952), 39.

128 **"ramparts"; "restraining and punishing . . ."**: Hamilton to Jonathan Dayton, October–November 1799, in *Papers of Alexander Hamilton,* ed. Syrett, 23:601, 604.

128 **"Friends of order and rational liberty"**: Elkins and McKitrick, *Age of Federalism,* 680.

128 **"common ideological ground"**: Ibid., 679.

128 **"resuscitation"**: Benjamin Rush to Jefferson, 12 March 1801, in Malone, *Jefferson and the Ordeal of Liberty,* 443.

128 **Cap of Liberty . . .**: Newman, *Parades and Politics,* 70.

128 **"A stronger one . . ."**: Madison to Jefferson, 14 February 1800, in *Republic of Letters,* ed. Smith, 2:1127.

128 **"bespeaks a luminous view . . ."**: Jefferson to Thomas Mann Randolph, 2 February 1800, in *Writings of Thomas Jefferson,* ed. Ford, 7:422.

129 **"character and situation . . . are materially different from the French"**: Jefferson to John Brekenridge, 29 January 1800, in *Writings of Thomas Jefferson,* ed. Ford, 7:418.

129 **"The jealousies, the hatred . . ."**: Jefferson to Martha Jefferson Randolph, 8 June 1797, in Jefferson, *Writings,* ed. Peterson, 1047.

129 **"Politics and party hatreds . . ."**: Jefferson to Martha Jefferson Randolph, 17 May 1798, in Ellis, *Founding Brothers,* 186.

129 **"political rancour & malevolence"**: Thomas Pinckney to John Rutledge, 23 September 1800, in Kerber, *Federalists in Dissent,* 194–95.

129 **"Opposition to the government"**: *Memorandum on Measures for Strengthening the Government,* 1799, in Hamilton, *Writings,* ed. Freeman, 916.

129 **"odious aspect"**: John Quincy Adams to Abigail Adams, 7 May 1799, in Sisson, *American Revolution of 1800,* 51.

129 **"prone to every Species"**: John Adams to Thomas Jefferson, 25 December 1813, in *Adams-Jefferson Letters,* ed. Cappon, 2:412.

129 **perverse pleasure of blocking:** Adams to Jefferson, 9 July 1813, in *Adams-Jefferson Letters,* ed. Cappon, 2:351.

130 **"political dissension"; "great evil"; "lethargy"**: Jefferson to Thomas Pinckney, 29 May 1797, in *Writings of Thomas Jefferson,* ed. Ford, 7:128.

130 **when tumult is absent:** Machiavelli, *Discourses,* Bk. 1, ch. 4, 5, 6, my translation.

130 **parties "will exist wherever . . ."**: Franklin, "The Internal State of America" [1785], in Koch, *American Enlightenment,* 141. See also Verner Crane, "Franklin's 'The Internal State of America 1786,'" *William and Mary Quarterly,* 3rd ser., 15 (April 1959):214–27.

130 **"so many blessings . . .":** Boston *American Herald,* 1 November 1790, in Stewart, "Jeffersonian Journalism," 775.

130 **"for when investigation ceases . . .":** *New York Argus,* 11 May 1795, in Stewart, "Jeffersonian Journalism," 776.

131 **"THE QUIET OF SUBMISSION":** Boston *Independent Chronicle,* 21, 25 January 1796, in Stewart, "Jeffersonian Journalism," 818.

131 **"Where there is no liberty . . . more desirable than slavery":** Eulogy on Washington, 8 February 1800, in *Works of Fisher Ames,* ed. Ames, 2:79.

131 **"middle course":** Washington to Hamilton, 26 August 1792, in Washington, *Writings,* ed. Rhodehamel, 819–20.

131 **"I hold it as honorable . . .":** Jefferson to William Branch Giles, 31 December 1795, in *Writings of Thomas Jefferson,* ed. Ford, 7:43, italics added.

132 **not open to women, blacks:** See Rosemarie Zagarri, "Gender and the First Party System," in Ben-Atar and Oberg, eds., *Federalists Reconsidered,* 119.

132 **galvanizing platform:** See Jefferson to Elbridge Gerry, 26 January 1799, in *Writings of Thomas Jefferson,* ed. Ford, 7:327–29.

132 **"bring our arguments home . . .":** Meriwether Jones to Creed Taylor, 9 April 1799, in Letters of Creed Taylor, Virginia State Archives, in Woodfin, "Contemporary Opinion," 59.

132 **Hamilton's suggested improvements to country's infrastructure:** Hamilton to Jonathan Dayton, October–November 1799, in *Papers of Alexander Hamilton,* ed. Syrett, 23:601–4.

133 **"If principles instead of men . . .":** Washington to Governor Jonathan Trumbull, 30 August 1799, in *Writings of George Washington,* ed. Ford, 14:200.

133 **"generous and emancipating":** Joyce Appleby, "Republicanism in Old and New Contexts," *William and Mary Quarterly,* 3rd ser., 43, no. 1 (1986):33.

133 **"ignorance of the value of public discussion":** Wood, "Democratization of Mind," 80.

133 **"A free government . . .":** Baltimore *Daily Intelligencer,* 24 May 1794, in Stewart, "Jeffersonian Journalism," 774.

133 **"real sovereign":** "Public Opinion," *National Gazette,* 19 December 1791, in Madison, *Writings,* ed. Rakove, 500.

134 **"America's 19th-century popular substitute":** Wood, "Democratization of Mind," 83.

134 **"pious and . . . philosophical resignation":** John Adams to Abigail Adams, 20 January 1796, in *Letters of John Adams, Addressed to His Wife,* ed. Adams.

134 **"misled and corrupted . . .":** William Smith Shaw to Arthur Maynard Walter, January 1801, in Kerber, *Federalists in Dissent,* 206.

134 **"is not true in fact":** Hamilton, 18 June 1787, Federal Convention Debates, in S. E. Morison, ed., *Sources and Documents Illustrating the American Revolution* (Oxford: Clarendon Press, 1923), 259.

135 **"mawkish":** Theron Metcalf, *An Address to the Phi Beta Kappa Society of Brown University, Delivered 5th September, 1832,* in Wood, "Democratization of Mind," 84.

135 **"instability and fluctuation . . .":** Daniel Dewey to Theodore Sedgwick, 8 December 1800, Massachusetts Historical Society.

135 **"Popular gales . . .":** George Cabot to Wolcott, 7 April 1797, in Fischer, *Revolution of American Conservatism,* 6.

135 **"public opinion should be enlightened":** Farewell Address, in Washington, *Writings*, ed. Rhodehamel, 972.

135 **"real voice" of the people:** Washington to Edward Carrington, 1 May 1796, in *Writings of George Washington*, ed. Fitzpatrick, 35:31–32.

135 **"nothing to give a proper direction . . .":** James McHenry to Oliver Wolcott, 22 July 1800, in Steiner, *Life and Correspondence of James McHenry*, 462.

136 **"more open and more enterprising":** Hamilton to Jonathan Dayton, October–November 1799, in *Papers of Alexander Hamilton*, ed. Syrett, 23:600.

136 **"neglected the cultivation":** Kenyon, "Alexander Hamilton, Rousseau of the Right," 171.

136 **Federalists had fought for too long:** Tocqueville, *De la Démocratie en Amérique*, ed. Mayer, Bk. 1. Pt. 2, ch. 2, 181.

7. The War of Words

137 **"pure unadulterated logocracy . . . immemorial custom":** Washington Irving, *Salmagundi*, 4 April and 19 September 1807, in Irving, *Letters of Jonathan Oldstyle, Gent.*, and *Salmagundi*, ed. Bruce I. Granger and Martha Hartzog (Boston: Twayne Publishers, 1977), 142–43, 234–36.

137 **"Words are things . . .":** Fischer, *Revolution of American Conservatism*, 238.

137 **"eloquence is power":** Ibid., 347.

138 **violence of opinion . . . :** François de La Rochefoucauld-Liancourt, *Travels Through the United States of North America* (London, 1799), in John R. Howe, "Republican Thought and the Political Violence of the 1790s," *American Quarterly* 19, no. 2 (1967):148.

138 **"names & appearances . . .":** Ames to Rutledge, 27 January 1801, in Kerber, *Federalists in Dissent*, 197.

138 **code words:** "Words," in *Life and Correspondence of Rufus King*, ed. King, 5:96.

138 **all-purpose "sounds":** Cunningham, "Election of 1800," 122.

138 **"signify any thing, every thing . . .":** Thompson, *John Adams and the Spirit of Liberty*, 186–87.

138 **gentlemen-politicians cling to educated style:** Wood, *Radicalism of the American Revolution*, 91. See also Wood, "Democratization of Mind."

139 **working-class pamphlet and debate culture:** See Cornell, *Other Founders*.

139 **impossible for a dozen Americans . . . :** Isaac Weld, Jr., *Travels Through the States of North America*, in Noble E. Cunningham, Jr., *The United States in 1800: Henry Adams Revisited* (Charlottesville: University Press of Virginia, 1988), 55.

139 **newspaper strategies:** See Fischer, *Revolution of American Conservatism*, ch. 7, "Federalists and the Press," 129–49. See also Donald H. Stewart, *The Opposition Press of the Federalist Period* (Albany: State University of New York Press, 1969), 19.

139 **"all the people read a newspaper":** Pierre Samuel Dupont de Nemours, *National Education in the United States of America*, in Cunningham, *The United States in 1800*, 20.

139 **newspapers in all parts of the country:** Main, *Social Structure of Revolutionary America*, 263.

139 **two hundred newspapers:** Stewart, *Opposition Press*, 16, 651–52; Pasley, "*Tyranny of Printers*," 201.

139 **"no party disputes to raise . . .":** Margaret Woodbury, *Public Opinion in Philadelphia, 1789–1801* (Durham, N.C.: Seaman Printery, 1919), 7–8.

140 **editors as "principal spokesman":** Pasley, "1800 as a Revolution," 135.

140 **"bring our arguments home":** Pasley, *"Tyranny of Printers,"* 160.

140 **"Christianity in the morning . . .":** *Baltimore American and Daily Advertiser,* 16 May 1799, in Cunningham, *Jeffersonian Republicans: Formation of Party Organization,* 168. See also Pasley, *"Tyranny of Printers,"* 162.

140 **too much at stake; "despicable impartiality"; "reservoir":** Pasley, *"Tyranny of Printers,"* 160–63.

140 **sale of printed matter:** Wood, "Democratization of Mind," 78–79.

140 **visitor from France, . . . :** La Rochefoucauld-Liancourt, *Travels Through the United States,* 2:215.

140 **English visitor:** Pasley, *"Tyranny of Printers,"* 202.

141 **friend who would work alongside others:** See Taylor, "From Fathers to Friends," 226–27.

141 **Philadelphia artillery company:** Newman, *Parades and Politics,* 80.

141 **True Republican Society of Philadelphia:** Toasts Drunk at the Anniversary Meeting, 7 May 1800, in Foner, *Democratic-Republican Societies,* 110.

141 **"embraced the rights . . .":** *Richmond* (Va.) *Argus,* 11 July 1800, in Cunningham, "Election of 1800," 145.

141 **"field of enjoyment . . .":** Newark (N.J.) *Centinel of Freedom,* 6 May 1800, in Stewart, *Opposition Press,* 584, italics added.

141 **"Under the administration of so good . . .":** *Aurora,* 31 July 1800, italics added.

141 **toasts are informal party platforms:** Pasley, "1800 as a Revolution," 133–34.

141 **"slaves of monarchy . . .":** Toasts Drunk on Fourth of July, 1799, in Foner, *Democratic-Republican Societies,* 219, italics added.

142 **"perceives no grade . . .":** *Vermont Gazette,* 4 August 1800.

142 **"friend and patron of agriculture":** *Albany Register,* 8 April 1800, in Charles Beard, *Economic Origins of Jeffersonian Democracy* (New York: Macmillan, 1915), 367–68.

142 **"most of them are farmers . . .":** *Aurora,* 1 and 2 August 1800, in Stewart, "Jeffersonian Journalism," 685.

142 **Federalists oppressing farmers:** "A Republican," Charleston (S.C.) *City Gazette,* 3 October 1800, in Beard, *Economic Origins,* 215, 373–74.

142 **"money from the pocket . . .":** A "Scots Correspondent," Richmond (Va.) *Examiner,* 10 January 1800, in Stewart, "Jeffersonian Journalism," 684.

142 **"bask in the sunshine of monarchy . . .":** Boston *Independent Chronicle,* 13 March 1800, in Stewart, "Jeffersonian Journalism," 828.

142 **Manning sought to awaken the "Many" . . . :** Manning, *Key of Liberty,* ed. Merrill and Wilentz, 155–57.

143 **"Dutch inhabitants":** Newark (N.J.) *Centinel of Freedom,* 7 October 1800, in Stewart, "Jeffersonian Journalism," 695.

143 **Federalists anti-Irish:** *Aurora,* 27 September 1800, in Stewart, "Jeffersonian Journalism," 696.

143 **anti-Semitic:** *Aurora,* 13 August 1800; Charleston (S.C.) *City Gazette,* 3 September 1800, in Stewart, "Jeffersonian Journalism," 696.

143 **"If we want to return . . .":** Cunningham, "Election of 1800," 121.

143 **"My theory has always been . . .":** Jefferson to Marbois, 14 May 1817, in Jefferson, *Writings*, ed. Peterson, 1411.

143 **"to risque a change":** An Address to the Citizens of North Carolina, July 1800, in Cunningham, *The United States in 1800,* 50.

143 **"stamped with all the babyhood imbecility . . . dying faction":** *Vermont Gazette,* 25 August 1800.

143 **"high time for a CHANGE?":** Cunningham, "Election of 1800," 121.

143 **"Take Your Choice!":** *Aurora,* 4 October 1800, in Noble E. Cunningham, Jr., ed., *The Making of the American Party System, 1789–1809* (Englewood Cliffs, N.J.: Prentice-Hall, 1965), 79.

144 **"The Republican LITANY":** *Vermont Gazette,* 31 March 1800.

144 **"sacrificed to serve . . . diffuse knowledge of all kinds":** Thomas Cooper, *Political Arithmetic* (Philadelphia, 1798), 4, 14–15, 20.

144 **Jefferson's *Notes on the State of Virginia*:** See Cunningham, *The United States in 1800,* 22.

144 **"for while I would be engaged . . .":** Burns, *Deadlock of Democracy,* 33.

145 **"The engine is the press . . .":** Jefferson to Madison, 5 February 1799, in *Republic of Letters,* ed. Smith, 2:1093.

145 **"either destroy our free system . . .":** Madison, *The Virginia Report,* in Meyers, ed., *Mind of the Founder,* 264.

145 **"It would be useless . . .":** Jefferson to Monroe, 11 February 1799, in *Writings of Thomas Jefferson,* ed. Ford, 7:346.

145 **"seldom republish . . .":** Nicholas to Hamilton, 4 August 1803, in Andrew W. Robertson, *The Language of Democracy: Political Rhetoric in the United States and Britain, 1790–1900* (Ithaca, N.Y.: Cornell University Press, 1995), 38–39 n.

145 **"the papers on our side . . .":** Oliver Wolcott to George Cabot, 16 June 1800, in Wolcott, *Memoirs,* ed. Gibbs, 2:371.

145 **"improper":** Oliver Wolcott to Fisher Ames, 1800, in Fischer, *Revolution of American Conservatism,* 134.

145 **"shaken by every prospect . . .":** Fisher Ames to Oliver Wolcott, 3 August 1800, in Wolcott, *Memoirs,* ed. Gibbs, 2:396.

146 **"zeal and ardor . . . whirlwind":** Fisher Ames, "Laocoon," No. 1, *Boston Gazette,* April 1799, in *Works of Fisher Ames,* ed. Ames, 2:112–13.

146 **"did not mingle . . .":** Samuel Goodrich, *Recollections,* 1:237, in Fischer, *Revolution of American Conservatism,* 95.

146 **"formidable in lies and cunning . . .":** Fisher Ames, "Laocoon," No. 1, *Boston Gazette,* April 1799, in *Works of Fisher Ames,* ed. Ames, 2:117.

146 **"sound the tocsin":** Cunningham, "Election of 1800," 121.

146 **"weakness of nerves . . .":** "A Short Address to the Voters of Delaware," 21 September 1800, in Cunningham, *Jeffersonian Republicans: Formation of Party Organization* , 223.

146 **"Born with a restless . . .":** *Gazette of the United States,* Letter III to Thomas Jefferson, 23 August 1800.

146 **"one day the parlour is in front . . .":** *Gazette of the United States,* 23 August 1800.

146 **"theorize about government":** "Burleigh," in *Connecticut Courant,* 12 July 1800.

147 **"*a philosophe* in the modern French sense":** *Address to the Citizens of South Carolina,* in Lerche, "Jefferson and the Election of 1800," 476.

147 **"man of the choice of France":** Ibid., 485.

147 **"Let these men get into power . . .":** "A Short Address to the Voters of Delaware," 21 September 1800, in Cunningham, "Election of 1800," 151.

147 **"timid men . . .":** Jefferson to Philip Mazzei, 24 April 1796, in Jefferson, *Writings*, ed. Peterson, 1037.

147 **"free, peaceful, and flourishing . . .":** "An Address to the Voters for Electors of President and Vice-president of the United States in the State of Virginia," 26 May 1800, in Cunningham, "Election of 1800," 149.

147 **"learn the principles of liberty . . .":** *Connecticut Courant*, in Cunningham, "Election of 1800," 122.

147 **When the state of Virginia "appears . . .":** "A Candid Address to the Freemen of the State of Rhode-Island," in Cunningham, "Election of 1800," 142.

148 **"Now as the only labourers . . .":** *Newark Gazette*, 1 July 1800, in Fischer, *Revolution of American Conservatism*, 165.

148 **"opinions unfriendly . . .":** "Address to the Citizens of South Carolina," in Lerche, "Jefferson and the Election of 1800," 486.

148 **"THE GRAND QUESTION STATED . . .":** *Gazette of the United States*, 11 and 27 September, 9 October 1800.

148 **"never to have known the meaning . . . none at all":** *Connecticut Courant*, 18 August 1800.

148 **"My eyes have been opened . . .":** "The Political Conversion, Number 1," *Gazette of the United States*, 11 September 1800.

148 **"it does me no injury . . .":** *Notes on the State of Virginia*, in Jefferson, *Writings*, ed. Peterson, 285.

148 **Linn and Mason:** William Linn, *Serious Considerations on the Election of a President*; John Mitchell Mason, *The Voice of Warning to Christians, on the Ensuing Election of a President*, in Buel, *Securing the Revolution*, 232–33. See also Cunningham, *Jeffersonian Republicans: Formation of Party Organization*, 224.

149 **timeline and history of Greece:** McDonald, "Was There a Religious Revolution of 1800?" 182–83.

149 **"What is a man who . . .":** *The Voice of Warning, to Christians, on the Ensuing Election of a President of the United States* (New York, 1800), 8, in Lerche, "Jefferson and the Election of 1800," 473.

149 **"theological inquisition . . . good citizen":** *Aurora*, 1 October 1800.

149 **"fanatics . . .":** John James Beckley, "Address to the People of the United States," 4 July 1800, in Beckley, *Justifying Jefferson*, 168.

149 **"the equal Brotherhood"; "does not think that a catholic . . .":** Cunningham, *Jeffersonian Republicans: Formation of Party Organization*, 219.

149 **"religion ought to be kept . . .":** McDonald, "Was There a Religious Revolution of 1800?" 186.

149 **only Republicans were true Christians . . . :** Newburgh (N.Y.) *Rights of Man*, 28 April 1800, in Stewart, "Jeffersonian Journalism," 765.

149 **"Jeff is pretty fiercely attacked . . .":** Robert Troup, September 1800, in Cunningham, "Election of 1800," 125.

149 **"indignation":** Fisher Ames to Rufus King, 24 September 1800, in *Life and Correspondence of Rufus King*, ed. King, 3:304.

149 **"shuffle the cards . . .":** Adams to John Trumbull, 10 September 1800, in *Works of John Adams*, ed. Adams, 9:83.

150 **"The democrats court the passions . . ."; "devoted to higher and more salutary . . .":** *Gazette of United States,* 26 January 1801, 21 August 1800.

150 **"infidels . . .":** *Gazette of the United States,* 4 October 1800.

150 **malapropisms, colloquialisms:** *Gazette of the United States,* 5 August 1800, in Murrin, "Escaping Perfidious Albion," 119. See also Schappes, "Anti-Semitism and Reaction," Part 2, 132ff.

150 **"fools" and "drunkards":** Richard Rosenfeld, *American Aurora* (New York: St. Martin's Press, 1997), 829–30.

151 **"Ode to Popularity":** "Ode to Popularity," *Gazette of the United States,* 28 October 1800.

151 **"There is nothing said . . .":** Oliver Wolcott to George Cabot, 18 June 1800, in *The Life and Letters of George Cabot,* ed. Henry Cabot Lodge (Boston: Little, Brown, 1878), 279.

151 **"If time ever permitted . . . stand or fall with their country":** "Candid Address to the Freemen of the State of Rhode-Island on the Subject of the Approaching Election," in Cunningham, "Election of 1800," 140–41.

151 **"men who are firm . . .":** *Connecticut Courant,* 21 March 1800.

152 **"bred in the old school . . .":** *Washington Federalist,* 7 October 1800, in McCullough, *John Adams,* 546.

152 **"12th year . . .":** Cunningham, "Election of 1800," 152, italics added.

152 **"In times less critical . . .":** Ibid., 140.

152 **What was their grievance . . . Republican hands?:** *Connecticut Courant,* 24 November 1800.

8. Storms in the Atmosphere

153 **"I like a little rebellion . . . Atmosphere":** Jefferson to Abigail Adams, 22 February 1787, in *Adams-Jefferson Letters,* ed. Cappon, 1:173.

153 **"ultimate appeal to arms . . .":** *Fredericksburg* (Va.) *Herald,* 9 May 1800, in Douglas R. Egerton, *Gabriel's Rebellion: The Virginia Slave Conspiracies of 1800 and 1802* (Chapel Hill: University of North Carolina Press, 1993), 37.

154 **skilled artisans in short supply:** Egerton, *Gabriel's Rebellion,* 26.

154 **whites and blacks working side by side:** Ibid., 27.

154 **"publick danger . . .":** Ibid., 15.

154 **"Sans-culotte *Richmond* . . .":** *Porcupine's Gazette,* 3 April 1798, in ibid., 39.

154 **"twilight . . .":** Egerton, *Gabriel's Rebellion,* 25.

154 **Gabriel in trouble with the law:** Ibid., 32.

155 **class lines:** Ibid., 49.

155 **"negro insurrection":** Monroe to Jefferson, 22 April 1800, in ibid., 49.

155 **Quersey, Beddenhurst, rumors reach Governor Monroe:** Egerton, *Gabriel's Rebellion,* 67.

155 **revolt in Saint Domingue:** Ibid., 46ff.

155 **"it is our duty . . .":** Ibid., 47.

155 **"leven":** Jefferson to Madison, 12 February 1799, in *Writings of Thomas Jefferson,* ed. Ford, 7:349.

155 **Robert Goodloe Harper:** 20 March 1799, in Egerton, *Gabriel's Rebellion,* 46.

155 **"Jefferson would call upon France . . .":** Egerton, *Gabriel's Rebellion,* 42.

155 **Wythe argues against slavery:** Ibid., 13.

156 **"outrageous violation . . .":** Ibid., 113.

156 **"the insurrection had blown":** Ibid., 73.

156 **"This alarm has kept me . . .":** Monroe to Madison, 9 September 1800, in *Papers of James Madison,* ed. Mattern et al., 17:408.

156 **"I beg, as a favour . . .":** Egerton, *Gabriel's Rebellion,* 81–82.

156 **"The plot has been . . .":** Ibid., 76.

157 **"Thirty or forty of the party . . .":** *Fredericksburg Herald,* 16 September 1800, in ibid., 80.

157 **"It is unquestionably . . .":** 15 September 1800, in Ammon, *James Monroe,* 187.

157 **"whether mercy or severity . . .":** Monroe to Jefferson, 15 September 1800, in Egerton, *Gabriel's Rebellion,* 89.

157 **"Where to stay the hand . . .":** Jefferson to Monroe, 20 September 1800, in *Writings of Thomas Jefferson,* ed. Ford, 7:457.

157 **"If white men were engaged . . .":** John Drayton, in Egerton, *Gabriel's Rebellion,* 114.

158 **"good joke":** Egerton, *Gabriel's Rebellion,* 115.

158 **"their eagerness and anxiety . . .":** *Gazette of the United States,* 1 October 1800.

158 **"we are truly to be pitied . . . over the mind of man":** Jefferson to Dr. Benjamin Rush, 23 September 1800, in *Writings of Thomas Jefferson,* ed. Ford, 7:460–61.

158 **"The gallows are in full operation . . . collect our strength!":** Troup to King, 1 October 1800, in *Life and Correspondence of Rufus King,* ed. King, 3:315. See King Papers for full text.

158 **"Unfortunately, there is too little . . .":** John Jay to Theophilus Parsons, 1 July 1800, in *Correspondence and Public Papers of John Jay,* ed. Johnston, 274.

159 **"pure Monocrats . . . hoop them together":** Jefferson to Madison, 26 November 1799, in *Republic of Letters,* ed. Smith, 2:1122.

159 **secret deal:** Cabot to Rufus King, 29 May 1800, in *Life and Correspondence of Rufus King,* ed. King, 3:249.

159 **"a more singular and mysterious state . . .":** Ames to King, 15 July 1800, in *Life and Correspondence of Rufus King,* ed. King, 3:275.

159 **"the very affectionate reception . . .":** Kurtz, *Presidency of John Adams,* 399.

159 **Adams in Newark:** Ibid., 399.

159 **Boston leaders don't call on Adams:** Cunningham, "Election of 1800," 116.

159 **"His language is bitter . . .":** Fisher Ames to Rufus King, 15 July 1800, in *Life and Correspondence of Rufus King,* ed King, 3:276.

159 **"did not hate nor dread . . .":** Ames to King, 26 August 1800, in *Life and Correspondence of Rufus King,* ed. King, 3:296.

160 **"no affair can be more involved . . .":** Fisher Ames to Rufus King, 15 July 1800, in *Life and Correspondence of Rufus King,* ed. King, 3:275–77; see also Ames to King, 24 September 1800, 3:303–6.

160 **"disgusting":** Wolcott to Hamilton, 7 July 1800, in *Papers of Alexander Hamilton,* ed. Syrett, 25:16.

160 **"actually insane":** McCullough, *John Adams,* 538.

160 **"creature of impulse . . .":** Ames to King, 24 September 1800, in *Life and Correspondence of Rufus King,* ed. King, 3:305.

160 **"liable to gusts of passion . . .":** Bayard to Hamilton, 18 August 1800, in *Papers of Alexander Hamilton,* ed. Syrett, 25:71.

160 "fits and starts": Troup to King, 5 June 1799, in *Life and Correspondence of Rufus King*, ed. King, 3:33.

160 "strong revolutionary taint . . .": Ames to King, 24 September 1800, in *Life and Correspondence of Rufus King*, ed. King, 3:304–5.

160 "in concert": Timothy Pickering to John Pickering, 17 May 1800, in *Papers of Alexander Hamilton*, ed. Syrett, 24:848, editorial note.

160 "attachment to the dictates of honour . . .": John Jay to Theophilus Parsons, 1 July 1800, in *Correspondence and Public Papers of John Jay*, ed. Johnston, 4:275.

161 "a bastard": Miller, *Federalist Era*, 262.

161 brusque letter to Adams: Hamilton to Adams, 1 August 1800, in *Papers of Alexander Hamilton*, ed. Syrett, 25:51; see also Hamilton to Wolcott, 1 July 1800, 25:5.

161 "opium": Adams to Benjamin Waterhouse, 21 May 1821, in Koch, *American Enlightenment*, 233.

161 "unreasonable conduct of the jacobins . . .": Adams to John Trumbull, 10 September 1800, in *Works of John Adams*, ed. Adams, 9:83–84.

161 "Aegis": Hamilton to Lear, 2 January 1800, in *Papers of Alexander Hamilton*, ed. Syrett, 24:155.

161 "perverseness and capriciousness . . . irreparable loss": Hamilton to King, 5 January 1800, in *Papers of Alexander Hamilton*, ed. Syrett, 24:168.

162 "My mind is made up . . . withdraw from the party": Hamilton to Sedgwick, 10 May 1800, in *Papers of Alexander Hamilton*, ed. Syrett, 24:475.

162 "very belligerent humour"; "I have serious thoughts"; "most authentic way": Hamilton to Wolcott, 3 August 1800, in *Papers of Alexander Hamilton*, ed. Syrett, 25:54, italics added.

162 "We must vote for . . .": Bayard to Hamilton, 18 August 1800, in *Papers of Alexander Hamilton*, ed. Syrett, 25: 71.

162 increase divisions among Federalists: Wolcott to Hamilton, 2 October 1800, in *Papers of Alexander Hamilton*, ed. Syrett, 25:145.

162 "It will be converted to a new proof . . .": Cabot to Hamilton, 21 August 1800, in *Papers of Alexander Hamilton*, ed. Syrett, 25:75.

163 "Where is the inconsistency . . .": Ames to Hamilton, 26 August 1800, in *Papers of Alexander Hamilton*, ed. Syrett, 25:87.

164 Burr discovers copy of Hamilton's pamphlet: Lomask, *Aaron Burr*, 257.

164 Hamilton's pamphlet: *Letter from Alexander Hamilton, Concerning the Public Conduct and Character of John Adams, Esq. President of the United States*, 24 October 1800, in *Papers of Alexander Hamilton*, ed. Syrett, 25:169–234. See also Miller, *Federalist Era*, 262.

164 Cooper wants Hamilton to be prosecuted: Miller, *Federalist Era*, 263.

164 "whether Republicanism is to be the victim . . .": Cooper, in Malone, *Jefferson and the Ordeal of Liberty*, 488.

164 Cooper's attempt to prosecute Hamilton: See Dumas Malone, "The Threatened Prosecution of Alexander Hamilton Under the Sedition Act by Thomas Cooper," *American Historical Review* 29 (1924): 76–81.

165 "with a union to be expected . . .": Theophilus Parsons to John Jay, 5 May 1800, in *Correspondence and Public Papers of John Jay*, ed. Johnston, 4:267ff.

165 "I am bound to tell you . . .": George Cabot to Alexander Hamilton, 29 November 1800, in *Life and Letters of George Cabot*, ed. Lodge, 300.

165 Webster's **"Letter to General Hamilton"**: Webster, "Letter to General Hamilton Occasioned by his letter to President Adams," in Cunningham, *Jeffersonian Republicans: Formation of Party Organization*, 230.

165 **every member of their circle of friends**: Troup to King, 9 November 1800, in *Life and Correspondence of Rufus King*, ed. King, 3:331.

165 **"staggering"**: Madison to Jefferson, 10 January 1801, in *Papers of James Madison*, ed. Mattern et al., 17:454.

166 **"fetters imposed on liberty at home"**: "Political Reflections," 23 February 1799, in Madison, *Writings*, ed. Rakove, 606.

166 **"Our opponents perceive . . ."**: Jefferson to Martha Jefferson Randolph, 22 April 1800, in *Family Letters of Thomas Jefferson*, ed. Betts and Bear, 187.

167 **"capable of base, dishonorable . . ."**: Pickering to George Cabot, 16 June 1800, in *Life and Letters of George Cabot*, ed. Lodge, 277.

167 **"A meaner, a more artful . . ."**: Adams to Pickering, 13 August 1799, in *Works of John Adams*, ed. Adams, 9:13–14.

167 **description of Cooper's trial**: Smith, *Freedom's Fetters*, 320–28.

168 **description of Madison**: George Tucker, Memoir, in Brant, *James Madison*, 4:13.

168 **"leveled against that right of freely examining . . . independent nation"**: "Report on the Alien and Sedition Acts," 7 January 1800, in Madison, *Writings*, ed. Rakove, 647ff.

168 **Adams intends to wed his daughter to son of George III**: Callender, *The Prospect Before Us* (1800).

168 **"between Adams, war and beggary . . ."**: Smith, *Freedom's Fetters*, 340.

168 **"abuse and scandel"**: Ibid., 341.

168 **"the sacrifice of all that Good men . . ."**: Abigail Adams to Marcy Cranch, 5 May 1800, in *New Letters of Abigail Adams*, ed. Mitchell, 251.

169 **"repulsive pedant . . ."**: McCullough, *John Adams*, 524.

169 **"oppose and vilify"**: Pickering to William Bingham, 22 September 1799, in Smith, *Freedom's Fetters*, 338–39.

169 **"I think it essentially just . . ."**: Jefferson to Monroe, 26 May 1800, in *Writings of Thomas Jefferson*, ed. Ford, 7:448.

169 **"thronged with spectators . . ."**: *Virginia Gazette*, June 1800, in Smith, *Freedom's Fetters*, 347.

169 **"It would deceive . . ."; prosecutor would not budge**: Smith, *Freedom's Fetters*, 353.

170 **pamphlet containing proceedings of trial**: Ibid., 358.

170 **"insolence and abuse of liberty . . ."**: Ibid., 357.

170 **Adams "super-eminently entitled . . ."**: Ibid., 358.

170 **government accusations against Holt**: Ibid., 380.

170 **"why the word standing is more seditious . . ."**: Ibid., 382.

170 **"only SLUMBER"**: *New London Bee*, 8 January 1800, in Stewart, "Jeffersonian Journalism," 896.

171 **"If the *Aurora* is not blown up . . ."**: *Palladium*, 10 April 1800, in Smith, *Freedom's Fetters*, 288.

171 **stalemates and disputes in several states about electors**: See Malone, *Jefferson and the Ordeal of Liberty*, 463.

171 **Ross bill and Grand Committee of Thirteen**: Smith, *Freedom's Fetters*, 289.

171   **"licentiousness in constructive perversions":** Madison to Jefferson, 15 March 1800, in *Republic of Letters*, ed. Smith, 2:1130.

171   **committee on Senate privileges; Tracy's move for Senate punishment of Duane:** Malone, *Jefferson and the Ordeal of Liberty*, 464. See also Smith, *Freedom's Fetters*, 291.

172   **Jefferson supposed to ask him . . . :** Malone, *Jefferson and the Ordeal of Liberty*, 464.

172   **Duane informed Jefferson of plan:** Cooper to Jefferson, 23 March 1800, Library of Congress, 20951. See Malone, *Jefferson and the Ordeal of Liberty*, 465.

172   **"I will not degrade myself . . .":** Smith, *Freedom's Fetters*, 297.

172   **Duane sends Jefferson correspondence:** *Aurora*, 27 March 1800. See Malone, *Jefferson and the Ordeal of Liberty*, 465.

173   **"The three most active and most notorious foreign emissaries . . .":** *Gazette of the United States*, 13 June 1800, in Rosenfeld, *American Aurora*, 810.

173   **"Firm to their purposes . . .":** Jefferson to Madison, 12 May 1800, in *Writings of Thomas Jefferson*, ed. Ford, 7:446–47.

173   **"cannot fail I think to aid . . .":** Madison to Jefferson, 4 April 1800, in *Papers of James Madison*, ed. Mattern et al., 17:377.

173   **"BE NOT INTIMIDATED . . .":** Frankfort (Ky.) *Palladium*, 15 May 1800, in Stewart, "Jeffersonian Journalism," 819.

174   **Adams guilty:** *Augusta* (Ga.) *Herald*, 8 October 1800, in Stewart, "Jeffersonian Journalism," 905.

174   **Why was Adams's conduct shielded . . . :** *Annapolis* (Md.) *Gazette*, 23 June 1800, in Stewart, "Jeffersonian Journalism," 905.

174   **"virtue to the level of vice"; "bane of freedom . . .":** Smith, *Freedom's Fetters*, 342, 355. On hollow Jacobin maxims, see Dunn, *Sister Revolutions*, ch. 4.

9. On the Campaign Trail

175   **"Politics are such a torment"; "daily wearing off":** Jefferson to Martha Jefferson Randolph, 11 February 1800, and Jefferson to Mary Jefferson Eppes, 12 February 1800, in *Family Letters of Thomas Jefferson*, ed. Betts and Bear, 184–85.

175   **Again and again; "indelicate":** Jefferson to Madison, 4 and 8 March 1800, 25 March 1800, in *Republic of Letters*, ed. Smith, 2:1129, 1131.

175   **"So much depends":** Madison to Jefferson, 4 April 1800, in *Republic of Letters*, ed. Smith, 2:1132.

176   **election hinged on New York City; "no doubt of the event of that election . . .":** Jefferson to Madison, 4 March 1800, in *Writings of Thomas Jefferson*, ed. Ford, 7:432–34.

176   **"unquestionably republicans . . . painful & doubtful questions":** Jefferson to Burr, 17 June 1797, in *Writings of Thomas Jefferson*, ed. Ford, 7:146–48.

176   **"At present there would be no doubt . . .":** Jefferson to Monroe, 12 January 1800, in *Writings of Thomas Jefferson*, ed. Ford, 7:401–2.

176   **Republicans might do worse than in 1796:** Jefferson to Madison, 4 March 1800, in *Writings of Thomas Jefferson*, ed. Ford, 7:433–34.

177   **"By his arts & intrigues . . .":** Robert Troup to Rufus King, 6 May 1799, in *Politi-*

cal Correspondence and Public Papers of Aaron Burr, ed. Mary-Jo Kline, 2 vols. (Princeton: Princeton University Press, 1983), 1:420, editorial note.

177 "**trimmer . . .**": pamphlet published in 1802 signed Aristides, in *Memoirs of Aaron Burr*, ed. Matthew Davis (New York: Harper Brothers, 1858), 2:59.

177 "**Amusement from Albany!**": Burr to Natalie Delage, 2 February 1800, in Bernard A. Weisberger, *America Afire: Jefferson, Adams, and the Revolutionary Election of 1800* (New York: William Morrow, 2000), 99.

178 "**as usual supine . . .**": Peter August Jay to John Jay, 7 April 1800, in Fischer, *Revolution of American Conservatism*, 96.

178 **two grocers . . .**: Matthew Davis to Gallatin, 15 April 1800, in Adams, *Life of Albert Gallatin*, 236.

178 "**read it over with great gravity . . .**": John Adams to James Lloyd, 17 February 1815, in *Works of John Adams*, ed. Adams, 10:125.

178 "**Never have I observed . . .**": Cunningham, "Election of 1800," 109.

178 "**We have labored hard**"; "**there is a most auspicious gloom . . .**": Livingston to Jefferson, 2 May 1800, in Cunningham, *Jeffersonian Republicans: Formation of Party Organization*, 184.

178 "**intrigue and management**": Matthew Davis to Albert Gallatin, 29 March 1800, in Cunningham, *Jeffersonian Republicans: Formation of Party Organization*, 177.

178 **very able lawyer**: Gouverneur Morris, in Lomask, *Aaron Burr*, 85.

178 **Burr and Hamilton in court**: General Erastus Root, in Lomask, *Aaron Burr*, 94.

179 "**fun and honor & profit**": Burr to Aaron Ward, 14 January 1832, in *Political Correspondence and Public Papers of Aaron Burr*, ed. Kline, 2:1211.

179 **voting lists in New York**: Arnold A. Rogow, *A Fatal Friendship: Alexander Hamilton and Aaron Burr* (New York: Hill and Wang, 1998), 240. See also John James Turner, "New-York in Presidential Politics" (Ph.D. diss., Columbia University, New York, 11968.171). See also Samuel P. Orth, *Five American Politicians: A Study in the Evolution of American Politics* (Cleveland: The Burrows Brothers Company, 1906), ch. 1, "Aaron Burr, Father of the Political Machine," 42.

179 "**kept open house . . .**": Journal of Benjamin Betterton Howell, in Lomask, *Aaron Burr*, 244.

179 "**If we carry this election . . .**": Matthew Davis to Albert Gallatin, 24 March 1800, in Lomask, *Aaron Burr*, 248.

179 "**extreme distaste**": Madison to Washington, 2 December 1788, in *Papers of James Madison*, ed. Rutland et al., 11:377.

179 **ban on solicitation of votes**: Jonathan Jackson, *Thoughts upon the Political Situation of the United States* [1788], in Fischer, "Myth of the Essex Junto," 209.

179 "**Every threshing floor . . .**"; "**never despairing . . .**": "Laocoon," No. 1, *Boston Gazette*, April 1799, in *Works of Fisher Ames*, ed. Ames, 2:115–16.

180 "**hurrying this way . . .**": *General Advertiser*, 3 April 1800, in Lomask, *Aaron Burr*, 244.

180 **whole financial system of the nation would tumble . . .**: *New York Spectator*, 26 April 1800, in Beard, *Economic Origins*, 368.

180 "**stoop so low . . .**": *Daily Advertiser*, 28 April 1800, in Lomask, *Aaron Burr*, 244.

180 **British cruiser arrives in New York:** See Miller, *Federalist Era*, 258.

180 **voters urged to cast ballots for party ticket:** Cunningham, *Jeffersonian Republicans: Formation of Party Organization*, 253–54.

180 **carriages; German-speaking operatives:** Lomask, *Aaron Burr*, 245.

180 **white horse:** Margaret C. S. Christman, *"The Spirit of Party": Hamilton and Jefferson at Odds* (Washington, D.C.: National Portrait Gallery, 1992), 47.

180 **"accomplished and courtly . . .":** *Memoirs of Aaron Burr*, ed. Davis, 60.

180 **"I have not eaten dinner . . .":** Troup to Peter Van Schaack, 2 May 1800, in Lomask, *Aaron Burr*, 244.

180 **posted guards:** Lomask, *Aaron Burr*, 245.

180 **houses were large and addresses fashionable:** Harp, "Patrician Partisans," 479–501.

181 **"We have beat you . . .":** Lomask, *Aaron Burr*, 246.

181 **"so miraculous a manner":** Nicholson to Gallatin, 6 and 7 May 1800, in Lomask, *Aaron Burr*, 250.

181 **Republicans caucus:** Lomask, *Aaron Burr*, 254.

181 **"The Goddess of Liberty . . .":** Goshen (N.Y.) *Orange Patrol*, 13 May 1800, in Stewart, *Opposition Press*, 583.

181 **"In a free country let no man . . .":** *Albany Register*, 30 May 1800, in Smith, *Freedom's Fetters*, 397–98.

181 **Senate adjourns:** Burns, *Deadlock of Democracy*, 34.

181 **Vice President Jefferson paid a call:** Jefferson to Benjamin Rush, 16 January 1811, in *Writings of Thomas Jefferson*, ed. Ford, 9:296–97.

181 **"Hamilton exhibits a figure of rage . . .":** Brant, *James Madison*, 4:17.

182 **"an Atheist in religion . . ."; "The reasonable part of the world . . . hostile to the system":** Hamilton to Jay, 7 May 1800, in *Papers of Alexander Hamilton*, ed. Syrett, 24:464–66.

182 **"embarrassment":** Schuyler to Jay, 7 May 1800, in *Correspondence and Public Papers of John Jay*, ed. Johnston, 4:273.

183 **Hamilton's letter published:** Lomask, *Aaron Burr*, 247.

183 **"it would not become me to adopt":** Hamilton to Jay, 7 May 1800, in *Correspondence and Public Papers of John Jay*, ed. Johnston, 4:272 n.

183 **women lose right to vote in New Jersey:** Zagarri, "Gender and the First Party System," 126.

183 **women vote in New Jersey:** *Gazette of United States*, 18 October 1800. See also Carl Prince, *New Jersey's Jeffersonian Republicans: The Genesis of an Early Party Machine, 1789–1817* (Chapel Hill: University of North Carolina Press for the Institute of Early American History and Culture, 1964), 9; Miller, *Federalist Era*, 264; Zagarri, "Gender and the First Party System," 126.

184 **"at a horse race . . .":** Cunningham, *Jeffersonian Republicans: Formation of Party Organization*, 190.

184 **election in Maryland:** Cunningham, "Election of 1800," 126.

184 **senator from South Carolina urges Madison to lead effort:** *Papers of James Madison*, ed. Mattern et al., editorial note, 17:415. See also Malone, *Jefferson and the Ordeal of Liberty*, 460.

184 ***Virginia Argus:*** Cunningham, *Jeffersonian Republicans: Formation of Party Organization*, 145.

184 **"the minority is entirely unrepresented":** Jefferson to Monroe, 12 January 1800, in *Writings of Thomas Jefferson,* ed. Ford, 7:401.

184 **"no time for qualms":** Cunningham, *Jeffersonian Republicans: Formation of Party Organization,* 144.

185 **"The American Republican Ticket":** Risjord, *Chesapeake Politics,* in Sharp, *American Politics in the Early Republic,* 246.

185 **"Virginia is sold":** Bayard, in Cunningham, "Election of 1800," 126.

185 **"reputable class" would "keep the people steady":** George Cabot, in Fischer, *Revolution of American Conservatism,* 4.

185 **any candidate found guilty of canvassing for votes:** Fischer, *Revolution of American Conservatism,* 91.

185 **"not a man had been spoken to . . .":** Van Schaack to Sedgwick, 7 April 1800, in ibid., 96.

185 **colored ballots:** Fischer, *Revolution of American Conservatism,* 95, n. 14.

186 **all "call themselves . . ."; Gerry:** Sharp, *American Politics in the Early Republic,* 248.

186 **"unite their parties . . .":** Formisano, *Transformation of Political Culture,* 72ff.

186 **"self-preservation":** Cunningham, *Jeffersonian Republicans: Formation of Party Organization,* 146.

186 **electoral rules in Pennsylvania in 1796:** Elkins and McKitrick, *Age of Federalism,* 520. See also Smith, "Election of 1796," 98.

186 **Federalists in control of the state Senate . . . :** See Malone, *Jefferson and the Ordeal of Liberty,* 463. See also Brant, *James Madison,* 4:13.

187 **"The issue of the election . . .":** Jefferson to Thomas Mann Randolph, 5 December 1800, in Cunningham, *Jeffersonian Republicans: Formation of Party Organization,* 231.

187 **"We have never been so pestered . . .":** Cunningham, *Jeffersonian Republicans: Formation of Party Organization,* 189.

188 **"It is said several Hundred . . ."; "began to despair":** Pinckney to Jefferson, 16 October 1800, and December 1800, in ibid., 232, 237.

188 **Pinckney promising patronage appointments:** Cunningham, *Jeffersonian Republicans: Formation of Party Organization,* 237–38.

188 **one Republican tried to prevent a compromise:** Timothy Green to Aaron Burr, 9 December 1800, in ibid., 235.

188 **"All depends on the vote . . .":** Cunningham, "Election of 1800," 126.

188 **"The Election is just finished . . .":** Pinckney to Jefferson, 2 December 1800, in Cunningham, *Jeffersonian Republicans: Formation of Party Organization,* 236.

189 **"adopt C. Pinkney's nominations":** Cunningham, *Jeffersonian Republicans: Formation of Party Organization,* 238.

189 **"I was turned out . . .":** Adams to Benjamin Rush, 12 June 1812, in Schutz and Adair, *Spur of Fame,* 225.

189 **"Our Country is yet safe . . .":** Freneau to Paine, 2 and 4 December 1800, in Cunningham, *Jeffersonian Republicans: Formation of Party Organization,* 236.

10. Showdown

190 **"My health still suffers . . . political Theatre":** Madison to Jefferson, 10 January 1801, in *Papers of James Madison,* ed. Mattern et al., 17:455–56.

190 **"Yesterday morning . . .":** Madison to Jefferson, 28 February 1801, in *Papers of James Madison,* ed. Mattern et al., 17:475.

190 **"An unhappy event . . .":** Monroe to Madison, 29 September 1800, in *Papers of James Madison,* ed. Mattern et al., 17:415.

191 **Jefferson goes to Washington:** Malone, *Jefferson and the Ordeal of Liberty,* 476–77.

191 **Jefferson stops in Montpelier:** Brant, *James Madison,* 4:27.

191 **"refectory of monks":** Gallatin to his wife, 15 January 1801, in Adams, *Life of Albert Gallatin,* 253. See also Smith, *First Forty Years,* ed. Hunt.

191 **boarding houses in Washington:** *List of Members of the Senate and House of Representatives, with Their Places of Abode* (December 1801), in Cunningham, *The United States in 1800,* 58.

191 **"embryo capital":** Sharp, *American Politics in the Early Republic,* 263.

191 **future greatness of the city:** L'Enfant to Washington, 11 September 1789, in Elisabeth S. Kite, *L'Enfant and Washington* (Baltimore: Johns Hopkins University Press, 1929), 34.

191 **"graced . . . by not a single vessel":** Gallatin to his wife, 15 January 1801, in Adams, *Life of Albert Gallatin,* 253.

192 **life in Washington:** See Anne H. Wharton, *Social Life in the Early Republic* (New York: Benjamin Blom, 1902), 60ff.

192 **"The republicans have triumphed . . .":** *National Intelligencer,* 24 December 1800.

192 **"the new Election of JEFFERSON . . .":** *Vermont Gazette,* 29 December 1800.

192 **"A Seditious People!":** Georgetown (D.C.) *Cabinet,* 30 December 1800, in Stewart, "Jeffersonian Journalism," 907.

192 **"The absurd policy . . .":** *Connecticut Courant,* 26 January 1801.

192 **contemporary political scientists:** Sharp, *American Politics in the Early Republic;* William Freehling, *The Road to Disunion: Secessionists at Bay, 1776–1854* (New York: Oxford University Press 1990).

192 **blacks would have voted Federalist:** Paul Finkelman, "The Problem of Slavery," in eds. Ben-Atar and Oberg, *Federalists Reconsidered,* 153.

193 **"The federal party has been so imprudently managed . . .":** John Adams to T. B. Adams, 16 January 1801, in Fischer, *Revolution of American Conservatism,* 57.

193 **"so vainly overrated . . .":** Adams to Benjamin Soddert, 31 March 1801, in *Works of John Adams,* ed. Adams, 9:582.

193 **"Mr. Hamilton has carried his eggs . . .":** Adams, 13 December 1800, in Smith, *John Adams,* 2:1053.

193 **"revolution of 1801":** Adams to James Lloyd, 24 April 1815, in *Works of John Adams,* ed. Adams, 10:162.

194 **"Yet . . . no one pretends to know . . .";** **Burr left a "chasm":** Jefferson to Burr, 15 December 1800, in *Writings of Thomas Jefferson,* ed. Ford, 7:467–68. See also Jefferson to Madison, 19 December 1800, 7:470.

194 **"the sincerity of a refined Jesuit":** *Memoirs of Aaron Burr,* ed. Davis, 2:69.

194 **"I will cheerfully abandon"; "diverting a single vote":** Burr to Jefferson, 23 December 1800, in *Political Correspondence and Public Papers of Aaron Burr,* ed. Kline, 1:473–74.

194 **"federal party can entertain . . .":** Burr to Samuel Smith, 16 December 1800, in *Political Correspondence and Public Papers of Aaron Burr,* ed. Kline, 1:471.

194 **"no confidence":** Mrs. Gallatin to Albert Gallatin, 7 May 1800, in Adams, *Life of Albert Gallatin*, 243.

194 **"It is highly improbable . . .":** Jefferson to Samuel Smith, 16 December 1800, in *Political Correspondence and Public Papers of Aaron Burr*, ed. Kline, 1:471, italics added.

195 **"tolerable well ascertained":** Jefferson to Caesar Rodney, 21 December 1800, in *Writings of Thomas Jefferson*, ed. Ford, 7:472.

195 **"great dismay and gloom":** Jefferson to Madison, 19 December 1800, in *Writings of Thomas Jefferson*, ed. Ford, 7:470.

195 **"What a glorious revolution . . .":** James Brown to John Brown, 8 January 1801, in Waldstreicher, *In the Midst of Perpetual Fetes*, 189.

195 **"How mighty a power . . .":** Adams to Elbridge Gerry, 30 December 1800, in *Works of John Adams*, ed. Adams, 9:577.

195 **Madison assured his friends:** See Brant, *James Madison*, 4:24.

196 **lame-duck House; voting in House:** Morton Grodzins, "Political Parties and the Crisis of Succession in the United States: The Case of 1800," in Joseph LaPalombara, ed., *Political Parties and Political Development* (Princeton: Princeton University Press, 1966), 316. See also Joyce Appleby, "Presidents, Congress, and Courts: Partisan Passions in Motion," *Journal of American History* 88, no. 2 (Fall 2001):408–14.

196 **"the candidates would certainly I think . . .":** Madison to James Monroe, 10 November 1800, in *Papers of James Madison*, ed. Mattern et al., 17:435.

196 **"The electors intended . . .":** *National Intelligencer*, 5 January 1801.

197 **"We have involved ourselves . . .":** John Francis Mercer to Madison, 5 January 1801, in *Papers of James Madison*, ed. Mattern et al., 17:452.

197 **"cast about . . . fulfill that intention . . .":** Gouverneur Morris to Hamilton, 19 December 1800, in *Papers of Alexander Hamilton*, ed. Syrett, 25:267, italics added.

197 **"The game of preventing an election . . .":** Hamilton to Gouverneur Morris, 9 January 1801, in *Papers of Alexander Hamilton*, ed. Syrett, 25:304.

197 **"reflect, that, in republicks . . .":** Caleb Strong, 4 January 1801, in Caleb Strong, *Patriotism and Piety: The Speeches of His Excellency Caleb Strong* (Newburyport, Mass.: Printed by Edmund M. Blunt, 1808), 39.

197 **"The Feds appeared determined . . .":** Jefferson to Madison, 26 December 1800, in *Republic of Letters*, ed. Smith, 2:1156.

198 **"strangle the election . . . proper decision":** Madison to Jefferson, 10 January 1801, in *Republic of Letters*, ed. Smith, 2:1157–58.

198 **"Rotten Apples":** James Gunn to Hamilton, in *Papers of Alexander Hamilton*, ed. Syrett, 25:263

198 **"There would be really cause to fear . . .":** Christman, *"The Spirit of Party,"* 50.

198 **"Stocks have fallen . . .":** Fisher Ames to Christopher Gore, 29 December 1800, in *Works of Fisher Ames*, ed. Ames, 1:288–89.

199 **debates on monument to Washington:** See *National Intelligencer*, 29 December 1800 through 5 January 1801.

199 **unable to appropriate money:** See John Marshall, *The Life of George Washington* (Philadelphia: James Crissy, 1838), 375–76.

199 **"mortal division":** Harrison Gray Otis to Hamilton, 17 December 1800, in *Papers*

of Alexander Hamilton, ed. Syrett, 25:259. See also Sedgwick to King, 24 May 1801, in *Life and Correspondence of Rufus King,* ed. King, 3:455.

199   **Burr was "actuated by ordinary ambition . . .":** Cabot to Hamilton, 20 August 1800, in *Papers of Alexander Hamilton,* ed. Syrett, 25:63–64.

199   **"It is granted . . .":** Orth, *Five American Politicians,* 46.

199   **"are of a negative nature . . .":** Sedgwick to Theodore Sedgwick, Jr., 11 January 1801, in *Political Correspondence and Public Papers of Aaron Burr,* ed. Kline, 1:482, italics added.

199   **"very selfishness"; "begin by democratizing . . .":** Theodore Sedgwick to Hamilton, 10 January 1801, and John Rutledge to Hamilton, 10 January 1801, in *Papers of Alexander Hamilton,* ed. Syrett, 25:308–13.

200   **willing "to consider the federalists as his friends . . .":** James Bayard to Hamilton, 7 January 1801, in *Papers of Alexander Hamilton,* ed. Syrett, 25:300.

200   **"Burr or no President":** William Cooper to John Jay, quoted in James E. Lewis, Jr., "'What Is to Become of Our Government?' The Revolutionary Potential of the Election of 1800," in Horn, Lewis, and Onuf, *Revolution of 1800,* 15.

200   **"resort to the sword":** Lomask, *Aaron Burr,* 288.

200   **"would dishonor my Views . . .":** Burr to Samuel Smith, 16 December 1800, in *Political Correspondence and Public Papers of Aaron Burr,* ed. Kline, 1:471.

200   **A certain "Gentleman":** Burr to Samuel Smith, 29 December 1800, in *Political Correspondence and Public Papers of Aaron Burr,* ed. Kline, 1:479.

200   **Mr. Burr had insinuated . . . :** *New York Gazette,* 8 January 1801, in *Political Correspondence and Public Papers of Aaron Burr,* ed. Kline, 1:483.

200   **report of meeting between Burr and Smith:** Gabriel Christie to Samuel Smith, 19 December 1800, in *Political Correspondence and Public Papers of Aaron Burr,* ed. Kline, 1:484.

201   **"The feds will attempt. . . . report to the contrary":** Smith to Burr, 11 January 1800, in *Political Correspondence and Public Papers of Aaron Burr,* ed. Kline, 1:488.

201   **"persons friendly . . .":** Bayard to Hamilton, 7 January 1801, in *Papers of Alexander Hamilton,* ed. Syrett, 25:300.

201   **"desperadoes":** See *Political Correspondence and Public Papers of Aaron Burr,* ed. Kline, 1:475, editorial note.

201   **"keep the game . . .":** Robert Goodloe Harper to Burr, 24 December 1800, in *Political Correspondence and Public Papers of Aaron Burr,* ed. Kline, 1:474.

201   **Smith reported to Burr:** Joanne B. Freeman, "Corruption and Compromise in the Election of 1800," in Horn, Lewis, and Onuf, *Revolution of 1800,* 107.

201   **Burr repeats his promise:** Burr to Samuel Smith, 16 January 1801, in *Political Correspondence and Public Papers of Aaron Burr,* ed. Kline, 1:493.

201   **Hamilton sends Morris contrary report:** Hamilton to Gouverneur Morris, 13 January 1801, in *Papers of Alexander Hamilton,* ed. Syrett, 25:314.

201   **"highly injurious . . . to be neglected":** Jefferson to Burr, 1 February 1801, in *Writings of Thomas Jefferson,* ed. Ford, 7:485–86.

202   **"most malignant Spirit . . .":** Burr to Jefferson, 12 February 1801, in *Political Correspondence and Public Papers of Aaron Burr,* ed. Kline, 1:501.

202   **Republicans caucused:** George Jackson to Madison, 5 February 1801, in *Papers of James Madison,* ed. Mattern et al., 17:460–61.

202 **"No man placed in his situation . . .":** Nathaniel Macon to Rodney, 20 February 1801, in Cunningham, *Jeffersonian Republicans: Formation of Party Organization*, 246.

202 **"feudalists":** Elbridge Gerry to Jefferson, 15 January 1801, in Worthington Chauncey Ford, ed., *Some Letters of Elbridge Gerry of Massachusetts, 1784–1804* (Brooklyn: Historical Printing Club, 1896), 13.

202 **"degraded . . . by the attempt . . .":** See Brant, *James Madison*, 4:27. See also Troup to King, 12 February 1801, in *Life and Correspondence of Rufus King*, ed. King, 3:391.

202 **Madison blames Burr:** Madison to Jefferson, 14 January 1824, in *Republic of Letters*, ed. Smith, 3:1891.

202 **"conduct has been honorable . . .":** Jefferson to Martha Jefferson Randolph, 4 January 1801, in Jefferson, *Writings of Thomas Jefferson*, ed. Ford, 7:478.

202 **"an honest, frank-dealing man . . .":** Jefferson to William Branch Giles, 20 April 1807, in *Writings*, ed. Peterson, 1175.

202 **"Burr is a cunning man . . .":** Morton Borden, *The Federalism of James Bayard* (New York: Columbia University Press, 1955), 81.

202 **"bankrupt beyond redemption":** Hamilton to Wolcott, 16 December 1800, in *Papers of Alexander Hamilton*, ed. Syrett, 25:257.

202 **"voluptuary":** Hamilton to John Rutledge, Jr., 4 January 1801, in *Papers of Alexander Hamilton*, ed. Syrett, 25:295.

202 **"permanent power":** Hamilton to Wolcott, 16 December 1800, in *Papers of Alexander Hamilton*, ed. Syrett, 25:257.

203 **"As to his theory . . .":** Hamilton to James Ross, 29 December 1800, in *Papers of Alexander Hamilton*, ed. Syrett, 25:280.

203 **"most unfit":** Hamilton to James Bayard, 27 December 1800, in *Papers of Alexander Hamilton*, ed. Syrett, 25:277.

203 **"he will laugh . . .":** Hamilton to James Bayard, 27 December 1800, in *Papers of Alexander Hamilton*, ed. Syrett, 25:277.

203 **"tools . . .":** Hamilton to Gouverneur Morris, [13] January 1801, in *Papers of Alexander Hamilton*, ed. Syrett, 25:315.

203 **"Grecian horse":** Hamilton to Wolcott, December 1800, in *Papers of Alexander Hamilton*, ed. Syrett, 25:288.

203 **"crafty":** Hamilton to Bayard, 16 January 1801, in *Papers of Alexander Hamilton*, ed. Syrett, 25:319.

203 **"with Burr I have always . . .":** Hamilton to Gouverneur Morris, 26 December 1800, in *Papers of Alexander Hamilton*, ed. Syrett, 25:275.

203 **"If Jefferson is president . . .":** Hamilton to Wolcott, December 1800, in *Papers of Alexander Hamilton*, ed. Syrett, 25:286.

203 **"disorganized and contemptible":** Hamilton to Bayard, 16 January 1801, in *Papers of Alexander Hamilton*, ed. Syrett, 25:324.

203 **"Depend upon it . . .":** Hamilton to Gouverneur Morris, [13] January 1801, in *Papers of Alexander Hamilton*, ed. Syrett, 25:315.

204 **"radically deficient . . .":** Troup to King, 31 December 1800, in *Life and Correspondence of Rufus King*, ed. King, 3:359.

204 **"declared that his influence . . .":** Troup to King, 12 February 1801, in *Life and Correspondence of Rufus King*, ed. King, 3:391.

204 **"I shall be obliged . . .":** Hamilton to Bayard, 16 January 1801, in *Papers of Alexander Hamilton*, ed. Syrett, 25:319.

204 **"has been increasing . . .":** Sedgwick, diary entry, 30 January 1801, in *Political Correspondence and Public Papers of Aaron Burr*, ed. Kline, editorial note, 1:485.

204 **"bold enough":** Gallatin to his wife, 29 January 1801, in Adams, *Life of Albert Gallatin*, 257.

204 **"What will be the plans . . .";** **"I see some danger . . .";** **"Shall we submit?":** Gallatin to his wife, 22 January 1801, in Adams, *Life of Albert Gallatin*, 255.

204 **"A few, indeed, drink . . .":** Albert Gallatin to his wife, 22 January 1801, in Adams, *Life of Albert Gallatin*, 255.

204 **"Rumors are various . . .":** Morris to Nicholas Low, 8 February 1801, in *Life of Gouverneur Morris*, ed. Sparks, 3:152.

204 **defeat:** Peterson, *Thomas Jefferson and the New Nation*, 654.

204 **"the delight of my Eyes . . .":** Adams to Jefferson, 24 March 1801, in *Adams-Jefferson Letters*, ed. Cappon, 1:264.

204 **"deep dejection":** T. Pickering to Rufus King, 5 January 1801, in *Life and Correspondence of Rufus King*, ed. King, 3:366.

205 **Jefferson calls on President Adams:** Jefferson to Dr. Benjamin Rush, 16 January 1811, in Jefferson, *Writings*, ed. Peterson, 1236–37.

205 **"incalculable consequences":** Jefferson to Dr. Benjamin Rush, 16 January 1811, in *Writings of Thomas Jefferson*, ed. Ford, 9:294. See also Peterson, *Thomas Jefferson and the New Nation*, 645.

205 **Pennsylvania Avenue; president of the Senate:** *Anas*, 1804, in Jefferson, *Writings*, ed. Peterson, 695.

205 **"Sir, the event of the election . . .":** Jefferson to Rush, 16 January 1811, in *Writings of Thomas Jefferson*, ed. Ford, 9:297.

205 **"Then . . . things must take their course":** Peterson, *Thomas Jefferson and the New Nation*, 645.

205 **"Mr. Burr's good fortune . . . at a loss":** Adams to Elbridge Gerry, 30 December 1800, in *Works of John Adams*, ed. Adams, 9:577–78.

205 **"political convulsion"; "The President would be as legal . . .":** Adams to Elbridge Gerry, 7 February 1801, in *Works of John Adams*, ed. Adams, 9:98.

206 **"infinitely sunk":** Madison to Jefferson, 10 January 1801, in *Republic of Letters*, ed. Smith, 2:1157.

206 **special session of the Senate:** Lewis, "'What Is to Become of Our Government?'" 19–20.

206 **"dead calm":** *New England Palladium*, reprinted 10 January 1801 in *Gazette of the United States*.

206 **only "bold resistance":** *Gazette of the United States*, 10 January 1801.

206 **"former Treasury Secretary . . .":** *Aurora General Advertiser*, 20 January 1801, in Rosenfeld, *American Aurora*, 897.

206 **Federalist support for slave rebellions:** Michael A. Bellesiles, "'The Soil Will Be Soaked with Blood': Taking the Revolution of 1800 Seriously," in Horn, Lewis, and Onuf, *Revolution of 1800*, 64.

206 *Aurora:* Sharp, *Politics in the Early American Republic*, 251. See also Wilhelmus Bogart Bryan, *A History of the National Capital* (New York: Macmillan, 1914), 1:384–85.

206 **"Philosopher" Jefferson . . . :** *Salem Federalist*, 29 January 1801, in Sharp, *American Politics in the Early Republic*, 252.

207 **"every democrat should be put . . .":** Sharp, *American Politics in the Early Republic*, 252.

207 **reports of violence and threats:** Ibid., 250–51.

207 **marines:** *Aurora*, 7 January, 10 January, 3 February 1801, in ibid., 257.

207 **seize forts and arsenals . . . :** Brackenridge to Jefferson, 19 January 181, in Sharp, *American Politics in the Early Republic*, 258. See also Henry Brackenridge to Jefferson, 19 January 1801, in Sharp, *American Politics in the Early Republic*, 258.

207 **"How could the rights of the people . . .":** *Gazette of the United States*, 29 January 1801.

207 **"You, who are temperate . . .":** Gouverneur Morris to Hamilton, 5 January 1801, in *Papers of Alexander Hamilton*, ed. Syrett, 25:299.

207 **"This is the morning of the election . . .":** Jefferson to Tench Coxe, 11 February 1801, in *Writings of Thomas Jefferson*, ed. Ford, 7:488–89.

207 **two miles; against doctors' advice:** Smith, *First Forty Years*, ed. Hunt, 23–24.

207 **wife threatens divorce:** See Miller, *Federalist Era*, 271.

208 **Jefferson reads tally:** Jefferson skipped over the irregularities of the Georgia ballot, which were ultimately inconsequential. See Bruce Ackerman and David Fontana, "How Jefferson Counted Himself In," *The Atlantic* 293, no. 2 (March 2004):84–95.

208 **Nicholson:** Lomask, *Aaron Burr*, 290.

208 **Nicholson's wife helps him write . . . :** Smith, *First Forty Years*, ed. Hunt, 24.

208 **"accommodation of those whom age or debility . . .":** Ibid., 23.

208 **"If our opponents . . .":** Lewis, "'What Is to Become of Our Government?'" 19.

209 **messengers running:** Smith, *First Forty Years*, ed. Hunt, 24.

209 **" I never lay down . . .":** Ibid., 24.

209 **"the happiness of five millions . . .":** *Washington Federalist*, 12 February 1801, reprinted in *Gazette of the United States*, 16 February 1801.

209 **eat, drink, sleep . . . :** Smith, *First Forty Years*, ed. Hunt, 23.

209 **"I have not closed my eyes . . .":** John Dawson to James Madison, 12 February 1801, in *Papers of James Madison*, ed. Mattern et al., 17:465.

209 **"If the union could be broken . . .":** Cunningham, "Election of 1800," 132.

209 **"prepared to take up arms . . .":** Tyler to Monroe, 11 February 1801, in Sharp, *American Politics in the Early Republic*, 269.

209 **"put Virginia to the Test":** Hamilton to Sedgwick, 2 February 1799, in Hamilton, *Writings*, ed. Freeman, 914.

209 **"guard against a situation truly awful":** Lewis, "'What Is to Become of Our Government?'" 19.

209 **"If anything requires . . .":** Monroe, 12 February 1801, in Ammon, *James Monroe*, 193.

210 **"By all means, preserve the city . . .":** Gallatin to Dallas, in Sharp, *American Politics in the Early Republic*, 268.

210 **"momentous":** *Washington Federalist*, quoted in *Aurora*, 19 February 1801, in Sharp, *American Politics in the Early Republic*, 268.

210 **"for the purpose of putting to death . . .":** Gallatin to Muhlenberg, 8 May 1848, in Adams, *Life of Albert Gallatin*, 249.

210 **"Nothing new to-day":** Gallatin to James Nicholson, 14 February 1801, in Adams, *Life of Albert Gallatin*, 261.

210 "**nothing but desperate measures remain**"; "**We broke up each time . . .**":
Bayard to Hamilton, 8 March 1801, in *Papers of Alexander Hamilton*, ed. Syrett,
25:345.

210 **three more ballots, voting postponed until Monday:** Gallatin to James Nicholson, 14 February 1801, in Adams, *Life of Albert Gallatin*, 261.

210 "**The scene passing here . . .**": Jefferson to Maria Eppes, 15 February 1801, in *Republic of Letters*, ed. Smith, 2:1143.

210 "**the whole labor of our lives**": Jefferson to Martha Jefferson Randolph, 5 February 1801, in *Family Letters of Thomas Jefferson*, ed. Betts and Bear, 195.

210 "**Four days of balloting . . . should be submitted to**": Jefferson to Monroe, 15 February 1801, in *Writings of Thomas Jefferson*, ed. Ford, 7:490, italics added.

210 **Jefferson would not object to the election of Burr; "usurpation":** Jefferson to
McKean, 9 March 1801, in Sharp, *American Politics in the Early Republic*, 274.

211 "**present democratical spirit . . . favorite morsels of the constitution**": Jefferson to Monroe, 15 February 1801, in *Writings of Thomas Jefferson*, ed. Ford,
7:491.

211 "**will irritate and inflame . . .**": Dallas to Gallatin, 15 February 1801, in Brant, *James
Madison*, 4:32.

211 "**Rest assured . . .**": Gallatin to James Nicholson, 14 February 1801, in Adams, *Life
of Albert Gallatin*, 261.

211 **Bayard's preference for Burr:** Bayard to Hamilton, 8 March 1801, in *Papers of Alexander Hamilton*, ed. Syrett, 244–45.

211 **Bayard's and Smith's versions of events:** John Pancake, "Aaron Burr: Would-Be
Usurper," *William and Mary Quarterly*, 3rd ser., 8 (April 1951):212.

211 "**I have declared to them unequivocally . . .**": Jefferson to Monroe, 15 February
1801, in *Writings of Thomas Jefferson*, ed. Ford, 7:490.

211 "**excited some anxiety**": Burr to Gallatin, 25 February 1801, in *Political Correspondence and Public Papers of Aaron Burr*, ed. Kline, 1:509.

211 "**at the expense . . .**": James Bayard to Samuel Bayard, 22 February 1801, in Malone,
Jefferson and the Ordeal of Liberty, 504.

212 "*I was chiefly influenced . . .*": Hofstadter, *Idea of a Party System*, 147.

212 "**Deserter!**": Lomask, *Aaron Burr*, 291.

212 "**the clamor . . .**"; "**such a wretch**": James Bayard to Samuel Bayard, 22 February
1801, in Miller, *Federalist Era*, 273.

212 "**We have balloted for the 34th time . . .**": Gallatin to James Nicholson, 16 February 1801, in Adams, *Life of Albert Gallatin*, 262.

212 **letters from Burr:** Elkins and McKitrick, *Age of Federalism*, 749.

212 "**explicitly resigns . . .**": Theodore Sedgwick to Theodore Sedgwick, Jr., 16 February 1801, in *Political Papers and Public Correspondence of Aaron Burr*, ed. Kline,
1:486, editorial note.

212 "**bold and imperious partisans . . .**": *Gazette of the United States*, 16 February 1801,
in Malone, *Jefferson and the Ordeal of Liberty*, 504.

212 "**During that period of deep suspence . . .**": *National Intelligencer*, 16 February
1801.

213 "**the step was not taken . . .**": Hofstadter, *Idea of a Party System*, 147.

213 "**political existence**" **of Delaware:** Lewis, "'What Is to Become of Our Government?'" 23.

213 **"The storm we have passed through . . .":** Jefferson to Lafayette, 13 March 1801, in Gilbert Chinard, ed., *The Letters of Lafayette and Jefferson* (Baltimore: Johns Hopkins University Press, 1929), 212.

213 **"tree of Liberty . . .":** Stewart, *Opposition Press*, 597.

213 **"an infidel":** Abigail Adams to John Adams, 21 February 1801, in Smith, *John Adams*, 2:1062.

213 **"Nothing could then equal . . .":** *National Intelligencer,* 18 February 1801.

213 **"alarming intelligence":** *Gazette of the United States,* 19 February 1801.

214 **"Now roar the cannon . . .":** Democraticus, *Jeffersoniad, or, An echo to the groans of an expiring faction* (Fredericktown, Md.: Bartgis, 1801).

214 *"simply turned over":* Seymour Martin Lipset, *Political Man: The Social Bases of Politics* (Garden City, N.Y.: Doubleday, 1960). 44.

215 **no future revolutionaries would emulate:** See Dunn, *Sister Revolutions,* ch. 6.

215 **"What a lesson . . .":** Madison to Jefferson, 28 February 1801, in *Republic of Letters,* ed. Smith, 2:1162.

215 **"Presidents, Secretaries . . .":** Rufus King to N. Low, 7 July 1800, in *Life and Correspondence of Rufus King,* ed. King, 3:269.

215 **"Because he is President . . .":** Hofstadter, *Idea of a Party System,* 148.

216 **"party spirit is blind . . .":** Abigail Adams to Jefferson, 18 August 1804, in *Letters of Mrs. Adams, The Wife of John Adams,* ed. Charles Francis Adams (Boston: Wilkins, Carter and Company, 1848), 395.

216 **parties may shake up society:** Tocqueville, *De la Démocratie en Amérique,* ed. Mayer, Bk. 1, Pt. 2, ch. 2, 179.

216 **"The Revolution of 1776 . . .":** *Aurora,* 20 February 1801, in McCullough, *John Adams,* 562, italics added.

217 **"one of the luckiest circumstances . . . doctrines they had opposed":** Tocqueville, *De la Démocratie en Amérique,* ed. Mayer, Bk. 1, Pt. 2, ch. 2, 181.

11. March 4, 1801

218 **Jefferson at breakfast:** Smith, *First Forty Years,* ed. Hunt, 12. Dumas Malone questions the authenticity of Smith's account, although he underscores that Jefferson was "personally unpretentious." Dumas Malone, *Jefferson the President: First Term, 1801–1805* (Boston: Little, Brown and Company, 1970), 29.

218 **elimination of "levees":** Jefferson to Nathaniel Macon, 14 May 1801, in *Writings of Thomas Jefferson,* ed. Ford, 8:51.

218 **"all our received notions of propriety . . .":** Sir Augustus John Foster, in Newman, *Parades and Politics,* 79.

218 **"to admit the smallest distinction . . .":** Malone, *Jefferson the President,* 93.

219 **"In social circles all are equal . . .":** Ibid., 499.

219 **"pêle mêle":** Jefferson, "A Memorandum on Rules of Etiquette," November 1803, in Jefferson, *Writings,* ed. Peterson, 705.

219 **round table:** Joyce Appleby, "Thomas Jefferson and the Psychology of Democracy," in Horn, Lewis, and Onuf, *Revolution of 1800,* 158.

219 **"arrogance of precedence":** Ibid., 158.

219 **"between writing to the highest . . . facilitate business":** Jefferson to Monroe, 29 May 1801, in *Writings of Thomas Jefferson,* ed. Ford, 8:59.

219   "no mysteries" in public administration: Burns, *Vineyard of Liberty,* 167.

219   Jefferson's entourage: Ellis, *American Sphinx,* 170.

220   "Sensible, moderate men . . .": *Massachusetts Spy,* 18 March 1801, in McCullough, *John Adams,* 564.

220   "sufficiently humbled": Bayard to Hamilton, 8 March 1801, in *Papers of Alexander Hamilton,* ed. Syrett, 25:344.

220   "You can have no idea . . .": Gallatin to his wife, 5 March 1801, in Adams, *Life of Albert Gallatin,* 265.

220   "In the future administration . . .": Adams to Jay, 19 December 1800, in *Correspondence and Public Papers of John Jay,* ed. Johnston, 4:284.

220   "I shall endeavor . . .": See Ellis, *American Sphinx,* 177.

220   "Instead of smoothing the path . . .": Madison to Jefferson, 28 February 1801, in *Republic of Letters,* ed. Smith, 2:1162.

220   "common justice": Jefferson to Abigail Adams, 13 June 1804, in *Adams-Jefferson Letters,* ed. Cappon, 1:270.

220   "indecent": Jefferson to Benjamin Rush, 24 March 1801, in *Writings of Thomas Jefferson,* ed. Ford, 8:32.

221   inauguration in Senate: See Constance McLaughlin Green, *Washington,* 2 vols. (Princeton: Princeton University Press, 1962–63), 1:135.

221   "one of the most interesting scenes a free people . . . disorder": Smith, *First Forty Years,* ed. Hunt, 25.

221   "speculative theorists . . .": John Marshall to Charles Cotesworth Pinckney, 4 March 1801, in Burns, *Vineyard of Liberty,* 161.

221   "in so low a tone": Smith, *First Forty Years,* ed. Hunt, 26.

221   "principles, institutions, or systems of education": "To the Young Men of Philadelphia," 7 May 1798, in *Works of John Adams,* ed. Adams, 9:186.

222   "This whole chapter . . .": Jefferson to Joseph Priestley, 21 March 1801, in *Writings of Thomas Jefferson,* ed. Ford, 8:22.

222   "Checks and Ballances, Jefferson . . .": Adams to Jefferson, 25 June 1813, in *Adams-Jefferson Letters,* ed. Cappon, 2:334.

222   "The will of the majority is in all cases . . ."; "absolute acquiescence . . ."; "We are all federalists . . .": First Inaugural Address, 4 March 1801, in Jefferson, *Writings,* ed. Peterson, 492–96.

222   three drafts: Peterson, *Thomas Jefferson and the New Nation,* 655.

223   national identity: See Onuf, *Jefferson's Empire,* 107.

223   "both parties claim to be federalists . . .": Jefferson to John Wise, 12 February 1798, in Malone, *Jefferson the President,* 20 n.

223   "more a political platitude . . .": Ellis, *American Sphinx,* 182.

223   "patriotic" Federalists . . . : Jefferson to Thomas Lomax, 25 February 1801, in *Writings of Thomas Jefferson,* ed. Ford, 7:500; see also Jefferson to Levi Lincoln, 25 October 1802, 8:175.

223   "nothing shall be spared . . .": Jefferson to Joseph Fay, 22 March 1801, in Noble E. Cunningham, Jr., *The Jeffersonian Republicans in Power* (Chapel Hill: University of North Carolina Press for the Institute of Early American History and Culture, 1963), 8, italics added.

223   moderates had begun "most anxiously" . . . : Jefferson to Madison, 18 February 1801, in *Writings of Thomas Jefferson,* ed. Ford, 7:494.

223 **"will cement & form . . .":** Jefferson to William Giles, 23 March 1801, in *Writings of Thomas Jefferson,* ed. Ford, 8:25.

224 **"strongest government on earth"; "*theoretic* and *visionary*" fear; "Sometimes it is said that . . .":** First Inaugural Address, in Jefferson, *Writings,* ed. Peterson, 493.

224 **"steady line of conciliation":** Jefferson to Rush, 24 March 1801, in *Writings of Thomas Jefferson,* ed. Ford, 8:32.

225 **"I shall often go wrong . . .":** First Inaugural Address, in Jefferson, *Writings,* ed. Peterson, 495–96.

225 **"curiosity"; "decent respect . . . better than we expected":** Bayard to Hamilton, 8 March 1801, in *Papers of Alexander Hamilton,* ed. Syrett, 25:344.

225 **"virtually a candid retraction . . .":** Address to the Electors of the State of New York, 21 March 1801, in *Papers of Alexander Hamilton,* ed. Syrett, 25:365.

225 **"shook hands with each other":** Rush to Jefferson, 12 March 1801, in *Letters of Benjamin Rush,* ed. Lyman Butterfield, 2 vols. (Princeton: Princeton University Press, 1951), 2:831.

225 **"We are all tranquil . . .":** Cabot to King, 20 March 1801, in *Life and Correspondence of Rufus King,* ed. King, 3:408.

225 **"it is strongly characteristic of the general cast . . .":** John Marshall to Charles Cotesworth Pinckney, 4 March 1801, in Burns, *Vineyard of Liberty,* 161.

225 **"smooth promises . . .":** Ames to Dwight, 19 March 1801, in *Works of Fisher Ames,* ed. Ames, 1:292.

226 **"aristocrat" removes clapper:** Malone, *Jefferson the President,* 16.

226 **New Jersey home builder:** L. Q. C. Elmer, *History of Cumberland County, New Jersey,* 43, in Fischer, *Revolution of American Conservatism,* 185.

226 **"YESTERDAY EXPIRED . . .":** Boston *Columbian Centinel,* 4 March 1801, in Malone, *Jefferson the President,* 4.

12. The New Politics

227 **"My dear friend . . .":** Gouverneur Morris to Robert Livingston, 20 February 1801, in *Life of Gouverneur Morris,* ed. Sparks, 3:154.

227 ***"Nil desperandum . . .":*** Morris to Rufus King, 4 June 1800, in *Life of Gouverneur Morris,* ed. Sparks, 3:128.

227 **"a champion who never flinches, . . .":** Ames to Theodore Dwight, 19 March 1801, in *Works of Fisher Ames,* ed. Ames, 1:293–94. See also Hofstadter, *Idea of a Party System,* 145.

228 **"A party can never be too high . . .":** A. J. Dallas to Gallatin, 21 May 1801, in Miller, *Federalist Era,* 274.

228 **"We are not dead yet":** Francis Crawford to Ebenezer Foote, 7 March 1801, in Cunningham, *Jeffersonian Republicans: Formation of Party Organization,* 260.

228 **"Mr. Jefferson, whose politics . . .":** *Gazette of the United States,* 5 March 1801, italics added.

228 **"the culpable desire of gaining . . .":** The Examination, No. 2, 21 December 1801, in *Papers of Alexander Hamilton,* ed. Syrett, 25:458.

228 ***"Good patriots must at all events . . .":*** The Examination, No. 1, 17 December 1801, in *Papers of Alexander Hamilton,* ed. Syrett, 25:454.

228 **"the collected wisdom"**: The Examination, No. 9, 18 January 1802, in *Papers of Alexander Hamilton*, ed. Syrett, 25:501.

229 **"LITTLE POLITICIANS"**: The Examination, No. 18, 8 April 1802, in *Papers of Alexander Hamilton*, ed. Syrett, 25:591, 597.

229 **"Those whose patriotism . . . *impure tide*"**: The Examination, No. 1, 17 December 1801, in *Papers of Alexander Hamilton*, ed. Syrett, 25:454, italics added.

229 **"will open their eyes and see . . . to destruction!"**: The Examination, No. 17, 20 March 1802, in *Papers of Alexander Hamilton*, ed. Syrett, 25:576.

229 **"Among federalists old errors . . ."**: Hamilton to King, 3 June 1802, in *Papers of Alexander Hamilton*, ed. Syrett, 26:15.

229 **"What can I do better than withdraw . . ."**: Hamilton to Gouverneur Morris, 29 February 1802, in *Papers of Alexander Hamilton*, ed. Syrett, 25:544.

229 **"It is perfectly proper . . ."**: Ames to Theodore Dwight, 19 March 1801, in *Works of Fisher Ames*, ed. Ames, 1:294.

229 **"We must study . . ."**: Ames to John Rutledge, 26 January 1801, in Fischer, *Revolution of American Conservatism*, 180.

229 **"We must speak . . ."**: Ames to Theodore Dwight, 19 March 1801, in *Works of Fisher Ames*, ed. Ames, 1:293.

230 **"Weary and disgusted . . ."**: Ames to Rutledge, 30 July 1801, in Fischer, "Myth of the Essex Junto," 227.

230 **"outside passenger"**: Ames to Christopher Gore, 3 October 1803, in *Works of Fisher Ames*, ed. Ames, 1:323.

230 **"Our defeat has taught us more . . ."**: *Gazette of the United States*, 18 February 1801.

230 **"palsied"**: John Quincy Adams to Rufus King, 8 October 1802, in *Life and Correspondence of Rufus King*, ed. King, 4:176–77. See also Thomas Dwight to Theodore Sedgwick, 5 December 1800, in Fischer, *Revolution of American Conservatism*, 58; George Cabot to Rufus King, 17 March 1804, in *Life and Letters of George Cabot*, ed. Lodge, 345; Sedgwick to Hamilton, 27 January 1803, in *Papers of Alexander Hamilton*, ed. Syrett, 26:80.

230 **"Federalism sits like a Turk . . ."**: *New England Palladium*, 4 January 1800, in Fischer, *Revolution of American Conservatism*, 58.

230 **"The party committed suicide . . ."**: Adams to James Lloyd, 6 February 1815, in *Works of John Adams*, ed. Adams, 10:115.

230 **"rallying point"; "Supreme Governor"**: Troup to King, 31 December 1800, in *Life and Correspondence of Rufus King*, ed. King, 3:359.

231 **"tyranny of what is called . . ."**: Ames, in Henry Adams, *History of the United States of America During the Administrations of Thomas Jefferson*, ed. Earl N. Harbert (New York: Library of America, 1986), 59.

231 **"to destroy every trace of civilization . . ."**: Theodore Dwight, in Arthur M. Schlesinger, *New Viewpoints in American History* (New York: Macmillan, 1922), 84.

231 **"Reason, common sense . . ."**: *New York Spectator*, 18 January 1804, in Dixon Ryan Fox, *The Decline of Aristocracy in the Politics of New York* (New York: Columbia University Press, 1919), 7.

231 **"Oh my Country . . ."**: John Adams to Benjamin Rush, 19 September 1806, in *Old Family Letters*, ed. Biddle, 113, italics added.

231 "Your people, sir . . .": Adams, *History of the United States of America*, ed. Harbert, 60–61.

231 "When the people have been long enough drunk . . .": Morris to Roger Griswold, 3 November 1803, in Fischer, *Revolution of American Conservatism*, 26.

231 "compel a reluctant people . . .": Morris to Mountflorence, 22 June 1805, in *Diary and Letters of Gouverneur Morris*, ed. Anne Cary Morris (New York: Charles Scribner's Sons, 1888), 2:468, italics added.

231 "What remains but to cultivate . . .": Morris to Livingston, 1805, in *Diary and Letters of Gouverneur Morris*, ed. Morris, 2:469–70.

231 fears of the ignorance of the people: Jefferson to Abigail Adams, 11 September 1804, in *Adams-Jefferson Letters*, ed. Cappon, 1:280.

231 "completely and irrevocably abandoned . . .": John Quincy Adams to Rufus King, 8 October 1802, in *Life and Correspondence of Rufus King*, ed. King, 4:176–77.

232 Hamilton convokes national meeting: Hamilton to C. C. Pinckney, 15 March 1802, in *Papers of Alexander Hamilton*, ed. Syrett, 25:562.

232 Morris proposes network of committees: Gouverneur Morris to Hamilton, 22 February 1802, in *Papers of Alexander Hamilton*, ed. Syrett, 25:528.

232 "I never will surrender . . .": William Davie, 2 May 1803, in Fischer, *Revolution of American Conservatism*, 151.

232 "To be counted one of [Washington's] disciples . . .": Rufus Putnam to Timothy Pickering, 5 January 1804, in Fischer, *Revolution of American Conservatism*, 408.

232 The duty of every federalist . . .: *Scioto Gazette*, 3 December 1800, in Fischer, *Revolution of American Conservatism*, 239–40.

232 "Federalists may as well go home": Fischer, *Revolution of American Conservatism*, 253.

232 Federalists scarcely dared to name a candidate . . .: John Quincy Adams to Rufus King, 8 October 1802, in *Life and Correspondence of Rufus King*, ed. King, 4:176.

232 no Federalists run in New York: New York *Evening Post*, 27 April 1802; see also Fox, *Decline of Aristocracy*, 61.

232 appealed to conservative Federalists: See Willard M. Wallace, Introduction, *Interview in Weehawken: The Burr-Hamilton Duel*, ed. Harold C. Syrett and Jean G. Cooke (Middletown, Conn.: Wesleyan University Press, 1960), 33–34.

232 Burr runs for governor of New York: see Lomask, *Aaron Burr*, 336ff.

232 tidal waves on sea: Dawn Stover, "Surf's Up in Nevada," *Popular Science* (December 2000):13.

233 "Every minutia . . .": Griswold to David Daggett, 8 December 1801, in Cunningham, *Jeffersonian Republicans in Power*, 20.

233 "He is tall in stature . . .": Dr. S. L. Mitchill to his wife, 10 January 1802, in Malone, *Jefferson the President*, 94.

233 Washington's funereal dinners: Theodore Sedgwick to Ephraim Williams, June 1789, in Joseph Charles, *The Origins of the American Party System* (Williamsburg, Va.: The Institute for Early American History and Culture, 1956), 38.

233 dinner conversation: *Memoirs of John Quincy Adams*, ed. Charles Francis Adams, 12 vols. (Philadelphia: J. B. Lippincott and Co., 1874–77), 23 November 1804, 1:316; see also 3 November 1807.

233 **"true politeness":** Joyce Appleby, *Thomas Jefferson* (New York: Times Books, 2003), 45.

233 **"His instincts . . .":** Adams, *History of the United States of America,* ed. Harbert, 99.

234 **ferociously partisan:** See David Waldstreicher, "The Nationalization and Racialization of American Politics," in *Contesting Democracy: Substance and Structure in American Political History, 1775–2000,* ed. Byron E. Shafer and Anthony Badger (Lawrence: University of Kansas Press, 2001), 47.

234 **"royalists or priests":** Jefferson to Dupont de Nemours, 18 January 1802, in *Writings of Thomas Jefferson,* ed. Ford, 8:126 n.

234 **"sink . . . into an abyss . . .":** Jefferson to Levi Lincoln, 25 October 1802, in *Writings of Thomas Jefferson,* ed. Ford, 8:176.

234 **"so scouted":** Jefferson to Joel Barlow, 3 May 1802, in *Writings of Thomas Jefferson,* ed. Ford, 8:150.

234 **"I wish nothing but their eternal hatred":** Hofstadter, *Idea of a Party System,* 165.

234 **"unanimous in their hate for me . . .":** Franklin D. Roosevelt, *Public Papers and Addresses,* 1936, Madison Square Garden Address, October 1936.

234 **"federal candidate would not get the vote . . .":** Jefferson to Dupont de Nemours, 18 January 1802, in *Writings of Thomas Jefferson,* ed. Ford, 8:126 n.

235 **"consolidated" in Republican principles:** Jefferson to Hawkins, 18 February 1803, in *Writings,* ed. Peterson, 114.

235 **"unequivocal in principle . . . no invasion from me":** Jefferson to Elbridge Gerry, 29 March 1801, in Jefferson, *Writings,* ed. Peterson, 1089–90.

235 **"errors of opinion":** Jefferson, First Inaugural Address, in Jefferson, *Writings,* ed. Peterson, 493.

235 **"dazzle . . . common sense":** Jefferson to John Tyler, 28 June 1804, in *Writings,* ed. Peterson, 1147.

235 **"the overwhelming torrent"; "we have ever asserted . . .":** Jefferson to Abigail Adams, 11 September 1804, in *Adams-Jefferson Letters,* ed. Cappon, 1:279.

235 **"a few prosecutions . . .":** Jefferson to Thomas McKean, 19 February 1803, in *Writings of Thomas Jefferson,* ed. Ford, 8:218–19.

235 **Jefferson's forays into suppression of criticism:** See Levy, *Emergence of a Free Press,* 304–8, 341–46.

236 **Jefferson a moderate:** See Richard R. Beeman, *The Old Dominion and the New Nation, 1788–1801* (Lexington: University Press of Virginia, 1972), 243.

236 **"noiseless course . . . must become happy":** Jefferson to Thomas Cooper, 29 November 1802, in *Writings,* ed. Peterson, 1110.

236 **Federalist raised too much money:** Jefferson to Cooper, 29 November 1802, in Jefferson, *Writings,* ed. Peterson, 1100.

236 **"bring the government to a simple . . .":** Jefferson to Monroe, 13 January 1803, in *Writings,* ed. Peterson, 1112.

236 **"lopping them . . .":** Jefferson to Monroe, 20 June 1801, in Noble E. Cunningham, Jr., *Jefferson and Monroe* (Monticello, Va.: Monticello Monograph Series, 2003), 36.

236 **"reduce the army . . .":** Jefferson to Thaddeus Kosciusko, 2 April 1802, in Jefferson, *Writings,* ed. Peterson, 1103.

236 **"mortifies me":** Jefferson to Dupont de Nemours, 18 January 1802, in Jefferson, *Writings,* ed. Peterson, 1101.

236 **new banks:** Appleby, *Thomas Jefferson*, 85.

237 **"We must now place the manufacturer . . . to our comfort":** Jefferson to Benjamin Austin, 9 January 1816, in *Writings of Thomas Jefferson*, ed. Ford, 10:10.

237 **Jefferson opposed to the exercise of federal power:** Onuf and Sadosky, *Jeffersonian America*, 170.

237 **"federal government took bolder steps . . .":** John L. Larson, "'Bind the Republic Together': The National Union and the Struggle for a System of Internal Improvements," in *Federalists and Republicans*, ed. Peter Onuf (New York: Garland, 1991), 288.

238 **Lance Banning:** Banning, *Jeffersonian Persuasion*, 284.

238 **Horace Mann:** Horace Mann, *Speech of Horace Mann of Massachusetts on the Fugitive Slave Law* (Boston: W. S. Damrell, 1851); Charles Beecher, *The duty of disobedience to wicked laws. A sermon on the fugitive slave law* (New York: J. A. Gray, 1851).

238 **"gradual consolidation of the states":** Madison, "Consolidation," 5 December 1791, in Madison, *Writings*, ed. Rakove, 499.

238 **"must always be a powerful barrier":** Madison, "Political Reflections," 23 February 1799, in *Papers of James Madison*, ed. Mattern et al., 17:242.

238 **"people over constitutions":** Madison, "Report of 1800," in *Papers of James Madison*, ed. Mattern et al., 17:312.

238 **natural right of revolution; "strategy of 1798":** Lance Banning, *The Sacred Fire of Liberty: James Madison and the Founding of the Federal Republic* (Ithaca, N.Y.: Cornell University Press, 1995), 394.

239 **the "Old Republican" opposition:** Harry Ammon, "James Monroe and the Election of 1809 in Virginia," *William and Mary Quarterly* (1963):35–39.

239 **"basic document of anti-governmentalism . . .":** Garry Wills, *A Necessary Evil: A History of American Distrust of Government* (New York: Simon and Schuster, 1999), 143–44.

239 **"a large construction . . .":** Hamilton to James Bayard, 16 January 1801, in *Papers of Alexander Hamilton*, ed. Syrett, 25:320.

239 **"We wish to remain well . . .":** Jefferson to Livingston, 10 October 1802, in *Writings of Thomas Jefferson*, ed. Ford, 8:173.

239 **"An American contending by stratagem . . .":** Jefferson to Madison, 19 March 1803, in *Republic of Letters*, ed. Smith, 2:1266.

240 **"give for the whole":** Jon Kukla, *A Wilderness So Immense: The Louisiana Purchase and the Destiny of America* (New York: Alfred A. Knopf, 2003), 249–50, 269.

240 **"casting behind them . . .":** Jefferson to Breckinridge, 12 August 1803, in *Writings of Thomas Jefferson*, ed. Ford, 8:244 n, italics added.

240 **"The less we say about constitutional difficulties . . .":** Jefferson to Madison, in Malone, *Jefferson the President*, 316.

240 **"What is practical . . .":** Jefferson to Dupont, 18 January 1802, in *Writings of Thomas Jefferson*, ed. Ford, 8:127 n.

241 **Supreme Court:** Sanford Levinson, "The Louisiana Purchase as Seminal Constitutional Event," in Peter J. Kastor, ed., *The Louisiana Purchase: Emergence of an American Nation* (Washington, D.C.: CQ Press, 2002), 114.

241 **"a great waste . . .":** Boston *Columbian Centinel*, 13 July 1803, in Malone, *Jefferson the President*, 297.

241 **"not valuable to the United States . . .":** Hamilton, unsigned article in the New York *Evening Post*, 5 July 1803, in *Papers of Alexander Hamilton*, ed. Syrett, 26:129–32; Stourzh, *Alexander Hamilton*, 193.

241 **"Let those who wish for the increase of slaves . . .":** Andrew Siegel, "The Defense of Federalism in Connecticut," in Ben-Atar and Oberg, eds., *Federalists Reconsidered*, 217.

242 **new market for slave trade; constitutional amendment:** Garry Wills, *"Negro President": Jefferson and the Slave Power* (Boston: Houghton Mifflin, 2003), 131–32.

242 **"negro Presidents":** Pickering to Rufus King, 4 March 1804, in *Life and Correspondence of Rufus King*, ed. King, 4:365.

242 **"fatal to its advocates":** Fischer, "Myth of the Essex Junto," 229–32. See also Wills, *"Negro President,"* 144.

242 **"for our descendants to the thousandth . . .":** Jefferson, First Inaugural Address, in Jefferson, *Writings*, ed. Peterson, 494.

243 **"an empire of liberty":** Jefferson, "To the President and Legislative Council," 28 December 1805, in Stourzh, *Alexander Hamilton*, 191–92.

243 **Plumer:** Malone, *Jefferson the President*, 328.

243 **"an assumption of implied power":** John Quincy Adams, 20 October 1821, in *Memoirs of John Quincy Adams*, ed. Adams, 5:364–65.

243 **"embraced strict construction:** Peter S. Onuf, "The Louisiana Purchase and American Federalism," in Kastor, *Louisiana Purchase*, 125.

243 **"not a friend to a very energetic government":** Jefferson to Madison, 20 December 1787, in *Republic of Letters*, ed. Smith, 1:514.

243 **"There never was a Government . . .":** Livingston to Madison, 1 September 1802, in *Papers of James Madison*, ed. Robert J. Brugger, David Mattern, et al., 3 vols., Secretary of State Series (Charlottesville: University of Virginia Press, 1986–95), 3:536.

244 **Jefferson as foremost party leader:** James W. Davis, *The President as Party Leader* (New York: Greenwood Press, 1992), 6.

244 **"There never arose . . .":** Jefferson to Destutt de Tracy, 26 January 1811, in *Writings of Thomas Jefferson*, ed. Ford, 9:307.

244 **"Behind the curtain . . .":** Skowronek, *The Politics Presidents Make*, 73.

244 **"successful in getting through Congress . . .":** Dumas Malone, "Presidential Leadership and National Unity: The Jeffersonian Example," *Journal of Southern History* 35, no. 1 (February 1969):6.

245 **Jefferson and the three-fifths clause:** Wills, *"Negro President,"* 1–18.

245 **"drunk deeper":** Jefferson to Elbridge Gerry, 29 March 1801, in Jefferson, *Writings*, ed. Peterson, 1088–89.

245 **"Nature . . . seems to have formed . . .":** Jefferson to Monroe, 24 November 1801, in Jefferson, *Writings*, ed. Peterson, 1098, italics added.

245 **Jefferson and patronage:** Richard H. Kohn, *Eagle and Sword: The Federalists and the Creation of the Military Establishment in America, 1783–1802* (New York: The Free Press, 1975), 303; Martin Shefter, *Political Parties and the State: The American Historical Experience* (Princeton: Princeton University Press, 1994), 64–65.

245 **"yet when vacancies happen . . .":** Pickering to Rufus King, 27 December 1800, in *Life and Correspondence of Rufus King*, ed. King, 3:353.

245 **"so as gradually . . .":** Beckley to Jefferson, 27 February 1801, in Malone, *Jefferson the President*, 71.

245 **"carry his displacing system . . .":** Troup to King, 23 March 1801, in *Life and Correspondence of Rufus King*, ed. King, 3:409. See Malone, *Jefferson the President*, 72.

245 **"attornies & marshals . . .":** Malone, *Jefferson the President*, 74.

246 **on repeal of Judiciary Act of 1801 and on Marbury v. Madison:** See Peterson, *Thomas Jefferson and the New Nation*, 695ff.

246 **"federal sect"; "mark on Cain":** Jefferson to Benjamin Hawkins, 18 February 1803, in Jefferson, *Writings*, ed. Peterson, 1114.

246 **"Does it violate . . .":** Jefferson to Elias Shipman and Others, a Committee of the Merchants of New Haven, 12 July 1801, in *Writings of Thomas Jefferson*, ed. Ford, 8:69–70.

246 **"noisy band of royalists":** Jefferson to Dupont de Nemours, 18 January 1802, in Jefferson, *Writings*, ed. Peterson, 1100.

246 **"appointments & disappointments":** Jefferson to Benjamin Rush, 24 March 1801, in *Writings of Thomas Jefferson*, ed. Ford, 8:31.

246 **"most painful":** Wood, *Radicalism of the American Revolution*, 301.

246 **"when the only questions":** Jefferson to Elias Shipman and Others, a Committee of the Merchants of New Haven, 12 July 1801, in *Writings of Thomas Jefferson*, ed. Ford, 8:69–70.

246 **"The appointment of a woman . . .":** Appleby, *Thomas Jefferson*, 39.

247 **"always at market":** *Anas* (1804), in Jefferson, *Writings*, ed. Peterson, 693.

247 **making connections:** See Gordon S. Wood, "The Real Treason of Aaron Burr," *Proceedings of the American Philosophical Society* 143, no. 2 (June 1999):288.

247 **"Davis is too important . . .":** Burr to Gallatin, 28 June 1801, in Cunningham, *Jeffersonian Republicans in Power*, 41.

247 **break with Burr:** Cunningham, *Jeffersonian Republicans in Power*, 42.

247 **"inspired me with distrust":** Jefferson, *Anas*, Memo of 26 January 1804, in *Writings of Thomas Jefferson*, ed. Ford, 1:304.

248 **Hamilton opposes Burr as minister to France:** See "List of Names from Whence to Take a Minister for France," 19 May 1794, in "The Duel," editorial note, in *Papers of Alexander Hamilton*, ed. Syrett, 26:238.

248 **Burr had had enough:** Burr to Charles Biddle, 28 July 1804, in "The Duel," editorial note, *Papers of Alexander Hamilton*, ed. Syrett, 26:240.

248 **Burr's brief letter to Hamilton:** Burr to Hamilton, 18 June 1804, in *Papers of Alexander Hamilton*, ed. Syrett, 26:242–43.

248 **Cooper:** Dr. Charles Cooper to Philip Schuyler, 23 April 1804, printed in the *Albany Register*, 24 April 1804, in "The Duel," editorial note, in *Papers of Alexander Hamilton*, ed. Syrett, 26:242.

248 **Hamilton asks Adams for explanation:** Hamilton to Adams, 1 August 1800, in *Papers of Alexander Hamilton*, ed. Syrett, 25:51.

248 **Hamilton considered not responding:** William P. Van Ness's Narrative of the Events of June 22, 1804, in *Papers of Alexander Hamilton*, ed. Syrett, 26:252.

248 **"I have maturely reflected . . .":** Hamilton to Burr, 20 June 1804, in *Papers of Alexander Hamilton*, ed. Syrett, 26:247–49.

249 **"I am importuned . . .":** Hamilton to Philip Schuyler, 18 February 1781, in Hamilton, *Writings*, ed. Freeman, 96.

249 **"Political opposition can never absolve . . .":** Burr to Hamilton, 21 June 1804, in *Papers of Alexander Hamilton*, ed. Syrett, 26:250, italics added.

249   **"ill-will"; "I have not censured him . . ."**: "Statement on Impending Duel with Aaron Burr," 28 June–10 July 1804, in *Papers of Alexander Hamilton,* ed. Syrett, 26:279–80.

249   **challenge to duel:** Burr to Hamilton, 22 June 1804, in *Papers of Alexander Hamilton,* ed. Syrett, 26:255–56.

249   **"Gothic and absurd":** Moncure Daniel Conway, ed., *The Writings of Thomas Paine* (New York: G. P. Putnam's Sons, 1894–99), 1:40.

249   **"absurd":** Jefferson to James Ogilvie, 23 June 1806, in *Collections of the Massachusetts Historical Society,* 7th ser., vol. 1 (Boston: Published by the Society, 1900), 116–17.

249   **"murderous Practice":** Benjamin Franklin, quoted in Evarts B. Greene, "The Code of Honor in Colonial and Revolutionary Times," in *Transactions: Publications of the Colonial Society of Massachusetts,* March 1926, 385.

250   **Jefferson's code penalizing duelers:** "A Bill for Proportioning Crimes and Punishments" [1779], in Jefferson, *Writings,* ed. Peterson, 351. See also *Writings of Thomas Jefferson,* ed. Ford, 2:207.

250   **Massachusetts law:** Greene, "Code of Honor," 387.

250   **"scarce a mail arrives . . .":** Walpole (N.H.) *Farmer's Museum,* 9 June 1800, in Fischer, *Revolution of American Conservatism,* 186.

250   **political motives for dueling:** Freeman, "Dueling as Politics," 308–9.

250   **"My character is not within . . .":** Jefferson to Thomas Jefferson Randolph, 24 November 1808, in Jefferson, *Writings,* ed. Peterson, 1196.

250   **1803 resolution:** Elliot, *Debates,* 4:451–52.

250   **No man should vote for a dueler:** Lyman Beecher, *The Remedy for Duelling, a sermon delivered before the Presbytery of Long Island, at Aquebogue,* 16 April 1806 (Boston: Leavitt and Alden, 1806).

250   **"The highest as well as the eldest hope . . .":** Hamilton to Benjamin Rush, 29 March 1802, in *Papers of Alexander Hamilton,* ed. Syrett, 25:583–84.

250   **"horrid custom":** Allan Nevins, *The Evening Post: A Century of Journalism* (New York: Boni and Liveright, 1922), 28.

250   **"we do not now live . . .":** Hamilton to William Gordon, 5 September 1779, in Hamilton, *Writings,* ed. Freeman, 62.

251   **eleven affairs of honor:** Freeman, "Dueling as Politics," 294. See also Joanne B. Freeman, *Affairs of Honor: National Politics in the New Republic* (New Haven: Yale University Press, 2001). See also Gustavus B. Wallace to James Madison, 20 April 1790, in *Papers of James Madison,* ed. Hobson and Rutland, 13:152. See also Jan Lewis, "'The Blessings of Domestic Society': Thomas Jefferson's Family and the Transformation of American Politics," in *Jeffersonian Legacies,* ed. Peter S. Onuf (Charlottesville: University Press of Virginia, 1993), 118–23.

251   **"true honor . . .":** *The Defence No. V,* 5 August 1795, in *Papers of Alexander Hamilton,* ed. Syrett, 19:91.

251   **"abhorr[ed] the practice of Duelling"; "a peculiar necessity . . .":** "Statement on Impending Duel with Aaron Burr" [28 June–10 July 1804], in *Papers of Alexander Hamilton,* ed. Syrett, 26:278, 280, italics added; probably written on 10 July. See Freeman, "Dueling as Politics," 289 n.

251   **America has no feudal past:** Louis Hartz, *The Liberal Tradition in America* (New York: Harcourt, Brace, 1955), 6, 20.

251 **"elitist, for small male in-groups":** Douglass Adair, *Fame and the Founding Fathers,* ed. Trevor Colbourn (New York: W. W. Norton for the Institute of Early American History and Culture, 1974), 10.

252 **"sportsmanlike decency":** Hofstadter, *Idea of a Party System,* 249.

252 **"thus giving a double opportunity to Col Burr":** "Statement on Impending Duel with Aaron Burr," in *Papers of Alexander Hamilton,* ed. Syrett, 26:280, italics added.

252 **"The scruples of a Christian . . .":** Hamilton to Elizabeth Hamilton, 10 July 1804, in *Papers of Alexander Hamilton,* ed. Syrett, 26:308.

252 **"Adieu best of wives . . .":** Hamilton to Elizabeth Hamilton, 4 July 1804, in *Papers of Alexander Hamilton,* ed. Syrett, 26:293.

253 **Hamilton puts on his glasses:** Burr to Charles Biddle, 18 July 1804, in *Papers of Alexander Hamilton,* ed. Syrett, 26:334–35, editorial note.

253 **the pistols were discharged within a few seconds . . . :** Joint Statement by William P. Van Ness and Nathaniel Pendleton on the Duel between Alexander Hamilton and Aaron Burr, 17 July 1804, in *Papers of Alexander Hamilton,* ed. Syrett, 26:333.

253 **smoke from Hamilton's pistol:** Van Ness to Charles Biddle, no date, in *Papers of Alexander Hamilton,* ed. Syrett, 26:335, editorial note.

253 **"This is a mortal wound"; description of Hamilton's death:** Dr. David Hosack to William Coleman, 17 August 1804, in *Papers of Alexander Hamilton,* ed. Syrett, 26:344. See also Syrett and Cooke, *Interview in Weehawken,* 160–65.

254 **"I have found, for some time past . . .":** Mason to Coleman, 18 July 1804, in Freeman, "Dueling as Politics," 317 n.

254 **"His most determined Enemies . . .":** Adams to Jefferson, 3 September 1816, in *Adams-Jefferson Letters,* ed. Cappon, 2:488.

254 **"Would Hamilton have done this thing? . . . majesty of the law":** Gouverneur Morris, Funeral Oration, 14 July 1804, in *Papers of Alexander Hamilton,* ed. Syrett, 26:328.

254 **"If we were truly brave . . .":** Clarkson to Morris, in *Diary and Letters of Gouverneur Morris,* ed. Morris, 2:458, italics added.

254 **"shot each other in juvenile displays . . .":** Ellis, *Founding Brothers,* 39.

254 **"falsest of honour":** Jefferson to Thomas Mann Randolph, 13 July 1806, in *Writings of Thomas Jefferson,* ed. Ford, 8:459.

254 **"a gentleman is free . . .":** Lomask, *Aaron Burr,* 69; see also Elkins and McKitrick, *Age of Federalism,* 746. See letter from Burr's future wife, Theodosia Prevost, 12 February 1781, in *Memoirs of Aaron Burr,* ed. Davis, 1:224.

254 **"the persecutions which are practised . . .":** Burr to Charles Biddle, 18 July 1804, in *Political Correspondence and Public Papers of Aaron Burr,* ed. Kline, 2:887–88.

255 **"If any male friend of yours . . .":** Burr to Theodosia Burr, 11 August 1804, in *Memoirs of Aaron Burr,* ed. Davis, 2:332.

255 **eighteenth-century novel:** Choderlos de Laclos, *Les Liaisons dangereuses* [1782].

255 **"Our real Disease . . .":** Hamilton to Theodore Sedgwick, 10 July 1804, in *Papers of Alexander Hamilton,* ed. Syrett, 26:309.

255 **"the ability to be in future useful . . .":** Hamilton, "Statement on Impending Duel with Aaron Burr" [28 June–10 July 1804], in *Papers of Alexander Hamilton,* ed. Syrett, 26:280.

255 **"General Hamilton hated republican government . . . fatal to liberty and honor":** Morris to Robert Walsh, 5 February 1811, in *Life of Gouverneur Morris,* ed. Sparks, 3:260–68, italics added.

255 **"Pride, Strength and Courage . . . twain":** Adams to Jefferson, 21 December 1819, in *Adams-Jefferson Letters,* ed. Cappon, 2:551.

255 **"This American world . . .";** **"frail and worthless"; "withdraw from the Scene":** Hamilton to Morris, 29 February 1802, in *Papers of Alexander Hamilton,* ed. Syrett, 25:544.

256 **"A garden . . .":** Hamilton to C. C. Pinckney, 29 December 1802, in *Papers of Alexander Hamilton,* ed. Syrett, 26:71.

256 **"disgusted with everything . . .":** Hamilton to John Laurens, 8 January 1780, in Hamilton, *Writings,* ed. Freeman, 66.

13. Would the System Work?

257 **"mere county of England":** Jefferson to Barnabas Bidwell, 5 July 1806, in Jefferson, *Writings,* ed. Peterson, 1163.

257 **"almost melted into one":** Jefferson to Volney, 8 February 1805, in Malone, *Jefferson the President,* 434.

258 **on young Federalists:** see Fischer, *Revolution of American Conservatism,* ch. 8, "A Party in Search of an Issue," 150–81; Steven Watts, "Ministers, Misanthropes, and Mandarins: The Federalists and the Culture of Capitalism, 1790–1820," in Ben-Atar and Oberg, *Federalists Reconsidered,* 157–78.

258 **statewide organizations; door-to-door canvassing:** Fischer, *Revolution of American Conservatism,* 60ff, 106–7.

258 **newspapers in the United States:** Pasley, *"Tyranny of Printers,"* 201.

258 **friends of the people:** Taylor, "From Fathers to Friends," 465–91.

258 **mob:** Jacob Bigelow, Jr., to Rev. Jacob Bigelow, 16 April 1807, in Fischer, *Revolution of American Conservatism,* 156.

258 **frugal government:** New York *Evening Post,* 8 March 1809, in Fischer, *Revolution of American Conservatism,* 172.

258 **"to protect better the property . . .":** Annals of Congress, 11 April 1808, in Fischer, *Revolution of American Conservatism,* 170.

258 **"not binding":** Wills, *Necessary Evil,* 158.

258 **Federalists recycle themselves as agrarians:** Fischer, *Revolution of American Conservatism,* 173.

258 **Anglophobia:** Ames to Timothy Pickering, 2 December 1805, in *Works of Fisher Ames,* ed. Ames, 1:344. On Federalist Anglophobia, see Vermont Federalist Josiah Dunham (1769–1844), in Fischer, *Revolution of American Conservatism,* 243. See also Josiah Quincy to Harrison Gray Otis, 26 November 1811, in Fischer, *Revolution of American Conservatism,* 174.

258 **bent on subverting Christianity:** *Hudson (N.Y.) Balance,* 6 November 1802, in Fischer, *Revolution of American Conservatism,* 169.

259 **Irish and Jews:** Fischer, *Revolution of American Conservatism,* 165.

259 **"enact publicly their friendship . . .":** Taylor, "From Fathers to Friends," 491.

259 **"Our two great parties . . .":** John Adams, New York *Evening Post,* 28 January 1808, in Fischer, *Revolution of American Conservatism,* 172.

259 **"They equally lay claim . . .":** Fischer, *Revolution of American Conservatism,* 163.

259 **Wolcott converts to democracy:** Nevins, *The Evening Post,* 31.

260 **"union of sentiment"; "think as they think":** Second Inaugural Address, 4 March 1805, in Jefferson, *Writings,* ed. Peterson, 522–23.

260 **"Twenty years peace . . .":** Washington to Charles Carroll of Carrollton, 1 May 1796, in *Writings of George Washington,* ed. Fitzpatrick, 35:30–31.

260 **"If we can keep at peace . . .":** Jefferson to James Monroe, 28 January 1809, in Jefferson, *Writings,* ed. Peterson, 1199–1200.

261 **Samuel Lyman:** Fischer, *Revolution of American Conservatism,* 358, 251.

261 **"those happy times . . .":** Thomas Sinnickson, *Plain Truth; or, an Address to the Citizens of New-Jersey* [1812], in Fischer, *Revolution of American Conservatism,* 326.

261 **"wisdom and virtue":** Gouverneur Morris to Robert Walsh, 5 February 1811, in *Life of Gouverneur Morris,* ed. Sparks, 3:268–69.

261 **"Ignorance and Presumption":** Morris, *An Address to the People of New York* [1812], in Fischer, *Revolution of American Conservatism,* 154.

261 **King proposes to vet Morris's speech:** Rufus King to John Jay, 20 June 1814, in *Correspondence and Public Papers of John Jay,* ed. Johnston, 4:374ff.

261 **"the means by which all popular governments . . .":** Webster to Rufus King, 6 July 1807, in *Life and Correspondence of Rufus King,* ed. King, 5:38.

261 **Bingham moves to England:** Fischer, *Revolution of American Conservatism,* 334.

261 **Federalists' flexibility, receptiveness toward women:** Zagarri, "Gender and the First Party System," 119.

262 **"Come on then! . . .":** New York *Evening Post,* 13 March 1816.

262 **"the Marats, the Dantons":** Jefferson to Lafayette, 14 February 1815, in Jefferson, *Writings,* ed. Peterson, 1364.

262 **Hartford convention:** Burns, *Vineyard of Liberty,* 217, 231.

262 **"The existence of parties is not necessary . . .":** Monroe to Andrew Jackson, 14 December 1816, in *The Writings of James Monroe,* ed. Stanislaus Murray Hamilton, 7 vols. (London: G. P. Putnam's Sons, 1898–1903), 5:345–46.

262 **"Now is the time to exterminate . . .":** Jackson to Monroe, 1816, in Burns, *Deadlock of Democracy,* 47, italics added.

262 **"constitute one great family . . .":** First Inaugural Address, 4 March 1817, in *Writings of James Monroe,* ed. Hamilton, 6:13, italics added.

263 **His job was not to be the head of a party . . . :** Monroe to Jackson, in Hofstadter, *Idea of a Party System,* 195.

263 **Monroe's tour of New England:** Ammon, *James Monroe,* 372ff.

264 **"the unanimity of indifference":** Lynn W. Turner, "Elections of 1816 and 1820," in *History of American Presidential Elections,* ed. Schlesinger, 314.

264 **"general safety of the Republic":** Ibid., 316.

264 **"Sir, I do not believe in this harmony . . .":** Henry Clay, 7 March 1818, in James F. Hopkins, ed., *The Papers of Henry Clay* (Lexington: University Press of Kentucky, 1959), 2:452.

265 **Crawford incident:** Burns, *Vineyard of Liberty,* 254.

265 **"schismatize":** Jefferson to Thomas Cooper, 9 July 1807, in *Writings of Thomas Jefferson,* ed. Ford, 9:102.

265 **"moved the bitter waters . . .":** Martin Van Buren, *Inquiry into the Origin and Curse of Political Parties in the United States* (New York: Hurd and Houghton, 1867), 4.

265 **"harmony"; "break up the remnant":** Hofstadter, *Idea of a Party System*, 233–34.

266 **"A respectable minority . . .":** Jefferson to Joel Barlow, 3 May 1802, in *Writings of Thomas Jefferson*, ed. Ford, 8:149.

266 **the "complete suppression of party":** Jefferson to Lafayette, 14 May 1817, in *Writings of Thomas Jefferson*, ed. Ford, 10:83.

266 **"sweetened society . . .":** Jefferson to Lafayette, 14 May 1817, in *Writings of Thomas Jefferson*, ed. Ford, 10:83.

266 **"I am no believer in the amalgamation . . .":** Jefferson to Henry Lee, 10 August 1824, in *Writings of Thomas Jefferson*, ed. Ford, 10:317.

266 **"Tories are Tories still . . .":** Jefferson to Martin Van Buren, 29 June 1824, in *Writings of Thomas Jefferson*, ed. Ford, 10:316. See also Jefferson to Lafayette, 4 November 1823, 10:281.

266 **"The same political parties . . ."; "gag of a despot":** Jefferson to Adams, 27 June 1813, in *Adams-Jefferson Letters*, ed. Cappon, 2:335–37.

266 **misconstrue, misrepresent . . . :** Adams to Jefferson, 9 July 1813, in *Adams-Jefferson Letters*, ed. Cappon, 2:351.

266 **"friends of order . . .":** *Massachusetts Mercury,* 1800, in John Zvesper, *Political Philosophy and Rhetoric: A Study of the Origins of American Party Politics* (Cambridge: Cambridge University Press, 1977), 182.

266 **"dangerous principle":** Jefferson to William Short, 8 January 1825, in *Writings of Thomas Jefferson*, ed. Ford, 10:335.

267 **"they strengthen the Union of the Whole":** Madison to Robert Walsh, 27 November 1819, in *Writings of James Madison*, ed. Hunt, 9:12.

267 **"perfectly sound":** Henry Clay, quoted in Ketcham, *James Madison*, 660.

267 **"overbearing," "unjust and interested":** Madison, *Federalist* No. 10.

267 **"interested combinations . . .":** Madison, *Federalist* No. 51.

268 **"The vital principle of republican . . .":** Madison to unknown, 1833, in *Writings of James Madison*, ed. Hunt, 9:520–28. See also Dahl, *How Democratic*, 36–37.

268 **"no free Country . . .":** Madison, "Note to His Speech on the Right of Suffrage," 1821, in Farrand, ed., *Records of the Federal Convention of 1787,* 3:452.

269 **strange hybrid:** Burns, *Deadlock of Democracy*, 46. See also Rahe, *Republics Ancient and Modern*, vol. 3, *Inventions of Prudence*, 105–6.

269 **new breed of party men:** See Hofstadter, *Idea of a Party System*, ch. 6, 212–71; Ketcham, *Presidents Above Party*, 140ff.

269 **"the last degradation . . .":** Jefferson to Francis Hopkinson, 13 March 1789, in *Papers of Thomas Jefferson*, ed. Boyd, 14:650.

269 ***"as indispensable as any other moral qualification":*** Ketcham, *Presidents Above Party*, 143.

269 **"very discord . . . public good":** Ibid., 144.

269 **"His Majesty's Opposition":** Ibid., 149.

270 **organizing, committees, newspapers, barbecues, clubs:** Robert V. Remini, "Election of 1828," in *History of American Presidential Elections,* ed. Schlesinger, 418–22.

270 **scrambling, romping, fighting; "Saturnalia":** Ibid., 435; Burns, *Vineyard of Liberty*, 323.

270 **antipartyism periodically emerges:** See Gerald Leonard, "The Ironies of Partyism and Antipartyism," *Illinois Historical Journal* 87 (Spring 1994):21–40.

270 **"second party system":** See Richard P. McCormick, *The Second American Party*

System: Party Formation in the Jacksonian Era (Chapel Hill: University of North Carolina Press, 1966).

271 **Tocqueville on citizens' engagement:** See Dunn, *Sister Revolutions*, 98–99. See also Tocqueville, *De la Démocratie en Amérique*, ed. Mayer, Bk. 1, Pt. 2, ch. 6, 252ff. Translations from the French are my own.

272 **"Freedom of association . . . strengthens the polity"; "art of coming together":** Tocqueville, *De la Démocratie en Amérique*, ed. Mayer, Bk. 2, Pt. 2, ch. 7, 2:125, 122.

Epilogue

273 **"fire not to be quenched":** Farewell Address, in Washington, *Writings*, ed. Rhodehamel, 969–70.

273 **partisan press:** See Pasley, *"Tyranny of Printers."*

274 **"as real a revolution in the principles . . . suffrage of the people":** Jefferson to Spencer Roane, 6 September 1819, in *Writings of Thomas Jefferson*, ed. Ford, 10:140.

274 **"with a view to sink her":** Jefferson to John Dickinson, 6 March 1801, in *Writings of Thomas Jefferson*, ed. Ford, 8:7.

274 **"with one heart and one mind":** First Inaugural Address, 4 March 1801, in Jefferson, *Writings*, ed. Peterson, 493, italics added.

275 **Beeman and Key:** Beeman, *Old Dominion*, 237–38; V. O. Key, *Southern Politics in State and Nation* (New York: Alfred. A. Knopf, 1949), 19.

275 **democratization of land purchases:** Andro Linklater, *Measuring America: How an Untamed Wilderness Shaped the United States and Fulfilled the Promise of Democracy* (New York: Walker and Co., 2002), 164, 171.

275 **elections in eighteen of the twenty-four states; voter participation:** Pasley, "1800 as a Revolution," 127–28.

275 **3 percent:** Beeman, *Old Dominion*, 239.

275 **"politics of inclusion":** Elkins and McKitrick, *Age of Federalism*, 27–28.

276 **"We are acting for all mankind":** Jefferson to Joseph Priestley, 19 June 1802, in *Writings of Thomas Jefferson*, ed. Ford, 8:159.

276 **Republicans did not reject gender and race:** Zagarri, "Gender and the First Party System," 132.

276 **improvements in women's education:** Linda Kerber, *Women of the Republic: Intellect and Ideology in Revolutionary America* (Chapel Hill: University of North Carolina Press, 1980), 193.

276 **women deprived of right to vote in New Jersey:** Ronald P. Formisano, "State Development in the Early Republic: Substance and Structure, 1780–1840," in Shafer and Badger, eds., *Contesting Democracy*, 9.

276 **"ardent love . . . their ancestors":** Ellis, *American Sphinx*, 201–2.

276 **"Instead of inviting Indians . . .":** Peterson, *Thomas Jefferson and the New Nation*, 774.

276 **free blacks in the North:** Wood, *American Revolution*, 128.

277 **postmaster general:** Bellesiles, "'Soil Will Be Soaked with Blood,'" 80.

277 **blacks in North Carolina:** Finkelman, "The Problem of Slavery," 153.

277 **"true" revolution of 1800:** James Sidbury, "Thomas Jefferson in Gabriel's Virginia," in Horn, Lewis, and Onuf, eds., *Revolution of 1800*, 201.

277 **"not a moral question"**: Jefferson to Lafayette, 26 December 1820, in *Writings of Thomas Jefferson,* ed. Ford, 10:180.

277 **"party trick"; separation of the North:** Jefferson to Charles Pinckney, 30 September 1820, in *Writings of Thomas Jefferson,* ed. Ford, 10:162.

277 **"declare that the condition . . ."**: Jefferson to Gallatin, 26 December 1820, in Jefferson, *Writings,* ed. Peterson, 1449–50.

278 **"rights of human nature"**: Jefferson, *A Summary View of the Rights of British America,* in *Papers of Thomas Jefferson,* ed. Boyd, 1:130.

278 **"has betrayed the secret . . ."**: Rahe, *Republics Ancient and Modern,* 2:227.

278 **Federalists more sensitive to the suffering of blacks:** Finkelman, "The Problem of Slavery," 135–56.

278 **"My proposition . . ."**: Jefferson to Gallatin, 26 December 1820, in Jefferson, *Writings,* ed. Peterson, 1449–50.

278 **"abandonment of the subject"**: Jefferson to William Short, 18 January 1826, in *Writings of Thomas Jefferson,* ed. Ford, 10:362. See D. B. Davis, *Was Thomas Jefferson an Authentic Enemy of Slavery?* (Oxford: Clarendon Press, 1970).

279 **"the momentum leading toward . . ."**: Rahe, *Republics Ancient and Modern,* 2:149.

279 **usurp "all the rights . . . without limitation of powers"**: Jefferson to William Giles, 26 December 1825, in *Writings of Thomas Jefferson,* ed. Ford, 10:354–55. See also Robert E. Shalhope, "Thomas Jefferson's Republicanism and Antebellum Southern Thought," *Journal of Southern History* 42, no. 4 (November 1976):548.

280 **"The nullifiers who make the name . . ."**: Madison to Nicholas Trist, 23 December 1832, in Madison, *Writings,* ed. Rakove, 862–63.

280 **"the advice nearest to my heart . . ."**: Rahe, *Republics Ancient and Modern,* 2:152.

280 **"caught a vision . . ."**: Bernard Bailyn, *To Begin the World Anew: The Genius and Ambiguities of the American Founders* (New York: Alfred A. Knopf, 2003), 47.

280 **"I have not perceived . . ."**: Jefferson to Thomas Humphreys, 8 February 1817, in *Writings of Thomas Jefferson,* ed. Ford, 10:77.

280 **"I tremble for my country . . ."**: *Notes on Virginia* [1781] in Jefferson, *Writings,* ed. Peterson, 289, 214. See also Onuf, *Jefferson's Empire,* 147–88.

281 **"All, all dead . . ."**: Jefferson to Francis Adrian Van Der Kemp, 11 January 1825, in *Writings of Thomas Jefferson,* ed. Ford, 10:337. On Jefferson's pessimism, see Wood, *Radicalism of the American Revolution,* 367–69.

281 **"our descendants . . ."**: Jefferson to Joseph Cabell, 14 January 1818, in *Writings of Thomas Jefferson,* ed. Ford, 10:102.

281 **"I cannot live to see it"; "My joy . . ."**: Jefferson to William Giles, 26 December 1825, in *Writings of Thomas Jefferson,* ed. Ford, 10:357.

281 **"It is a good world on the whole . . ."; "I steer my bark . . ."; "labors are lost . . ."**: Jefferson to Adams, 8 April 1816, 12 September 1821, in *Adams-Jefferson Letters,* ed. Cappon, 2:467, 575.

281 **"a leaf of our history . . ."**: Jefferson to Edward Coles, 25 August 1814, in Jefferson, *Writings,* ed. Peterson, 1345.

281 **"All eyes are opened . . ."**: Jefferson to Roger Weightman, 24 June 1826, in *Writings of Thomas Jefferson,* ed. Ford, 10:391.

Acknowledgments

I am deeply grateful to many friends and colleagues for their help and encouragement in this project. Joyce Appleby, Milton Djuric, Ralph Lerner, Michael McGiffert, Paul Rahe, and C. Bradley Thompson all generously offered constructive criticism of portions of this manuscript. Warm appreciation goes to Robert Dalzell for his helpful and insightful advice. Special thanks go to Peter Onuf for his careful reading of my manuscript, for his invaluable comments and suggestions, and for sharing with me his deep knowledge of the period.

My editor, Anton Mueller, offered many useful recommendations for the manuscript. Donna Chenail and her colleagues in the Faculty Secretarial Office, as well as Alison O'Grady, Walter Komorowski, Linda Hall, and Rebecca Ohm at the Williams College Library, my agent, Fifi Oscard, and my student David Riskin, all contributed their able and cheerful assistance. And I am indebted to Williams College and to Thomas Kohut, Dean of Faculty, for his collegial support.

Finally, I would like to express my profound gratitude to James MacGregor Burns for his patient readings and rereadings of my manuscript, his Jeffersonian optimism and encouragement, his countless, illuminating discussions of history and politics, and, of course, for far more.

Index